Labor Mobility and the World Economy

Federico Foders
Rolf J. Langhammer
Editors

Labor Mobility and the World Economy

 Springer

Rolf J. Langhammer
Kiel Institute for World Economics
D–24100 Kiel
rolf.langhammer@ifw-kiel.de

Federico Foders
Kiel Institute for World Economics
D–24100 Kiel
federico.foders@ifw-kiel.de

Cataloging-in-Publication Data:
Library of Congress Control Number: 2005937737

ISBN-10   3-540-31044-4   Springer Berlin Heidelberg New York
ISBN-13   978-3-540-31044-0   Springer Berlin Heidelberg New York

Springer-Verlag is a part of Springer Science+Business Media

springeronline.com

© Springer-Verlag Berlin · Heidelberg 2006
Printed in Germany

Hardcover-Design: Erich Kirchner, Heidelberg

Printed on acid-free paper   42/3153-5 4 3 2 1 0

Contents

I. Labor Mobility and Globalization

II. Integrated Labor Markets and Global Governance

III. Labor Mobility and Public Policy

Preface

An increasing number of landings of illegal migrants on the coast of Italy and Spain, but also the recent riots, car-burnings, and street battles that occurred all across France and that have been attributed to the migrant community, seem to indicate that migration is likely to stay high on the European policy agenda for some time. The flow of migrants from poor to rich countries does not, however, constitute a typically European problem. U.S. public policy has also been facing a continued (legal and illegal) inflow of labor from different regions, notably Mexico and other Latin American countries. And similar developments in other advanced countries (Australia, Canada) as well as in selected fast-growing emerging markets in Eastern Europe and East Asia imply that these countries too are being compelled to adjust their public policies in order to relieve migratory pressures and deal with their consequences.

The world economy already saw rising cross-border labor flows in the 1990s and most forecasts predict that South-North and South-South migration will remain at relatively high levels over the next decades and possibly even turn into a major global challenge for policy makers in the 21st century. Although migrants currently amount to less than 3 percent of the world's population, the concentration of immigrants in only a few host countries and regions raises some important questions in the receiving and sending countries as well as at the supranational level: What structural relationships exist between labor, trade, and capital flows? Are they substitutes or complements? Over the recent past, has there been any progress in modeling labor mobility in a globalization framework? Does immigration (emigration) spur or slow down long-run economic growth? What forces hamper the international integration of labor markets? Do we need improved coordination and/or harmonization of national immigration policies at the regional and global level? Do we need an international/regional regime to manage labor flows?

Against this background, the 2004 Kiel Week Conference on "Labor Mobility and the World Economy" provided economists, other social scientists, and policy makers with a forum to discuss current developments in migration theory and policy.

The first paper included in the conference volume was written jointly by Timothy J. Hatton and Jeffrey G. Williamson. It draws heavily on economic history and focuses on the secular drift from the very positive to much more negative immigrant selection that took place in the first global century after 1820 and in the second era of globalization after 1950, and aims at finding explanations for that drift. It then explores the political economy of immigrant restriction in the past, in an attempt to derive lessons for the present. In doing so, the authors critically review around two centuries of immigration trends and policies in Europe and the United States.

Given the broad scope of this starting point, Frank Barry asks whether economic theory, especially some models of imperfect labor mobility, may be useful in explaining migration in a globalized world in which all factors of production are highly mobile. Although the standard approach consists in adopting a heterogeneous-agent framework, he introduces an alternative model and claims that his approach contributes, among other things, to simplifying welfare evaluations. He builds a model based on the well-known Harris–Todaro model, which allows labor-market-disequilibrium-cum-emigration to be analyzed. Moreover, his model incorporates a variable representing the role of governance in development which enables him to extend the standard analysis in a new way to assess the impact of migration on welfare under different governance regimes.

In their paper, Gabriel Felbermayr and Wilhelm Kohler focus on a phenomenon known as skill-based selection in immigration policies and propose a model of the Ricardo–Viner type featuring three levels of skills. They apply the latter to work out both the wage and welfare effects of alternative immigration scenarios, thereby taking into account several of the adjustment mechanisms suggested by the related empirical literature dealing with changes in the prices of tradable and nontradable goods. A crucial thrust of the paper is that it considers the general equilibrium repercussions of endogenous price adjustments and draws largely counterintuitive conclusions about the welfare effects of skill-based immigration policies.

There is a well-established literature on the role of networks, particularly ethnic networks, in international trade. Ethnic networks are seen as a way to overcome informal barriers to trade such as information costs, risk, and uncertainty by building trust and, to a certain degree, by substituting for the difficulty of enforcing contracts internationally. The networks studied by Gil S. Epstein and Ira N. Gang are those which emerge from the interaction (i) between migrants and natives in the host country and (ii) between migrants and natives in their home country. One of the central issues addressed is the extent to which ethnic networks need to be associated with incomplete assimilation of migrants in the host country for them to have a major impact on exports and imports. A related issue, the relationship between international capital movements and international labor movements, has been discussed before in the literature on foreign direct investment and remittances. In this volume, it is touched upon by Kar-yiu Wong who, employing a model of two economies of different size featuring identical technologies and factor endowment ratios, investigates whether capital and labor movements may be substitutes in a world that enjoys a free flow of goods and services. His analyses encompass substitution in both the price sense and the quantity sense.

The paper by Sheetal K. Chand and Martin Paldam deals with the economic consequences of migration from a less developed country to a developed country and asks whether cultural differences and the institutions of the developed country can cause both a shortfall in and a redistribution of the potential benefits of migration. They explicitly differentiate two mechanisms, the selection of immigrants and the incentives for labor market participation faced by immigrants, in three stylized cases, a Dubai-like guest worker society, a U.S.-like immigrant society, and a Nordic-like tax-based welfare state.

The political economy of worker displacement in an environment characterized by individual-specific uncertainty about the precise distributional consequences of a change in immigration policy is analyzed by Sanjay Jain, Devesh Kapur, and Sharun W. Mukand. The policy shift is assumed to lead to the displacement of high-paid Northern workers by low-paid, skilled Southern workers who were previously barred from entering the country and directly competing with Northern workers. The authors show that in an attempt to contain adverse distributional consequences, the dilemma faced by the Northern politician is that limiting the inflow of human capital might exacerbate the outflow of jobs, as firms "outsource" or "offshore" tasks that had previously been performed domestically. They then go on to ask several questions: Does the outsourcing of service sector jobs raise larger political concerns than the loss of manufacturing jobs and if so, why? Why does the displacement of information technology workers seem to generate a disproportionate amount of political backlash?

The next contribution refers to the pros and cons of international regimes for migration. Since more and more countries are being affected by migration, either as a country of origin, of destination, or of transit, or all of these simultaneously, migration has become an international phenomenon which, in the opinion of Stefania Pasquetti, requires multilateral, rather than unilateral action, by all the states concerned. The European Union is one of the areas of the world economy that has adopted a regional policy with respect to the full mobility of its citizens within the EU as well as with respect to the immigration and asylum of third-country citizens, including a new approach to foster the latter's integration. Her paper focuses on the record of the EU migration policies in the field of (legal) migration and cooperation with the countries of origin. Moreover, it also addresses the conditions that should be met by the European Commission to provide improved management of labor flows at the supranational level.

The link between the traditional determinants of migration and the role of social values in the context of European integration is scrutinized from an empirical point of view by Holger Wolf. Choosing the empirical fact that Europeans tend to be relatively immobile across borders as a starting point, he sets out to investigate the reasons for this behavior. He gives particular attention to location-specific utility and explores the importance of formal and informal barriers to migration and the perceived benefits and costs of migration, thereby extending the traditional approach to encompass the contribution of social values in shaping the individual's decision to migrate.

In 2004, the number of refugees worldwide reached 12 million, up from 3 million in the early 1970s. And the number of people seeking asylum in the developed world increased tenfold, from about 50,000 per annum to half a million over the same period. Governments and international agencies have grappled with the twin problems of providing adequate humanitarian assistance in the Third World and avoiding floods of unwanted asylum seekers arriving on the doorsteps of the First World. In another contribution to the conference, Timothy J. Hatton and Jeffrey G. Williamson draw on the recent literature and ongoing research to address a series of questions that are relevant to the refugee debate. First, they examine the causes of refugee displacements and asylum flows, focusing on the effects of conflict, political upheaval, and economic incentives to migrate. Then, they analyze the evolution of policies towards asylum seekers and the consequences of those policies for Europe. Finally, they ask whether greater international coordination could produce better outcomes for refugee-receiving countries as well as for the refugees themselves.

The question whether the domestic politics of international trade differ in any fundamental way from the domestic politics of immigration has been raised before. It has to be acknowledged, however, that it is still extremely difficult to say exactly how and, more importantly, why both politics tend to differ. The paper by David Greenaway and Douglas R. Nelson uses a common frame of reference, namely endogenous policy models, as a tool to inquire into this topic. These models capture the essential insight underlying much of political economy analyses, namely that material interests tend to drive policy preferences. The paper aims at establishing whether both trade and immigration politics appear to be essentially about material interest and whether the differences between trade and immigration politics also show up in institutional aspects such as the way both areas of public policy are organized.

In the final contribution, Per Lundborg investigates the effects on growth and welfare of emigration-related variables such as (i) the emigration of educated and uneducated labor and (ii) the emigration probability itself. Using a Grossman–Helpman model of endogenous growth, he seeks to find answers to the question whether the prospects of emigration to a high-wage country raise the expected returns to education, stimulate human capital formation, and augment the rate of economic growth in the sending country. In addition, he also touches upon the role played by tuition fees in economic growth within the broader context of migration.

As editors we are highly indebted to the participants of the 2004 Kiel Week Conference for the innovative ideas they contributed and for the lively discussion they sparked on a central topic of international public policy. Our thanks go to the Volkswagen Foundation and the German Marshall Fund of the United States from which we received financial support. We would also like to thank Bosch und Siemens Hausgeräte, Deutsche Bank, Dresdner Bank, HSH Nordbank, and Mobilcom for co-sponsoring the conference. Moreover, we gratefully acknowledge the help received from colleagues in the Institute: we were excellently assisted by Olivier Godart (research assistant), Rita Halbfas and Silke Matthiesen-Goß (conference office), and by members of the Institute's technical and administrative staff. Finally, we owe gratitude to Dietmar Gebert, Paul Kramer, and Britta Thun, who prepared the conference volume for publication.

Kiel, January 2006   Federico Foders
                                                               Rolf J. Langhammer

Timothy J. Hatton and Jeffrey G. Williamson

International Migration in the Long Run: Positive Selection, Negative Selection, and Policy

Abstract:

Most labor-scarce overseas countries moved decisively to restrict their immigration during the first third of the 20th century. This autarchic retreat from unrestricted immigration in the first global century before World War I to the quotas and other restrictions introduced afterwards was the result of a combination of factors, one of which was public hostility toward new immigrants with lower education and labor market skills. The paper documents the secular drift from very positive to much more negative immigrant selection which took place in the first global century after 1820 and in the second era of globalization after 1950, and seeks explanations for it. It then explores the political economy of immigrant restriction.

Prologue

The autarchic retreat from unrestricted and even subsidized immigration in the first global century before World War I to the quotas and other restrictions introduced afterwards was the result of a combination of factors: public hostility toward new immigrants with lower education and skills, public assessment of the impact of those immigrants on a deteriorating labor market, political participation of those affected, and, as a triggering mechanism, the sudden shocks to the

Remark: This paper draws heavily on our forthcoming book *Global Migration and the World Economy: Two Centuries of Policy and Performance* (MIT Press). We are grateful to the conference organizers for their hospitality and to the participants for their comments. Hatton acknowledges support through a British Academy Research Readership and Williamson acknowledges financial support from the National Science Foundation SES-0001362. We are both grateful to the Australian National University for providing us with the opportunity and the environment for collaboration on this research project. Williamson also thanks the University of Wisconsin Economics Department, where this paper was completed while on leave from Harvard.

labor market delivered by the 1890s depression, the Great War,[1] and postwar adjustment. The United States led the way with quotas in the 1920s, and the great depression helped persuade others to follow (e.g., South African quotas in 1930, Brazilian quotas in 1934, and restrictions by Australia in 1930, New Zealand in 1931, and Canada in 1932). This paper documents the secular drift from very positive to much more negative immigrant selection which took place in the first global century after 1820 and in the second era of globalization after 1950. It then seeks explanations for it. Finally, it explores the political economy of immigrant restriction in the past and seeks historical lessons for the present.

1   Immigrant Policy and Immigrant Prejudice

1.1   Backlash: Attitudes toward Immigrants in the First Global Century

Public attitude towards immigration became increasingly negative as North America moved into the long and deep depression of the 1890s, in part as a response to the imagined or real economic threats delivered by the immigrant flood. When asked for their opinions by state labor bureau interviewers in the middle of the 1890s depression, here is how some workingmen in the Midwest responded: almost 63 percent of the Kansas wage earners surveyed in 1895 thought immigration should be restricted and another 24 percent thought it should be outright suppressed, adding up to 87 percent who wanted to retreat from the free-immigration status quo; almost 68 percent of the Kansas wage earners surveyed in 1897 thought immigration should be restricted and another 24 percent thought it should be suppressed, adding up to 92 percent favoring a retreat from the status quo; in 1895, about half of the railway workers and almost 62 percent of the owners of public conveyances surveyed in Michigan thought that immigration hurt their occupation, and more than 92 percent of those Michigan workers favored restriction (Hatton and Williamson 2005: Chapter 8).

   The 1890s was not the first time that a powerful immigrant backlash had its public expression in America, since loud and hostile voices could be heard a half-century earlier when the first great immigration waves pounded U.S. labor markets.[2] The first immigration surge into the United States which occurred in the three decades following 1820 turned out to be the biggest. At the start of the

---

[1]   In addition, the impact of the sinking of the Lusitania in 1915 helped make for anti-European public sentiment.

[2]   The classic account of American nativism is Higham (1988); see also Jones (1992).

boom in 1820, the United States was a nation of natives and the immigration rate was only 1 per thousand. By 1845–1846 and even before the Irish famine, the immigration rate had soared to 11.2 per thousand (Chickering 1848: Table III, 14). By 1850 the immigration rate was more than 15 per thousand, a figure never to be exceeded even in the much-vaunted pre–World War I boom.[3] The surge was driven by American growth and settlement, by declining transatlantic steerage costs, by declining passenger costs from European interior to port, by industrial revolutions in Europe (helping to release poverty constraints), and, of course, by the great Irish famine. The share of the foreign-born in the U.S. resident population was 9.7 percent in 1850, 13.1 percent in 1860, and 14 percent in 1870 (U.S. Department of Commerce 1975: 8, 117–118). While these foreign-born shares were certainly enormous by the standards of that time, note that the 1850 figure is exceeded by those for North America and Western Europe today (Table 1).

But it was not just a rise in the *quantity* of immigrants that distinguished this first and biggest surge, since their *quality* fell too. By "quality" we mean the education, ability, occupation and language skills that are rewarded in the labor market. By the 1850s, U.S. immigrants had become increasingly unskilled as declining passenger costs and economic development back home brought overseas emigration within reach of much poorer, severely capital-constrained Europeans. So, how did Americans respond to the *rise in immigrant quantity* and the *fall in immigrant quality*?

> The pressures immigration placed on labor markets, particularly in the urban Northeast, produced a remarkable backlash in the 1850s. The first response of native workers was increased labor militancy. . . . The second response was political: increasing support for those who preached the nativist creed. . . . The popular press took up the anti-immigrant cry with equal fervor: an editorial in the Philadelphia Sun asserted that "the enormous influx of foreigners will in the end prove ruinous to American workingmen." (Ferrie 1999: 162–163)

The economics underlying that *Philadelphia Sun* editorial and the Know-Nothing political party rhetoric is pretty obvious: a glut in the labor supply lowered the unskilled wage relative to profits and land rents. Since capital and land were held by those at the top of the distribution pyramid, immigration-induced labor supply growth must have created more inequality and the demise of immi-

---

[3]   Ferrie (1999: 35). The immigration rate increased by more than *seven times* between the early 1820s and the early 1840s, even before the big leap to 15 per thousand in 1850. The U.S. immigration rate averaged "only" about 10 per thousand during the 1901–1910 boom decade (Hatton and Williamson 1998: Table 2.1).

Table 1:
The Migrant Stock as a Percent of Population, 1965–2000

	1965	1975	1985	1990a	1990b	2000
World	2.3	2.1	2.2	2.3	2.9	2.9
Emigrant Regions						
Africa	2.5	2.7	2.3	2.5	2.6	2.1
Asia	1.7	1.3	1.4	1.4	1.6	1.4
Latin Am. & Carib.	2.4	1.8	1.6	1.7	1.6	1.1
Immigrant Regions						
North America	6.0	6.3	7.8	8.6	9.8	13.0
Europe	2.2	2.7	3.0	3.2	6.7	7.7
Western Europe	*3.6*	*4.9*	*5.8*	*6.1*	*8.6*	*10.3*
Oceania	14.4	15.6	16.9	17.8	18.0	19.1

Note: There are differences of definition in the figures for 1965–1990a and 1990b–2000. The most important is due to the breakup of the Soviet Union, which is included with Europe for the earlier years, but the reclassified republics added about 27 million to the world international migrant stock in 2000.

Source: Hatton and Williamson (2005: Table 10.1).

gration would have created less, ceteris paribus. In addition, since immigrants were more unskilled than the native-born, immigration must have raised the premium on skills over the common laborer's wage as skills got relatively scarce and the demise of immigration would have reduced the premium on skills as they got relatively abundant, ceteris paribus. However, few native workers were so skilled that they might have been complements to the unskilled, but rather most were near-substitutes for the unskilled. Immigration-induced changes in skill premia and earnings distributions would be a problem for the next century, not this one.

The Know-Nothings, or the Order of the Star-Spangled Banner, had about a million followers in 1854. All white males had the vote in the United States at that time, and these numbered 5.7 million. Thus, this third party was able to get more than a sixth of the potential voters, and in only two years! The Know-Nothings elected eight state governors, perhaps one hundred congressmen, and the mayors of Boston, Philadelphia, and Chicago (Ferrie 1999: 162), an impressive achievement.

1.2   Backlash: Attitudes toward Immigrants Today

Negative public opinion is on the rise today too, as the quantity of immigrants entering OECD labor markets has surged and, as we shall see, their quality has fallen. The rise in quantity has been impressive, as Table 1 confirms. When President John F. Kennedy wrote his book *A Nation of Immigrants* in 1964, it was not. But the migrant stock as a share of the local population rose in North America from 6 to 13 percent between 1965 and 2000, more than a doubling. Western Europe experienced an even bigger increase, from 3.6 percent in 1965 to 10.3 percent in 2000, a near tripling.

How has public opinion responded to the rise in quantity and the fall in quality of immigration this time? A 1995 international survey asked whether immigration should be reduced in their country, where a score of 3 meant "remain the same," 4 meant "reduce a little," and 5 meant "reduce a lot." The figures for three big immigrating countries were Germany 4.2, Britain 4.1, and the United States 3.9—ranging between "reduce a little" and "reduce a lot" (O'Rourke and Sinnott 2004: Table 1; see also Mayda 2003). Furthermore, these responses were, like those in the 1850s, given during boom times in host country labor markets. One can well imagine what they would be now as the OECD struggles out of the recent slump, perhaps as hostile as were those Midwest workers in the middle of the 1890s depression. While the labor market effects of immigration are again an issue, fiscal effects matter today as well, and they matter far more than in 1850s or even in the 1890s when governments were much smaller and immigrants were never a big net fiscal burden or bonus.

Voters in rich countries may be hostile toward immigrants and immigration for both economic and noneconomic reasons. Racism, xenophobia, and nationalist sentiment can push citizens to vote for immigration restriction. O'Rourke and Sinnott (2004) find that hostility towards immigrants in 1995 had much of its source in this kind of sentiment. They also find that economic motives help explain attitudes towards immigrants and immigration, and in predictable ways: it is the unskilled worker in rich countries who has the most negative sentiment; and the unskilled worker's negative sentiment is much stronger in more egalitarian countries (e.g., more so on the European continent than in the United States). But the more relevant question is how much of the recent *rise* in immigrant hostility is driven by a *rise* in racism, xenophobia, and nationalist sentiment? The 1995 survey cannot answer this question, but history will, as we shall see. Our strong prior, however, is that it is *changing* economic conditions and *changing* labor market quality of the immigrants that drives *changing* voter attitude.

1.3   Political Action at the End of the First Global Century

What was the impact of the immigrant backlash a century ago? New World host countries gradually closed their doors to immigrants after the 1890s. The doors did not suddenly slam shut on American immigrants when the United States Congress overrode President Wilson's veto of the Immigrant Literacy Act in February 1917, or when it passed the Emergency Quota Act of May 1921, since there was plenty of precedent and warning. Over the half-century prior to the Literacy Act, the United States had been imposing restrictions on what had been free immigration (e.g., contract labor laws, Chinese exclusion acts, excludable classes, head taxes, and so on). And the United States was hardly alone. Argentina, Australia, Brazil, and Canada enacted restrictive measures, although the timing was sometimes different, and the policies often took the form of an enormous drop in, or even disappearance of, large immigrant subsidies rather than a move to outright exclusion. Thus, travel and job search subsidies disappeared, and offers of free land did too.

The United States illustrates this long political process best. The U.S. debate over immigration restriction started on the House floor in 1895, in the depths of the depression. It continued with the first House roll call in 1897 when 86 percent of the representatives voting went for restriction (Goldin 1994). But American three-legged politics require that the House, the Senate, and the President all agree, and the latter two disagreed with the former. Thus, the debate continued with the creation of the fact-finding Immigration (Dillingham) Commission in 1906, which reported its blockbuster findings in 1911—that immigrants were low-skilled, crowded out native born, were poor citizens or even refused citizenship,[4] and contributed to poverty. The debate was resolved when Congress overrode President Woodrow Wilson's veto in 1917. Recall that the legislation passed was an immigrant literacy requirement, a hurdle that Congress thought would be high enough to keep out poorly educated immigrants. As it turned out, the hurdle was not high enough, since in the meantime a European schooling revolution had armed young adults pondering the move with the literacy necessary to leap over the U.S. bar (Hatton and Williamson 2005: Chapter 8). [5]

---

[4]   The Dillingham Commission stressed that "new" immigrants were much more frequently temporary and had far higher return migration rates than did the "old" immigrants. By refusing citizenship, they refused assimilation, and thus remained strangers in the United States. This was an important source of hostility, something that is well worth remembering when politicians push for temporary immigration status today.

[5]   It should be noted that the literacy test required immigrants to have a basic level of literacy in *any* language. Had literacy in English been required, the literacy test might have been more effective in blocking out immigrants from Southern and Eastern Europe.

When the underlying fundamentals favor immigration restrictions, they are usually not imposed until an economic crisis occurs, that is, when short-run labor market problems are most acute and affected citizens are most verbal. These are precisely the episodes when labor demand slumps, labor markets go slack, potential emigrants postpone their move, and previous immigrants return home disappointed. Under those conditions, net immigration falls to low levels even in the absence of any policy restriction. Indeed, if immigrants flee poor labor market conditions in the host country, then their departure should tend to ease unemployment and prop up sagging earnings of the native-born. Of course, these benign labor market effects never stopped politicians and labor unions from using inflammatory, anti-immigrant rhetoric during industrial crises. Immigrants have always been convenient nonvoting scapegoats.

Contrary to the conventional wisdom, therefore, while there was a big regime switch in policy around World War I from unrestricted (and often subsidized) immigration to quotas, there was no big switch in public attitude. Rather, there had been a continued toughening of attitudes towards immigration in the high-wage New World. Attitudes did not change overnight, but it took a powerful triggering mechanism to convert the underlying anti-immigration sentiment to anti-immigration action.

2   Positive Selection, Negative Selection, and Declining Immigrant "Quality"

2.1   Declining Immigrant Quality Today

Annual immigration to North America and Oceania rose gradually to the mid-1970s before surging to a million per year in the 1990s. The absolute numbers were by then similar to those reached during the age of mass migration about a century earlier, but they were smaller relative to the destination country populations that had to absorb them. Thus, the U.S. annual immigration rate fell from 11.6 immigrants per thousand in the 1900s to 0.4 immigrants per thousand in the 1940s, before rising again to 4 immigrants per thousand in the 1990s. The proportion of the foreign-born U.S. population had fallen from a 1910 peak of 15 percent to an all-century low of 4.7 percent in 1970. The postwar immigration boom increased the proportion of the foreign-born to more than 8 percent in 1990 and more than 10 percent in 2000. Thus, the United States has today reclaimed two-thirds of the title "a nation of immigrants" after a half-century retreat.

What happened to the United States after World War II also happened world-wide. Table 1 reports trends in the foreign-born around the world over the thirty-five years since the mid-1960s. The data are based on country censuses, and because they measure the immigrant stock rather than the flow, they deal with unambiguous net permanent moves.[6] The most revealing entries appear in the last four rows of the table. There we see that the foreign-born share in the total population increased by about a third in Oceania between 1965 and 2000 (from 14.4 to 19.1 percent), more than doubled in North America (from 6 to 13 percent), and more than tripled in Europe (from 2.2 to 7.7 percent). North America is defined to exclude emigrating Mexico, so in this case we are talking exclusively about a high-wage immigrant-absorbing region. The same is not true of Europe, since the latter is defined to include Eastern Europe and the former Soviet Union, two net emigrating regions and, increasingly, a significant source of migrants for the European Union. The foreign-born share in *Western* Europe rose from 3.6 percent in 1965 to 10.3 percent in 2000, an increase of more than three times, even bigger than for North America. Of course, the addition of undocumented immigrants would raise these foreign-born shares, and perhaps even raise their increase over time.

While OECD immigration has surged, the labor market quality of these immigrants has declined. For example, U.S. immigrant males earned 4.1 percent *more* than native-born men in 1960, but they earned 16.3 percent *less* in 1990 (Borjas 1999: 1724). Some of this was due to the decline in immigrant educational attainment, but when we control for this effect, the adjusted relative wage still fell by 13.3 percent over these thirty years. Recently arrived immigrants always suffer an earnings disadvantage before they assimilate, and that was even true in 1960. But their initial relative wage deteriorated by 24 percentage points over those thirty years. Although the average educational attainment of immigrants improved, it did not increase as rapidly as that of the native-born. The percentage with less than 12 years education (equivalent to less than high school) is greater among immigrants and that gap increased dramatically between 1970 and 1990. For newly arrived immigrants, that share was 5.6 percentage points higher than for the native-born in 1970, but 20.4 percentage points higher in 1990, an increase of almost *four times* (Hatton and Williamson 2005: Table 15.1). Our guess is that this educational quality decline took place before 1970 and after 1990 as well.

---

[6]   We use the term foreign-born here although for some countries, particularly in Europe, the data record those holding foreign nationality rather than those born abroad. Since the foreign-born generally exceed foreign nationals (by proportion that reflects the country's naturalization laws, among other things), the proportion of foreigners is underestimated in some parts of the world relative to others.

Most of this decline in immigrant education and earnings is due to changes in the source country composition of U.S. immigrants (Table 2; see also Borjas 1999), and it reflects four seismic shifts in world migration patterns by source over the half century since World War II. The first seismic shift involved Europe's decline as an emigrant source: European emigration to North America and Oceania collapsed from 400,000 per annum in the early 1950s to less than 100,000 per annum in the early 1990s. Part of this drop can be explained by the resurgence of migration *within* Europe. To take only one example, the share of Portuguese emigrants moving *within* Europe rose from a tiny minority of 1.5 percent in 1950–1954 to a large majority of 57.1 percent in 1970–1974 (United Nations 1979). Migration *within* Europe (including Turkey) grew rapidly in the early postwar years through guestworker arrangements, particularly in Germany, where by 1973 one out of nine workers was foreign-born. Foreign nationals increased from 1.3 percent of the Western European population in 1950 to 3.6 percent in 1965 and 10.3 percent 1990. The 2000 figure would be even higher if it included the foreign-born that had become naturalized (Stalker 1994: 189–190).

Table 2:
Composition of U.S. Immigration by Sending Region, 1951–2000 (% of total)

Region of origin	1951–1960	1961–1970	1971–1980	1981–1990	1991–2000
Europe	52.7	33.8	17.8	10.3	14.9
West	47.1	30.2	14.5	7.2	5.6
East	5.6	3.6	3.3	3.1	9.4
Asia	6.1	12.9	35.3	37.3	30.7
Americas	39.6	51.7	44.1	49.3	49.3
Canada	15.0	12.4	3.8	2.1	2.1
Mexico	11.9	13.7	14.2	22.6	24.7
Caribbean	4.9	14.2	16.5	11.9	10.8
Central America	1.8	3.1	3.0	6.4	5.8
South America	3.6	7.8	6.6	6.3	5.9
Africa	0.6	0.9	1.8	2.4	3.9
Oceania	0.5	0.8	0.9	0.6	0.6
Total (000's)	2,515	3,322	4,493	7,338	9,095

Note: National origin based on country of last residence. Totals include 2.7 million former illegal aliens receiving permanent resident status under the Immigration Reform and Control Act 1986. Of these, 1.3 million fall in the decade 1981–1990 and 1.4 million in the decade 1991–2000. The subheadings under "Americas" do not include "other."

Source: Hatton and Williamson (2004: Table 10.2).

More recently, Western and Southern Europe have become destinations for immigrants from Asia, the Middle East and Africa, and since the demise of the Soviet Union in the 1990s Western Europe has also absorbed immigrants from the East, including the former Soviet republics. As a result, annual net immigration into the European Union (EU) rose from 200,000 in the 1980s to over a million in 1989–1993: over the decade between the 1980s and 1990s, EU immigration more than tripled. Indeed, EU immigration now surpasses that of the United States and would exceed it by even more if (estimated) illegal immigrants were included.

The second seismic shift involved the transformation of Latin America from a major emigrant destination to a major immigrant source. The Latin American evolution is a mirror image of the European transformation from a major source to a major destination, and it appears to be unique. We have come to expect that poor, low-wage, and agrarian countries should send out emigrants, especially during early industrialization, but at some point these countries should start to receive immigrants as they get rich, industrial, and high-wage. Latin America is an exception to this rule, and the explanation appears to be that the region has an even richer and faster growing neighbor to the north. Since the 1920s, Latin American income per capita has lagged further behind that of North America, and the gap in living standards has progressively widened. Thus, it is hardly surprising that the stock of immigrants in Latin America and the Caribbean who were born outside the region fell from 3.7 million in 1960 to 3 million in 1980, while Latin Americans and Caribbeans residing outside the region increased from 1.9 million to 4.8 million over the same two decades. The magnitude of this change has been really quite phenomenal: Latin America underwent a secular regime switch from hosting (net) 1.8 million foreign-born, to having (net) 1.8 million Latin Americans hosted abroad, a regime switch adding up to a net change of 3.6 million over only two decades!

The changing source of United States immigrants is particularly instructive in illustrating this Latin American migration revolution (Table 2). Whereas only about a fifth (22.2 percent) of all U.S. immigrants came from south of the border in the 1950s, almost half (47.2 percent) did so in the 1990s, the latter about equally split between Mexico and the rest of Latin America and the Caribbean. Mexicans themselves increased their share of U.S. (legal) immigration from almost 12 percent in the 1950s to almost 25 percent in the 1990s. No doubt, the measured share would have increased even more had it included illegals. Some observers argue that the sustained increase in the number of Mexican-Americans presents a challenge to U.S. assimilation capabilities that has no equal in its long immigration history (Huntington 2004).

The third seismic shift during the postwar decades involved Asian and African immigrants, whose numbers rose from negligible to a very large flow. Asian migrants to the United States have come mainly from India, Pakistan, China, Korea, the Philippines, and Vietnam. Europe has undergone the same surge in Asian immigration as well as a surge from Africa and the Middle East. Annual immigration from the developing world into five major European destination countries—Belgium, Germany, the Netherlands, Sweden, and the United Kingdom—rose from 97,000 in 1975–1979 to 225,000 in 1990–1993 (United Nations 1997: 32–33). For Germany alone, annual immigration from North Africa and Western Asia more than tripled from 20,000 in 1975–1979 to 67,000 in 1990–1993, while the numbers from sub-Saharan Africa rose from 1,200 to 22,000.

The fourth seismic shift involved emigration from Eastern Europe.[7] The movement of European labor from the less industrial and poor East to the more industrial and rich West has a long history that goes back to the industrial revolution almost two centuries ago. Even during the troubled interwar years, migration from Poland and Czechoslovakia to Belgium and France was extensive. In the five years following the end of WWII, something like 12 million ethnic Germans returned to Austria or Germany from Poland, Czechoslovakia, and the Soviet Union. When the Soviet Union annexed eastern parts of Poland at the end of the war, some 1.5 million Poles emigrated.

This traditional east-west flow of European migrants was stopped cold by postwar emigration policy in the centrally planned economies (United Nations 2002: 12). Thus, a historically important world migration flow almost ceased for those three or four decades after 1950. Things changed dramatically in the 1980s when Poland and Romania opened up, and they changed even more dramatically when the Berlin Wall fell in November of 1989. Emigration from what came to be called the transition economies increased by five times between 1985 and 1989, from about 240,000 to about 1.2 million. The annual outflows stayed at those high levels until 1993, when they eased off a bit, averaging around 700,000

---

[7]   A fifth seismic shift involved the Persian Gulf. The development of oil production and exports in the countries bordering the Persian Gulf led to a large labor demand boom which spilled over into an increasing demand for foreign workers. The rapid job creation appeared in construction and trade and low-skilled service industries, as well as in occupations requiring more highly educated workers, such as teachers, engineers, and doctors. Initially, the rising excess demand for labor was satisfied by importing temporary contract workers from nearby parts of the Arab world, like Egypt, Palestine, and Yemen. With the formation of the OPEC cartel and with the continuing increase in world demand for oil, crude oil prices reached unprecedented heights. This price boom raised local income and generated an extraordinary increase in the demand for labor, an excess demand that spilled over into a demand for foreign workers. While contract workers from other Arab states continued to move to the Persian Gulf, they were soon far outnumbered by the millions of temporary workers from nearly all parts of Asia. The annual flow of Asian workers to the Middle East increased from less than 100,000 in 1975 to nearly one million in 1991, with the sources moving eastward as time went on. This sharp upward trend ceased after the first Gulf War and the economic changes that flowed in its wake.

in 1997 and 1998 (United Nations 2002: Tables 3 and 5). Since illegal immigrants from the rest of the world are using Europe's east as a door to its west, these legal migration figures no doubt understate the magnitude of the total immigrant surge in Western Europe. In short, Europe seems to have reestablished its old east–west migration tradition.

2.2   Declining Immigrant Quality due to Changing Source in the First Global Century

The current discussion over the impact of shifting immigrant source on the labor market quality of immigrants certainly has its parallel in the pre-1914 era, years that culminated in the influential Dillingham Commission Report and the subsequent country-of-origin quotas imposed a decade later. An ominous comparison, perhaps, but it provides an obvious benchmark. So how do the two eras match up?

The figures for (gross) intercontinental emigration from Europe are plotted as five-year averages in Figure 1. In the first three decades after 1846, the numbers averaged about 300,000 per annum; in the next two decades, they more than doubled; and after the turn of the century, they rose to over a million per annum. European emigrant sources also changed dramatically. In the first half of the century, the dominant emigration stream was from the British Isles, followed by Germany. A rising tide of Scandinavian and other northwest European emigrants joined these "old" emigrant streams by mid-century. Southern and Eastern Europeans followed suit in the 1880s. This "new" emigrant stream from the south and east accounted for most of the rising emigrant totals in the late 19th century. It came first from Italy and parts of Austria–Hungary, but from the 1890s it swelled to include Poland, Russia, Spain, and Portugal. This shift in country-of-origin implied a decline in immigrant education, literacy, and skills as more and more came from low-wage, low-skilled, and low-schooled regions.

Observers and voters noted the decline in immigrant quality before World War I, and it became an important issue in debates over policy. So much for political realities, but what was the economic impact of the decline in immigrant quality? In 1909 the wage for the average male immigrant in industry was 6.4 percent lower than for native-born males; a figure comparable with the late 1970s. Male immigrants in 1909 who were newly arrived earned 20.4 percent less than natives, a figure that is also similar to the 1970s. But note this important fact: the variation in immigrant quality by source is *five times greater* in modern times than it was in the past. Thus, the standard deviation of the log wage across immigrant nationalities was 0.056 in 1909 as compared with 0.295 across immigrant nationalities in 1980. Stated another way, much of the source country difference in labor market performance is accounted for by the wage gap between "old" and "new" immigrants (Hatton 2000: 520–525): the wage gap in 1909 between immigrants from northwest Europe (old) and the rest (new) was 6.7 percent; by contrast, the wage gap in 1980 between Europeans and those from Africa, Asia, and South America was 30.7 percent.

Figure 1:
Emigration from Europe, 1871–1939 (five-year averages)

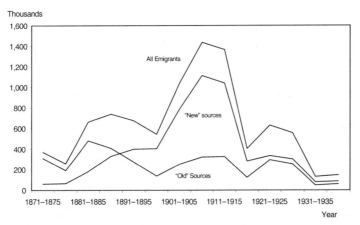

Source: Underlying data from Kirk (1946: 289).

Since wage gaps among newly arrived immigrants are much wider in more recent times, the effects of changing nationality mix are potentially more powerful. Between 1873 and 1913, the effect of shifting immigrant origins toward less developed countries was to reduce the immigrant wage by only 4.7 percentage points (2.3 percentage points after 1893). Between 1940 and 1980, however, source country composition shifts reduced the immigrant wage by 27 percentage points (17 percentage points after 1960). Thus, the decline in the labor market quality of immigrants in the four decades before 1980 was *much* greater than that which prevailed in the four decades before World War I, and it continued into the 1990s. Furthermore, these calculations understate the downward drift in immigrant quality to the extent that it only considers *legal* immigrants. Illegal immigrants tend to be less skilled and it appears that they have increased in relative importance over the past half century.

2.3   Individual Selection versus Country Source Effects

What about the selection of immigrants from a given country? According to the Roy model, immigrants should be more negatively selected the higher the return to skills is (and the greater earnings inequality is) at the origin relative to that in the destination (Borjas 1987). Given that Mexican inequality exceeds American inequality, theory suggests that Mexican emigrants should be unskilled. In terms of observable skills, however, immigrants from Mexico were drawn predominantly from the *middle* of the distribution, not from the bottom (Chiquiar and Hanson 2002). Some evidence of this is offered by Table 3, which reports education data for adult migrants in OECD host countries by sending source and for adults in the same sending source countries. While migrants in the OECD have 7.2 more years of education than the adults they left back home, Mexican migrants (mostly in the United States) had only 1.2 more years of education than Mexican adults back home. The data in Table 3 do not adjust for the fact that immigrants are younger than the average adult back home, or for the fact that immigrants may have received some education in host countries after their arrival. However, it is very clear that the gap between mover and stayer is much smaller for Mexicans, who are close to the United States, than for East Europeans, Balkans, and Turks, who are close to the EU.

Table 3:
Education of Sending Country Stayers and of Its Emigrants in Host Countries, ca. 1990

Region (No. of sending countries)	Years of schooling		
	Stayers in the sending country	Migrants in the host countries	Difference (migrants–stayers)
Africa (4)	4.6	15.4	10.8
Mexico (1)	6.3	7.5	1.2
Caribbean and Central America (14)	5.4	11.2	5.8
South America (10)	5.9	12.5	6.6
Asia (15)	5.8	14.4	8.6
Eastern Europe, the Balkans, and Turkey (3)	7.8	12.6	4.8
Total (47)	5.7	12.9	7.2

Note: All figures are unweighted averages. The stayer column is based on Barro–Lee, while the migrant column is based on OECD censuses around 1990. The two columns use country observations only if they supply both the stayer and the migrant information.

Source: Based on Hendricks (2002: Table B1).

Although Latin American immigrants are not, on the whole, negatively selected, it seems that they are less positively selected than migrants from poorer and more distant sources. One reason for the weaker positive selection revealed in immigration from sources close by is that, as a share of income, migration costs decrease sharply with skill level, offsetting the positive selection effects of greater inequality at the source. Thus, the higher the migration costs the more positive immigrant selection is (Chiswick 2000). Mexico is close enough to the United States, and countries to the immediate east and southeast are close enough to the EU, so that all share lower migration costs and thus can send poorer and less skilled migrants. Greater distances, lower source country inequality, a weaker friends and relatives effect, and (for the poorest regions) the poverty constraint all imply that U.S. and EU migrants coming from farther away should be more positively selected. So it was that the 1990 share of U.S. immigrants with tertiary schooling was more than three times higher for Asians and Africans than it was for Mexicans and Central Americans. And so it was that the gap in education level between movers and stayers was greatest for Asians and Africans (Table 3).

While the United States and other overseas regions faced *rising immigrant quantity* before World War I, they also faced *falling immigrant quality*. The OECD is facing similar trends again today. In both global centuries, it was the shift in source from richer to poorer regions that lowered the education and skills of the typical immigrant.

3   Why the Drift from Highly Positive toward More Negative Selection?

3.1   Selection by Sending Region in the First Global Century

The emigrants in 1900 were certainly different from those in 1800. Early 19th century migrations often took place as family groups, intent on acquiring land and settling at some overseas frontier. While many still had rural roots in the late 19th century, the emigrants from any given country were increasingly drawn from cities, towns, and urban occupations. Thus, emigrants from Britain in the 1830s, a country that by then had already undergone a half-century of industrialization, were mainly from nonfarm occupations. This industrialization-induced trend was overwhelmed by the shift from old emigrant sources, the industrial leaders, to new emigrant sources, the industrial followers. In short, the 19th century shift in source dominated immigrant selectivity, and it served to lower the average skills of immigrants to the United States. So it was that this shift in source left its mark on trends in the occupational composition of immigrants across the century (Table 4). Thus, the share of the immigrants that were unskilled rose from 16 percent in the 1820s to 55 percent in the 1890s, while the share that were skilled fell from 61 to 30 percent. The trends from very positive selection to negative selection were probably even more dramatic than these figures suggest, and for two reasons. First, "farmers" were individuals with assets, coming from the middle of the European income distribution. If these are added to the skilled, that share falls from 84 to 42 percent. Second, between the 1820s and the 1890s, the United States underwent an industrialization rate that was the envy of the world. Along the way, the unskilled fell as a share of the resident labor force, and the share of the skilled, professional, and commercial increased. Thus, *relative* to the host country labor force, the quality of the immigrants declined even more spectacularly across the century. The same, of course, has been true over the last half century.

Table 4:
The Occupations of U.S. Immigrants, 1820–1898

Occupation	1820–1831	1832–1846	1847–1854	1855–1864	1865–1873	1873–1880	1881–1893	1894–1898
Skilled	61	40	24	36	31	30	24	30
Farmers	23	33	33	23	18	18	14	12
Unskilled	16	26	43	41	51	48	60	55
Miscellaneous	–	–	–	0	1	5	3	3
Percent male	70	62	59	58	62	63	61	57

Note: Skilled = professional, commercial, and skilled artisans; unskilled = servants and laborers.

Source: http//:www.eh.net/encyclopedia/cohn.immigration.us.php.

The Immigration Commission concluded that the new immigrants were inferior to the old. True, the commission failed to allow for the assimilation process when comparing new and old immigrants. But even when such adjustments are made, it appears that significant differences between origin groups remain and that these can be traced largely to their characteristics upon arrival. Drawing on the commission's evidence, Jenks and Lauck (1926) demonstrated that among those admitted in 1899–1909, 22 percent of old immigrants but only 9.2 percent of new immigrants were classified as either professional or skilled (1926: 36). They also found that among adults only 2.7 percent of old immigrant arrivals were illiterate compared with 35.8 percent of new immigrants. Jenks and Lauck interpreted this as powerful evidence that immigrant quality had fallen as a result of the shift in immigrant source. Yet, as Table 4 shows, there is little evidence of any decline in the share of immigrants that were classified as having skilled, professional, or commercial occupations after the 1870s, when new immigrants arrived in such large numbers.[8] Even so, the immigrants would have declined in quality relative to the host labor force, as it gained in schooling and skills.

Positive or negative selection should be judged relative to the sending or the host country. When it is the former, the discussion is about brain drain. When it is the latter, the discussion is about assimilation. Table 5 offers some proxies describing trends in U.S. population and thus labor force quality after 1870, and in the schooling dimension. School enrollment rates rose from 48.4 in 1870 to 69.9 percent in 1930. Attendance rates (days in school per enrolled student) doubled, from 78.4 in 1870 to 151.7 in 1930. As a result of these educational investments, illiteracy dropped steadily over the six decades, from 20 to 4.3 percent. (In 1900, just six years before the Immigration Commission was formed, the U.S. illiteracy rate was 10.7 percent, while it was 35.8 percent for "new" immigrants. No wonder concern about low quality immigrants became a public issue.) High school graduates were only 2 percent of all 17-year-olds in 1870, but 8.6 percent in 1910 and 28.8 percent in 1930. Thus, even if immigrant educational attainment had been constant over the period, their *relative* attainment would have declined

Table 5:
Quality Proxies for the U.S. Population, 1870–1930

	Enrollment rates per 100 population	Attendance rates per student	% 17-year-olds graduating high school	Illiteracy rate
1870	48.4	78.4	2.0	20.0
1880	57.8	81.1	2.5	17.0
1890	54.3	86.3	3.5	13.3
1900	50.5	99.0	6.3	10.7
1910	59.2	113.0	8.6	7.7
1920	64.3	121.2	16.3	6.0
1930	69.9	151.7	28.8	4.3

Source: U.S. Department of Commerce (1975: 370, 375–376, 379–380, 382).

---

8   Douglas (1919) made the same point in his critique of the commission: specifically, he argued that the proportion of the skilled among the new immigrants in 1899-1909 was no lower than that among the old immigrants at a time when they formed the bulk of the inflow.

significantly. Any absolute decline in observed immigrant educational quality must be augmented to reflect an even greater relative decline.

In spite of the unambiguous evidence of declining relative education, opposing views about the evolution of immigrant labor market quality persisted, but perhaps they can be reconciled by noting two trends that were pushing in opposite directions. On the one hand, immigrants from each country were becoming more skilled and educated as industrialization proceeded and schooling expanded at home (but perhaps not as fast as in the United States). On the other hand, the immigrant composition was shifting towards the less developed sending regions. The right question to ask is: What effect did the shift in source-country composition have *by itself* on the average skills of immigrants? If we focus only on European males and only on those who reported an occupation, the share of the skilled and professional fell by 4.3 percentage points between 1873 and 1913 (Hatton 2000: Tables 1 and 4). But had the source-country composition stayed constant, the share of the skilled and professional would have *increased* by 2.7 percentage points, a difference of 7 percentage points (from –4.3 to 2.7). More dramatic still, between 1893 and 1913 the share of adult immigrants who were literate (in any language) fell by 4 percentage points, whereas it would have *increased* by more than 6 percentage points if source-country composition had remained constant, a difference of 10 percentage points.

It appears that Jenks and Lauck are vindicated: source-country composition effects reduced immigrant quality by quite a bit, at least according to literacy and occupational status; and they reduced it still more relative to U.S. literacy rates. But how much difference did those attributes make to their labor market performance? That is, did the destination labor market place high value on those home-acquired attributes? The decline in immigrant earnings relative to the native-born that can be attributed to the changing country of origin has been estimated to be less than 5 percentage points, a decline that was associated mostly with the effects of the shifting source-country composition on the proportions who were literate and skilled (Hatton 2000: 520).

Is a five percent decline in the relative earnings capacity of the immigrant inflow over forty years big or small? Perhaps a comparison with more recent experience might help gauge its impact. Source-country composition effects account for a 26 percentage point fall in the relative earnings of newly arrived immigrants between 1940 and 1980 (Borjas 1992). This is five times as large as the composition effects on immigrant earnings that occurred between 1873 and 1913. Part of the reason for the big difference is that the earnings gap between the new and old immigrants of the 1960s and 1970s were *much* larger than those between the new and old immigrants of the 1890s and 1900s. Had the Immigration Commission been able to look forward 70 years they might have had a higher opinion of the new immigrants of their own day.

3.2   Were Immigrants Positively Selected? Controlling by Source

Even if the labor market quality of U.S. immigrants declined as a result of the changing origin, it might still have been true that immigrants were positively selected. Indeed, it is widely believed that international migrants were and are the best and brightest—that on average they are more skilled, more ambitious, and more enterprising than those who stay home. Although it may be widely believed, the late 19th century evidence is far from clear-cut. Selection could occur along a number of observable characteristics like education, skill, wealth, and family background, but what about unobservable characteristics like ambition, energy, and motivation? The issue of selection is further complicated by the fact that we cannot observe how migrants would have done had they stayed in the home country. In addition, are we interested in selection relative to home or host country populations? If the focus is on the political economy of immigration restrictions, then it is the host country that matters. In any case, we do not have the evidence to be very precise about host or home country labor force quality. Given these complications, much of what follows should be viewed as informed speculation.

Inferences about selection can be drawn from immigrant performance in destination labor markets. Given sufficient time to assimilate, those from northwest Europe often achieved higher earnings than the native-born. This fact implies that the advantage of positive selection eventually outweighed the initial disadvantage of being an immigrant. Those from Southern and Eastern Europe may also have been positively selected, but even if they were, the positive selection effect failed to outweigh the immigrant disadvantage, since their skills, particularly language, were of much lower value in the destination country. A further piece of evidence comes from second-generation immigrants who inherit some of their parents' characteristics but who do not suffer their initial immigrant disadvantage. Native-born workers with one or two foreign-born parents had earnings that were 6.5 percent *higher* than those with native-born parents (Hatton 1997, 2000; Minns 2000). Second generation immigrants appear to have had an advantage over those with native-born parents, implying an element of inherited positive selection.

What about evidence from immigrant origins? Emigrants before the mid-19th century—the pioneers of mass transatlantic migration—were frequently farmers and artisans. While they were not upper class—like the most powerful merchants and the landed rich—these pioneer migrants *were* from the middle class of their day. For example, emigrants from the German region of Hesse-Cassel were in 1832–1857 "positively selected because the highest skilled were over-represented. In terms of financial wealth, the emigrant population was negatively selected because the richest were under-represented" (Wegge 2002: 390). Emigrants who moved later in the 19th century reveal similar patterns. Thus, among emigrants from Denmark between 1868 and 1900 craftsmen and artisans were overrepresented—their share among emigrants was about twice that among the source population; laborers were underrepresented even though they were the majority of the emigrants (Hvidt 1975: 113).[9] Thus, for most countries the poorest were underrepresented in emigrant flows. Still, the important issue is not whether selection was positive or negative, but whether it became less positive, and strongly so.

3.3   Constraints, Incentives, and Immigrant Selection

Low representation of the very poor in immigrant flows is consistent with the view that poverty constrained the volume of emigration from the poorer parts of Europe. It is also consistent with the view that transatlantic migrants were more positively selected than they would have been in the absence of poverty constraints. The very poor had the most to gain by a long distance move to high-wage labor markets, but they were least able to marshal the resources needed to invest in the move. These poverty constraints facing Europe's poor declined over the first global century due to the combined effect of the following forces (Hatton and Williamson 1998; 2005: Chapters 3 and 4): transport revolutions lowered the steerage costs from port to port and lowered the cost of getting from interior to port; the same transport revolutions reduced the time in transit, thus lowering income foregone; industrial revolutions at home raised working class earnings, making it easier for potential emigrants to find the surplus to invest in the move; and previous pioneer emigrants sent prepaid tickets and other remittances home, helping to finance the next wave. As the poverty constraint on immigration was released, positive selection diminished and negative selection increased. This fact helps explain an emigration paradox. The emigration rate was low for poorer European countries and regions, and higher for richer countries and regions. Furthermore, European countries went through emigration life cycles, emigration rates *rising*, not falling, as industrial revolutions unfolded at home. Since the incentive to move fell as incomes rose at home, it must have been an even bigger decline in constraints that explains this life cycle.

---

[9]   The underrepresentation of unskilled laborers among new emigrants was not always true, as the Irish illustrate. Long after the famine, Irish laborers were still 80 percent of male emigrants in 1881 but only 22 percent of the Irish labor force, and 84 percent of female emigrants were servants compared with 33 percent of the population. It appears that the poor Irish found another way out of the poverty trap: the huge post-famine emigrant stock abroad generated huge remittances which made subsequent emigration possible for poor and unskilled Irish, long after the famine years.

What about incentives? The modern literature on migration suggests that one factor determining immigrant selection is the relative return on skills at home and abroad. If the return to skills is higher in the (rich) destination country than in the (poor) origin country, then the skilled have a greater incentive to emigrate than the unskilled. Was that the case in the 19th century? Truly comparable cross-country evidence is sparse for most of the 19th century, but Table 6 presents skill premia for blue-collar occupations for four Atlantic regions in 1890. The premium for semiskilled and skilled workers over the unskilled was considerably larger in the United States than in Great Britain, Germany, and Switzerland. Other things equal, this would imply a greater incentive for skilled emigration from these countries. The same was not true of France and Belgium and it may not have been true of less developed, early industrializing, "new" European countries for which we do not have comparable data.

Table 6:
Skill Premia in the United States and Europe, 1890

	United States	Great Britain	France/ Belgium	Germany/ Switzerland
Premium for semiskilled over unskilled	28.4	16.1	25.2	17.9
Premium for skilled over unskilled	53.0	32.6	63.1	35.2

Note: These are the coefficients from a regression of log earnings for male household heads on age, age-squared, industry dummies (that differ between Europe and the United States) and skill by country dummies. All the coefficients reported here are significant at the 5 percent level.

Source: Hatton et al. (1994).

Hard evidence on the skilled premium is almost absent for the early 19th century, but there is a tradition that points out expensive unskilled labor and cheap skills in the early industrial United States compared with Britain (Habakkuk 1962; Rosenberg 1967). For example, while U.S. skilled machine makers in the 1820s received a wage only 2 percent more than their British counterparts, unskilled U.S. labor manning those machines earned 22 percent more. Thus, compared with the United States, the British skill premium was 20 percent higher in the 1820s. Such evidence suggests that, *in the absence of poverty constraints*, Anglo-American migration should have *negatively* selected British unskilled labor early in the century. We should repeat the important qualification "in the absence of poverty constraints," since that was the force that probably dominated even in the antebellum period. Anglo-American migration should have *positively* selected British skilled labor in the 1890s, after 50 or 60 years of hot-house American industrialization when the skill premium was pushed up so high by an explosion of skilled labor demands. Income incentive (negative selection) and poverty constraints (positive selection) were working against each other early in the century, while they were working together late in the century.

We should also observe systematic differences across destinations that offered different incentives or costs to the migrant. The skill composition of the flows to Canada and the United States were very similar at the turn of the century. New evidence suggests a good reason for this: skill premia were also very similar in the two countries (Green et al. 2002: 681).[10] It seems likely that skill premia were similar in Australia. Yet, British emigrants to Australia were much more skilled compared with those heading for North America (Pope and Withers 1994). Since the costs of migration to Australia were so much larger (even when subsidized), any difference in positive selection favoring Australia was likely to have been driven by poverty constraints (only the best could afford the move) rather than by wage relatives.

What about other streams of mass migration? One puzzle is why Italians from the *mezzogiorno* (the southern regions of Italy) who crossed the Atlantic typically went to the United States, while those from the more industrial north typically went to South America.[11] On the face of it, this fact seems anomalous, since the more literate, skilled, and urban northern Italians would seem to be better matched with United States labor markets, while the less literate, less skilled, and more rural Southern Italians would have been better matched with South American labor markets. Historians have argued that those at the bottom of the occupational ladder in the poor and backward *mezzogiorno* gained most by working as unskilled laborers in cities like New York, while those from the north had better opportunities to become middle class entrepreneurs or skilled workers in places like Buenos Aires (Klein 1983; Baily 1983: 296). The costs of migration mattered too, of course: the subsidies for migration to the Sao Paulo coffee plantations were offered exclusively to northern Italians.[12] But as the coffee

---

10 Similarities in the wage distributions are striking: in Canada, the log wage premia for operatives and craft workers over unskilled laborers were 0.14 and 0.39, respectively; in the United States, they were 0.19 and 0.40, respectively.

11 Among Italians who went to the United States between 1876 and 1930, 80 percent came from the south; among those who went to Argentina only 47 percent came from the south (Klein 1983: 309).

12 It is sometimes suggested that Italian flow to the United States was characterized by exceptionally high return migration rates. Although Italian return rates were higher than for most other immigrant groups in the United States, they were not much higher than the return rates of the Italians who went to Argentina. Between 1861 and

boom faded and as living standards in North America outstripped those in South America, *all* Italian emigrants, from north and south, shifted increasingly to the United States.

Clearly, cultural affinities, location preferences, and the friends and relatives effect all influenced who emigrated and where they went. But we can also detect the influence of strong economic forces on immigrant selection. It seems plausible to conclude that while positive selection was driven by wage incentives for British and German emigrants, it was driven more by poverty constraints in the poorer parts of Europe. It also seems likely that the degree of positive selection differed across destinations: the more distant the destination, the greater the costs of emigration and the more likely immigrants would be positively selected. Finally, to the extent that declining migration costs were the dominant force, thus releasing the emigration constraint, positive selection fell and negative selection rose across the first global century.

3.4   Policy and the Modern Drift to Poorer Immigrant Sources

In the first global century, shifts in the source-country composition were the result of rising incomes and demographic booms in Europe combined with falling transport costs between sending and receiving regions—forces that were amplified by the friends and relatives effect. These forces slowly reduced positive selection: the really poor could finance the move only late in the first global century, as their incomes at home rose and as the cost of passage fell. The same forces have also been at work in the modern era but policy served to accelerate the demise of positive selection. These policy changes included the abolition of the country-of-origin quotas that had previously favored Europe, the shift to a worldwide quota, and the emphasis on family reunification over skills as the key criteria for admission. Other OECD countries also opened their doors more widely and experienced shifts in immigrant composition and quality, but the effects have not been as dramatic. For example, as the sources of Canadian immigration widened after the 1960s, immigrant quality fell, but by less than it did in the United States (Baker and Benjamin 1994). Some have argued that the difference can be explained by policy, the Canadian points system selecting immigrants with higher average labor quality (Borjas 1993). Perhaps, but note that the difference is accounted for by one dominant fact: Latin Americans are 47 percent of U.S. immigrants but only 14 percent of Canadian immigrants, and Mexicans account for most of that disparity (Antecol et al. 2003). While this Latin differ-

---

1914, repatriation rates were 47 percent for the United States and 52 percent for Argentina (Baily 1983: 296).

ence may be partly due to immigration policy, it also reflects location. Distance matters enormously in explaining who migrates to the United States (Clark et al. 2002). Because of its closer proximity to Latin America and its long land border with Mexico, the United States would need an even more skill-selective immigration policy than Canada (or even quotas for Latin Americans) in order to raise immigrant quality to the Canadian level.

4   Why Do We Care? The Political Economy of Restriction

What explains the evolution of immigration policy? Increasing racism, xenophobia, and widening ethnicity gaps between previous and current immigrants have always been popular candidates. But political economy candidates turn out to be equally important: more immigrants, the declining labor market quality of those immigrants and the threat of further declines, crowded-out native unskilled workers, rising inequality, greater awareness of that inequality by the powerful (informed by activist reformers), and greater voting power in the hands of those hurt most—the working poor.

We now know a lot about the underlying determinants of changing immigration policy between 1860 and 1930 (Goldin 1994; Timmer and Williamson 1998; O'Rourke and Williamson 1999: Chapter 10). The most consistent effect is that immigration policy was slow to change. This was especially true of Brazil and the United States: in the latter case, the result is driven by the 1895–1917 period, which included two decades of public scrutiny and congressional debate, ending in the 1917 Immigration Act and the quotas which followed; and in the former case, the result is driven by the 1890–1920 period, when heavily subsidized immigration, financed by fat export earnings generated by high coffee prices, was replaced by restriction and no subsidies when plunging coffee prices generated lean export earnings. It is worth noting that where historical persistence was strongest, the switch in policy, from open to closed, was biggest. Big immigration policy changes typically require long periods of debate, and the longer the debate, the bigger the change.

Measures of macroeconomic conditions—like unemployment rates—were, predictably, of little help in accounting for long-run policy changes. However, the *timing* of the introduction of such policies was powerfully influenced by short-run macroeconomic conditions, often serving as the triggering mechanism. This was certainly true of the 1890s depression, the Great War, and postwar readjustment in the United States. It was true of the great depression for South African quotas in 1930, Brazilian quotas in 1934, and tough restrictions by Australia in 1930, New Zealand in 1931, and Canada in 1932. It was true of 1973–1974 in Europe, when the first oil price shock and subsequent rising unemployment provoked the end of the guestworker era. And it was true of European toughening on asylum seekers in the late 1990s, when host countries underwent a slowdown and falling employment rates.

Whether immigration has a big impact on labor markets in host countries or not (Williamson 1982, 1986, 1996, 1997, 1998; Hatton and Williamson 2004: Chapters 6 and 14), labor market conditions had a consistent influence on immigration policy, and they did so both through the absolute and relative income performance of unskilled workers. Real wage growth mattered most in the United States, nominal wage growth mattered most in Australia, while real wage levels mattered most in Brazil. In all cases, poor wage performance was associated with more restrictive policy. However, the most consistently significant explanatory variable is the ratio of the unskilled wage to per capita income, or of income near the bottom of the distribution to income in the middle. Rising inequality was associated with increasingly restrictive immigration policy. As we have seen, new immigrants tended to cluster at the bottom of the income distribution, a fact that was increasingly true as positive selection diminished over the century. Regardless of what else is included in the regression equation, this measure of labor's relative economic position stands up as an important influence on policy. Rising relative labor scarcity encouraged more open immigration policies; declining relative labor scarcity encouraged more restrictive immigration policies.

The evidence just summarized speaks to the *indirect* impact of immigration on policy by looking at absolute and relative wage performance in labor markets. What about the *direct* impact of immigration on policy? Perhaps the size and character of the current and expected future immigrant flows precipitated policy change, the latter serving to anticipate the labor market impact. Two variables serve to proxy direct immigration effects. One is a measure of *quality* of the immigrants—the real wage of urban workers in the source countries. Another is a measure of the *quantity* of the immigrants—the foreign-born population share. Low and falling immigrant quality tended to precipitate immigration restrictions in Australia, Canada, and the United States, even after controlling for other forces: policy in these countries anticipated the impact of rising numbers of low-quality immigrants on unskilled wages and moved to exclude them. In addition, Argentina seems to have looked to the north across the Rio de la Plata to watch labor market events in Brazil, acting as if they knew that those events in that bigger neighbor would divert immigrants to or from Argentina's labor markets. Thus, rising relative and absolute wages in Brazil tended to produce more open policy in Argentina, and deteriorating Brazilian labor market conditions made Argentina close off immigration. In contrast, the United States was never responsive to competitors' immigration policies, presumably because it was too big to care and thus was a policy leader. For the smaller immigrating countries, however, policy abroad mattered a great deal.

The difference in ethnic composition between the current immigration flow and the foreign population stock seems to have had little bearing on policy. This is not the relationship that the popular literature favors: according to that view, a rising gap between the ethnic origins of previous immigrants—who had become residents and probably voting citizens—and those of current immigrants would serve to erode commitments to free immigration. We should be quick to add that we are speaking here almost entirely about immigrants of *European* ethnic origin. The United States and other high-wage countries had already acted to exclude most Asians, and free Africans rarely tried to gain admission into the historically slave-based New World.

To summarize, while the *size* of the immigrant flow did not seem to have any consistent impact on New World policy up to 1930, its *low and declining quality* certainly did, provoking restriction. Racism and xenophobia do not seem to have been at work in driving the evolution of policy (which is not, of course, to deny that they existed). But in terms of changes over time, it was immigrant quality, labor market conditions, and policies abroad—especially those set by the economic leader, the United States—that mattered most for policy. New World countries acted in a way that revealed an effort to defend the economic interests of their scarce factor, unskilled labor.

5   Policy in Two Eras of Globalization

It has become a commonplace to compare policy trends during the two global centuries, the first up to the 1920s, and the second after the 1950s. Policies which promote world economic integration evolved very differently in the two centuries. Tariff and nontariff barriers have been progressively removed so that trade is at least as free now as it was then. International capital markets have also been liberalized to the extent that world financial markets may be even more integrated now than they were then. In sharp contrast, immigration policies have not returned to anything like the unrestricted openness that prevailed in the age of free mass migration.

This costly anomaly demands explanation. After all, estimates of the effects of eliminating barriers to world migration range between 10 and 100 percent of global GNP. These estimated gains to world migration are much bigger than those that might be reaped from removing the remaining barriers to trade or capital flows. As Rodrik (2002) has stressed, commodity prices rarely exceed a ratio of two to one; by contrast, the ratio of wages of similarly qualified individuals in developed countries are at least ten times that of less developed countries. Thus, if "policymakers were really interested in maximizing worldwide efficiency they would spend little of their energies on a new trade round or on the international financial architecture. They would all be busy at work liberalizing immigration restrictions" (Rodrik 2002: 314).

Thus, for Rodrik and most other observers the key question seems to be why the current immigration regime is so restrictive, when the potential gains to liberalization are so great. We think this is the wrong question. We think the right question is why OECD immigration policies are not *more* restrictive! As world migration increased across the first global century, its sources shifted to the poorer preindustrial periphery. This shift in immigrant origin towards poorer sending countries resulted in immigrants of lower skill and schooling *relative to host country native-born*. This decline in immigrant quality played an important role in provoking hostile attitudes towards immigrants as the first global century unfolded. And those hostile anti-immigrant attitudes were converted into political support for quality control, quotas, bans, and restrictions (Williamson 1997, 1998). From the 1890s to the 1930s, macroeconomic crises offered the trigger which converted the underlying fundamentals into policy action.

Now compare the first global century with current experience. The shift in emigrant source has been even more dramatic, and the induced labor productivity gap between source and destination has also become much bigger. As a result, the relative skills and schooling of newer immigrants into high-wage host countries have fallen even more rapidly than they did during the 50 years before 1914. Nowhere has this experience been more marked than in the United States. So, why has there not been the same hostile policy reaction in the thirty years after the 1970s as the reaction that took place in the thirty years after the 1890s?

We need some answers. One might be that the labor market effects of immigration are more benign today than they were a century ago, when land and other natural resources were more important and diminishing returns to labor had far more bite than it does today. In addition, perhaps spatial labor markets were more segmented then (best illustrated by the post-slavery South), which served to heighten the impact of immigration on urban gateways in the Northeast and Midwest. Certainly most studies of contemporary labor markets find that immigration's impact on the earnings and employment rates of natives are much more modest than they were a century ago. Another explanation might be that today's "new" immigrants compete far less directly with the median native-born worker (and voter) compared with a century ago, when the gaps in skills and schooling were smaller and when the market for manual labor was far more extensive. While all of these factors may help explain the anomaly, another makes it even more puzzling: the fiscal effects of immigration are *much* larger now, especially in Europe, than they were a century ago, when the welfare state was all but absent. The less skilled and educated the immigrants are, the bigger their net fiscal burden is likely to be. Thus, the declining "quality" of immigrants over recent decades implied a rising net fiscal burden on taxpaying natives. We have indirect support for the hypothesis, since we know that the richer the destination country is and the greater negative selectivity is, the greater popular antipathy to immigration is (O'Rourke and Sinnott 2001). We also have direct support for the hypothesis, since respondents often state that concerns about fiscal burden are important ingredients to their negative attitudes towards immigrants (Dustmann and Preston 2002).

True, attitudes toward immigrants have hardened in some countries. Yet, policy has not. Why the difference? Is the macroeconomic trigger missing? Recall that against a background of anti-immigrant sentiment, cumulative change in the economic fundamentals did not lead to policy backlash in the first global century until a major economic shock occurred. Indeed, there is evidence in the more recent past of episodes when cumulative anti-immigration pressures led to sharp changes in policy when a bad macroeconomic event triggered it. One example is the sudden and permanent guestworker recruitment stop that took place in Germany, the Netherlands, and elsewhere in Europe in the recession of 1973–1974 following the first oil price shock. Another is the dramatic toughening in policy towards asylum seekers that took place across the EU in the early 1990s after a couple of decades of rising OECD inequality (Hatton 2004). While these restrictive policy reactions are consistent with what happened in the past, they have not been nearly as dramatic as the policy reversals that took place during the interwar period. Perhaps the macroeconomic shocks have not been large enough to provide the political impetus for seismic reforms in immigration policy.

We hope to have shed light on current immigration policy by appealing to history. Still, we are left with that critical question: why have the trends in immigration policy been so different from those involving world trade and world finance? The fact that immigration policies are set unilaterally rather than through the sort of multilateralism that characterizes the World Trade Organization should make collective trade policy harder to achieve, not easier. Perhaps history matters here too: the politics surrounding the International Labor Organization were simply not as propitious for multilateralism as those that later underlay the GATT and the WTO (O'Rourke and Sinnott 2004). But that fact does not explain why greater efforts have not been made to establish multilateral migration agreements.

World migration differs from world trade in two important ways. First, permanent migration is a one-way street: migration imports are not matched by migration exports as they usually are on the trade balance sheet. Thus, there is less scope for the bilateral agreements (like the most-favored-nation clause) that spawned multilateralism in world trade. Second, the biggest gainers from trade liberalization are easily identifiable and have political voice. By contrast, the biggest gainers from liberalizing world migration are the migrants themselves, and they are the only ones who have absolutely no vote over policy whatsoever.

Bibliography

Antecol, H., D.A. Cobb–Clark, and S.K. Trejo (2003). Immigration Policy and the Skills of Immigrants to Australia, Canada and the United States. *Journal of Human Resources* 38 (1): 192–218.

Baily, S.L. (1983). The Adjustment of Italian Immigrants in Buenos Aires and New York, 1870–1914. *American Historical Review* 88 (2): 281–305.

Baker, M., and D. Benjamin (1994). The Performance of Immigrants in the Canadian Labor Market. *Journal of Labor Economics* 12 (3): 455–471.

Borjas, G.J. (1987). Self-Selection and the Earnings of Immigrants. *American Economic Review* 77 (4): 531–553.

Borjas, G.J. (1992). National Origin and the Skills of Immigrants in the Postwar Period. In G. Borjas and R. B. Freeman (eds.), *Immigration and the Workforce: Economic Consequences for the United States and Source Areas.* Chicago: University of Chicago Press.

Borjas, G.J. (1993). Immigration Policy, National Origin, and Immigrant Skills: A Comparison of Canada and the United States. In D. Card and R. B. Freeman (eds.), *Small Differences that Matter: Labor Markets and Income Maintenance in Canada and The United States.* Chicago: University of Chicago Press.

Borjas, G.J. (1999). The Economic Analysis of Immigration. In O. Ashenfelter and D. Card (eds.), *Handbook of Labor Economics.* Vol. 3A. New York: North Holland.

Chickering, J. (1848). *Immigration into the United States.* Boston: Little Brown.

Chiquiar, D., and G.H. Hanson (2002). International Migration, Self-Selection, and the Distribution of Wages: Evidence from Mexico and the United States. NBER Working Paper 9242. NBER, Cambridge, Mass.

Chiswick, B.R. (2000). Are Immigrants Favorably Selected? In C. B. Brettell and J. F. Hollifield (eds.), *Migration Theory: Talking Across Disciplines.* New York: Routledge.

Clark, X., T.J. Hatton, and J.G. Williamson (2002). Where Do US Immigrants Come From? Policy and Sending Country Fundamentals. NBER Working Paper 8998. NBER, Cambridge, Mass.

Douglas, P.H. (1919). Is the New Immigration More Unskilled than the Old? *Journal of the American Statistical Association* 16: 393–403.

Douglas, P.H. (1930). *Real Wages in the United States, 1890–1926.* New York: Augustus Kelley. Reprinted 1966.

Dustmann, C., and I. Preston (2002). Racial and Economic Factors in Attitudes to Immigration. Unpublished paper. University College London.

Ferrie, J.P. (1999). *Yankeys Now: Immigrants in the Antebellum United States, 1840–1860.* New York: Oxford University Press.

Goldin, C. (1994). The Political Economy of Immigration Restriction in the United States, 1890 to 1921. In C. Goldin and G. D. Libecap (eds.), *The Regulated Economy: A Historical Approach to Political Economy.* Chicago: University of Chicago Press.

Green A., M. MacKinnon, and C. Minns (2002). Dominion or Republic? Migrants to North America from the United Kingdom, 1870–1910. *Economic History Review* 55 (2): 666–696.

Habakkuk, H.J. (1962). *American and British Technology in the Nineteenth Century.* Cambridge: Cambridge University Press.

Hatton, T.J. (1997). The Immigrant Assimilation Puzzle in Late Nineteenth Century America. *Journal of Economic History* 57 (1): 34–62.

Hatton, T.J. (2000). How Much Did Immigrant "Quality" Decline in Late Nineteenth Century America? *Journal of Population Economics* 13 (3): 509–525.

Hatton, T.J. (2004). Seeking Asylum in Europe. *Economic Policy* 38: 5–62.

Hatton, T.J., and J.G. Williamson (1998). *The Age of Mass Migration: An Economic Analysis.* New York: Oxford University Press.

Hatton, T.J., and J.G. Williamson (2005). *Global Migration and the World Economy: Two Centuries of Policy and Performance.* Cambridge, Mass.: MIT Press.

Hatton, T.J., G.R. Boyer, and R.E. Bailey (1994). The Union Wage Effect in Late Nineteenth Century Britain. *Economica* 61 (20): 435–456.

Hendricks, L. (2002). How Important Is Human Capital for Development? Evidence from Immigrant Earnings. *American Economic Review* 92 (1): 198–219.

Higham, J. (1988). *Strangers in the Land: Patterns of American Nativism, 1860–1925.* 2nd ed. Piscataway, New Jersey: Rutgers University Press.

Huntington, S.P. (2004). Jose, Can You See? *Foreign Policy* 20 (March/April): 30–45.

Hvidt, C. (1975). *Flight to America.* New York: Academic Press.

Jenks, J.W., and W.J. Lauck (1926). *The Immigration Problem.* 6th ed. New York: Huebsch.

Jones, M.A. (1992). *American Immigration.* 2nd ed. Chicago: University of Chicago Press.

Kennedy, J.F. (1964). *A Nation of Immigrants.* New York: Harper Row.

Kirk, D. (1946). *Europe's Population in the Interwar Years.* Princeton: Princeton University Press for the League of Nations.

Klein, H.S. (1983). The Integration of Italian Immigrants into the United States and Argentina: A Comparative Analysis. *American Historical Review* 88 (2): 306–329.

Mayda, A.M. (2003). Who Is Against Immigration? A Cross-Country Investigation of Individual Attitudes Towards Immigrants. Mimeo. Harvard University (January). Cambridge, Mass.

Minns, C. (2000). Income, Cohort Effects, and Occupational Mobility: A New Look at Immigration to the United States at the Turn of the 20th Century. *Explorations in Economic History* 37 (4): 326–350.

O'Rourke, K.H., and R. Sinnott (2004). The Determinants of Individual Attitudes towards Immigration. Mimeo. Trinity College Dublin (January).

O'Rourke, K H., and J.G. Williamson (1999). *Globalization and History: The Evolution of a Nineteenth-Century Atlantic Economy.* Cambridge, Mass.: MIT Press.

Pope, D., and G. Withers (1994). Wage Effects of Immigration in Late-Nineteenth Century Australia. In T. J. Hatton and J. G. Williamson (eds.), *Migration and the International Labor Market, 1850–1939.* London: Routledge.

Rodrik, D. (2002). Final Remarks. In T. Boeri, G. Hanson and B. McCormick (eds.), *Immigration Policy and the Welfare System.* Oxford: Oxford University Press.

Rosenberg, N. (1967). Anglo-American Wage Differences in the 1820s. *Journal of Economic History* 27 (2): 221–229.

Stalker, P. (1994). *The Work of Strangers: A Survey of International Labor Migration.* Geneva: International Labor Organisation.

Timmer, A., and J.G. Williamson (1998). Immigration Policy Prior to the Thirties: Labor Markets, Policy Interaction, and Globalization Backlash. *Population and Development Review* 24 (4): 739–771.

United Nations (1979). *Trends and Characteristics of International Migration since 1950.* New York: United Nations.

United Nations (2002). *International Migration Report, 2002.* New York: United Nations.

U.S. Department of Commerce (1975). *Historical Statistics of the United States, Colonial Times to 1970.* Washington, D. C.: Bureau of the Census.

Wegge, S.A. (2002). Occupational Self-Selection of European Emigrants: Evidence from Nineteenth Century Hesse-Cassel. *European Review of Economic History* 6 (3): 365–394.

Williamson, J.G. (1982). Immigrant-Inequality Trade-Offs in the Promised Land: American Growth, Distribution and Immigration Prior to the Quotas. In B. Chiswick (ed.), *The Gateway: U.S. Immigration Issues and Policies.* Washington, D.C.: AEA Press.

Williamson, J.G. (1986). The Impact of the Irish on British Labor Markets During the Industrial Revolution. *Journal of Economic History* 46 (3): 693–720.

Williamson, J.G. (1996). Globalization, Convergence and History. *Journal of Economic History* 56 (2): 1–30.

Williamson, J.G. (1997). Globalization and Inequality, Past and Present. *World Bank Research Observer* 12 (2): 117–135.

Williamson, J.G. (1998). Globalization, Labor Markets and Policy Backlash in the Past. *Journal of Economic Perspectives* 35 (3): 51–72.

I.

Labor Mobility
and Globalization

Frank Barry

Modelling Migration and Development in Economic History and Geography

Abstract:

Models of imperfect labour mobility are useful in a world in which many other factors of production are highly mobile. The standard approach is to adopt a heterogeneous-agent framework. The present paper introduces an alternative model that makes welfare evaluation easier. It uses this as background to the development of a variant of the Harris–Todaro model that can rationalize simultaneous labour-market disequilibrium and emigration. The final and main part of the paper models the role of governance in development and contrasts the impact of migration under different governance regimes. Emigration, in the model, raises wages under poor governance, while immigration has this same effect when governance is improved.

1   Introduction

Globalization is primarily defined by freer flows of goods, information and factors of production. Other papers in this volume chart the migration flows of recent times, and O'Rourke and Williamson (1999) document the substantial flows of the 19th century. Both trade and FDI are known to have expanded more rapidly than GDP over the period since World War II, suggesting that technology transfer is more fluid today. And financial capital is highly mobile of course; as Anne Krueger (1998) points out, even middle-income developing countries no longer face constraints on access to financial capital through the private international capital market.

A first aim of the present paper is to discuss ways of modelling labour mobility at the theoretical level in circumstances in which mobility of goods and factors is so ubiquitous. In circumstances where one might wish to assume perfect international mobility of factors such as capital, it is useful to have a way of modelling *imperfect* mobility of a factor such as labour. One such model is presented here.

A second aim is to look more closely at one well-known migration equilibrium—the Harris–Todaro model. Kevin O'Rourke and I have clearly had this model in mind in some of our writings on the pre-Celtic Tiger Irish economy: an era of high unemployment combined with high emigration. Here, some of the shortcomings of the model are exposed and one alternative is briefly explored.

In a world of widespread factor mobility, individual economies—at the theoretical level—must still be defined with reference to some fixed factor. Land is the first one that usually springs to mind. (In economic geography models such as Krugman (1991), this is transmuted into a fixed number of farmers.) For policy analysis, however, it is arguably more useful to consider a factor whose quality varies with governance. Let us call this 'infrastructure'. In its broadest sense this will include roads, telecommunications, educational establishments, national systems of innovation, etc. The third and final aim of the present paper is to explore the relationship between governance/infrastructure and the impact of migration. In tackling this topic, the paper seeks to bridge the gap between the perspective of economic historians such as O'Rourke and Williamson (1999)—who show that emigration played a large part in raising living standards across much of the European periphery, and thus promoted convergence—and that of economic geographers for whom immigration serves to maintain the lead of the core over the periphery, leading to divergence.

In most theoretical economic geography models (e.g., Krugman 1991) it is random as to which area emerges as the core and which becomes the periphery, though economic historians such as Pollard (1981) and Berend and Ranki (1982) have added much meat to these bare bones. The present paper presents a unified model in which emigration raises wages in the periphery, immigration raises wages in the core, and differences in standards of governance contribute to the emergence of the core-periphery divide.

This model draws a distinction between economic development and emigration-driven wage growth. While O'Rourke and Williamson (1999) focus primarily on the latter, the distinction is clearly crucial, as their own numbers verify. Thus (pages 126 and 155), even though Norway, Sweden and Denmark came next in line to Ireland and Italy in terms of the labour force lost to migration between 1870 and 1913, emigration accounted for only 5–10 per cent of the more than 100 per cent real wage growth in Scandinavia over that period, while accounting for 40 per cent of real wage growth in Ireland and Portugal and 100 per cent in the case of Spain—the countries that remained underdeveloped.

The Scandinavian economies used industrialization to achieve strong convergence on the leaders. Ireland partially converged without industrialization, while the Iberian countries actually diverged. As O'Rourke and Williamson (1997) put it, some economies exploited globalization well and others badly, a view consistent with the model developed here.

2   Modelling Labour Mobility

Under perfect labour mobility, as in the Harris–Todaro approach, for example, migration equalizes utility across locations or else leads to complete depopulation of one or other of the economies involved, as in Krugman (1991).[1] Perfect mobility generates the very restrictive result, however, that if the outside option remains constant nothing can affect individuals' welfare. For example, if the utility of working elsewhere in the EU is independent of conditions in small open economy i, then if EU country i issues work visas to immigrants from outside the EU, this simply displaces would-be immigrants from other EU countries without impacting on their welfare.[2]

Faini (1996) and Andersson and Forslid (2004), on the other hand, assume population heterogeneity. In this case, the greater the utility difference across locations, the greater the proportion of the population that will choose to migrate. The drawback of the heterogeneity assumption, however, is that it makes welfare analysis particularly difficult.

Barry (2002) surmounts both of these restrictions by modelling migration using a 'love of variety' approach. The proportion of their lives that individuals choose to spend in two locations—i.e., at home and abroad—is determined by the relative attractiveness of the locations. This yields a type of imperfect labour mobility, as in the population-heterogeneity approach, without sacrificing the ability to evaluate welfare effects easily.[3]

Specifically, the model works as follows. Given a fixed amount of labour time (set at unity), individuals choose to work l_i hours in their home location, and $l_j = 1-l_i$ hours abroad, in order to maximize

$$(1.1) \quad U = (y)^{\varphi} \left(\sum_{i=1,2} \mu_i l_i^{\theta} \right)^{1-\varphi},$$

where $\theta < 1$ and $y = w_1 l_1 + w_2 l_2$.

---

[1] A common way to maintain the assumption of perfect factor mobility, but to slow down the movement to full equilibrium, is to assume a rising marginal cost of migration, where the cost of moving for the marginal migrant rises with the number of migrants, as in Barro and Sala-i-Martin (1995: Chapter 9).

[2] Dascher (2000) allows for land ownership, with land prices endogenous, allowing a distinction to be made between the utility levels of indigenous and immigrant workers.

[3] Care must be taken, however, in deciding whose welfare exactly is taken into account in the social welfare function.

This yields the first-order condition

$$(1.2) \quad \left(y/\sum l_i^{\theta}\right)\left[(1-\phi)/\phi\right]\theta\left[u_1 l_1^{\theta-1} - u_2 l_2^{\theta-1}\right] = [w_2 - w_1],$$

which yields positively-sloped labour supply functions: dl_1/dw_1 and $dl_2/dw_2 > 0$.

The ratio l_1/l_2 emerges as a positive function of μ_2/μ_1 and w_1/w_2; thus, agents allocate their working life across locations in accordance with relative wages and their locational-preference bias.

This approach will prove useful in the next few sections of the paper.

3   Extending the Harris–Todaro Model

Kevin O'Rourke (1995) argues that labour-market disequilibrium prevailed in Ireland over a long historical time period. He cites International Labor Organization data from the 1920s onwards that show, when adjusted for purchasing power differences between Ireland and Britain, that for most years and most occupations, real wages were higher in Dublin than in London. This situation co-existed with high unemployment in Ireland and consistent emigration to the United Kingdom, in a pattern which he suggests is reminiscent of the well-known model of rural-urban migration of Harris and Todaro (1970).

The Harris–Todaro model postulates a fixed wage in the rural sector, w^*, and a higher wage, w, in the urban sector, with a migration equilibrium established by higher unemployment in the urban sector (i.e., lower L/N, where L and N represent employment and population in the urban area); i.e.,

$$(2.1) \quad w L/N = w^*.$$

Barry (2003) notes that such a situation appeared to prevail right up to the arrival of the Celtic Tiger era of the 1990s in Ireland. With Irish wages set at too high a level for labour-intensive industries to prosper in the wake of the move to free trade in the 1960s, Irish domestically-owned firms failed to gain foreign market share, while seeing their share of the home market eroded. Only the significant levels of FDI entering the economy propped up the Irish manufacturing sector.[4]

---

[4]   Barry (2003) contrasts developments in 1960s Ireland with those in the other EU cohesion countries. Thus, Portuguese and Greek export growth was based on labour-intensive industries, while Ireland was developing—against its apparent comparative advantage—into capital-intensive sectors. Such a possibility, of developing against apparent comparative advantage when wages are set above equilibrium levels, is modelled theoretically by Brecher (1974).

One would like to have an optimizing model, of course, of how such a situation might have developed. The monopoly union model presented by Oswald (1985) suggests itself as an appropriate candidate. In this setup, the microfoundations of which are consistent with the insider-outsider perspective of Lindbeck and Snower (1986), wages are set by a "closed shop" union, which restricts employment levels in order to drive up wages.

The union chooses a wage to maximize the aggregate income of its members, as given by $wL + (N_j - L)b$, where N_j represents union-j membership and b represents, for ease of exposition, the social-welfare benefit level. As the union takes the employment response of the firm—easily derived from a production function such as $Y = AK^\alpha L^{1-\alpha}$—into account, the optimal level of the wage is given by

(2.2) $w = b/(1-\alpha)$.

Thus, the union-determined wage is above the opportunity cost of labour, b.

Many such models assume that employment is then distributed equally across union members. If the entire (periphery) population enjoys union membership, the Harris–Todaro equation, with the social welfare benefit taken into account, becomes

(2.3) $[wL + b (N-L)]/N = w^*$.

The difficulty with this setup, however, is that, since the union maximizes the left-hand-side numerator, equilibrium will require an equivalent increase in the denominator N; i.e., this type of labour-market disequilibrium triggers a labour inflow rather than an outflow—the opposite of the situation that one wishes to model!

To rescue the notion of a monopolized labour market that triggers emigration, we could instead assume that the jobs paying the high wage in the periphery are tied up by a smaller group of insiders and only become available at rate δ, while workers, to be eligible, need to queue at the social-welfare benefit rate. This is similar to the 'segmented labour market' model of MacDonald and Solow (1985). An equilibrium entailing perfect labour mobility would then require that the expected pay rate of workers queuing in the periphery be equal to the alternative rate available in the core economy, w^*:

(2.4) $\delta L/U [w] + [1-\delta L/U] b = w^*$.

The problem with this, however, is that the combination of δ (the rate at which well-paid jobs become available) and b (the social-welfare benefit) will in many circumstances be too low for the equation to solve. In this case, no one would be content to remain unemployed in the periphery; all will emigrate to the core, and the model will be unable to explain the situation that needs to be modelled—excessively high wages in the periphery leading to a combination of unemployment and emigration.

The imperfect-labour-mobility formulation derived above, however, implies that a lower utility level for those unemployed in the periphery will trigger a less than infinite shift of labour to the core. Such a combination of elements—imperfect labour mobility, a monopoly union and the requirement to queue for highly-paid jobs—is thus capable of rationalizing the outcome that one wishes to model.

4   Modelling Development and Underdevelopment

I now wish to extend the discussion to embrace some broader issues in economic history and geography. Here I will be concerned with the role of good and bad governance in infrastructural provision, and with the impact of migration under these alternative scenarios.[5]

There are two industries in the model. One produces an internationally traded final good, Y, under constant returns to scale, using capital and a CES bundle of non-tradeable intermediates, Z:

(3.1) $Y = K^a Z^{1-a}$,

where

(3.2) $Z = [\sum_i x_i^{\sigma-1/\sigma}]^{\sigma/(\sigma-1)}$.

The rationale for introducing intermediates in this way is as in Romer (1987). The output of final goods is an increasing function of the total number of specialized intermediate inputs, which "loosely captures the idea that a ceteris paribus increase in the degree of specialisation increases output" (page 57).

With capital internationally mobile at a fixed rate of return r^*, final goods production will be a linear function of Z, implying that the elasticities of Y and of Z with respect to labour are equal: $\varepsilon(Y; L) = \varepsilon(Z; L)$.

Labour is the only factor used in the production of intermediates. Letting x be the output of a representative firm in the intermediate-goods sector, and w the national wage, the cost function for production of intermediates, with fixed and variable cost components, is

---

5   In equating poor infrastructural provision with bad governance, I have in mind, with respect to history, some forms of colonialism and, with respect to developing economies today, dictatorial regimes such as that of Mobutu in Zaire, which inherited reasonably good infrastructure and allowed it to deteriorate massively.

(3.3) $C(x_i) = (A + bx_i) w.$

With monopolistic competition in intermediates, the price charged for each variety i is an identical fixed mark-up on marginal costs:

(3.4) $q_i = q = \mu w,$

where $\mu = [\sigma b /(\sigma-1)]$, and $\sigma (> 1)$ is the elasticity of substitution between intermediates.

Free entry and exit in the intermediate-goods sector yields

(3.5) $x = A (\sigma-1)/b,$

where the subscript i has now been dropped, since all varieties are symmetric.

Labour-market equilibrium entails

(3.6) $L = n(A+bX)$, which, given (3.5), $= n\sigma A.$

The price index for the CES bundle of intermediates is

(3.7) $Q = \left[\sum_i q_i^{1-\sigma} \right]^{1/(1-\sigma)} = n^{[1/(1-\sigma)]} q = n^{[1/(1-\sigma)]} \mu w.$

Since the final good is produced under constant returns, the unit cost function is

(3.8) $p^* = c(r^*, Q).$

With the price of final goods and the return to capital both determined exogenously on international markets, the price index for intermediates is thus also exogenous. Setting the total differential of Q in (3.7) to zero yields

$$n^{[1/(1-\sigma)]} dq = - [1/(1-\sigma)] n^{[\sigma/(1-\sigma)]} q \, dn,$$

which indicates a positive relationship between the cost of each individual variety, q, and the number of varieties, n (since $\sigma > 1$).

Since the price of an intermediate is a mark-up on wages, this means that the wage rate is increasing in the number of varieties: $\varepsilon(n; L) = (\sigma-1) \varepsilon(w; L)$. Whether the wage rises or falls with the size of the labour force then depends on the relationship between L and the number of intermediate varieties, n.

What does this in turn depend on? Equation (3.6) reveals that

(3.9) $\varepsilon(n; L) = [1-\varepsilon(A; L)].$

Thus, everything hinges on the size and sign of $\varepsilon(A; L)$, the elasticity of the fixed cost with respect to employment or population. This is the issue that remains to be explored.

We allow fixed costs, as in Bougheas et al. (2000), to depend on the level of infrastructure, G, relative to the size of the economy.[6] Specifically in the present model fixed costs depend negatively on infrastructure per head, G/L, in the following way:

(3.10) $A = a[L / G)]^\varphi$,

where $\varphi > 0$.

A constant tax rate, t, is levied on labour income wL.[7] An economy characterized by poor governance has an unchanging level of infrastructure, G_0. The government pockets all tax revenues for itself![8] In this case, $\varepsilon(A; L) = \varphi$, and $\varepsilon(w; L) = [1/(\sigma-1)] (1-\varphi)$.

In this 'poor governance' case, an increase in L exerts offsetting pressures on the wage. The increasing-returns dimension of the model causes L to exert upward pressure on the wage, while the rise in fixed costs as infrastructure per head declines tends to reduce the number of varieties, exerting downward pressure on the wage. If the latter effect dominates (i.e., for $\varphi > 1$), the model behaves like a diminishing-returns economy: emigration raises the wage level, as in O'Rourke and Williamson (1999). Henceforth, we will assume that this condition is met.

In an economy characterized by good governance on the other hand, these tax revenues are ploughed back into infrastructure. The level of infrastructure is now given by:

(3.11) $G/L = tw$, and the fixed cost $A = a[1/tw)]^\varphi$.

This implies $\varepsilon(A; L) = -\varphi \, \varepsilon(w; L)$, which yields $\varepsilon(w; L) = 1/(\sigma-\varphi-1)$.

For a sufficiently large value of σ this is positive. What does this mean? It means that for a range of parameter values, the decline in fixed costs as the labour force increases accentuates the market-growth effects to encourage further specialization. In this case, an increase in L is associated with an increase in wages.

---

6   They argue that it is plausible to expect that fixed costs are largely determined by the availability and quality of transport and telecommunications infrastructure.

7   It is common in the growth literature to assume a constant tax rate on national income. With international capital mobility in the present model, however, the effective incidence of the tax will fall on labour.

8   The model is not defined for $L=0$. For present purposes, we can assume that the level of infrastructure in the periphery is the same as would prevail in the core for the minimum level of L for which the model is defined.

These two cases are depicted in Figure 1, where the wage in the alternative location (the rest of the world) is set at $w*$.[9] There are two ways in which real
wages in the small open economy can be raised: (i) through emigration, or (ii)
through better governance, which causes the slope of the labour-market locus to
become positive.

Figure 1: The Small Open Economy Model with Emigration under Bad
Governance and Immigration under Good Governance

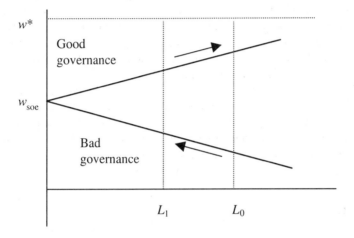

As O'Rourke and Williamson (1999) and various other papers of O'Rourke's
point out, Ireland had traditionally relied on the first of these mechanisms. Beginning with a 'closed labour market' equilibrium at L_0 in the bad governance
case, and in line with the model of imperfect labour mobility developed earlier,
the opening up of migration opportunities will lead to emigration and higher
wages, and the establishment of a new equilibrium at L_1.

All elements of Irish policy improved substantially over the Celtic Tiger era,
however (Barry 2000). If Ireland has indeed been transformed into the case represented in the good governance scenario, then the starting equilibrium at L_1
will now trigger labour inflows and strong convergence, exactly as has happened
over the last 15 years or so.[10]

---

9   Since only the small open economy case is being considered, emigration has no im-
    pact on wages in the rest of the world.

10 Note that the implications of this model are quite different from the standard one in
    which improved policy induces a rightward shift of a downward-sloping labour de-

5   Conclusions

Models of imperfect international labour mobility are useful, particularly when other factors can be assumed to be more mobile. The present paper introduced one such model, whose microfoundations allow for simple welfare evaluations, which is not the case if the alternative assumption of population heterogeneity is adopted.

The paper also presented a brief discussion of the Harris–Todaro model. It pointed out that when this model is set in an optimizing framework, immigration into the economy with unemployment is a more likely outcome than emigration, which is not consistent with many of the situations in which the model has been implicitly or explicitly invoked. The imperfect-labour-mobility model discussed above, when wedded to a version of the Harris–Todaro model, does allow for an equilibrium in which emigration and unemployment coexist.

Finally, the paper introduced governance as a determining factor in the emergence of a core-periphery divide, and presented a set of circumstances in which emigration can lead to wage growth under poor governance, while immigration can drive wage growth under good governance. The model is of course highly stylized, but would seem to offer potential for further elaboration.

Bibliography

Andersson, F., and R. Forslid (2004). A Fundamental Asymmetry of Asymmetric Shocks. *European Economic Review* 48 (2): 337–351.

Barro, R., and X. Sala-i-Martin (1995). *Economic Growth*. New York: McGraw-Hill.

Barry, F. (2000). Convergence Is not Automatic: Lessons from Ireland for Central and Eastern Europe. *World Economy* 23 (10): 1379–1394.

Barry, F. (2002). FDI, Infrastructure and the Welfare Effects of Labour Migration. *Manchester School* 70 (3): 364–379.

Barry, F. (2003). Economic Integration and Convergence Processes in the EU Cohesion Countries. *Journal of Common Market Studies* 41 (5): 897–921.

Berend, I.T., and G. Ranki (1982). *The European Periphery and Industrialisation, 1780–1914*. Cambridge: Cambridge University Press.

Bougheas, S., P. Demetriades, and T. Mamuneas (2000). Infrastructure, Specialization and Economic Growth. *Canadian Journal of Economics* 33 (2): 506–522.

---

mand function. In such a model, immigration per se reduces the wages of indigenous workers. In the present case, immigration has the opposite effect.

Brecher, R. (1974). Minimum Wage Rates and the Pure Theory of International Trade. *Quarterly Journal of Economics* 88 (1): 98–116.

Dascher, K. (2000). Trade, FDI and Congestion: The Small and Very Open Economy, CEPR Working Paper 2526. London. Available at: http://www.ucd.ie/~economic/workingpapers/2000.htm

Faini, R. (1996). Increasing Returns, Migrations and Convergence. *Journal of Development Economics* 49 (1): 121–136.

Krueger, A. (1998). Whither the World Bank and the IMF? *Journal of Economic Literature* 36 (4): 1983–2020.

Krugman, P. (1991). Increasing Returns and Economic Geography. *Journal of Political Economy* 99 (31): 483–499.

Lindbeck, A., and D. Snower (1986). Wage Setting, Unemployment, and Insider-Outsider Relations. *American Economic Review, Papers and Proceedings* 76 (2): 235–239.

McDonald, I., and R. Solow (1985). Wages and Employment in a Segmented Labor Market. *Quarterly Journal of Economics* 100 (4): 1115–1141.

O'Rourke, K. (1995). Emigration and Living Standards in Ireland since the Famine. *Journal of Population Economics* 8 (4): 407–421.

O'Rourke, K., and J. Williamson (1997). Around the European Periphery 1870–1913: Globalization, Schooling and Growth. *European Review of Economic History* 1 (2): 153–191.

O'Rourke, K., and J. Williamson (1999). *Globalization and History: The Evolution of a Nineteenth-Century Atlantic Economy.* Cambridge: MIT Press.

Oswald, A. (1985). The Economic Theory of Trade Unions: An Introductory Survey. *Scandinavian Journal of Economics* 87 (2): 160–193.

Pollard, S. (1981). *Peaceful Conquest: the Industrialisation of Europe 1760–1970.* Oxford: Oxford University Press.

Romer, P. (1987). Growth Based on Increasing Returns due to Specialization. *American Economic Review, Papers and Proceedings* 77 (2): 56–62.

Comment on Frank Barry

Timothy J. Hatton

In this paper, Frank Barry provides an interesting perspective on models that are used to study international migration, an analysis that is motivated by the migration experience of Ireland in the century and a half since the famine. There are essentially three themes in the paper: an interpretation of migration and labour markets in Ireland, a critique of the Harris–Todaro model as an analytical framework, and a new model that focuses on infrastructure and governance. I will comment on each in turn.

What happened in Ireland? The chapter notes that during the twentieth century Irish wages adjusted for purchasing power parity were higher than those prevailing across the Irish Sea in Britain. That is true for urban wages from the 1920s onwards, but before 1914 things were a little different. The Irish urban unskilled wage was below that of Britain, but it rose from 58 percent of the British wage in 1860 to 72 percent in 1913. The Irish agricultural wage also rose, from 61 percent to 75 percent of the British agricultural wage over the same period. What drove this dramatic convergence in Irish wages relative to British? George Boyer, Kevin O'Rourke and I showed that it was mostly due to the massive emigration from Ireland that saw the Irish population fall from 6.5 million in 1851 to 4.3 million in 1911 (Boyer et al. 1994). Using a computable general equilibrium model, we found that all of this wage convergence can be accounted for by higher rates of emigration from Ireland (some of which was to Britain). As this emigration proceeded, it soaked up the rural surplus and relieved the downward pressure of rural-urban migration on Irish urban wages. Thus, both urban and rural wages rose relative to their British counterparts.

That raises the question: what determined these migration flows? Can Todaro-style models account for it? Let us turn first to rural-urban migration. We do not have the unemployment data for Ireland but we do have some evidence from Britain. Robin Gowers and I estimated a model of the agricultural wage from 1872 to 1913 that embeds in it the (unobserved) rural-urban migration rate (Gowers and Hatton 1997).[1] The result is as follows:[2]

---

[1] This model is derived as follows:

Labour demand in agriculture (in changes): $\Delta \ln L_t^D = -\alpha \Delta \ln (W^A/P^A)_t + r$, where r reflects exogenous productivity change. Change in rural labour supply: $\Delta \ln L_t^S = n_t - m_t$,

$$\Delta \ln W_t^A = -0.06 + 0.10 \, \Delta \ln P_t^A + 0.12 \Delta \ln P_t^A + 0.13 \ln\left(W^B / W^A\right)_{t-1} + 0.21 \ln(1 - U_{t-1})$$
$$\quad (2.0) \quad (2.5) \qquad\quad (2.6) \qquad\quad (2.5) \qquad\qquad\quad (2.9)$$

$$(R^2 = 0.73; \text{DW} = 1.35; \text{LM} = 2.09),$$

where W^A is the agricultural wage, W^B is the urban wage, P^A is the farm output price, and U is urban unemployment. Both the relative wage and urban unemployment have the predicted effects. In the long run (setting the Δ's to zero), the urban-rural wage gap depends on the urban unemployment rate, as the Todaro model suggests. So we can easily account for these wage gaps in Britain, and presumably also in Ireland.

What drove emigration from Ireland? Here we do observe the migration rate so we can model it directly. As Jeffrey Williamson and I showed, it too can be explained by wage gaps and unemployment (Hatton and Williamson 1998: Ch. 5). A typical result for the emigration rate from Ireland to all foreign destinations from 1876 to 1913 is as follows:[3]

$$M_t = -18.4 - 25.9 \, \Delta \ln Q_{t-1}^H + 77.5 \ln(1 - U^F)_t + 15.5 \ln(W^F/W^H)_t + 37.5 \, MST_t$$
$$\quad (3.5) \quad (3.8) \qquad\quad (3.8) \qquad\qquad (3.7) \qquad\qquad (3.6)$$

$$+ 0.39 \, M_{t-1} - 0.16 \, M_{t-2}$$
$$\quad (2.9) \qquad\quad (1.2)$$

$$(R^2 = 0.85; \text{DW} = 1.79; \text{LM} = 0.45),$$

where M is the emigration rate per thousand of the Irish population, Q^H is Irish farm output, U^F is the destination unemployment rate, W^F/W^H is the foreign to home wage ratio, and MST is the stock of previous emigrants living in overseas destinations. While unemployment is statistically important, most of the long-run trend in Irish migration can be explained by the diminishing wage gap between Ireland and the destination countries. As we have noted, emigration reduced the wage gap between the 1860s and 1913. And in turn, according to our estimates,

---

where n is natural increase and m is net outmigration. Rural-urban migration: $m_t = \mu \left[\ln\left(W^B/W^A\right)_{t-1} + \ln(1 - U_{t-1})\right]$. Substituting migration into the labour supply equation and equating labour demand and labour supply in the agricultural sector gives $\Delta \ln W_t^A = (r-n)/\alpha + \Delta \ln P^A + (\mu + \alpha) \ln\left(W^B/W^A\right)_{t-1} + (\mu + \alpha) \ln(1 - U_{t-1})$.

[2] t-statistics in parentheses; LM is the Lagrange multiplier test for serial correlation $(\chi^2_{(1)})$. The model also includes a dummy (not reported here) for the years of agricultural unionism, 1872–1876.

[3] t-statistics in parentheses; LM is the Lagrange multiplier test for serial correlation $(\chi^2_{(1)})$.

this diminishing wag gap reduced the annual emigration rate by 4 per thousand between 1876–1880 and 1909–1913, and by 8.4 per thousand between 1852–1856 and 1909–1913.

These simple models in the tradition of Harris and Todaro work well and they tell a consistent story about developments in Ireland, particularly before the First World War. While acknowledging this, Frank Barry seeks to reinterpret the model using the "love of variety" approach. Essentially, this says that individuals have convex preferences over location and they therefore spend some of their time at home and some of it abroad. This of course gives the same empirical prediction as before—migration is driven by unemployment and wage differentials. The key difference is that we do not need to have heterogeneous individuals to explain why some people emigrate and others do not. However, it is difficult to square this interpretation with the historical record. In the case of Ireland, the vast bulk of those who emigrated never came back. These emigrants were choosing one country over another—not diversifying across two countries on either side of the Atlantic.

One reason for the love of variety approach is that it provides a model in which individuals are identical but not everyone emigrates, and it therefore makes welfare comparisons easier in the theoretical model. But even for this purpose there are problems. The standard analysis of immigration distinguishes between the residents of one country and those of another. From a policy point of view, we may want to ask what the effects of liberalizing policy are on three main groups: the original residents of the destination, the migrants themselves, and the nonmigrant residents of the origin country. The assumption that each of the original residents in the origin country migrates in some proportion clouds this sharp distinction.

The final part of the paper develops a model in which a migration-induced increase in the population could either increase or reduce the real wage. If there are increasing returns to population, then the gap in living standards between the poor origin country and the rich destination country will widen with migration. On the other hand, if diminishing returns dominate, then the gap will narrow as migration drives down the wage in the rich country and pulls it up in the poor country. That seems to be what happened in the Atlantic economy from the middle of the nineteenth century. And it occurred in the presence of well-integrated goods and capital markets. Diminishing returns were largely the result of the importance of the land as a country-specific factor. Thus, the ratio of wages to land rents increased in Europe as labour became relatively more scarce and it fell in the New World as labour became relatively more abundant.

Frank Barry's model offers a different twist: it suggests that infrastructure is a key underpinning of a country's living standards and that "good governance" matters in determining how that infrastructure increases as the population expands. In the "good governance" case, the additional tax revenues that population growth produces are ploughed into a cost-reducing expansion of infrastructure. In the "bad governance" case, additional tax revenues are not spent productively and hence diminishing returns dominate. While differently motivated, this approach has much in common with that of Alesina and Spolaore (2003), who set out to explain the size of nations. In their analysis, there is a tradeoff between the benefits of scale, which flow from the provision of public goods, and the costs of heterogeneity in tastes, which increase with population size. This tradeoff is shifted by two additional factors. One is economic openness which reduces the economic importance of scale. The other is nondemocratic institutions which suppress the rising costs of heterogeneity as a means through which autocrats maximize rent extraction.

Barry uses his model to explain Ireland's recent experience: rapidly rising per capita income, a switch from emigration to immigration, and a faster rate of population growth. But it seems worthwhile to enrich the model somewhat and to use it to motivate Irish history over a longer sweep. Such a story might be told as follows. In post-famine Ireland, there was free trade and poor governance—but it was not Irish governance. Under British rule, there were conflicts over land and stunted industrial growth. As a result, there were strongly diminishing returns to population size, and mass emigration helped to raise living standards. After 1921, trade became less free and governance (now home grown) did little to promote growth. Emigration declined further, but largely because the opportunities for emigrating were restricted by rising barriers overseas. The Irish miracle emerged in the postwar period partly as a result of improvements in governance, but above all, as a result of joining the European Union. This had two important effects. One was the increase in trade openness provided by the common market. The other was the EU-financed investment in infrastructure from which Ireland benefited more than most.

This has implications for the future. One is that the gains to further population growth might be small provided that the economy stays open. And now that Ireland is a rich country (relative to many others in the enlarged European Union), infrastructure investments have become more expensive. The other is that as immigration proceeds population heterogeneity may increase. Thus, it is far from clear that Ireland will reap further benefits from the virtuous cycle that the model presented in this paper envisages.

Bibliography

Alesina, A., and E. Spolaore (2003). *The Size of Nations*. Cambridge, Mass: MIT Press.

Boyer, G.R., T.J. Hatton, and K.H. O'Rourke (1994). The Impact of Emigration on Real Wages in Ireland, 1850–1914. In T.J. Hatton and J.G. Williamson (eds.), *Migration and the International Labor Market, 1850–1939*. London: Routledge.

Gowers, R., and T.J. Hatton (1997). The Origins and Early Impact of the Minimum Wage in Agriculture. *Economic History Review* 50 (1): 82–103.

Hatton, T.J., and J.G. Williamson (1998). *The Age of Mass Migration: Causes and Economic Impact*. New York: Oxford University Press.

Gabriel Felbermayr and Wilhelm Kohler

Immigration and Wages in General Equilibrium: A Theoretical Perspective

Abstract:

We propose a variant of the Ricardo–Viner model featuring three skill levels to analyze skill-based selection in immigration policies. We analyze both wage and welfare effects of alternative types of immigration scenarios. The model incorporates various adjustment mechanisms that may be responsible for why host country wage effects of immigration may in some cases be low, and large in others, as suggested by the empirical literature. A crucial thrust of the paper is to take into account the general equilibrium repercussions from an endogenous price adjustment for both tradable and nontradable goods. We identify conditions under which goods price effects dominate the effects of factor complementarity, potentially leading to welfare losses.

1   Introduction and Policy Background

If judged against the large share of the world's population persistently living under enormously deprived conditions, relative to the affluent parts of the world, international migration flows look surprisingly small. Economic differences between countries are increasing. The ratio of average GDP per capita in what the World Bank classifies as high-income countries to that in low-income countries rose from 0.41 in 1975 to 0.66 in the year 2000. Yet, the migrant share of the world's population remains small. It was 2.1 percent in 1975, and rose to a mere

Remark: We are grateful to Joaquim Ramos Silva, our discussant at the Kiel Week Conference. Thanks are also due to Timothy Hatton, Douglas Nelson, and Jeffrey Williamson for thought-provoking comments and discussion during the conference.

    Research on this paper was conducted while both of us were members of the Economics Department at Johannes Kepler University Linz. It is part of a research project entitled "Public Finance, Unemployment, and Growth" and was supported by the Austrian Science Fund (FWF) under grant P14702.

2.9 percent by 2000.[1] This reflects restrictive policies, particularly in immigration countries, but it also reflects limited mobility, either through deliberate choice or limited capacity to bear the sheer cost of moving. Limited mobility is also evidenced by large and persistent gaps in income and employment perspectives between regions within countries, where policy-induced restrictions on migration are absent. If huge disparities in living conditions are a result of disparities in natural conditions and national institutions, and if it is true that institutions are difficult to build and do not travel well across countries, then international migration ought to be part and parcel of any serious attempt to alleviate world poverty.[2] Indeed, one should expect that any credible policy commitment towards reducing poverty and worldwide inequality should include incentives and provisions for enhanced international migration. The cause is not restricted to humanitarian and equity considerations. If income disparities reflect productivity gaps, then any migration driven by market signals should also increase overall world output. It has been estimated that moving 100 million migrants from low- to high-income countries would increase average and global GDP by as much as 8 percent.[3]

In fact, however, the *policy landscape* is not at all characterized by promigration attitudes, but rather by restrictive policies, mostly imposed by *im*migrant countries. Externalities in both sending and receiving countries give ample reasons to interfere with migration flows driven by market signals. However, it is hard to imagine that the restrictive immigration policies observed in many OECD countries are merely a reflection of relevant market failures. Nor do they appear to be driven by concerns about alleviating world poverty and inequality, all policy commitments towards ambitious international development goals notwithstanding. Instead, immigrant countries typically attempt to tailor restrictions to their own needs, more or less openly pursuing *native gains* from immigration (see Martin 2004). One might be tempted to charge immigration countries with deplorable self-interest, and to some extent that may be true. On the other hand, selecting migrants such that immigration is to the benefit also of the receiving country need not be at the expense, or exploitation, of migrants or of their poor home countries. Migration is *not* a zero-sum game. And if securing native benefits is a means to maintain domestic support of immigration, this should also

---

[1]   See Martin (2004). The migrant share is defined as the stock of persons outside their country of birth or citizenship for 12 months or more. To give an idea about the absolute numbers involved, the migrant share of 2.9 percent in 2000 amounted to 175 million people.

[2]   The principal other cause of income disparities is differences in individuals' abilities. But these should not be considered as exogenous in the same sense as natural conditions. In particular, they are importantly determined by a country's institutions.

[3]   See again Martin (2004).

serve an enhanced role of international migration in the global attempt to alleviate world poverty.

The present policy discussion revolves around three issues. First and foremost, there is widespread fear that labor inflows may adversely affect the income and employment perspectives of certain kinds of domestic workers, particularly those with low skills. In the history of world migration, this is not a novel issue, although the formation of systematic immigration policies as a response to these concerns is a relatively recent phenomenon. It was sparked in the early 20th century in the United States (see, for instance, Chiswick and Hatton 2003, and Williamson 2004). Depending on the details of migrants' self-selection, relative to the skill distribution of the domestic labor force, unfettered immigration may be conducive, or run counter to, the domestic distributional policy goal, but perhaps the "default case" is one where the host country would sooner want to exercise restrictions geared towards a higher skill content of immigration.

The second issue is some perceived shortage of domestic labor supply. A prominent example, of course, is the policy of active recruitment in the form of the "guest-worker" programs run by some European countries in the 1960s and 1970s. More recently, some countries have perceived that they have shortages of high-skilled labor and have turned to "green-card-type" programs that are, in a fundamental sense, quite similar to "guest-worker" programs, although the target is somewhat different. The policy discussion usually does not pin down in precise analytical terms what is meant by "shortage." In some sense, it must mean that a boost in supply of certain types of goods seems attractive to the domestic economy. For instance, an immigration-induced increase in domestic supply of low-skilled labor might lead to an enhanced and, therefore, cheaper supply of nontraded goods if these are low-skill-intensive. On the other hand, a country might want to improve its supply conditions for high-skilled tradable goods, although for exported goods it may thus run the risk of a terms-of-trade deterioration.

Finally, the third issue relates to the concern that immigrant workers may contribute less to the welfare state than what they receive through unemployment benefits and other welfare entitlements. This is a novel issue in the history of migration, since in the earlier periods of "mass migration," the welfare state in its present form simply did not exist. Obviously, the details of this problem hinge on the idiosyncrasies of an immigrant country's welfare state. Generally, however, the "default case" here again is one where the immigrant country expects to increase its benefit by selecting young and well-educated migrants.

Notice the potential for conflict inherent in this policy landscape. Alleviating a perceived shortage may run counter to the distributional objective, as may the attempt to ease fiscal pressure from the welfare state. Notice also that an active recruitment policy in a fundamental sense is not much different from a restrictive policy in the face of emigrant tides. In both cases, the immigrant country tries to exercise a quantitative control over the size of the domestic labor force by means of a "cross-border instrument." Moving down to the individual level, conflicting interests abound. Given a host of different *alleged* effects of immigration, different parts of society will often have conflicting views on the desirability of immigration, and on the specific form of policy to pursue. In other words, the native benefit a country may want to pursue by an active immigration policy is a somewhat elusive concept, at least on the practical policy level. And to make matters worse, controversy in policy formation is aggravated by a shortage of solid knowledge about the effects of immigration on the domestic economy. This holds true with respect to both a principal understanding of the effects to be expected and the empirical magnitudes involved. All too often, policy formation is based on vague anxieties and concerns focusing only on alleged directly observable effects, and less on economy-wide implications.

As to the first issue, *economic theory* emphasizes the factor price effect of an increase in an economy's endowment with labor of various skill types. Obviously, if immigration just increases the entire endowment base of an economy, one would not expect much need for a factor price adjustment. Moreover, if the economy is open, even an unbalanced change in domestic endowment, say due to a certain type of skill selection in immigration, may be absorbed through internal adjustment without much, or any, factor price or wage effects. Relying on canonical trade theory, trade economists tend to make a distinction between Heckscher–Ohlin models, where wage effects of immigration are completely absent, at least over certain ranges of domestic endowment, and specific-factor (or Ricardo–Viner) models, which are commonly seen as featuring sensitivity of domestic wages to immigration.[4] We shall return to this below.

Whatever the details of adjustment, economic theory points out a further effect that somehow escapes attention in much of the policy debate. If a discrete labor inflow leads to a downward adjustment of wages for the type of labor received, then under competitive labor markets, immigrants as a whole contribute more to domestic output than what they receive in terms of wage payments. The difference is a so-called immigration surplus that accrues to some domestic factor owners. At the same time, if immigrants are perfect substitutes for some nations, these natives will lose. Hence, the immigration surplus is inextricably connected to a redistributive effect among natives.

As to the second issue, the notion that immigration might help relax "shortages" implies that shortages will normally show up in high prices, which should then fall as a result of enhanced supply. Such price changes ought to be taken

---

[4]   See Srinivasan (1983) for an early discussion of this dichotomy in the context of labor migration.

into account in the aforementioned immigration surplus to the immigrant country. Lower prices directly affect well-being through lower expenditure per unit of welfare. The effect of cheaper nontraded goods is thus clearly positive (for discrete labor inflows), but for traded goods there is the distinct possibility of a terms-of-trade loss, as we shall see in more detail below. In addition, goods price adjustments have indirect effects on factor prices engendered by general equilibrium repercussions, usually captured by the zero-profit conditions of a competitive equilibrium. This will, indeed, be a key ingredient of the analysis below. One might add that there is a further potential meaning of "shortage" that may implicitly underlie some of the "green-card-type" policies geared towards immigration of high-skilled labor. If domestic firms earn pure rents in certain export markets because they enjoy market power, then an additional supply of certain types of labor might enable them to increase those rents.

As to the third issue of the welfare-state effects of immigration, theory suggests that, with the coexistence of labor market imperfections and unemployment benefits, any unregulated, nonmarginal inflow of labor might temporarily increase unemployment. Much depends on the nature of labor market imperfection, and on the institutional details of the welfare state, but in principle there is the potential of a direct loss of native employment and income, and the possibility that immigrants as a whole contribute less to the welfare state than they receive in the form of entitlements. Moreover, although labor market performance and institutions probably play the greatest role in determining the welfare-state implications of immigration, in the long run educational and retirement policies also play a role.

Empirical studies on the wage effects of immigration have shown mixed results. However, a consensus interpretation of the literature is that immigration exerts downward pressure on domestic wages, particularly for low-skilled labor, but that the orders of magnitude are rather low. A notable exception is a recent study by Borjas (2003).[5] While this seems comforting against the background of distributional concerns, we must conclude from theory that it also indicates that a relatively modest immigration surplus occurs. If sizable flows of migration fail to significantly affect domestic wages, it is because the domestic economy features adjustment mechanisms, primarily the reallocation of factors (not necessarily the ones migrating), that enable the economy as a whole to absorb an increased labor supply with full employment of all factors at unchanged marginal productivities. Typically, however, empirical studies leave the precise nature of

---

5   Borjas estimates that an 11 percent increase in U.S. labor supply, as induced by immigration between 1980 and 2000, has depressed average U.S. wages by about 3 percent. For earlier studies with lower estimates, see in particular Card (2001). Surveys are found in Borjas (1994), Friedberg and Hunt (1995), Borjas (1999) and Hanson et al. (2002). For Europe, see DeNew and Zimmermann (1994).

such mechanisms unspecified. Hence, the results found are often somewhat difficult to interpret. In particular, one would want to know more precisely why it is that the wage effects of immigration that are revealed are very tiny in some cases and episodes, but larger in others.[6]

In a recent study using calibration techniques based on a model ruling out all factor price effects, Davis and Weinstein (2002) have calculated that immigration into the United States over the past two decades may have caused a welfare loss to natives equal to 0.8 percent of GDP. This was the result of a deterioration of the terms of trade, and it is in marked contrast to earlier calculations by Borjas (1995, 1999), who rules out such price effects and arrives at an immigration surplus between 0.1 and 0.5 percent of GDP.[7] The Davis–Weinstein result is a powerful reminder of the potential shortcoming of any analysis that fails to explicitly take commodity price adjustments into account, as is typically the case with studies focusing on wage effects of immigration.

The empirical literature, thus, seems far from conclusive. There are somewhat mixed results on the wage effects, and conflicting results on welfare effects, based on opposite assumptions about goods price adjustments. At first sight, the above-mentioned theoretical dichotomy with respect to the factor price effects of immigration seems ill-suited for providing any further insight, since it suggests that it is necessary to subscribe, a priori via model choice, to the factor-price insensitivity view associated with Heckscher–Ohlin-type models, or with the opposite view that there are strong wage effects due to sector-specific factors. It would seem preferable, instead, to have a model in which adjustment mechanisms that mitigate wage effects of immigration are present, but present in a parameterized way that allows us to spell out why it is that there are cases and episodes where immigration has wage effects, and others where it does not. A model of this kind would be a helpful framework with which to interpret the mixed results generated by the empirical literature.

In this paper, we provide a model which serves this purpose. It is a model of the specific-factors variety, but it is sufficiently flexible to allow for a wide range of wage effects of immigration, including the extreme case of complete wage insensitivity. Moreover, it is sufficiently rich in structure in order to address the

---

6   It is interesting to note in this context that present migration flows appear to be fundamentally different as regards their host-country wage effects from migration flows in the first wave of globalization that took place in the second half of the 19th century and the early 20th century up to the first World War. Extensive studies by O'Rourke and Williamson (1999) have shown that those early "mass migrations" have had profound wage effects in sending and receiving countries. This is in marked contrast to the difficulties that researchers have had finding sizable wage effects in the present wave of globalization.

7   Similar calculations are presented in Razin and Sadka (1997) and Bauer and Zimmermann (1997).

key issues mentioned above, including endogenous adjustment of prices for traded and nontraded goods. In addition, it allows us to mirror a stylized fact of immigration flows in most OECD countries, which seems very important from the above discussion: labor inflows often exhibit a bimodal skill distribution, with some skewedness towards the low-skill end. This seems to be true in particular for the United States.[8] In other words, while migrants are on average less skilled than natives, they tend to be concentrated at the high and low ends of the skill distribution. This may reflect both elements of self-selection and selective immigration policy.[9] It is obvious that any model that aims at capturing these elements of the policy discussion and stylized facts should feature at least three different skill levels. And it should contain a minimum of structural details regarding the skill intensity of traded and nontraded goods. In this paper, we propose a model featuring a labor force separated into three skill levels, with high-skilled labor used in the production of exportables, while low-skilled labor serves the production of nontradables, and labor with a medium level of skills is used in both sectors.

The remainder of the paper proceeds as follows. Section 2 briefly presents some historical background on the magnitudes of international labor migration in the two waves of globalization, focusing in particular on the receiving-country perspective. Section 3 introduces our specific-factors model of immigration, featuring three different skill levels and an endogenous adjustment of the terms of trade and the price of a nontradable good. Section 4 introduces what we call "augmented" wage frontiers and "augmented" labor demand functions as the analytical tools that we subsequently use for comparative static analysis. Section 5 then turns to the analysis of various immigration scenarios, focusing on both wage effects and native welfare effects. Section 6 concludes with a brief summary and suggestions for future research.

2   Empirical View of Immigration

We have mentioned before that, starting in the United States in the early 20th century, world migration flows came under the decisive influence of active immigrant-country policies. These policies have been mainly restrictive in nature, which may partly explain why international migration has contributed rela-

---

[8]   See OECD (2001: Table 5.8) for evidence based on educational categories, and Jasso et al. (2002) on U.S. bimodality. Bimodality has also been observed for some EU countries (see Brücker et al. 2002: 24).

[9]   Williamson (2004) points out that changes in the source have typically also had profound implications for the skill composition of international migration.

Table 1:
Migration in the First and Second Wave of Globalization
Average yearly migration rates in percent of the population

	First wave				Second wave				
	1871–1880	1881–1890	1891–1900	1900–1910	1960–1969	1970–1979	1980–1989	1990–1999	2000–2010
Emigration countries (*)					(***)				(*****)
Belgium	–	-0.086	-0.035	-0.061	0.165	0.080	0.005	0.526	0.090
Denmark	-0.206	-0.394	-0.223	-0.653	0.020	0.085	0.070	0.383	0.110
Germany	-0.147	-0.287	-0.101	-0.282	0.255	0.120	0.210	1.001	0.180
Finland	–	-0.132	-0.232	-0.545	-0.330	-0.060	0.065	0.171	0.045
France	-0.015	-0.031	-0.013	-0.014	0.420	0.140	0.095	0.176	0.060
Great Britain	-0.504	-0.702	-0.438	-0.045	0.055	-0.040	0.040	0.379	0.050
Ireland	-0.661	-1.417	-0.885	-0.698	-0.625	0.325	-0.570	0.520	0.230
Italy	-0.105	-0.336	-0.502	-1.077	-0.180	-0.035	-0.025	0.335	0.075
Netherlands	-0.046	-0.123	-0.050	-0.051	0.055	0.230	0.145	0.511	0.075
Norway	-0.473	-0.952	-0.449	-0.833	0.000	0.090	0.140	0.467	0.275
Austria	-0.029	-0.106	-0.161	-0.476	0.075	0.105	0.175	1.440	0.165
Portugal	-0.289	-0.380	-0.508	-0.569	-1.390	0.225	-0.200	0.073	0.015
Sweden	-0.235	-0.701	-0.412	-0.566	0.225	0.145	0.175	0.498	0.085
Switzerland	-0.130	-0.320	-0.141	-0.420	0.285	-0.200	0.320	1.315	0.045
Spain	–	-0.362	-0.438	-0.139	-0.220	-0.005	-0.030	0.222	0.060

	First wave				Second wave				
	1871–1880	1881–1890	1891–1900	1900–1910	1961–1970	1971–1980	1981–1990	1991–1996	2000–2010
Immigration countries (*)						(****)			(*****)
Argentina	1.170	2.217	1.639	2.918	–	–	–	–	–
Brazil	0.204	0.411	0.723	0.338	–	–	–	–	–
Canada	0.548	0.784	0.488	1.676	–	–	–	–	0.425
USA	0.546	0.858	0.530	1.020	0.170	0.210	0.310	0.667	0.240

Table 1:
Continued

	First wave			
	1871–1880	1881–1890	1891–1900	1900–1910
Emigration countries (**)				
Great Britain	—	-0.305	-0.520	-0.204
Italy	—	-0.165	-0.337	-0.487
Spain	—	-0.151	-0.601	-0.518
Sweden	—	-0.290	-0.720	-0.351
Portugal	—	-0.352	-0.416	-0.594
Immigration countries (**)				
USA	—	0.569	0.894	0.402
Canada	—	0.227	0.489	0.371
Australia	—	1.128	1.659	0.077
Argentina	—	0.450	2.560	0.950
Brazil	—	0.198	0.382	0.844
New Zealand	—	5.352	0.408	0.415

Source: (*): O'Rourke and Williamson (2000: Table 7.1). 1/10 of decadal rates. Austria–Hungary for Austria.
(**): Baldwin and Martin (1999: Table 16). 1/10 of decadal rates.
(***): *The Economist* (1999: 40–41). Austria instead of Austria–Hungary.
(****): Temin (1999: Table 2). 1/10 of decadal rates.
(*****): World Bank (2002), *World Development Indicators 2002.* 1990–1991: Gross migration, average yearly rates (Italy, Austria, Spain: Inflow of workers in percent of labor force); 2000–2010: Projections, yearly net migration flows.

tively little to the alleviation of world poverty and inequality. Before plunging into the theoretical analysis of migration effects from an immigrant country point of view, it seems worth presenting a numerical perspective on international migration during the two big waves of economic globalization towards the end of the 19th and 20th century. We do not intend to go into great deal, but simply highlight the quantitative importance of cross-border migration for the *receiving* countries during the two waves of globalization. The main presumption is that the size of the inflow relative to the domestic population is crucial for the perceived pressure of adjustment in the immigrant country.

It is sometimes argued that immigration generally was a more important and pervasive phenomenon in the first wave of economic globalization than in the second. A meaningful comparison requires looking at migration rates, rather than absolute numbers. Drawing on various sources, Table 1 therefore compares the average yearly migration rates for various decades across the two waves of globalization. Obviously, the direction of international migration has changed. In particular, while European countries were main sources of migration in the first wave, they have now become important destination and host countries. In view of the policy background outlined above, it seems particularly interesting to compare immigration rates, i.e., the inflow of migrants expressed in percent of the receiving country's population. These rates were generally smaller in the second wave up to the 1980s than towards the end of the 19th and in first decade of the 20th century. But in the 1990s, they rose to levels that for many European countries are comparable to those of the main receiving countries one hundred years ago. Moreover, since "natural" growth rates of the domestic populations are now typically lower, a given rate of immigration is probably perceived differently now than in the earlier periods. European immigration rates towards the end of the 20th century are importantly driven by emigration from formerly socialist European countries. The intercountry pattern clearly indicates that richer countries tend to receive more migration, although in the case of European east-west migration this has no doubt also been reinforced by geographic proximity and cultural ties. World Bank projections for 2000–2010 indicate that there was a temporary upsurge in European immigration during the 1990s and that future migration will be importantly affected by immigration policy, which is subject to debate and change.

A more detailed empirical picture of immigration would involve the source country pattern of migration, as well as its skill distribution. The two dimensions are often closely related, with the skills of migrants available to an immigrant country depending on where these come from (see Williamson 2004). As was mentioned before, immigration policies are particularly concerned with the skill content of immigration for various reasons. While the systems chosen to control the skill pattern of immigration vary across immigration countries (see Martin 2004), the principle idea seems to be the same, namely to maximize the benefit of immigration to the host country. The particular policy that a country follows in pursuit of this aim depends on how benefits are defined, and on the host country effects expected from immigrants with various skills, given the country's economic structure and its adjustment mechanisms. Generally, OECD countries typically receive immigrants that are on average less skilled than the domestic labor force. However, migrants often also exhibit what we have called a bimodal distribution. By this, we mean that they are concentrated on both the low *and* the high end of the skill distribution. This may, however, be due not only to deliberate policy design, but also to self-selection, or to specific conditions in the source country. We now turn to a model that serves to highlight these adjustment mechanisms, whereby we place particular emphasis on the bimodality of the skill distribution and on incorporating goods price adjustments when identifying the wage effects of immigration.

3   A Skill-Oriented Model of Immigration

3.1   Model Assumptions

We divide the labor force into high-skilled labor (H), labor with a medium level of skills (M), and unskilled labor (U). Using an asterisk to denote foreign (immigrant) stock, domestic endowments are denoted by $H = \overline{H} + H^*$, $M = \overline{M} + M^*$, and $U = \overline{U} + U^*$, where a bar indicates the given native labor force of the respective skill level. The associated wage rates are denoted by W^h, W^m, and W^u.

Trade based on product differentiation implies that, relative to a well-diversified pattern of consumption, production is specialized on a subset of goods. We model this by assuming three goods: an exportable good X, an importable good Z, and a nontradable good N. Residents consume all of these goods, whereas production is specialized in the exportable and the nontradable good. In our core interpretation of the model, we thus assume no domestic production of the importable good. However, we shall also offer alternative interpretations where good N is a traded good. Moreover, in line with trade based on product differentiation, our core interpretation features finitely elastic export demand for good X; but to establish a reference case we alternatively shut down all price effects by treating both goods X and N as traded goods with given world prices.

In OECD countries, the nontradable goods sector, particularly market-oriented activities (construction, services), is typically less skill-intensive than the exportables sector (see, for instance, Dimaranan and McDougall 2002). We model this by assuming that exportables use high-skilled labor, together with medium-skilled labor, which is in turn also used in the nontradable sector, together with unskilled labor. Outputs in the X and N sectors, denoted by Q^x and Q^n, are generated according to the production functions $Q^n = q^n(U, M^n)$ and $Q^x = q^x(H, M - M^x)$, which are linearly homogeneous and strictly concave.[10] Producers are maximizing profits under perfect competition. This yields a specific-factors structure that has been used extensively in the study of international migration; see Jones (1979), Srinivasan (1983), and, more recently, Razin and Sadka (1997), and Bilal et al. (2003).[11]

In our model, capital plays no apparent role in production. However, this must not be taken literally. On the contrary, it should be interpreted as reflecting the stylized fact of a high degree of international capital mobility. Specifically, we assume that the immigrant country is entirely open to world capital markets and accumulates capital stocks subject to given world rates of return. In other words, the economy is modeled, not as quantity-constrained by its own capital ownership, but as price-constrained with an endogenous adjustment of capital stocks invested domestically. Invoking a general result established by Neary (1985), we may then treat the economy as behaving, in qualitative terms, like an economy where production takes place without capital.[12]

Preferences are represented, identically for natives and immigrants, by a strictly quasi-concave utility function, $u(D^x, D^n, D^z)$, where D^j indicates consumption of good j. We denote goods prices by P^x, P^n, and P^z, whereby $P^z = 1$ by choice of the numéraire. Utility maximization subject to an expenditure constraint, $P^n D^n + P^x D^x + D^z \leq E$, , leads to the Marshallian demand functions

---

[10] Throughout this paper, we use upper-case letters to denote variables and lower-case letters to denote corresponding functional symbols.

[11] In a stylized model, any assumption about factor intensities is likely to draw criticism, as one can easily find counterexamples. However, opposite assumptions are easily implemented by relabeling sectors and/or labor types. Indeed, the model can even be interpreted without any reference to skill levels at all. The fundamental assumption is that immigrant labor is either specific to the tradable or the nontradable goods sector, while there is a third class of labor which is entirely native and perfectly mobile across sectors. While migrant labor may be spatially highly mobile within the immigrant country (see Borjas 2002), it is often highly specific to sectors. Sector specificity of migrant labor may also be due to regulation pertaining to immigrant employment (see Engerman and Jones 1996, and Müller 2003).

[12] In quantitative terms, of course, the economy behaves differently, due to the Le Chatelier–Samuelson principle, implying that price reactions are more moderate with an implicit adjustment of capital stocks than without. For more details, see Felbermayr and Kohler (2004).

$D^j = d^j\,(P^x,\ P^n,\ E)$, where $j = x,\ n,\ z$. Finally, we add a foreign demand function for good X, $D^{x*} = d^{x*}\,(\cdot\,\cdot)$, which we allow to be finitely elastic in P^x. A more detailed discussion of this closure will follow below.

3.2   General Equilibrium

In equilibrium, profit-maximizing labor demands must equal domestic endowments, including native labor and immigrants. Using subscripts for partial derivatives, labor market equilibrium conditions may be written as

(1) $P^x q_H^x\left(\overline{H} + H^*,\overline{M} - M^n\right) = W^h$ and $P^x q_M^x\left(\overline{H} + H^*,\overline{M} - M^n\right) = W^m,$

(2) $P^n q_U^n\left(\overline{U} + U^*,M^n\right) = W^u$ and $P^n q_M^n\left(\overline{U} + U^*,M^n\right) = W^m.$

The first equation in each line refers to high- and low-skilled labor, while the second relates to mobile labor with medium skills, which features a common wage rate, W^m, in both sectors. Moreover, the endowment constraint implies $M^x = \overline{M} - M^n$, whereby we assume $M^* = 0$ in order to capture in a stylized way the above-mentioned bimodality of migration in skills. Linear homogeneity of $q^x(\cdot)$ and $q^n(\cdot)$ implies the usual zero-profit conditions: $P^x = c^x\left(W^h, W^m\right)$ and $P^n = c^n\left(W^u, W^m\right)$, where $c^x(\cdot)$ and $c^n(\cdot)$ are concave minimum unit-cost functions.

   Commodity market equilibrium requires that

(3) $d^x\left(P^x,\,P^n,\,E\right) + d^{x*}\left(P^x,\,Y^*\,\right) = q^x\left(\overline{H} + H^*,\overline{M} - M^n\,\right)$

(4)   and $d^n\left(P^x,\,P^n,\,E\right) = q^n\left(\overline{U} + U^*,\,M^n\,\right).$

Expressions (1) through (4) constitute a system of 6 equations determining 6 endogenous variables: W^h, W^m, W^u, M^n, P^x, and P^n. Outputs are determined by equilibrium allocation of mobile labor, according to the production functions $q^x(\cdot)$ and $q^n(\cdot)$. Invoking the "adding up condition" $d^z\left(P^x, P^n, E\right) \equiv E - P^x d^x\left(P^x, P^n, E\right) - P^n d^n\left(P^x, P^n, E\right)$, commodity market clearing implies the usual current account equation: $D^z - P^x D^x \equiv E - \left(P^x Q^x + P^n Q^n\right)$. The reason why we do not require expenditure to be equal to domestic product will become evident below.

4   Comparative Statics of Wages with Endogenous Goods Prices

4.1   General Remarks

We model immigration policy as quota-driven changes in the domestic supply of high-skilled and unskilled labor, H and U. Assuming for simplicity that $U^* = 0$ and $H^* = 0$ initially, we have $\hat{H} = dH^*/H > 0$ and $\hat{U} = dU^*/U > 0$, with $dM^* = 0$. Full employment of medium-skilled labor implies $\hat{M}^x = -\mu\hat{M}^n$, where $\mu \equiv M^x/M^n$. Dividing the relevant factor market equilibrium conditions in (1) and (2) yields the familiar equality of relative wage rates and the marginal rates of substitution in each of the two sectors. Introducing elasticities of labor substitution in the two sectors, $\sigma^x > 0$ and $\sigma^n > 0$, yields equations (5) and (6) below. Inserting the zero-profit conditions, $P^x = c^x(W^h, W^m)$ and $P^n = c^n(W^u, W^m)$, into (3) and (4) and differentiating then gives rise to (7) and (8), where θ^x and θ^n are the usual cost shares of medium-skilled labor in sector X and N, respectively. On the right-hand side of (7) and (8), they are also interpreted as output elasticities:

$$(5) \qquad \hat{H} + \mu\hat{M}^n = \sigma^x(\hat{W}^m - \hat{W}^h),$$

$$(6) \qquad \hat{U} - \hat{M}^n = \sigma^n(\hat{W}^m - \hat{W}^u),$$

$$(7) \qquad -\eta[\theta^x\hat{W}^h + (1-\theta^x)\hat{W}^m] + \alpha\hat{E} + (1-\alpha)\hat{Y}^* = \theta^x\hat{H} - (1-\theta^x)\mu\hat{M}^n,$$

$$(8) \qquad -[\theta^n\hat{W}^u + (1-\theta^n)\hat{W}^m] + \hat{E} = \theta^n\hat{U} + (1-\theta^n)\hat{M}^n.$$

Equations (7) and (8) assume Cobb–Douglas preferences with respect to goods X and N. There are, thus, no cross-price effects, and we may write $\hat{D}^x = -\hat{P}^x + \hat{E}$, and similarly for good N. The elasticity of export demand with respect to P^x is denoted by $\eta^* > 0$, whence, with homothetic foreign preferences, we have $\hat{D}^{x^*} = -\eta^*\hat{P}^x + \hat{Y}^*$. Overall demand for the exportable then evolves according to $-[\alpha + (1-\alpha)\eta^*]\hat{P}^x + \alpha\hat{E} + (1-\alpha)\hat{Y}^*$, where α denotes the initial share of domestic demand. Thus, in (7), η is defined as $[\alpha + (1-\alpha)\eta^*]$.

Before we can proceed with the solution of the system (5) through (8), we need to know how expenditure E behaves in the adjustment process following $\hat{H} > 0$ and $\hat{U} > 0$. Generally, one would expect expenditure to be affected by immigration, first through a change in domestic factor prices and, thus, incomes of native factor owners, but also through a change in the domestic labor force, i.e., through migrant labor income. This interdependency generates substantial complexity in the analysis, and the question is whether one can simplify by suitable assumptions. A first assumption might be that all, or a large part, of the wage income earned by migrant workers is remitted to their home country. In this case, E is not affected, or not affected much, by the immigration-induced change in domestic endowment. One might call this a guest-worker, or repatriated-income system. It allows us to hold domestic expenditure constant in (8), the equilibrium condition for nontradables. If migrant workers become true residents, then their income feeds fully into domestic expenditure. Other things equal, any immigration would then require a larger increase (or a lower decrease) of P^n, with an associated Stolper–Samuelson repercussion on wages. In Felbermayr and Kohler (2004), we provide a full solution of the system incorporating this effect. Here, we assume a repatriated-income system, whence there is no endowment effect on domestic expenditure.

As regards native income effects, one may envisage two simplifying assumptions. One is that preferences are quasi-linear in the imported good Z, which rules out domestic income effects on expenditure for goods X and N in (7) and (8). The other is that the domestic government stabilizes domestic expenditure by means of a suitable macroeconomic policy. In this case, any change in GDP directly feeds through into a change in the current account, rather than any change in domestic expenditure. For our purposes, the two assumptions serve equally well, and in the solution presented below we consider migration scenarios where E is held constant.[13]

A further issue is whether equilibrium on world commodity markets is appropriately modeled in the present context by means of an export demand function with a finite price elasticity, η^*. Indeed, one might question any need for a terms-of-trade adjustment in the migration scenario considered by saying that there are offsetting Rybczynski-type reallocations in the sending and the receiving country. A first response might be that, in a migration scenario with unequal factor prices, the Rybczynski-type effects would not offset each other exactly, even for identical technologies, unless the model is linear. However, the net effect is probably not large enough to worry about terms-of-trade adjustments. Nor would we expect any need for such an adjustment if there are *neutral* technological differences between the two countries. But things look different if such differences are *nonneutral*, or if one assumes trade based on product differentiation, which may be seen as an extreme case of nonneutral differences. Under nonneutrality,

---

[13]   Again, we may refer to Felbermayr and Kohler (2004), which gives the full solution for the case where native income changes feed into changes in domestic expenditure.

any increase in domestic output of sector X is less than fully offset by lower supply of the sending country. In the realistic case of product differentiation, this is immediately obvious, as the two countries produce different sets of goods. Notice that an equivalent case also arises without product differentiation on the firm level if one assumes Ricardian trade, where countries specialize in disjoint subsets of goods. This is, indeed, the assumption underlying the case considered in Davis and Weinstein (2002), where terms-of-trade adjustments are the driving force behind a migration scenario which is detrimental to the receiving country as a whole, without having any distributional effect at all. Turning to our export price elasticity $\eta^* < \infty$, this should be seen as a convenient modeling device to capture the substitution relationship between the range of goods produced by the domestic economy and the goods produced abroad, the underlying assumption being that trade is based on product differentiation with complete specialization in production.[14] Notice that this elasticity is assumed to govern *overall* demand, given constant overall expenditure, due to the above-mentioned assumptions relating to domestic expenditure and repatriation of migrant income. With this interpretation, we may thus also set $\hat{Y}^* = 0$ in (7) above.

With these assumptions, we may now interpret equations (5) through (8) as jointly determining domestic wage effects $\hat{W}^n$, $\hat{W}^m$, and $\hat{W}^h$, as well as the accompanying reallocation of medium-skilled labor, $\hat{M}^n$, resulting from a policy-induced change in the stock of foreign labor, $\hat{H}$ and $\hat{U}$, say via a change in allocated quota. Even for constant E, however, the analytical solutions look messy.[15] We therefore resort to a more intuitive approach based on a graphical representation using labor demand schedules and wage frontiers which are augmented to incorporate equilibrating goods price adjustments.

4.2   Augmented Wage Frontiers

Traditional factor price frontiers depict alternative combinations of factor prices that are consistent with zero-profit conditions, given product prices. Our augmented wage frontiers now incorporate the relevant goods market equilibrium, given sector-specific endowments. Unlike traditional frontiers, the augmented frontiers are not necessarily downward-sloping. For instance, while a fall in W^m would facilitate an increase in W^h for a given P^x, the attendant increase in M^x

---

[14] Our view is supported by empirical estimates of export price elasticities that do not appear to systematically vary with country size, with elasticity values well below infinity even for small countries (Marquez 2002).

[15] The full solution may be found in Felbermayr and Kohler (2004).

would depress the equilibrium goods price and, thus, the rental for the specific factor H. Depending on the ease of factor substitution and the price elasticity of demand, W^h may in fact fall. A complete analogy obtains for sector N. Formal expressions may be obtained by combining (5) and (7), which yields (9), as well as by combining (6) and (8), which yields (10):

$$(9) \qquad \hat{W}^m = \frac{\hat{H}}{(1-\theta^x)(\eta-\sigma^x)} - \frac{\sigma^x + \eta\theta^x/(1-\theta^x)}{\eta-\sigma^x}\hat{W}^h,$$

$$(10) \qquad \hat{W}^m = \frac{\hat{U}}{(1-\theta^n)(1-\sigma^n)} - \frac{\sigma^n + \theta^n/(1-\theta^n)}{1-\sigma^n}\hat{W}^u.$$

In line with the above discussion on domestic and foreign expenditure effects of migration, the first terms on the right assume zero expenditure changes. Equations (9) and (10) highlight two opposing forces which are crucial not only for the wage effects of immigration, but also for whether or not the receiving country as a whole will enjoy an immigration surplus. One is the *complementarity effect*, which is conducive to the immigration surplus, and which is larger, the smaller the two elasticities of labor substitution in production are. The other is the price sensitivity of demand, which governs the *goods price effects* of immigration. A low value of η^* in $\eta \equiv \alpha + (1-\alpha)\,\eta^*$ is conducive to a deterioration of the terms of trade, which potentially offsets the complementarity effect. If the country is small, then $\eta \to \infty$ and the augmented wage frontier collapses to a standard factor price frontier, with its elasticity given by $-\theta^x/(1-\theta^x)$. On the other hand, if $\sigma^x \to \infty$, the slope of the frontier is equal to 1, and if $\sigma^x \to 0$, it is equal to $-\theta^x/(1-\theta^x)$. Similar results obtain for σ^n. If the elasticity of substitution and the elasticity of demand coincide, the augmented wage frontier is a vertical line. Figure 1 depicts augmented wage frontiers for sector N in the left-hand panel (labeled AWF^n), and for the export sector, X, in the right-hand panel (labeled AWF^x). Obviously, the slopes depend on the signs of $\eta - \sigma^x$ and $1 - \sigma^n$, respectively, with their absolute values increasing in the respective elasticities of substitution in labor use, and decreasing in the price elasticities of demand. In Figure 1, we assume "normal" slopes for the baseline case. The subscript labels refer to alternative scenarios (see below).

Immigration-induced increases in H or U shift the augmented wage frontiers, with the direction again depending on the signs of $\eta - \sigma^x$ and $1 - \sigma^n$. The smaller the difference between the elasticity of substitution and the elasticity of supply, the larger the shift of the frontiers. If either is infinity, the curves do not shift at all. It is worth spending a few words on the intuition behind these shifts. Generally, one would expect immigration of high-skilled labor to lower W^h and raise W^m, the wage for complementary medium-skilled labor. Whether or not this will

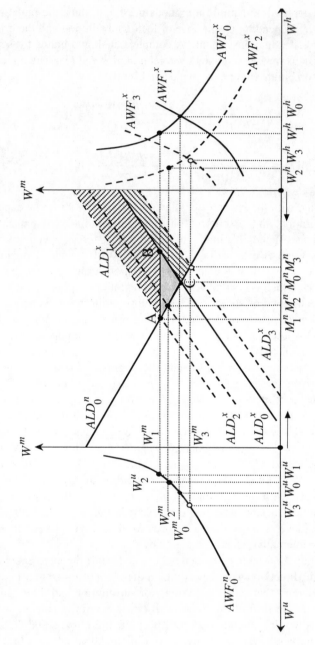

Figure 1:
The Wage and Welfare Effects of Immigration

eventually occur cannot be determined from the wage frontier for sector X alone, but in some sense the intuition is borne out, provided that complementarity is strong, relative to the price effect to be expected from a larger supply of good X, i.e., if $\eta - \sigma^x > 0$. The wage frontier shifts down, suggesting that it will not be possible for *both* factors to gain from this immigration. However, if the price effect dominates complementarity, $\eta - \sigma^x < 0$, then high-skilled immigration leads to an upward shift in the wage frontier, which generates room for an increase in the wage rates for both types of labor.

4.3   Augmented Labor Demand Schedules

The augmented demand schedules for mobile labor describe labor demand as functions of W^m, again incorporating market clearing in the respective goods markets. Setting expenditure changes equal to zero again, we obtain the following differentiated inverse labor demand schedules:

(11) $$\hat{W}^m = \theta^x \frac{\eta - \sigma^x}{\sigma^x \eta} \hat{H} - \frac{\eta \theta^x + \sigma^x(1 - \theta^x)}{\sigma^x \eta} \hat{M}^x,$$

(12) $$\hat{W}^m = \theta^n \frac{1 - \sigma^n}{\sigma^n} \hat{U} - \frac{\theta^n + \sigma^n(1 - \theta^n)}{\sigma^n} \hat{M}^n,$$

Like traditional labor demand schedules, augmented schedules are downward sloping. A high value of σ^x implies easy substitution between medium- and high-skilled labor in X and, thus, a large quantity reaction to changes in W^m. In turn, a large value of η makes the marginal value productivity of medium-skilled labor less sensitive to changes in employment. All of this results in a flatter demand curve. As $\eta \to \infty$, the slope approaches $-\theta^x / \sigma^x$, and as $\eta \to 0$, it approaches $-\infty$, regardless of the value of σ^x. On the other hand, as $\sigma^x \to -\infty$, the slope approaches $-(1 - \theta^x)/\eta$, and if $\sigma^x = 0$, it converges to $-\infty$.

More interestingly for our purpose, commodity market clearing may require counterintuitive shifts due to immigration-induced changes in the stock of the specific factor, the crucial factors again being $\eta - \sigma^x$ and $1 - \sigma^n$. For instance, a sufficiently low price elasticity of demand coupled with a high elasticity of substitution, $\eta - \sigma^x < 0$, implies that the marginal value productivity of M^x falls as H rises, shifting the labor demand schedule down. Moreover, for a given sign of $\eta - \sigma^x$, the vertical shift in the labor demand schedule is larger, the higher the degree of complementarity and the smaller the demand elasticity. The augmented demand schedules for medium-skilled labor (labeled ALD^n and ALD^x) in the center panel of Figure 1 complete the diagrammatical illustration, which we may now use for a full comparative static analysis of various immigration scenarios.[16]

5   Immigration Scenarios

Labor market equilibrium is identified by the intersection of the augmented labor demand curves, which determines the allocation M^n and the wage rate W^m for medium-skilled labor. Equilibrium wage rates for high-skilled and low-skilled labor are then read off the two augmented wage frontiers AWF^n and AWF^x, respectively. We use the subscript 0 to indicate the initial equilibrium. The immigration scenarios considered feature alternative combinations of high- and low-skilled labor inflows, $\hat{H} > 0$ and $\hat{U} > 0$, as motivated in the introduction. We first establish a reference case in which we interpret both goods as tradables, with constant prices given from world markets. We then increase realism and complexity by allowing for terms-of-trade effects for tradables, and returning to the case in which good N is treated as a nontradable whose price is endogenously determined by domestic demand and supply. The adjustment mechanism alluded to in the introduction is captured by the elasticities of substitution in production, and by the price elasticities of demand.

5.1   The Reference Case of a Small Open Economy

Suppose goods X and N are both traded and that the economy is small in world markets. This implies that $\eta \to \infty$, and the elasticity of demand for good N is no longer equal to unity, but also infinite. From the above discussion, we know that in this case immigration shifts the augmented labor demand schedules upward by $(\theta^x/\sigma^x)\,\hat{H}$ and $(\theta^n/\sigma^n)\,\hat{U}$, in relative terms, while leaving the wage frontiers unaffected. Note that the vertical shifts in the labor demand schedules are larger, the higher the degree of complementarity (low values of σ^x and σ^n). To avoid clutter in the figure, we draw shifts only for sector X, labeling the new equilibrium using the subscript 1. The generalization to simultaneous inflows of both types of labor is obvious.

Immigration of high-skilled labor initiates a reallocation of medium-skilled labor into the X sector, driving up W^m and pushing down wages for both high-skilled *and* low-skilled labor. More generally, *high-skilled* immigration harms

---

[16]   The diagram is a generalized version of Mussa's (1974) "scissors diagram."

unskilled workers if it draws mobile resources away from the sector in which un-skilled labor finds employment.[17] The hatched area between the ALD_0^x and ALD_1^x lines and above the ALD_0^n line measures the immigration-induced in-crease in GDP. However, part of this accrues to migrant labor that receives in-come according to the new wage rate W_1^h. Native factor owners *as a whole* en-joy an income gain equal to the triangle ABC. This is best understood by first identifying the income gain to medium-skilled labor as $\overline{M}(W_1^m - W_0^m)$, and then asking how much of this is a mere redistribution at the expense of high-skilled and low-skilled labor. Income to these workers before and after immigration, re-spectively, is found as the areas underneath the ALD_0^x and ALD_0^n lines between W_1^m and W_0^m. Hence, the extent to which the income gain to medium-skilled la-bor is not due to mere redistribution from other types of labor is measured by the triangle ABC. This triangle measures the Borjas-type immigration surplus, which normally appears underneath conventional labor demand functions.

Turning to the bimodal immigration scenario, it is clear from the above that any such inflow of whatever composition unambiguously benefits medium-skilled labor at the expense of both high- and low-skilled labor, provided that both elasticities of substitution, σ^x *and* σ^n are finite. By the same token, it follows that immigration at the two ends of the skill distribution, independent of its de-tailed pattern, is devoid of any wage effect if either σ^x *or* σ^n is infinite and if both goods continue to be produced domestically. In these circumstances, there will also be no immigration surplus to the domestic economy. Conversely, a positive immigration effect arises whenever σ^x *and* σ^n are both finite.

Note that if any one of the substitution elasticities is infinite, this effectively establishes a case with an equal number of goods and factors, hence the zero-profit conditions alone determine factor rewards, independently on endowments. Moreover, the direction of wage changes is determined by the factor intensity ranking, and does not depend on the magnitudes of the elasticities, provided both are finite. An important general conclusion is that a low elasticity of substitution within a sector receiving industry-specific migration is not enough to establish a complementarity-based immigration surplus. If that industry faces perfectly elastic domestic supply of some other factor which is mobile within the country, then the immigration surplus vanishes. In other words, reallocation of the mobile factor erodes complementarity *in general equilibrium*, and it alleviates wage

---

[17] This is the *sectoral* equivalent to the *spatial* effect emphasized by Borjas (2002), where an inflow of labor into a certain region causes movement of labor to other re-gions. Borjas emphasizes that this may explain the lack of wage effects from immi-gration found in empirical studies, and he therefore calls for a national focus in the empirical search for immigration effects. From the above analysis, it follows that in-tersectoral mobility may also be the reason for low effects in nationwide empirical studies.

pressure in the receiving sector, but only to have it reappear on specific factors in other sectors. This type of adjustment mechanism disappears, however, if the bimodal inflow is *symmetric* in the sense of shifting both *ALD* lines in Figure 1, such that equilibrium requires no reallocation in mobile labor employment. A further point worth mentioning is that, for any given overall size of the labor inflow, the parameter ratios θ^x/σ^x and θ^n/σ^n determine an *optimal skill composition* of the inflow, optimality here meaning a maximum overall gain for natives.[18]

5.2   A Large and Entirely Open Economy

Suppose that the economy is "large" in the sense that $\eta < \infty$, but there is no non-tradable good, which is what we mean by "entirely open." We should like to stress here that this arises even with small economies if their trade is based on product differentiation (see the above discussion). In fact, there need not even be product differentiation in the strict sense of the word. Whenever there is complete specialization in the sense that a country is the sole supplier of its specific traded goods, then we should expect terms-of-trade effects also in connection with immigration. This has recently been stressed by Davis and Weinstein for the United States, which is, of course a large economy by any measure (see Davis and Weinstein 2002). But the very model that they use, which is the Dornbusch–Fischer–Samuelson multigood version of the Ricardian model, also generates a qualitatively similar case for an economy which in the usual sense would be considered small. Moreover, a qualitatively similar case can also easily be imagined for other determinants of trade.[19]

In terms of Figure 1, the impact of high-skilled immigration is best understood as arising in two steps. First, the ALD^x line shifts up due to the complementarity effect, as in the previous scenario, but then it is forced down again to ALD_2^x due to an equilibrating reduction in P^x, the extent of which is determined by the value of η. This latter effect yields a Ricardo–Viner-type redistribution: W^m falls, but less than proportionally with P^x, and W^h falls more than proportionally with P^x. One could say that the worsened terms of trade are shouldered by three factors, viz. domestic high-skilled labor, foreign high-skilled labor, and domestic medium-skilled labor. Unskilled natives, on the other hand, are now clearly better off, relative to the previous (small-country) case, since the price ef-

---

[18]   See Felbermayr and Kohler (2004) for a calibrated numerical analysis of this issue.

[19]   In the context of the gravity approach to bilateral trade, Deardorff (1998) has identified conditions leading to the above-mentioned pattern of specialization in a world where trade is based on Heckscher–Ohin-type differences in endowments.

fect mitigates the immigration-induced reallocation of mobile labor into the tradables sector.

Clearly, the condition $\eta - \sigma^x = 0$ marks a dividing line. If $\eta - \sigma^x > 0$, then the complementarity effect still dominates the terms-of-trade effect, and in qualitative terms the *distributional* consequences are the same here as in the previous case. Note that the adverse effect on the wage for high-skilled labor is aggravated by a shift of the augmented wage frontier for the export sector down to AFW_2^x, leading to a wage rate equal to W_2^x. However, the *welfare* consequences may differ from the previous case even if $\eta - \sigma^x > 0$. In terms of Figure 1, the deterioration of the terms of trade has a direct negative effect on domestic high-skilled workers whose income is no longer depicted underneath the initial ALD_0^x line. Hence, the reasoning applied to the ABC triangle can no longer be applied in this case.

Welfare considerations in this case are further complicated by domestic consumption of the exported good, whence any terms-of-trade deterioration also holds benefits for domestic workers. Suppose, then, that good X is a pure export good, with $D^x = 0$ and $\eta = \eta^*$. Any native income gain is then equivalent to a welfare gain, and vice versa. Now, let $\eta - \sigma^x$ converge to zero. In the limit, there is no vertical shift in the ALD^x line; the output effect of high-skilled immigration is completely offset by deteriorated terms of trade. Moreover, there is no reallocation of medium-skilled labor, and GDP remains constant. But since the labor force has increased as a result of immigration, there is a loss in GDP *per capita*. Since immigrant wages are paid from an unchanged GDP, there is an income loss to *native* workers, which in this case also amounts to a welfare loss.

A fortiori, native income and welfare are reduced if $\eta - \sigma^x < 0$, in which case the ALD^x line shifts down below its initial position to a position like ALD_3^x in Figure 1. Moreover, if $\sigma^n < 1$, then both ALD^n and AWF^n are downward sloping, and high-skilled immigration causes *reverse reallocation* of medium-skilled labor into sector N, up to employment M_3^n, with a lower wage W_3^m. But it should be noted that $\eta - \sigma^x < 0$ implies an *upward*-sloping AWF_0^x line, and an immigration-induced upward shift to AWF_3^x. With the price effect dominating complementarity, therefore, cheaper medium-skilled labor does not really help high-skilled labor in the exportable sector. The distributional consequences of immigration are thus markedly different from the previous case. The terms-of-trade loss from high-skilled immigration that occurs here is more than fully accommodated by a real income loss to domestic high-skilled workers, as well as a loss to medium-skilled labor. Hence, in this case unskilled labor gains, with an increase in the wage rate up to W_3^n. We may thus portray this case as establishing a Davis–Weinstein-type negative result (Davis and Weinstein 2002), but with an added distributional change. It is worth emphasizing that in the present analysis the Davis–Weinstein case emerges in a unified modeling framework which, for a different parameter constellation, also incorporates the more conventional case of a Borjas-type immigration surplus (see Borjas 1995 and 1999).

5.3   A Large Open Economy with a Nontraded Goods Sector

We now turn to the core interpretation of our model, where N is a nontradable good with a unitary price elasticity of demand. Bimodal immigration now involves a simultaneous shift also of the augmented labor demand schedule ALD^n, and of the augmented wage frontier AWF^n. Moreover, the welfare calculation is necessarily complicated by the price effect, as is the case if there is also domestic consumption of the export good. A full welfare analysis would require capturing such price effects via the unit-expenditure function, which we have not introduced up to this point. One might also expect ambiguities to arise, depending on the details of demand. However, a number of things can be derived even without explicit reference to the expenditure function.

First, it is important to recognize that there is no *first-order* welfare effect from a price change for nontradable goods, since for these goods domestic demand and supply are always equal. For *marginal* immigration, therefore, the nontraded goods price effect may be ignored, whereas the terms-of-trade effect is a *first-order* magnitude. Now suppose that for the export sector, complementarity is dominated by the price effect, $\eta - \sigma^x < 0$, while for the nontraded goods sector, complementarity prevails, i.e., $\sigma^n < 1$. Suppose, moreover, that the economy already has some foreign unskilled labor to start with, i.e., $U^* > 0$. Then marginal immigration of high-skilled labor is harmful for native workers as a whole. The reason for this is that a (first-order) negative terms-of-trade effect, a result that has already been established above, is now coupled with a rise in wages for unskilled labor. But given $U^* > 0$, this implies that the negative overall terms-of-trade effect (Davis–Weinstein effect) is now aggravated by an income drain caused by higher wage income to foreign labor U^*.

This, of course, is a slightly provocative result, given the large preference that immigrant countries tend to give to high-skilled immigrants. It should be noted, however, that it is not so much the skill level *per se* that makes immigration harmful as its employment—exclusively in our stylized model—in the exportable sector, coupled with the dominance there of the price effect on complementarity. Moreover, this harmful effect would be mitigated if complementarity is similarly low in the nontraded goods sector, i.e., if $\sigma^n > 1$. In this case, we would still have reverse reallocation of the mobile factor, i.e., movement into the sector which is not favored by immigration of *its* specific factor, but this would now cause a fall in wage income to preexisting foreign unskilled workers, the reason being that the augmented wage frontier is rising.

What about immigration of the opposite skill pattern, i.e., immigration only of unskilled labor. It is quite clear from Figure 1 that there would be no harmful terms-of-trade effect in this case, independent of the sign of $\eta - \sigma^x$, and the distribution and surplus story of the small open economy would obtain for marginal immigration.[20] Not surprisingly, if the export price effect dominates complementarity, then this scenario even holds a wage increase for high-skilled labor. In other words, with low complementarity between high-skilled labor and the mobile factor, high-skilled labor becomes complementary to unskilled labor, even though unskilled labor is not used in tradable goods. Again, we recognize the importance of looking at nationwide reallocation as a crucial adjustment mechanism determining the wage and welfare effects of immigration.

A much less favorable picture emerges, of course, if there is complete dominance of price effects, $\eta - \sigma^x < 0$ and $\sigma^n > 1$. Figure 1 implies that any labor inflow of whatever skill pattern will cause a fall in *all* wage rates. This seems like an extreme Davis–Weinstein result, but one needs to be cautious, as there are price effects that need to be set against the changes in wage rates, in order to obtain real wage effects that are relevant for welfare. It is also quite obvious that the migration system matters a lot for the price effect for nontradable goods. Under a repatriated-income system, immigrant labor contributes in full to enhanced supply, without any significant demand effect. Hence, the fall in nontraded goods prices should be particularly large.

6   Conclusions

International migration is heavily influenced by active, and largely restrictive immigration policies. Relying primarily on skill-oriented quota-like systems, immigrant countries apparently want to secure benefits from immigration, and to avoid unwelcome wage and labor market effects. Empirically, such effects seem rather moderate, but anxiety still prevails. Low wage effects may seem comforting to policy, but might also be seen as troubling, since they indicate moderate overall host country benefits. Some researchers even point out that terms-of-trade effects may even cause sizable welfare losses from immigration.

Against this policy background, we have attempted to shed light on the wage and welfare effects of immigration, focusing on alternative skill distributions of

---

[20]   To avoid clutter and save space, we do not draw these shifts in Figure 1 and abstain from reiterating the graph for this scenario.

migrants, and on general equilibrium repercussions from adjustments in goods prices. Although somewhat less visible and less acknowledged in the policy debate, goods price effects seem important, a priori, because trade of immigrant countries is often based on product differentiation, and because of the presence of a nontraded goods sector. In rich immigrant countries, the traded goods sector is typically high-skill intensive, which often induces countries to follow a somewhat more generous policy for high-skilled migrants. However, if export demand is finitely elastic due to product differentiation, then an increased supply is likely to depress export prices. At the same time, the nontradable goods sector in these countries often relies on certain low-skilled labor, hence low-skilled immigration may be a welcome source for an increased, and therefore cheaper, supply of nontraded goods. Obviously, these price effects operate in different directions on overall host country welfare. Moreover, they have important repercussions on domestic wages.

In this paper, we have used a model of the specific-factors variety that reflects these facts, albeit in a highly stylized way. It allows us to identify the general equilibrium adjustment mechanisms that explain why wage effects of immigration may in some cases be low, and large in others. Moreover, we are able to identify conditions under which goods price effects dominate the effects of factor complementarity, potentially leading to welfare losses.

In concluding, we now try to give a flavor of the results obtained by briefly, but non-exhaustively, summarizing some of the results obtained. One set of crucial parameters is the elasticities of labor substitution that determine the extent and direction of complementarity between migrants and the domestic labor force. Immigration of whatever skill pattern is devoid of wage effects if this elasticity is large, either in the tradable goods or the nontradable goods sector. Moreover, whatever the skill pattern of immigration, it always tends to hurt both native high-skilled and low-skilled workers if both sectors feature a low elasticity of substitution.

As regards the price effect, we find a crucial dividing line where the elasticities of demand for the export good or the nontraded good are equal to the elasticity of labor substitution in that sector. The aforementioned effects tend to continue to obtain if, within these sectors, the price elasticity is larger than the elasticity of substitution. In the opposite case, the complementarity effect of immigration is dominated by the price effect. In this case, some of the conventional wage effects are reversed, and immigration of high-skilled labor generates an adverse terms-of-trade effect that causes a welfare loss which is shouldered through more than proportional real wage cuts by high-skilled labor and medium-skilled labor, while unskilled labor gains.

If this summary does not indicate a firm basis for a specific policy recommendation, this should, in and of itself, give rise to skepticism about the notion of tailoring immigration restrictions to specific home-country goals. General equilibrium repercussions of immigration-induced changes in the size and skill composition of the domestic labor force are of a complex nature, leading to results which sometimes are in marked contrast to expectations based on common sense. Hopes may be ill-guided, and anxieties may turn out to be unfounded, particularly if goods price adjustments, often ignored in research as well as policy discussions, are taken into account. Such effects arise in an indirect way, which often makes them difficult to relate to specific flows of immigration, and even less so to specific policy initiatives.

A promising route to follow in future research would be to use empirical data in such models and to pursue numerical simulations based on empirical information on the key magnitudes involved. This would also allow one to go beyond the confines of analytical tractability, and in particular to place more emphasis on expenditure effects related on nontraded goods, and to explore potential nonlinearities associated with variations in the size of the labor inflow.[21]

An important limitation of this paper that needs to be borne in mind relates to *welfare-state* effects of immigration. These are very much on the minds of policy makers and the general public, as emphasized in the introduction. Indeed, given the low empirical estimates of direct wage and labor market effects, alleged welfare-state effects seem to be of overriding concern in many of the OECD countries. This is perhaps the most important distinctive feature of migration in the second wave of globalization, as opposed to the first wave one hundred years ago. Abstracting from all welfare-state aspects, as we have done in this paper, might thus seem like a serious omission. However, our focus was different and, we should like to argue, no less important. Welfare-state issues of immigration are typically treated in abstracting from, or at least grossly simplifying, structural characteristics that may give rise, through adjustment forces on goods and factor markets, to an immigration surplus. The primary aim of our paper was to contribute to a better understanding of how immigration affects native wages and welfare through these adjustment mechanisms. In proposing a reasonably general framework to identify these channels, we hope to pave the ground for subsequent introduction of additional features reflecting welfare state and labor market imperfections.

---

[21]   See Felbermayr and Kohler (2004), where we take a first step in this direction.

Bibliography

Baldwin, R.E., and P. Martin (1999). Two Waves of Globalization: Superficial Similarities, Fundamental Differences. NBER Working Paper 6921. National Bureau of Economic Research, Cambridge, Mass.

Bauer, T., and K.F. Zimmermann (1997). Looking South and East: Labor Market Implications of Migration in Europe and LDCs. In O. Memedovic, A. Kuyenhoven, and W.T.M. Molle (eds.), *Globalization and Labor Markets. Challenges, Adjustment and Policy Responses in the EU and the LDCs*. Dordrecht: Kluwer Academic Publishers.

Bilal, S., J.M. Grether, and J. de Melo (2003). Attitudes Towards Immigration: A Trade Theoretic Approach. *Review of International Economics* 11 (2): 253–267.

Borjas, G.J. (1994). The Economics of Immigration. *Journal of Economic Literature* 32 (December): 1667–1717.

Borjas, G.J. (1995). The Economic Benefits from Immigration. *Journal of Economic Perspectives* 9 (2): 3–22.

Borjas, G.J. (1999). The Economic Analysis of Immigration. In O. Ashenfelter and D. Card (eds.), *Handbook of Labor Economics 3*. Amsterdam: Elsevier Science.

Borjas, G.J. (2002). Comments. In T. Boeri, G. Hanson, and B. McCormick (eds.), *Immigration Policy and the Welfare System*. Oxford: Oxford University Press.

Borjas, G.J. (2003). The Labor Demand Curve Is Downward Sloping: Reexamining the Impact of Immigration on the Labor Market. *Quarterly Journal of Economics* 118 (4): 1335–1374.

Brücker, H., G.S. Epstein, B. McCormick, G. Saint-Paul, A. Venturini, and K. Zimmermann (2002). Managing Migration in the European Welfare State. In T. Boeri, G. Hanson, and B. McCormick (eds.), *Immigration Policy and the Welfare System*. Oxford: Oxford University Press.

Card, D. (2001). Immigrant Inflows, Native Outflows, and the Local Labor Market Impacts of Higher Immigration. *Journal of Labor Economics* 19 (1): 22–64.

Chiswick, B.R., and T.J. Hatton (2003). International Migration and the Integration of Labor Markets. In M.D. Bordo, A.M. Taylor, and J.G. Williamson (eds.), *Globalization in Historical Perspective*. Chicago: University of Chicago Press.

Davis, D.R., and D.E. Weinstein (2002). Technological Superiority and the Losses from Migration. NBER Working Paper 8971. National Bureau of Economic Research, Cambridge, Mass.

Deardorff, A.V. (1998). Determinants of Bilateral Trade: Does Gravity Work in a Neoclassical World? In J.A. Frankel (ed.), *The Regionalization of the World Economy*. Chicago: University of Chicago Press.

De New, J., and K.F. Zimmermann (1994). Native Wage Impacts of Foreign Labor: A Random Effects Panel Analysis. *Journal of Population Economics* 7 (2): 177–192.

Dimaranan, B.V., and R.A. McDougall (2002). *Global Trade, Assistance and Production: The GTAP 5 Data Base.* West-Lafayette: Center for Global Trade Analysis (Purdue University).

The Economist (1999). *Pocket Europe in Figures.* 3rd ed. London: *The Economist,* with Profile Books.

Engerman, S.L., and R.W. Jones (1996). International Labor Flows and National Wages. *American Economic Review, Papers and Proceedings* 87 (May): 200–204.

Felbermayr, G.J., and W. Kohler (2004). Immigration and Native Welfare. Working Paper 0401. JKU Linz, Department of Economics, Linz.

Friedberg, R.M., and J. Hunt (1995). The Impact of Immigrants on Host Country Wages, Employment and Growth. *Journal of Economic Perspectives* 9 (2): 23–44.

Hanson, G.H., K.F. Scheve, M.J. Slaughter, and A. Spilimbergo (2002). Immigration and the US Economy: Labour-Market Impacts, Illegal Entry, and Policy Choices. In T. Boeri, G. Hanson, and B. McCormick (eds.), *Immigration Policy and the Welfare System.* Oxford: Oxford University Press.

Jasso, G., M.P. Rosenzweig, and J.P. Smith (2002). The Earnings of US Immigrants: World Skill Prices, Skill Transferability and Selectivity. Working Paper. The Rand Corporation, Santa Monica.

Jones, R.W. (1979).Comment. In R. Dornbusch and J.A. Frenkel (eds.), *International Economic Policy: Theory and Evidence.* Baltimore and London: Johns Hopkins University Press.

Marquez, J. (2002). *Estimating Trade Elasticities.* Advanced Studies in Theoretical and Applied Econometrics 39. Boston: Kluwer Academic Publishers.

Martin, P. (2004). *Challenge Paper on Population and Migration.* Copenhagen: Copenhagen Consensus.

Müller, T. (2003). Migration, Unemployment and Discrimination. *European Economic Review* 47 (3): 409–427.

Mussa, M. (1974). Tariffs and the Distribution of Income: The Importance of Factor Specificity, Substitutability, and Intensity in the Short and Long Run. *Journal of Political Economy* 82 (6): 1191–1203.

Neary, J.P. (1985). International Factor Mobility, Minimum Wage Rates and Factor Price Equalization: A Synthesis. *Quarterly Journal of Economics* 100 (August): 551–570.

OECD (2001). *Employment Outlook.* Paris: OECD.

Razin, A., and E. Sadka (1997). International Migration and International Trade. In M.K. Rosenzweig and O. Stark (eds.), *Handbook of Population and Family Economics.* 1B. Amsterdam: Elsevier Science.

O'Rourke, K.H., and J.G. Williamson (1999). *Globalization and History: The Evolution of a Nineteenth-Century Atlantic Economy.* Cambridge, Mass.: MIT Press.

Srinivasan, T.N. (1983). International Factor Movements, Commodity Trade and Commercial Policy in a Specific Factor Model. *Journal of International Economics* 14 (May): 289–312.

Temin, P. (1999). Globalization. *Oxford Review of Economic Policy* 15 (4): 76–89.

Williamson, J.G. (2004): The Political Economy of World Mass Migration. American Enterprise Institute for Public Policy Research, Washington, D.C.

World Bank (2002). *World Development Indicators 2000*. CD-ROM. Washington, D.C.: World Bank.

Comment on Gabriel Felbermayr and Wilhelm Kohler

Joaquim Ramos Silva

Felbermayr and Kohler's paper is an excellent presentation of a central issue of immigration within the context of the second globalization wave, particularly in OECD countries: its effects on wages and domestic welfare. As noted by the authors, the issue analyzed in the paper is of great interest, not only for theoretical and empirical reasons, but also for policy purposes. They have also methodologically privileged a theoretical perspective under the framework of the general equilibrium, where price adjustment mechanisms play a pivotal role. In my view, the emphasis on theory is quite necessary because, since the time of classical economics, theoretical approaches to immigration have not been developed or have been dismissed in the name of the immobility of factors so convincingly expounded by Adam Smith and David Ricardo. As is well known, the basic assumptions underlying this theory have remained, through various ways, widely accepted up to recent decades.

The present paper is a very substantial enhancement of the earlier version. It is more focused on the central point, using theoretical representative cases, for example, of the levels of skilled labor (high, medium, and low) or of small and large economies. In spite of the theoretical emphasis, empirical foundations and historical trends have not been forgotten. In addition, an effort has been made to link the theoretical approach to immigration to the major theorems of international economics, particularly those concerning trade and specialization as they relate to factors (specific-factors theory of the Ricardo–Viner type versus the Heckscher–Ohlin model). Indeed, even if we could accept that we are dealing with a phenomenon that is rather different from trade, the in-depth study of immigration requires that it must be compared with other international flows in a comprehensive way. Other improvements could also be mentioned here but the paper has mainly gained in clarity and precision, and I am sure it will be a useful instrument for researchers.

On the basis of the theoretical achievements in Felbermayr and Kohler's paper, its central issue must now be expanded in several directions. I will refer to some of them below, those that seem to have more theoretical and empirical potential, in order to increase our knowledge about immigration flows.

Firstly, the main theoretical assumptions now have to be empirically tested. As is natural in a theoretical paper like this, it must be followed by empirical findings. The authors themselves stress this necessity in the conclusions. Indeed, empirical investigation is justified not only in order to sustain and to adjust the theoretical assumptions but also to improve policies. In this regard, Felbermayr and Kohler (p. 54) are clear from the beginning:

> Controversy in policy formation is aggravated by a shortage of solid knowledge about the effects of immigration on the domestic economy. This holds true with respect to both a principal understanding of the effects to be expected and the empirical magnitudes involved. All too often, policy formation is based on vague anxieties and concerns focusing only on alleged directly observable effects, and less on economy-wide implications.

The previous considerations mean that we still know too little on the subject, and that the policies implemented are based more on superficial effects and feelings than on economic thinking. So, testing the theoretical assumptions, in a solid way, is a necessary step to the following up of the paper.

Secondly, as far as concerns the domestic welfare effects of immigration, a key issue of the paper, the references throughout the text show a very wide range of situations. According to the views presented, with the likely exception of the low-skilled domestic workers that can be easily replaced, there is no clear line about who benefits or not, and to what extent, from immigration. Nevertheless, even if, as a result of immigration, welfare decreases for some categories of wage earners, why is there such a continuous flow of foreign workers into OECD countries? Moreover, restrictive laws are often circumvented, and despite generalized quotas, new waves of legalization are sometimes allowed in the most diverse countries. Is it only the consequence of the pressure of external flows and migrant people? My answer is clearly "no." It seems to me that a major dimension of the process has not been sufficiently highlighted in the paper. Putting it straightforwardly: even in countries in which xenophobia is popular, what has really counted is the role of employers, for example, through political lobbying, in making a larger workforce available at a relatively lower cost. Under these circumstances, which are decisive for the economic process and for firms, capital is expected to have higher returns from immigration, notwithstanding the level of the employed immigrant skilled labor. Among other consequences, this may lead to an increase in domestic investment. Therefore, we may even assume that the capital owners contribute more than any other agent to the liberalization of international labor movements, and their role and implications cannot be ignored as far as national welfare effects are concerned.

Thirdly, the similarity of effects of restrictions on immigration and trade should be further explored. In Felbermayr and Kohler's paper, the different policies towards the three levels of skilled immigrant labor are apparently neutral in this respect. However, this does not seem to be the case. When the OECD countries favor the entry of high-skilled workers (some countries even subsidize the "import" of scientists and engineers (Romer 2000)), and discourage the coming of low-skilled workers, no matter whether these policies are successful or not, this may have similar effects as some arguments on protection and, consequently, cause distortions in welfare. In fact, the practices of attempting to attract the workers of high productivity call to mind the Manoïlescu argument for protection (Irwin 1996), leading to a result that may not be a positive sum for the partners in the game. Moreover, opportunely, Felbermayr and Kohler start their paper by reminding us that international inequality between countries (particularly the richest and the poorest countries) has increased over the three last decades.[1] Probably, immigration policies are not a significant determinant of this evolution, but they should not contribute to the aggravation of the inequalities either.

Still concerning the same point, despite the specificity of immigration, as with other international flows, it should also be analyzed in the light of free trade and transparency concerns. This is all the more important, since we know the institutional weakness of immigration from this point of view well. As was stressed by Hufbauer (2003: 256): "The world economy is within sight of achieving the free movement of goods and capital. The free movement of services is more distant, but the real laggard is the free movement of people." In conclusion, if, say, a WTO for migration is not foreseeable in the medium term, we should not let pass, without criticism, the old protectionist arguments in their new clothes (immigration policies).

Fourthly, for the sake of simplicity, the paper is focused on the effects on wages in host countries. However, in the future, it will be highly necessary to take into account the feedback of immigration in the country of origin, and to relate the whole impact of the movement. Indeed, we must not forget that we are in an increasingly interdependent and integrated world. For instance, in Europe and the neighboring area (Western Europe/Eastern Europe; Europe/Northern Africa), many of the immigration flows have simultaneously significant effects in both the host and the home countries. Perhaps immigration flows will still have more impact in the sending country (as was the case with Southern European

---

[1] It must be added, however, that the countries sending more immigrants are often not those whose economy is in stagnation or is totally backward, but, rather, those that are growing, sometimes at high growth rates, like China and India during the two last decades. This is perhaps due to the fact that, in an economy in motion, large parts of the population raise their expectations of rapid improvement in welfare that, in spite of the favorable trends, cannot be satisfied in the national context in a short period of time, perhaps because of local rigidities or other reasons.

countries— Portugal, Greece, and Spain—in the 1960s), but that is not the most interesting point here. In this perspective, what really matters is the fact that, in the integration and globalization era, home and host countries involved in the immigration process are more and more connected, particularly through trade and foreign direct investment. So, in the economic analysis of immigration we cannot ignore these reciprocal effects. Of course, in the public judgement it is not easy to separate the levels just mentioned (national, international, or regional), and national governments (even in closely integrated areas like the European Union, where there is a parliament and other common political structures), given their electoral basis, are above all responsible of their own territory and resident population. However, from the point of view of economic theory, including the welfare dimension, in order to assess the advantages or disadvantages of the immigration phenomenon, it is critically necessary to investigate all its domestic and external linkages in a dynamic way. So, even if governments are more geographically circumscribed in their concerns, economic theorists have the possibility of contributing to overcoming the limited perspective of national frontiers, in favor of a more global approach.

Bibliography

Hufbauer, G.C. (2003). Looking 30 Years Ahead in Global Governance. In H. Siebert, (ed.), *Global Governance: An Architecture for the World Economy*. Berlin: Springer.

Irwin, D.A. (1996). *Against the Tide: An Intellectual History of Free Trade*. Princeton: Princeton University Press.

Romer, P. (2000). Should the Government Subsidize Supply or Demand in the Market for Scientists and Engineers? NBER Working Paper. May. Cambridge, Mass.

Gil S. Epstein and Ira N. Gang

Ethnic Networks and International Trade

Abstract:

There is a well-established high-quality literature on the role of networks, particularly ethnic networks, in international trade. Ethnic networks are a way of overcoming informal barriers (information costs, risk and uncertainty) to trade by building trust and substituting for the difficulty of enforcing contracts internationally. The networks we are interested in are those that form between migrants and natives in the host country and between migrants and their home country. Ethnic networks exist when assimilation is not complete. We consider the struggle of migrants to assimilate and, at the same time, the struggle of the local population to prevent such assimilation. These activities affect trade possibilities. Moreover, we show that it may well be in the interest of migrants who specialize in trade to, at some point in time, turn from investing in assimilation activities and instead invest in antiassimilation activities in order to preserve immigrants' preferences for home country goods.

1   Introduction

There is a well-established high-quality literature on the role of networks, particularly ethnic networks, in international trade.[1] Ethnic networks are a way of overcoming informal barriers (information costs, risk and uncertainty) to trade by building trust and substituting for the difficulty of enforcing contracts internationally. The networks we are interested in are those that form between mi-

---

Remark: We are grateful for the helpful comments made by the participants in the Kiel Week Conference,

[1]   The literature is extensive and largely empirical. It is succinctly summarized and synthesized by Rauch (2001), who himself has made many of the seminal contributions. The fundamental insight is the role of ethnic networks in overcoming the inherent contract enforcement difficulties in international transactions. In this, it bears striking similarities to the literature on informal credit markets and microfinance institutions. These have been nicely reviewed in Morduch (1999).

grants and natives in the host country and between migrants and their home country.

Migrant assimilation is a topic of active research. The literature discusses the speed of the assimilation, the factors advancing and obstructing assimilation, attitudes towards indigenous immigrants, and intergenerational issues. To a degree, the question is, how long does it take for immigrants and their families to assimilate into the economic and social structure of the host country? The literature examines first-generation immigrants and the length of time, and the factors involved, in achieving earnings parity with the native-born.[2] There is also some evidence on intergenerational aspects of assimilation (Gang and Zimmermann 2000). While the evidence is mixed, the view that ethnic differences melt away does not hold sway. Though there is much individual variation, on average some ethnic groups do well and some do not. And within ethnic groups, some assimilate, some do not, and some maintain the middle ground.

We examine the consequences of the structure of immigrant assimilation on ethnic trading networks and on international trade. Natives and immigrants may battle each other over the position of the immigrant in the host country economy (Gradstein and Schiff 2005). Natives' views of immigrants, and the conflicts they may form the catalyst for, generate policy towards migrants in the host country. Moreover, immigrants, while desiring to assimilate into the host country culture, may at some point decide their native heritage is something to hold onto. These forces will impact international trade.

Ethnic networks are not fixed, and we expect them to change as immigrants assimilate. In the simplest world, if immigrants completely assimilate and very quickly do so, then there will be no ethnic networks and no gains from them for international trade. At the other extreme, where immigrant groups live and work in their own ghetto, with little or no contact with natives, the ethnic enclave is really an extension of the home country and it is questionable whether the effects on international trade will be any more than marginally positive. With just a little less isolation we should see trade gains. Over time, and as a result of immigrant desires for assimilation and host country attitudes, the role networks play changes, with consequences for the international economy.

Our paper is unique in that as far as we know it is the first to explicitly model the role immigrant assimilation plays in international trade. We proceed by constructing a model in which there are three groups of actors, the native-born and two groups of migrants, those who are involved in international trade and those

---

2   The classic paper by Chiswick (1978) starts the modern literature on immigrant wage assimilation. The controversies are summarized by Duleep and Regets (2002) who resolve the main issues. This and other strands of the literature are synthesized in Bauer and Zimmermann (1997). Also see the volume edited by Bauer and Zimmermann (2002) for highlights of the literature.

who are not. Migrants are assumed to all be from one home country, and the discussion of trade is with respect to the migrants' host and home countries only.[3] In this simple model, competition from migrants may lower native-born wages so natives undertake costly discrimination actions against the migrants, while migrants generally are assimilating into the host country culture.[4] We examine the consequences for assimilation and discrimination of increased migration, time, and traders' rents. We also analyze how increased migration, and traders' rents affect trade possibilities. Over time, migrant traders and employees exhibit different interests in assimilation and in maintaining their cultural identity, and we discuss how this affects trade possibilities over time.

2   The Model

Consider a host country that has two types of employed workers: Local workers and migrants. Denote the number of local workers by L_N (natives) and migrants (foreigners) by L_F. Moreover, consider the case where we have one group of migrants who are employees, and a second group of migrants who are self-employed and engaged in international trade between the host country and the home country.

2.1   Local Population's Utility

Let us consider the utility of the representative local worker. This individual consumes at level C and has positive utility from consumption. Consumption, C, is a function of wages of the local worker and as the level of wages is higher, consumption increases. Wages are set equal to the value of marginal product. We normalize the efficiency level of local workers to unity; migrants' efficiency level will be less than unity. The values of the efficiency level of the migrants will be a function of the discrimination activities of the local population and the

---

[3]   One could also think of networks of migrants from different countries but with the "same" cultural background (for example Asians, Africans, Arabs, etc.) or a common language. The assumption that all are from the same host country is to simplify our discussion.

[4]   In other words, we are assuming migrants are substitutes for natives in the work force. This is a simplification, as the degree of substitutability and complementarity between natives and migrants depends on the package of productive characteristics each possesses (Gang and Rivera-Batiz 1994).

assimilation activities of the migrants. The efficiency level of the migrants is a function of two elements:

(1) The effort invested by the local population in order to prevent migrants from assimilating into the population: not cooperating with them, antiassimilation activities, discrimination, and so on (hereafter "discrimination"). Such activities decrease the productivity levels of the migrants and thus their efficiency level.[5] Denote by d the amount of discrimination (or discrimination activities) against migrants.

(2) The effort invested by migrants to assimilate. These activities affect the migrants' efficiency level positively. The more the migrants assimilate, the more their productivity level increases, as it increases cooperation between the local population and the migrants. Denote assimilation activity by a.[6]

The local individual also has other benefits from the migrants not assimilating into the host country. In general, let us assume that the local worker receives a rent of n_N if the migrants are not at all assimilated. This rent is a function of the size of the labor market of local workers, L_N, and the number of migrants employed by the local population, L_F: $n_N(L_N, L_F)$ such that

$$(1) \qquad \frac{\partial n_N(L_N, L_F)}{\partial L_N} > 0 \text{ and } \frac{\partial n_N(L_N, L_F)}{\partial L_F} < 0.$$

As the local population increases (decreasing the relative size of the migrants), rent increases, while as the number of migrants increase (also equaling an increase in the relative number of migrants, as we are talking about the partial derivative), the rent of the local population decreases.

We assume that the proportion of migrants who assimilate will be given by the Tullock (1980) function where assimilation and discrimination activities have the following effect: $a/(a + d)$.[7] Thus, assimilation is relative to the amount of discrimination. For example, if both groups invest one unit in their respective activities, then 50 percent of the immigrants will assimilate. The proportion is also 50 percent if each invests 50 units. There is no cooperation between the groups and therefore the equilibrium level of investment in assimilation and discrimination activities will not be at the minimum level. Here, the proportion of migrants who do not assimilate equals $1 - [a/(a + d)] = d/(a + d)$.

---

[5]   This is similar to insider-outsider theory by Lindbeck and Snower (1988).

[6]   Assimilation is not always beneficial for migrants (Epstein 2003). For now, we ignore such possibilities; we will return to discuss them later in this paper.

[7]   See also Lockard and Tullock (2001).

The utility of a representative local worker is given by

$$(2) \quad u_N(\cdot) = \frac{d}{d+a} n_N(L_N, L_F) - d,$$

where d is the level of discrimination. We assume natives face costs in discriminating against migrants and thus it appears negatively in their utility function. As we are considering a representative local worker, it is clear that we may well have a problem of free riding, as it is optimal for all local workers to discriminate together against the migrants. However, each worker by himself will not have a reason to discriminate. We assume here that we have solved the free-riding problem. An alternative way of looking at this is to think of a case where a union represents the local workers and the union organizes discrimination against migrants. The union, a type of club, overcomes the free-rider problem. Of course, one could think of native utility as increasing in the discrimination level, as the native may have a positive utility just from discrimination. This may be the case for some natives; however, overall we assume that it costs natives to participate in discrimination activities. These activities take time and effort and thus decrease the utility of the native. Moreover, note that the effect discrimination activities have on the local worker's utility is also a function of economic conditions in the host country and could well be a function of the wages of the local population. In order to focus our discussion we disregard these effects.

The native's objective is to maximize his utility by determining his optimal discrimination level. The first-order condition determining optimal discrimination against migrants in the host country is given by $\partial u_N(\cdot)/\partial d = 0$. We therefore obtain that the first-order conditions can be written in the following way:

$$(3) \quad \frac{\partial u_N(\cdot)}{\partial d} = \frac{a}{(d+a)^2} n_N(L_N, L_F) - 1 = 0.$$

The first-order condition therefore satisfies

$$(4) \quad \frac{a}{(d+a)^2} = \frac{1}{n_N(L_N, L_F)}.$$

In order for the discrimination level determined in (3) to maximize the native's utility, the second-order condition must hold. The second-order condition for maximization is given by $\partial^2 u_N(\cdot)/\partial d^2 < 0$. The second-order condition can be calculated and shown to be equal to

(5) $$\frac{\partial^2 u_N(\cdot)}{\partial d^2} = -2\frac{a}{(d+a)^3}n_N(L_N,L_F) < 0.$$

Given the first- and second-order conditions, we can conclude the following:

LEMMA 1: *An increase in the natives' rent, either from an increase in the size of the local population or a decrease in the size of the migrant population, will, for a given level of assimilation activities, increase discrimination activities.*

2.2   The Migrant's Utility

We assume that a migrant can either be employed as described above or can be self-employed (Lofstrom 2002; Le 1999), trading with his home country. Migrants who have entered the host country may well maintain strong connections with their home country. This gives them an advantage in trading with their home country and in selling their products, which they import, to the residents of the host country. Moreover, the migrants may also sell products of the host country to their home country. To focus our discussion, let us think of the migrants as importing products from their home country to their host country.

A different way of looking at this is that many migrants want to continue consuming products that they are used to. The agents who import the products are naturally those who have connections in their home country, and these agents are migrants themselves. Networks to, and in, the home country help self-employed migrants import products and decrease their costs of importing. However, the migrants also need networks in the host country to further decrease the cost of importing (the same would apply in the case of exporting products from the host country to the home country). As the number of migrants who assimilate into the host country increases, the migrants' network externalities increase, enabling them to increase their profits and increase the quantity of imported products, thus increasing the utility of the international importer (exporter) migrant. We therefore have two types of networks that help the migrant increase his rent in importing (exporting) from (to) his home country to (from) the host country: (1) local networks in the host country—this is measured by the level of migrant assimilation into the host country; and (2) the network in the home country where the migrant still has ties. These ties enable the migrant to trade easier with the different groups in his home country.

As described above, the international trader migrant will benefit from the assimilation of his fellow migrants into the local population. A different way of looking at this is that as the level of assimilation increases, the migrants' wages increase and the consumption of products from their home country increases.[8]

Under this scenario, both employed migrants and self-employed international trade migrants want to increase their level of assimilation. As described above, it is clear that the employed migrant's wage and utility will increase from assimilation; the rent obtained by the international trader migrant will also increase from assimilation. We could think of the total level of assimilation activities, a, as the sum of both activities: the assimilation activities of the employed and the traders' assimilation activities. This, however, opens the problem of free riding by both groups. In order to focus our discussion, we assume that *only* one group engages in assimilation activities. For now, we assume that only self-employed international trade migrants invest in the assimilation process. Of course, one could think of both parties as investing in this process. However, we simplify matters in order to reduce the problem to a one-variable problem. One way of thinking about this is that if the stock of migrants—the employed and the self-employed—is assumed to be constant, these two levels of investment are proportional to the size of each group. Therefore, we only need to look at one of them. Later in the paper we will relax this assumption.

The utility of the self-employed international trader migrant, IT, at time t is given by

$$(6) \qquad u(\cdot)_{IT} = R\left(\frac{a}{d+a} n_{IT}(L_F)\right) - a.$$

$R(\cdot)$ is the rent associated with trade with the home country. The trader's rent is assumed to be a positive function of the number of migrants or their level of assimilation into the host country. This level of assimilation is represented by the term $[a/(d + a)]\, n_F(L_F)$. It is assumed that as the level of assimilation increases, $[a/(d + a)]\, n_{IT}(L_F)$ increases, that is, the rent also increases. These migrants participate in assimilation activities and thus have a cost of a for each a units of effort for the purpose of assimilation. To simplify, we assume that the rent from trade equals

$$R\left(\frac{a}{d+a} n_{IT}(L_F)\right) = r \frac{a}{d+a} n_{IT}(L_F).$$

---

[8] What we are modeling here is "differential" imports, that is, an import structure that is different from what it would be without the migrants. When we discuss imports increasing or decreasing, we are referring to imports from the home country only. Later, we will make clear that as assimilation proceeds, migrants' consumption pattern converges to that of natives.

Therefore, the utility of the self-employed international trader migrant becomes

(7) $u(\cdot)_{IT} = r \dfrac{a}{d+a} n_{IT}(L_F) - a$.

The first-order condition for maximization of the migrant's utility is given by $\partial u(\cdot)_{IT} / \partial a = 0$, namely,

(8) $\dfrac{\partial u(\cdot)_{IT}}{\partial a} = \dfrac{d}{(d+a)^2} n_{IT}(L_F) r - 1 = 0$.

The first-order condition is satisfied if

(9) $\dfrac{d}{(a+d)^2} = \dfrac{1}{n_{IT}(L_F) r}$.

In order to insure that the solution is the level that maximizes the migrant's utility it must hold that $\partial^2 u(\cdot)_{IT} / \partial a^2 < 0$. Given the function $a/(d+a)$ and the assumptions regarding the production function, it is clear that the second-order conditions hold true:

(10) $\dfrac{\partial^2 u(\cdot)_{IT}}{\partial a^2} = -2 \dfrac{d}{(d+a)^3} n_{IT}(L_F) r < 0$.

From (9) and (10) we can conclude the following:

LEMMA 2: *Given the level of discrimination, increasing the number of migrants, L_F, or the trade possibilities, r, will increase the level of assimilation activities.*

The reason for these results is that increasing these different variables increases the benefits the trader can obtain and thus increases their returns to investing in assimilation. With time, the migrants naturally integrate into the local population, as increasing assimilation activities further enhances integration.

2.3   Equilibrium

Natives invest in discrimination activities and migrants invest in assimilation activities (a and d are positive). We focus on the unique interior Nash equilibria.

Let us calculate the equilibrium discrimination and assimilation activity levels. For this, we must simultaneously solve (3) and (8), presented below as (3') and (8'):

(3') $\dfrac{\partial u_N(\cdot)}{\partial d} = \dfrac{d}{(d+a)^2} n_N(L_N, L_F) - 1 = 0$

and

(8') $\dfrac{\partial u(\cdot)_{IT}}{\partial a} = \dfrac{d}{(d+a)^2} n_{IT}(L_F)r - 1 = 0.$

Solving (3') and (8') we obtain that the equilibrium assimilation level of activities and the equilibrium level of discrimination activities equals

(9) $a^* = \dfrac{(r n_{IT}(L_F))^2 n_N(L_N, L_F)}{(r n_{IT}(L_F) + n_N(L_N, L_F))^2}$

and

(10) $d^* = \dfrac{(n_N(L_N, L_F))^2 r n_{IT}(L_F)}{(r n_{IT}(L_F) + n_N(L_N, L_F))^2}.$

It is clear from the above that the following holds:

LEMMA 3: *Increasing the rents of each group will increase their investment levels. That is, increasing the rent of the local population, given a constant level of the rent for the international trader, will increase discrimination activities. Increasing the rent of the international trader, given a certain level of the rent for the local population, will increase the assimilation activities.*

As a change in each of the parameters affects both levels in equilibrium, what effect changes in them will have on equilibrium discrimination and assimilation activities is not straightforward. We now wish to consider the effects changes in the size of the local population have on equilibrium levels of discrimination and assimilation activities.

Note that increasing the size of the local population means increasing the local population's rent. From (9) and (10) we obtain

(11) $\dfrac{\partial a^*}{\partial L_N} = \dfrac{r^2 n_{IT}^2 (rn_{IT} - n_N)\dfrac{\partial n_N}{\partial L_N}}{(r n_{IT}(L_F) + n_N(L_N, L_F))^3}$

and

$$(12) \quad \frac{\partial d^*}{\partial L_N} = \frac{2r^2 n_{IT}^2 n_N \frac{\partial n_N}{\partial L_N}}{\left(r n_{IT}(L_F) + n_N (L_N, L_F) \right)^3}.$$

PROPOSITION 1: *As the size of the local population increases, or as the local population's rent increases, discrimination activities will increase. However, assimilation activities will increase (decrease) if and only if the rent the migrant population can obtain from assimilation activities is greater (smaller) than the local population's rent,* $r n_{IT} > n_N$ ($r n_{IT} < n_N$).

This proposition states that local population growth or, equivalently, an increase in the local population's rent, will increase the discrimination activities that the local population undertakes. At the same time, local population growth or an increase in the local population's rent may decrease immigrants' assimilation activities if the rent migrants gain from assimilation activities is smaller than the benefit the local population can obtain. In other words, strengthening the local population may cause the migrants to decrease their assimilation activities.

This proposition is especially useful for comparing different-sized countries. Larger countries, ceteris paribus, will discriminate more against migrants than small countries. Moreover, under certain conditions, in larger countries migrants will assimilate less, maintaining their ethnic enclaves.

Now let is consider the effect an increase in the migrant population has on both types of activities. From (9) and (10 we obtain

$$(13) \quad \frac{\partial a^*}{\partial L_F} = \frac{r^2 n_{IT} \left(2n_N^2 \frac{\partial n_{IT}}{\partial L_F} + \left(r n_{IT} - n_N \right) n_{IT} \frac{\partial n_N}{\partial L_F} \right)}{\left(r n_{IT}(L_F) + n_N (L_N, L_F) \right)^3}$$

and

$$(14) \quad \frac{\partial d^*}{\partial L_F} = \frac{r n_N \left(n_N \frac{\partial n_{IT}}{\partial L_F} (n_N - r n_{IT}) + 2 r n_{IT}^2 \frac{\partial n_N}{\partial L_F} \right)}{\left(r n_{IT}(L_F) + n_N (L_N, L_F) \right)^3}.$$

Note that increasing the migrant population size increases the rent associated with assimilation activities, $\partial n_{IT} / \partial L_F > 0$, while increasing the size of the migrant population decreases the rent associated with the discrimination activities, $\partial n_N / \partial L_F < 0$.

PROPOSITION 2a: *Increasing the size of the migrant population will increase as-similation activities and decrease discrimination activities if and only if the rent the migrant population can obtain from assimilation activities is greater than that of the rent of the local population from discrimination activities, $rn_{IT} > n_N$ ($rn_{IT} < n_N$).*

PROPOSITION 2b: *If the size of the local population increases, it is not clear whether discrimination and assimilation activities will increase or decrease. This will depend on the relative and absolute size of the rents associated with the assimilation and discrimination activities.*

By Proposition 2b, the outcome depends on the asymmetry of the contestants in turning effort into performance and on the value of their benefit from assimilation and discrimination activities.

Now let us consider how a change in the rent, r, associated with the trade possibilities affects discrimination and assimilation activities. From (9) and (10) we obtain

$$(15) \quad \frac{\partial a^*}{\partial r} = \frac{2r n_{IT}^2 \, n_N^2}{\left(r n_{IT}(L_F) + n_N(L_N, L_F)\right)^3}$$

and

$$(16) \quad \frac{\partial d^*}{\partial r} = \frac{n_{IT} n_N^2 (n_N - r n_{IT})}{\left(r n_{IT}(L_F) + n_N(L_N, L_F)\right)^3}.$$

We thus obtain the following:

PROPOSITION 3a: *Assimilation activities will increase from increasing the rent associated with international trade, while discrimination (antiassimilation) activities may increase or decrease.*

PROPOSITION 3b: *Discrimination (antiassimilation) activities will decrease (increase) if and only if the rent the migrant population can obtain from assimilation activities is greater than that of the rent of the local population, $rn_{IT} > n_N$ ($rn_{IT} < n_N$).*

2.4   Trade Possibilities

Now let us consider how the above changes—changes in the size of the migrant population L_F and the rent received by the trader r—affect trade possibilities, $R = r\left(a/(a+d)\right) L_F = \left(a/(a+d)\right)bc$, where $bc = r\, L_F$. In general, we can write the following:

$$(17)\quad \frac{\partial R}{\partial b} = c\left(\underbrace{\frac{d}{(d+a)^2}\frac{\partial a^*}{\partial b}b - \frac{a}{(d+a)^2}\frac{\partial d^*}{\partial b}b}_{\text{indirect effect}} + \underbrace{\frac{a}{(d+a)}}_{\text{direct effect}}\right).$$

Of course, this equation will be modified for each of the variables L_F, and r. First, it is clear that one has to determine whether the direct effect is stronger or weaker than the indirect effect. This is important to establish, for the two effects may have different signs. The direct effect will be stronger than the indirect effect if $\eta + 1 > 0$, where

$$\eta = \frac{\dfrac{d}{(d+a)^2}\dfrac{\partial a^*}{\partial b}\,b}{\dfrac{a}{(d+a)}}$$

is the total elasticity of $a/(d+a)$ with respect to a change in b. It is not clear which effect is stronger. The second ambiguity that must be resolved is with respect to the elasticity

$$\eta = \frac{\dfrac{d}{(d+a)^2}\dfrac{\partial a^*}{\partial b}\,b}{\dfrac{a}{(d+a)}},$$

itself. It is clear that $d/(d+a)^2 > 0$ and $-a/(d+a)^2$ and the values of $\partial a^*/\partial b$ and $\partial d^*/\partial b$ are given in the analysis presented above. In this case, we know that natives increase their discrimination activities and migrants their assimilation activities. The sign of $\partial R/\partial L_F$ will be equal to the sign of

$$(18)\quad \frac{\partial R}{\partial L_F} = -rg(t)\left(\left(\frac{d}{(d+a)^2}\frac{-2d}{(d+a)^3}r + \frac{-a}{(d+a)^3}\frac{-2a}{(d+a)^3}L_N^2 f''\right) + \frac{a}{d+a}\right).$$

As we can see from (18), even though the effect of a change in the size of the migrant population has a positive effect on discrimination and assimilation activities, it is not clear which effect dominates overall trade possibilities. This will be a function of the strength in terms of gains and losses from such activities, as presented in Proposition 1. This result is similar for changes in the other parameters r and t, both of which determine the effect of trade possibilities.

PROPOSITION 4: *Changes in the size of the migrant population, L_F, time, and the rent, r, have ambiguous effects on trade possibilities. The total effect is a result of the relative strength of the two groups in terms of benefits and ability to turn effort into gains, described in Propositions 1–3.*

The ambiguity regarding what will happen to the assimilation and antiassimilation (discrimination) activities is resolved by looking at the results presented in the different propositions to see which of the groups has a stronger impact on the different activities.

3   Trade Possibilities over Time

Here we look at the effect of networks over time. As assimilation progresses, one network may grow stronger while the other becomes weaker. However, even though one becomes stronger, it may no longer be needed.

Each nonfully assimilated migrant is a representative of his home country and is a sales promoter of products from his home country. When migrants are not fully assimilated, they continue to consume products from their home country, this consumption is observed by the natives of the host country and has a positive effect on the natives' consumption of products from the migrants' home country. When migrants become fully assimilated, their consumption of products from their home country decreases and their consumption patterns are identical to those of the native population. As assimilation increases, the advantages migrant traders have over native traders decline.

Earlier in the paper, we discussed how assimilation increases trade opportunities. What is happening now is that international trader migrants want to increase ties with the local population in order to increase trade possibilities. As migrants assimilate, trade options may increase as a result of having more local networks and ties. However, the demand for products decreases as a result of the migrants themselves not consuming as many home products and this "promoter" of home products—the nonfully assimilated trader migrant—loses. We will observe over time the opposite consequences that these two effects have on trade possibilities. With time and assimilation, after a certain point the increase in benefits from assimilation are smaller than the losses from the decrease in the consumption of the imported products from the migrant's country of origin.

As the assimilation process moves forward, the trader migrant has more ties to the local population and can increase his trade possibilities with his home country. However, with time, even as his ties in the host country increase, his ties to his home country may well decrease. The trader migrant may now have fewer contacts in his home country and thus his trade possibilities decrease. Hence, we assume that after some point in time, increasing assimilation does not have additional positive effects on trade possibilities from the host country. In terms of ties to the home country, with time there is a decrease in these ties.

To summarize, it is assumed that the rent from trade $R(a/(a + d)\, g(t)\, L_F)$ has two effects over time:

$$(19) \qquad \frac{dR_t\left(\dfrac{a}{a+d} L_F\right)}{dt} = \underbrace{\frac{\partial R_t\left(\dfrac{a}{a+d} L_F\right)}{\partial t}}_{\text{direct effect}} + \underbrace{\frac{\partial R_t\left(\dfrac{a}{a+d} L_F\right)}{\partial\left(\dfrac{a}{a+d} L_F\right)} \frac{\partial\left(\dfrac{a}{a+d} L_F\right)}{\partial t}}_{\text{indirect effect}}.$$

The first component of the right-hand side of (19) represents the direct effect of time on the size of the rent from trade. For example, this can represent the decrease in trading possibilities as a result of a decrease in ties to the home country. The second component represents the indirect effect as a result of a change in ties to the host country. For example, it may capture an increase in ties to the local population and a decrease in the importation of home-country goods as a result of a high level of assimilation.

In one scenario we could think of the case where until time $\bar{t}$, it is assumed that the effect of assimilation and the creation of host-country ties is stronger than the loss of ties in the home country and thus $\left.(dR_t\,(a/(a+d\,)L_F)/dt)\right|_{t\leq\bar{t}}$ > 0. However, over time and assimilation, the effect of the increase in ties to the host country has a very small effect on the trade possibilities, while there is a substantial decrease in the ties to the home country, therefore decreasing overall trade possibilities over time, $\left.(dR_t\,(a/(a+d\,)L_F)/dt)\right|_{t>\bar{t}} < 0$. In this case, we would see that until point $\bar{t}$, the trader migrant will gain from assimilation: with time, his benefits from assimilation are initially increasing. However, after time $\bar{t}$, the trader will lose ties and his benefits from trade will decrease.

Consider the international trader migrant's utility as given by

$$(20) \qquad u_t(\cdot)_{IT} = R_t\left(\frac{a}{a+d} L_F\right) - |a_{1t}|,$$

where a_1 is assimilation activities, either for assimilation $a_1 > 0$ or against assimilation $a_1 < 0$. Denote by a_2 the activities of employed migrants. Therefore, $a = a_1 + a_2$. Under the assumption presented above we can conclude the following:

PROPOSITION 5: *There exists an inverse U-shaped relationship between the rent obtained from trade and time for the ethnic migrant. Moreover, with time the local population may well continue to invest in discrimination activities against the migrants, whereas the employed migrant population will invest in assimilation activities, while the international trader migrants will increase assimilation activities until a certain point in time, $\bar{t}$, and beyond this time will decrease assimilation activities and may even invest in antiassimilating activities ($a_1 < 0$).*

This proposition states that employed migrants benefit from assimilation and will invest in assimilation activities, $a_2 > 0$. At the beginning, the traders will benefit from assimilation and thus will increase their investment in assimilation activities (see Figure 1 until point $\bar{t}$). Over time, after $\bar{t}$, the trader benefits less from insider ties and trade possibilities decrease (see Figure 1). As a result, after

Figure 1:
Trade Possibilities

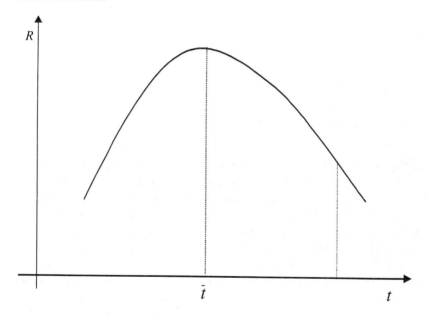

period $\bar{t}$, assimilation activities by trader migrants decrease (see Figure 2) and may even become negative. Negative assimilation activities can be thought of as antiassimilation activities $(a_1 < 0)$, and include activities aimed at preserving home country traditions and emphasizing the differences between the local population and the migrants. At the same time, the local population continues discriminating against migrants, while employed migrants continue to invest in assimilation activities.

Figure 2:
Assimilation Activities

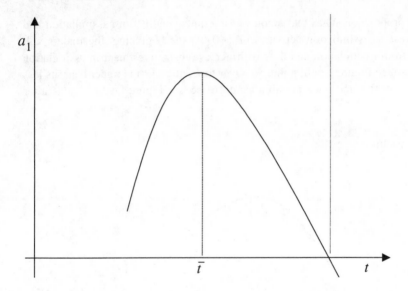

It may well be the case that as employed migrants continue in their assimilation activities after a level of a_2^* and international traders invest effort in antiassimilation activities, a_1 becomes negative. Thus, we see that the traders are fighting to prevent assimilation, or at least full assimilation, while the employed migrants from the same home country of the trader migrants' are fighting to increase assimilation. Both the local population and the traders will be fighting assimilation and the employed migrants will be fighting to increase assimilation. Over time, therefore, we may well see that the international trader migrants initially raise their assimilation efforts and fight discrimination, but after a certain point they go against their fellow countrymen and decrease their assimilation activities, even engaging in antiassimilation activities to hold on to their rent and not let the migrants fully integrate into the host country.

4   Concluding Remarks

Rauch (2001) asks whether ethnic networks in international trade will grow or shrink in importance over time. His answer is twofold. On the one hand, he appeals to the argument that in our increasingly integrated world international contracts now have some formal bite to them, diminishing the need for the sorts of "collateral" that ethnic networks can offer for traders. On the other hand, he points out that the information intensity of trade seems to complement transnational networks of the type that we have discussed. Our paper offers additional insights on this question, examining how those actors interact, affecting the assimilation path and international trade between the migrant's host and home countries.

Our picture of assimilation is simplified, focusing on the essential elements of migrant behavior in a host country, and the host country's receptivity to immigrants. Migrants want to assimilate, and as they assimilate their consumption patterns come to mimic those of natives. Natives, fearful of losing earnings, try to keep immigrants isolated. Over time, subgroups of migrants who cater to the migrant community will take action against assimilation, arguing for maintaining elements of their cultural heritage and therefore the subgroups' own rents. Though basic, the model allows us to gain insights that are helpful for understanding more complex assimilation scenarios (Gang and Zimmermann 2000; Rapoport and Weiss 2001).

Migrants and natives may possess asymmetrical ability and productivity. The degree of asymmetry will play a role in determining the intensity of assimilation activities by migrants and discrimination activities by natives. In turn, these determine the expansion and contraction of trade between migrants' host and home country. Over time, migrant traders and migrant employees exhibit different interests in assimilation and in maintaining their cultural identity, and the interplay of their conflict with the actions of the native-born over time provides further insights on the connection between ethnic networks and international trade.

Bibliography

Bauer, T., and K.F. Zimmermann (1997). Causes of International Migration: A Survey. In C. Gorter, P. Nijkamp, and J. Poot (eds.), *Immigrants, the City and the Labour Market*. Aldershot: Ashgate.

Bauer, T., and K.F. Zimmermann (2002). T*he Economics of Migration: Assimilation of Migrants*. Vol. II. Cheltenham: Edward Elgar Publishing Ltd.

Chiswick, B. (1978). The Effect of Americanization on the Earnings of Foreign-Born Men. *Journal of Political Economy* 86 (5): 897–922.

Duleep, H., and M. Regets (2002). The Elusive Concept of Immigrant Quality: Evidence from 1970–1990. Discussion Paper 631. IZA (Institute for the Study of Labor), Bonn.

Epstein, G.S. (2003). Labor Market Interactions between Legal and Illegal Immigrants. *Review of Development Economics* 7 (1): 30–43.

Epstein, G.S., and S. Nitzan (2005). Reduced Prizes and Increased Effort in Contests. *Social Choice and Welfare*. Forthcoming.

Gang, I.N., and F. Rivera-Batiz (1994). Labor Market Effects of Immigration in the United States and Europe: Substitution vs. Complementarity. *Journal of Population Economics* 7: 157–175.

Gang, I.N., and K.F. Zimmermann (2000). Is Child like Parent? Educational Attainment and Ethnic Origin. *Journal of Human Resources* 35: 550–569.

Gradstrein, M., and M. Schiff (2005). The Political Economy of Social Exclusion, with Implementations for Immigration Policy. *Journal of Population Economics*, forthcoming.

Le, A.T. (1999). Empirical Studies of Self-Employment. *Journal of Economic Surveys* 13 (4): 381–416.

Lindbeck, A., and D.J. Snower (1988). Cooperation, Harassment, and Involuntary Unemployment: An Insider–Outsider Approach. *American Economic Review* 78 (1): 167–188.

Lockard, A., and G. Tullock (2001). *Efficient Rent Seeking: Chronicle of an Intellectual Quaqmire*. Boston: Kluwer.

Lofstrom, M. (2002). Labor Market Assimilation and the Self-Employment Decision of Immigrant Entrepreneurs. *Journal of Population Economics* 15 (1): 83–114.

Morduch, J. (1999). The Microfinance Promise. *Journal of Economic Literature* 37 (4): 1569–1614.

Rapoport, H., and A. Weiss (2001). The Optimal Size for a Minority. Discussion Paper 284. IZA (Institute for the Study of Labor), Bonn.

Rauch, J.E. (2001). Business and Social Networks in International Trade. *Journal of Economic Literature* 39 (4): 1177–1203.

Tullock, G. (1980). Efficient Rent-Seeking. In J.M. Buchanan, R.D. Tollison, and G. Tullock (eds.), *Toward a Theory of the Rent-Seeking Society*. College Station: Texas A&T Press.

Comment on Gil S. Epstein and Ira N. Gang

Jutta Allmendinger and Christian Gaggermeier

The paper by Epstein and Gang is a major step forward in modeling the impact of ethnic networks on trade in times of increasing globalization.[1]

Gil Epstein and Ira Gang build a model in which they analyze—as the first ones, as far as they know—possible consequences of migrants' assimilation for production in the host country and for their trading with their home countries. By ethnic networks, Epstein and Gang mean the relations between immigrants, on the one hand, and their (trading) partners among the nationals in the host country as well as in their home country, on the other hand.

In the model, three types of employed are considered: native employees, foreign employees, and foreign self-employed (traders). The model's specific feature is that the productivity of the foreign employees is higher, the more they engage in assimilation activities, and lower, the more the natives harass them in order to prevent them from assimilating. Furthermore, the foreign traders' profit (their "rent") is proportional to the productivity of the foreign employees in the basic model version. The paper's results are based on the representative individuals' optimally determining their assimilation or harassment activities.

We have a few comments, some quite general, others focusing more specifically on the model's structure, including its explicit and implicit assumptions and their consequences.

General Remarks

First, labor markets matter. Hence, it seems to be crucial to distinguish economically "good" and "bad" times. In times of high unemployment rates, such as the ones that we are facing today, harassment activities will be much higher than otherwise. Labor markets and the mix of qualifications they need matter and must be considered as intervening variables. Second, we all know that harassment activities also depend on where migrants come from. Survey results show

---

[1] Please note that this comment refers to the original version of the paper. The revised version, published in this volume, does already take into account many of our suggestions made.

over and over that Germans, like other people, distinguish between people who seem closer or more familiar to them and those who seem less close or less familiar. Reference theories make this point. We accept white Americans much more than we accept Turkish people, and our harassment activities depend upon our acceptance of their ethnicity. As for labor markets, the nationality of the migrants needs to be seen as an intervening variable. Third, it is implicitly assumed that all natives behave alike. This is not the case, however. We know that prejudices and harassment depend upon the sex and the educational level of the natives, as well as on their prior experience with migrants. Fourth, harassment activities also depend on the absolute number of migrants as well as on the proportion between natives and migrants. This fact has less to do with migrants' respective nationality than simply with their number: the more people enter and try to assimilate, the more natives feel threatened and harassed. As Kanter (1977) has shown, the proportion of migrants to natives also plays a big structural role. Hence, harassment as well as assimilation depends on the number of immigrants and the proportion of immigrants to natives.

So far, our comments have dealt with the context in which assimilation takes place. We now turn to the specific model proposed by Epstein and Gang.

Basic Mechanisms of the Model and Individuals' Decision Problems

The representative native faces the following problem. The more he or she harasses foreigners, the lower their productivity is absolutely as well as in comparison to the natives' productivity at a given number of native and foreign employees. As the numbers of native and foreign workers are constant, less labor in efficiency units (which are defined such that a native worker just corresponds to one efficiency unit) is available then. But, the fewer efficiency units that are available, the higher the (marginal) productivity of one unit, i.e., of a native, is and the higher the wage is that firms are willing to pay for a native employee. This means higher income and thus a higher level of welfare for the representative native. On the other hand, however, harassment activities directly lower his or her utility as they cause disutility to him or her.[2] The native maximizes his or her utility, choosing the optimal amount of harassment.[3]

The mechanisms described in the preceding paragraph are subject to one of our main criticisms of Epstein and Gang's model. They implicitly assume that each native behaves as if the behavior of all other natives concerning their har-

---

[2]   All this is an interpretation of equation (7).

[3]   For example, expressed in time units, units of goods, or money.

assment activities is determined by and is the same as his or her own. This is formally reflected by the fact that Epstein and Gang substitute $h_1 L_N$ for h in equation (7) before they differentiate this utility function for h_1. In our opinion, however, this implicit assumption cannot be rationalized. Reasonably, h would have to remain in equation (7) before deriving it with respect to h_1. Consequently, Δ_N would equal minus one—which is the negative utility of increasing harassment by one unit, because a positive effect would not exist—and equation (8) could not be fulfilled. Harassment would not have any advantage and thus, would not be committed. As the same argument applies for assimilation activities, the whole model would crash. In other words: harassing is collectively rational, but not individually. All natives' choosing the amount of harassment calculated by Epstein and Gang (the collectively optimal amount) would be best for all of them, but given any behavior of all other individuals, not harassing is optimal for each individual. Even if all natives agreed on a certain level of harassment, each individual would have an incentive to deviate from that agreement. Epstein and Gang call the outcome of their computations a "Nash equilibrium," but in fact, that is what it is not.

Can this problem be resolved? One could view decisions over time as a repeated game and assume that the collectively optimal h can be enforced as an equilibrium by a trigger strategy in accordance with which a deviation from the optimal h or a implies the Nash equilibrium of $h = 0$ forever afterwards. But this is hardly plausible in a context with very many individuals who would have to coordinate among themselves. It could also be assumed that migrants' productivity depends directly on the harassment h_1 of each individual, which does not seem plausible either and would probably have different effects on the outcome of the model. Alternatively, it is possible to formulate the problem as a normative one, that is, to ask how the natives should behave in order to maximize their utility at the cost of the foreigners. But, this does not seem to be the aim of Epstein and Gang's paper.

Material Advantages Deriving from Harassment?

We doubt that people, collectively, can rationally expect to derive any material advantages from harassment. While they may nevertheless do so in certain special cases, the average (representative) individual will most likely not do so. If one can think of individuals who harass others as being rational individuals at all, we would assume that they engage in harassment because it makes them feel better, that is, because harassing increases their utility, while on the other hand, it brings about material disadvantages like foregone income or an expected value of penalties. Using poor cooperation as a harassment activity is similar. In this case, the disadvantage is also material (e.g., because of foregone deals), while the advantage is psychological. Thus, the natives' decision problem can be described as being the opposite of Epstein and Gang's description. Then, there is an advantage (a direct utility gain) as well as a (material) disadvantage that derives from individuals' behavior, even without assuming collectively rational behavior.

Harassment as Endogenous or Exogenous Variable?

But, why is harassment endogenously determined at all? According to the paper's title, ethnic networks and international trade are the main objects to be assessed in the paper. But, the natives, who determine the degree of harassment, are not involved in trade at all and, especially, do not profit from it in this model. They play a role only insofar as their harassment affects the profitability of trade relations via productivity and income of the foreign employees (see equation (13)). In other words, through modeling h as an exogenous variable the analysis could be simplified a lot.

The Effects of Harassment on the Profitability of International Trade

The representative (immigrant) trader faces the following problem. He or she tries to assimilate, because his/her assimilation activities—which also determine (how?) those of the employees among the foreigners—increase the productivity and income of the employees, raising their demand for products from their home country and thus, affecting positively the profitability of international trade.

For assimilating, the same applies as for harassing: why and how should a single trader be able to determine or at least influence the average assimilation effort of all other immigrants?[4] If he or she were, it is plausible that there is a positive income effect of assimilation on the demand for foreign goods, but there would also have to be a negative effect, since increasing the degree of assimilation decreases the preference for goods from the country of origin, as Epstein and

---

4   And, why is there not any distinction between the individual and the aggregate degree of assimilation efforts as there is between h_1 and h for harassment?

Gang assume in connection with the course of time.[5] The total effect would be undetermined.

Equilibria

After having described the model and the individuals' decision problems, Epstein and Gang assess how changing exogenous variables and parameters (number of foreign employees, ratio of trade profits and efficiency units of foreign employees, time) affects the optimal individual degree of harassment, the optimal degree of assimilation efforts, and trade profits. Hereby, Epstein and Gang have assumed—but not shown—that there are "unique interior Nash equilibria." Apart from our remarks above, we must mention that an interior equilibrium is not natural, as can be seen in the augmented model version in which foreign employees and traders make different assimilation efforts.[6] This is why an assessment of the existence and the properties of possible equilibria seems desirable to us.

Modeling Change over Time

At the end of the paper, Epstein and Gang present an extension of their model, in which they analyze how harassment and assimilation activities develop over time under certain assumptions. Now, it is assumed, as before, that time has a positive effect on trade profits. This is, unlike before, justified with improving local networks in the host country (but formally described in exactly the same way). Furthermore, it is assumed that time also has a negative effect on trade profits. As a consequence of increasing assimilation, the migrants' demand for home-country goods decreases (we have criticized above that this assumption is not made) and the migrated traders' networks in their home countries also decrease. Moreover, Epstein and Gang assume that the positive effect vanishes over the course of time, while the negative effect does not. That is, the time path of trading profits has an inverse U shape (which is part of Proposition 5). However, the assumption that the negative effect remains relatively constant over time appears to be unrealistic. The migrants' home-country-goods demand may asymptoti-

---

[5]   To be strict, *a* is modeled as the *activity* of assimilation, not as the *level* of assimilation. There is no reason to assume that the *activity* itself should reduce the preferences for home-country goods. Similarly, why should the activity itself increase productivity?

[6]   Where the trader's optimal *a* becomes zero sooner or later, see below.

cally approach zero (such that the decrease becomes smaller and smaller), but it cannot become negative. The same applies for the traders' relations to their countries of origin. Given this, however, one could equally assume that the total effect develops just the other way around. But, the validity of Proposition 5 depends almost directly on these assumptions.

What is in any case wrong in Proposition 5 under the given model assumptions is the statement that the traders would sooner or later engage in anti-assimilation activities (which is a negative a_1). That, namely, would decrease their utility according to their utility function (31): first, because anti-assimilation activities would reduce the foreign employees' productivity as well as their income and their demand for goods from home (see the left term) and, second, because the traders themselves would suffer from these activities (see the right term). a_1 must be set to zero whenever it would be negative according to Epstein and Gang's computations (see also figures 2 and 3 in the Appendix of the paper).

Alternative Approaches of Modeling

Epstein and Gang use a static model—augmented by ad hoc assumptions about the time dependence of productivity and trading profits—to analyze development over time. We doubt that this is the right formal approach. We think that assimilation activities should be viewed as investment (as Epstein and Gang call them), whose returns arise in the future. In the paper, nothing is said about what kind of immigrant one is supposed to imagine, whether the very same individual is looked at over the entire time horizon or a "dynasty" (i.e., different generations of the same family) or completely different persons who immigrate and emigrate again. Anyway, Epstein and Gang assume (by means of $g(t)$) that assimilation increases over time; staying at a certain time affects assimilation at a later time. Consequently, assimilation activities should also have effects in later periods. In the model of Epstein and Gang, however, these efforts only have immediate effects and are equivalently denoted as the "level of assimilation" (see text below equation (13)).

Moreover, a_1 and a_2 tend towards minus infinity and infinity, respectively, according to Epstein and Gang. What consequences does this have for the model economy? Does there exist a long-run equilibrium and how is it defined? Instead, one could model productivity as a function of a weighted sum (which is a weighted integral in this continuous-time context) of all preceding assimilation activities. One might be able to construct an intertemporal optimization problem whose solution results in a differential equation (or possibly in two or more independent differential equations) upon which the development of the model economy as well as the existence of a long-run equilibrium depend.

Ideally, such a macroeconomic problem should be analyzed in a general macroeconomic model which also includes second-order effects, e.g., on the number of immigrants, on the labor supply in the host country, on the ratio of employees to self-employed, or on wages.

Bibliography

Kanter, R.M., (1977). *Men and Women of the Corporation*. New York: Basic Books.

Kar-yiu Wong

Are International Capital Movement and International Labor Migration Substitutes under National Externality?

Abstract:

This paper examines the relationship between international capital movement (ICM) and international labor movement (ILM). Considering two economies that have identical technologies and factor endowment ratios but different sizes, this paper investigates whether ICM and ILM between the countries, when free trade in goods is allowed, are substitutes both in the price sense and in the quantity sense. Cases in which they are substitutes and those in which they are complements are described.

1   Introduction

With the growing importance of labor migration and foreign direct investment among countries, the theory of international trade has been putting more and more emphasis on international factor movements and their relations with trade in goods. Most of the analysis is given to the features of international factor movements and their relations with trade in goods.[1] There is, however, much less discussion about the relationship between different types of factor movements.

Nowadays, governments are facing many pressing issues related to factor movements and their relationship. For example, the United States has been receiving a substantial number of migrants from Mexico, some entering the United States legally but some making their ways into the country illegally. The United States has been spending resources on preventing the inflow of these undocumented immigrants and on deporting those who came illegally. Similar situations exist in Europe and Asia. Many Western European countries are receiving large numbers of legal and illegal immigrants from Eastern European countries. Japan, on the other hand, is a favorite destination for migrants from many other coun-

---

[1]   See, for example, Mundell (1957), Markusen (1983), and Wong (1986).

tries in Asia. These poor migrants, who are seeking better economic lives, are making tremendous efforts to come to and stay in Japan, mostly illegally.

For the governments of these destination countries, getting the inflow of labor immigration, especially illegal immigration, under control is an important issue. On the destination side, these governments have spent a lot of resources on patrolling the border, catching illegal workers, prohibiting local employment of illegal workers, and deporting them. There has been limited success. Attention has been paid to the source side, and discussion has been made about how to discourage people there from trying to come to the destination countries. One suggestion made, which has been drawing a lot of attention, is to encourage more investment from the destination country to the source countries, especially in areas of the source countries close to the destination country. The reason behind this argument is that the investment will improve the income of workers in those areas, making the workers less interested in coming to the destination country. Implicit in this argument is that international capital movement can replace or diminish international labor movement.

The objective of this paper is to investigate the substitutability between international capital movement (ICM) and international labor movement (ILM). In particular, we want to find out whether more international capital movement could have the effect of discouraging international labor movement. For our analysis, we will use a model that is close to the neoclassical framework, except that one of the sectors is subject to external economies of scale. Such a model, which is common in the theory of international trade, has the advantage of examining the roles of increasing returns in determining trade in goods and factor movements.

In the literature, several different definitions of substitutability between trade in goods and factor movements have been suggested. Following Wong (1986, 1995), the relationship between ICM (international capital movement) and ILM (international labor movement) is defined in the present paper in two different ways:

1. Price Sense—ICM and ILM are said to be substitutes if each of them is sufficient to give efficient allocation of resources in the world. This means that either of them will lead to equalization of factor prices. Implicit in this statement is that goods are allowed to flow freely, and that the factor that is allowed to flow is not under any impediments, so that the final equilibrium is characterized by equalization of the prices of that factor in the countries. Thus, substitutability between ICM and ILM means that equalization of the prices of one of them in the countries will lead to equalization of the other prices, and vice versa. They are then said to be complements if both of them are needed to reach efficiency in the world, i.e., equalization of the prices of

one factor in both countries does not lead to equalization of the prices of the other factor. Obviously, assessing the substitutability of ICM and ILM will be meaningful in cases in which the countries have identical technologies (and, in some cases, identical preferences as well).[2]

2. Quantity Sense—ICM and ILM are said to be substitutes (complements) if a small exogenous increase in the volume of flow of one of them leads to a decrease (an increase) in the volume of flow of the other, and vice versa.[3] Note that assessing substitutability between ICM and ILM using this sense does not require that the countries have the same technologies.

In many cases, governments may be more interested in the impacts of an exogenous change in either capital movement or labor movement. Thus, the relationship between ICM and ILM in the quantity case may be more important and relevant. However, our analysis will cover both senses of substitutability between ICM and ILM.

The rest of the paper is organized as follows. Section 2 describes a simple model of Marshallian externality (Marshall 1879, 1890). Section 3 explains the features of a two-country model in which free trade in goods plus factor movement are present. The section focuses on the equilibrium under free trade, with ICM and ILM given exogenously. Section 4 analyzes the case in which free trade in goods plus free capital movement are allowed, while Section 5 examines the case in which free trade in goods plus free labor movement exist. Section 6 examines the relationship between ICM and ILM, and investigates whether they are substitutes or complements. The last section concludes.

2   A Model with Marshallian Externality

We consider two countries labeled home and foreign, with similar production structures. Our analysis begins with home, which is endowed with capital and labor of exogenously given amounts, $\bar{K}$ and $\bar{L}$, respectively. Two homogeneous goods, which are labeled 1 and 2, are produced with the following production functions:

---

[2]   If the countries have different technologies, free trade in goods and free movement of one factor will generally not equalize the prices of the immobile factor.

[3]   This definition, which is adopted from the one for international trade in goods and international factor mobility defined in Wong (1986), is stricter than the corresponding one in the literature, where in most cases only the effects of more factor movement on the volume of trade, but not the effects of bigger volumes of trade on factor movement, are examined.

(1a) $Q_1 = h(Q_1) F_1(K_1, L_1)$,

(1b) $Q_2 = F_2(K_2, L_2)$,

where Q_i is the output of good i, $i = 1$, 2, and K_i and L_i are the capital and labor inputs in sector i, respectively. Sector 1 is assumed to be labor-intensive at all possible factor prices. Function $F_i(K_i, L_i)$ is increasing, linearly homogeneous, concave, and differentiable in factor inputs. The Inada conditions for $F_i(K_i, L_i)$ are also assumed, although they are generally stronger than what is needed. Function $h(Q_1)$, which is regarded as constant by all firms, depends on the sectoral output and satisfies the following conditions: $h = h(Q_1) > 0$ for all $Q_1 > 0$, $h(0) = 0$, and $h'(Q_1) \equiv dh/dQ_1 > 0$.[4] The production functions in (1) mean that sector 1 is subject to positive externality and thus increasing returns, while no externality exists in sector 2. Similar models have been analyzed and applied in the literature, and are useful for investigating the implications of externality because they reduce to the neoclassical framework when $h'(Q_1) = 0$.

Define $\varepsilon \equiv Q_1 h'(Q_1)/h(Q_1) > 0$ for all $Q_1 > 0$ as the rate of variable returns to scale (VRS) of sector 1.[5] To obtain positive social marginal products of factors in sector 1, it is assumed that $\varepsilon < 1$. Denote the relative supply price of good 1 by p^s.[6]

Employing the concept of virtual system introduced in Wong (1995), define the virtual output of sector i by

(2) $\tilde{Q}_i = F_i(K_i, L_i)$.

A comparison of equation (2) with the production functions (1) reveals that $\tilde{Q}_1 = Q_1/h$ and $\tilde{Q}_2 = Q_2$. Since function $F_i(K_i, L_i)$ has the properties of a neoclassical production function, the virtual system behaves like the neoclassical framework.[7] Define the virtual relative supply price of good 1 as $\tilde{p}^s \equiv hp^s$. We can also define the virtual GDP (gross domestic product) function,

---

[4]   For some fundamental concepts of externality and its use in the theory of international trade, see Wong (2001).

[5]   Equation (1) can be inverted to give the reduced-form production function $Q_1 = H_1(K_1, L_1)$, which is homothetic. See Wong (2001) for the proof and more discussion.

[6]   The supply price of good 1 is defined as the minimum price of the good that will make the profits of the firms in the sector 1 nonnegative.

[7]   Recall that the present framework is the same as the neoclassical framework except that sector 1 is subject to external economies of scale. The objective of the virtual system is to neutralize the economies-of-scale effect.

$g\left(\tilde{p}^{s}, K, L\right)$, where K and L are the capital and labor stocks in the economy. This function behaves like the neoclassical GDP function; in particular, its derivatives with respect to the virtual prices represent the virtual outputs, $\tilde{Q}_{1}\left(\tilde{p}^{s}, K, L\right)$. Using the definition of $\tilde{Q}_{i}$, we have

(3a) $Q_{1} = h(Q_{1})\,\tilde{Q}_{1}\left(\tilde{p}^{s}, K, L\right)$,

(3a) $Q_{2} = \tilde{Q}_{2}\left(\tilde{p}^{s}, K, L\right)$.

Equations (3) give the link between the virtual and real systems. Differentiating these two equations and using the definition of $\tilde{p}^{s}$, rearrange the terms to yield

(4) $\begin{bmatrix} \alpha_{11} & 0 \\ \alpha_{21} & 1 \end{bmatrix} \begin{bmatrix} dQ_{1} \\ dQ_{2} \end{bmatrix} = \begin{bmatrix} h^{2}\tilde{Q}_{1p} \\ h\tilde{Q}_{2p} \end{bmatrix} dp^{s} + \begin{bmatrix} h\tilde{Q}_{1K} \\ \tilde{Q}_{2K} \end{bmatrix} dK + \begin{bmatrix} h\tilde{Q}_{1L} \\ \tilde{Q}_{2L} \end{bmatrix} dL$,

where $\alpha_{11} = 1 - \varepsilon - \varepsilon\eta_{1p}$, $\alpha_{21} = -\varepsilon\eta_{2p} > 0$, $\eta_{ip} \equiv \tilde{p}^{s}\tilde{Q}_{ip}/\tilde{Q}_{1}$, and $\tilde{Q}_{ip} \equiv \partial\tilde{Q}_{i}/\partial\tilde{p}^{s}$. Note that η_{1p} is the price elasticity of the virtual supply of good 1, while η_{2p} is the negative of the price elasticity of the virtual supply of good 2. Assuming a strictly concave virtual production possibility frontier, we have $\tilde{Q}_{1p}, \eta_{1p} > 0$ and $\tilde{Q}_{2p}, \eta_{2p} < 0$. Denote the determinant of the matrix in (4) by Φ, and we have $\Phi = \alpha_{11}$. Consider the following condition:

CONDITION E: $\varepsilon < 1/(1+\eta_{1p})$.

LEMMA 1: *If sector 1 is subject to mild increasing returns, so that condition E holds, then $\Phi > 0$.* [8]

Define $\tilde{Q}_{ij} \equiv \partial\tilde{Q}_{i}/\partial j$ and η_{ij} as the elasticity of the virtual output of good i with respect to the endowment of factor j, while prices are kept constant, $i = 1, 2$ and $j = K, L$; for example, $\eta_{1K} = K\tilde{Q}_{1K}/\tilde{Q}_{1}$. Note that $\tilde{Q}_{ij}$ and η_{ij} have the same sign. For the virtual system, the Rybczynski theorem is valid, implying that $\eta_{1L}, \eta_{2K} > 1$ and $\eta_{1K}, \eta_{2L} < 0$. Condition (4) is solved for output changes:

(5a) $\hat{Q}_{1} = \dfrac{\eta_{1p}}{\Phi}\hat{p}^{s} + \dfrac{\eta_{1K}}{\Phi}\hat{K} + \dfrac{\eta_{1L}}{\Phi}\hat{L}$,

---

[8]   Note that another sufficient condition for $\Phi > 0$ is that sector 1 is subject to decreasing returns to scale.

(5b) $\hat{Q}_2 = -\dfrac{(1-\varepsilon)\eta_{2p}}{\varPhi}\hat{p}^s + \left[\eta_{2K} - \dfrac{\varepsilon\eta_{2p}\,\eta_{1K}}{\varPhi}\right]\hat{K} + \left[\eta_{2L} - \dfrac{\varepsilon\eta_{2p}\,\eta_{1L}}{\varPhi}\right]\hat{L},$

where $\wedge$ denotes the proportionate change of a variable; for example, $\hat{K} \equiv dK/K$. Defining the output ratio as $z \equiv Q_1/Q_2$, combine conditions (5) to give

(6) $\hat{z} = \dfrac{\mu}{\varPhi}\hat{p}^s + \dfrac{\sigma}{\varPhi}\hat{K} + \dfrac{\zeta}{\varPhi}\hat{L},$

where

$$\mu = \eta_{1p} - (1-\varepsilon)\eta_{2p} > 0,$$
$$\sigma = \eta_{1K}(1-\varepsilon\eta_{2p}) - \eta_{2K}\varPhi,$$
$$\zeta = \eta_{1L}(1-\varepsilon\eta_{2p}) - \eta_{2L}\varPhi,$$
$$\sigma + \zeta = (\eta_{1K} + \eta_{1L})(1-\varepsilon\eta_{2p}) - (\eta_{2K} + \eta_{2L})\varPhi,$$
$$= \varepsilon\left(1 + \frac{g\eta_{1p}}{Q_2}\right) > 0.$$

A possible relation between z and p^s (with given factor stocks) is illustrated by the curve labeled p^s in Figure 1 (either panel). The curve is positively sloped if and only if $\varPhi > 0$. The diagram shows the case in which the curve is positively sloped when z is small or very large in value, but it is negatively sloped when z has values in between.[9]

LEMMA 2: *If condition E is satisfied, then* (a) $\sigma < 0$ *and* (b) $\zeta > 0$.

PROOF: *This lemma can be proved by noting* (i) *by Lemma 1, condition E implies that* $\varPhi > 0$; (ii) η_{1L}, $\eta_{2K} > 0$, *and* η_{1K}, $\eta_{2L} < 0$; *and* (iii) $\eta_{2p} < 0$.[10]

---

[9]   The supply-price curve in Figure 1 is based on the assumption that the supply price is sufficiently small when z is small, while the supply price is very large when z is very large.

[10]   It is noted that condition E is only a sufficient condition for $\sigma > 0$.

Figure 1:
Stability of the Autarkic Equilibrium

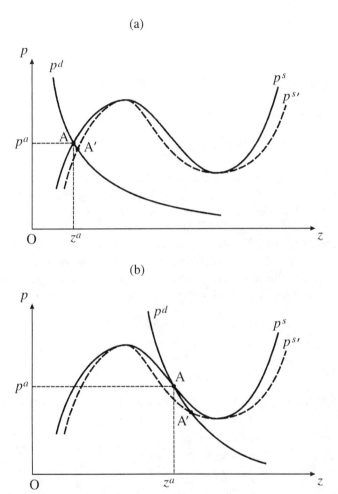

An alternative, but sometimes useful, formulation of (6) is

$$(7) \qquad \hat{z} = \frac{\mu}{\Phi}\hat{p}^s + \frac{\sigma+\zeta}{\Phi}\hat{K} - \frac{\zeta}{\Phi}(\hat{K}-\hat{L}).$$

For an economy with fixed endowments, the supply price elasticity of z is equal to μ/Φ.

Factor prices can be obtained from the virtual GDP function:

$$(8a) \qquad w = g_L(\tilde{p}^s, K, L) = g_L(h(Q_1)p^s, K, L),$$

$$(8b) \qquad r = g_K(\tilde{p}^s, K, L) = g_K(h(Q_1)p^s, K, L).$$

There has been discussion in the literature about whether with Marshallian externality an economy behaves normally to shocks like changes in prices or factor endowments.[11] Equation (7) shows that the output ratio responds normally to changes in prices and factor endowments if the increasing returns are mild, so that $\Phi > 0$. However, using the Marshallian adjustment mechanism as outlined in Ide and Takayama (1991, 1993), Wong (1995, 2001) demonstrates that if global adjustments are allowed, the responses are normal even if $\Phi < 0$.[12]

For any given factor stocks in the economy, factor-market equilibria are described by

$$(9a) \qquad L_1 + L_2 = L,$$

$$(9b) \qquad K_1 + K_2 = K.$$

To derive the autarkic equilibrium, we assume a homothetic, quasi-concave, and differentiable social utility function, so that the demand price can be defined as[13]

$$(10) \qquad p^d = f(z),$$

where z is the ratio of consumption of good 1 to consumption of good 2. Function $f(\cdot)$ is decreasing and differentiable. Figure 1 (both panels) shows a possi-

---

[11]   See, for example, Jones (1968), Inoue (1981), and Tawada (1989).

[12]   Wong (2001) argues that if global adjustments are allowed and are allowed with Marshallian adjustment, a certain form of the five fundamental trade theorems are valid under some conditions.

[13]   The demand price, p^d, is defined as the maximum price that the consumers are willing to pay for a basket consisting of a given ratio of good 1 to good 2, z.

ble downward-sloping demand price curve labeled p^d. Define $\psi \equiv -\hat{z}/\hat{p} > 0$ as the price elasticity of demand.

An autarkic equilibrium of the economy is represented by the output ratio that gives

(11) $p^s = p^d = p^a,$

where superscript a denotes the autarkic equilibrium value of a variable. A stable autarkic equilibrium in a Marshallian sense requires that the demand price curve cuts the supply price curve from above.[14] Figure 1 shows two possible autarkic equilibria. In panel (a), the demand price curve cuts the supply price curve from above at a point on its positively sloped part, and in panel (b), it cuts the supply curve, also from above, but at a point on the negatively sloped region of curve p^s. In both panels, the autarkic equilibrium point is at point A. In each of these cases, the autarkic equilibrium is stable in a Marshallian sense.

To facilitate the analysis given below, let us examine the effects of an expansion of the scale of the economy. Using (7), the effects of changes in factor endowments on the autarkic equilibrium price ratio are equal to

(12) $\hat{p}^a = -\theta[\sigma \hat{K} + \zeta \hat{L}] = -\theta[(\sigma + \zeta)\hat{K} - \zeta(\hat{K} - \hat{L})],$

where $\theta \equiv 1/(\psi \Phi + \mu)$, which is positive if and only if $\Phi > -\mu/\psi$. For a locally stable autarkic equilibrium, it is assumed that $\theta > 0$, which holds if $\Phi > 0$. [15]

If $\hat{K} = \hat{L} > 0$, (12) reduces to

(13) $\hat{p}^a = -\theta(\sigma + \zeta)\hat{K} < 0.$

Condition (13) implies that an expansion of the economy will lower its autarkic price ratio. This result can be illustrated graphically in Figure 1. By (7), an expansion of the economy lowers the supply-price curve to, say, the one labeled $p^{s'}$. The new autarkic equilibrium is at point A', representing a drop in the relative price of good 1.[16]

---

[14]   See Wong (2001) for more details.

[15]   See Wong (2001) for a proof and more discussion.

[16]   A locally stable autarkic equilibrium is only a sufficient condition for a drop in the autarkic price ratio as the economy gets bigger. Wong (2001) argues that even if the autarkic equilibrium is not locally stable, as long as the economy adjusts in a Marshallian sense, the price ratio will drop as the economy expands.

3   A Two-Country Model of Free Trade

We now turn to the analysis of both countries. In particular, we will analyze the equilibria under international trade and/or international factor movements.

3.1   Features of the Model

Consider two countries labeled home and foreign. Both countries have the same technology and factor endowment ratios, i.e., $\overline{K}/\overline{L} = \overline{K}^*/\overline{L}^*$, but home is uniformly bigger in size, i.e., $\overline{K} > \overline{K}^*$, where foreign variables are distinguished by asterisks. The production functions of the two sectors in each country are described by (1). Such a framework represents convenience in our analysis, as the assumption of identical technologies eliminates the Ricardian factor of comparative advantage, while the assumption of identical factor endowment ratio avoids the Heckscher–Ohlin factor of comparative advantage.[17] The present model, which reduces to the neoclassical framework if sector 1 is subject to constant returns, is suitable for analyzing the roles of externality. We further assume that the countries have identical preferences.

The speed of adjustment of the international goods markets is much faster than that of either factor market, so that as labor/capital moves gradually between the countries, the goods markets are always in equilibrium under free trade. The features of the model are meant to capture the following observations:

1. Goods usually move faster in response to price differential than factors do.
2. In general, the restrictions imposed by governments on the movement of goods are less than those on the movements of factors. In particular, the United States, Canada, and Mexico are members of the North American Free Trade Area and many European countries are members of the European Union, within which free trade in goods is allowed.[18]
3. By allowing free trade, this paper can focus more on the interactions between ICM and ILM.

---

[17]   In the Ricardian model, comparative advantage is explained in terms of differences in technologies between the countries, while the Heckscher–Ohlin theorem explains comparative advantage in terms of the difference between the countries' factor endowment ratios. In the neoclassical framework with identical technologies and identical factor endowment ratios, the countries have no comparative advantage.

[18]   It is true that NAFTA allows intraregional free capital movement, and that the EU permits intraregional free factor movements as well. However, governments usually remain more liberal in allowing trade in goods than in allowing factor movements.

This paper examines a model in which the two economies allow free trade in goods plus ICM and/or ILM. Denote the amount of capital flowing from home to foreign by k, and the amount of labor flowing from foreign to home by ℓ. A negative k or ℓ represents factor movement in an opposite direction, and a zero value means no international movement. Thus, the capital and labor stocks of the countries are, respectively,

(14a) $K = \overline{K} - k; \quad L = \overline{L} + \ell,$

(14b) $K^* = \overline{K}^* + k, \quad L^* = \overline{L}^* - \ell.$

It is assumed that factors that are working in the host country are paid the on-going market factor prices, and can remit earnings out of the country to be consumed in the source country free of any tax burden.

In the presence of factor mobility, a reduced-form output function of each sector can be written as

(15a) $Q_1 = h(Q_1)\,\tilde{Q}_1(\tilde{p}, K, L) \equiv \mathbf{Q}_1(p, k, \ell),$

(15b) $Q_2 = \tilde{Q}_2(\tilde{p}, K, L) = \mathbf{Q}_2(p, k, \ell,),$

where in the functions $\mathbf{Q}_i(p, k, \ell)$ the exogenously given factor endowments are not shown for simplicity.[19] Using equation (5a), the derivatives of $\mathbf{Q}_1(p, k, \ell)$ are

(16a) $\mathbf{Q}_{1p} = \dfrac{h^2 \tilde{Q}_{1\tilde{p}}}{\varPhi},$

(16b) $\mathbf{Q}_{1k} = \dfrac{h\tilde{Q}_{1K}}{\varPhi},$

(16c) $\mathbf{Q}_{1\ell} = \dfrac{h\tilde{Q}_{1L}}{\varPhi}.$

From now on we make the assumption that condition E is satisfied so that $\varPhi > 0$ in order to get normal comparative-static results.[20] Equations (8) can be used to define the following reduced-form factor price functions:

---

[19] Note that equation (15a) is used in deriving (15b).

[20] This assumption is stronger than needed. As Wong (1995, 2001) shows, comparative-static effects can still be normal if global changes are considered.

(17a) $w = \mathbf{W}(p,k,\ell) = g_L(h(Q_1)p,K,L)$,

(17b) $r = \mathbf{R}(p,k,\ell) = g_K(h(Q_1)p,K,L)$.

Differentiate both sides of (17) to give the derivatives of the factor prices:[21]

(18a)
$$\hat{w} = \frac{\eta_{wp}(1-\varepsilon)}{\Phi}\hat{p} - \left(\frac{\varepsilon\eta_{wp}\,\eta_{1K}}{\Phi} + \eta_{wK}\right)\frac{k}{\overline{K}-k}\hat{k}$$
$$+ \left(\frac{\varepsilon\eta_{wp}\,\eta_{1L}}{\Phi} + \eta_{wL}\right)\frac{\ell}{\overline{L}+\ell}\hat{\ell},$$

(18b) $\hat{r} = \dfrac{\eta_{rp}(1-\varepsilon)}{\Phi}\hat{p} - \left(\dfrac{\varepsilon\eta_{rp}\,\eta_{1K}}{\Phi} + \eta_{rK}\right)\dfrac{k}{\overline{K}-k}\hat{k} + \left(\dfrac{\varepsilon\eta_{rp}\,\eta_{1L}}{\Phi} + \eta_{rL}\right)\dfrac{\ell}{\overline{L}+\ell}\hat{\ell}$.

Since sector 1 is labor-intensive, $\eta_{wp} > 0$ and $\eta_{rp} < 0$. The derivatives in (18) can be simplified if the pattern of production is known. Suppose that the economy is diversified. In the virtual system, factor prices depend on virtual prices only, but not on factor endowments, i.e., $\eta_{ij} = 0$ for $i = w$, r, and $j = K$, L. In the real system, however, equations (18) show that even if commodity prices are fixed and the economy is diversified, factor endowments and factor movements could affect factor prices through a change in the output of good 1 and thus the virtual prices.

LEMMA 3: *Given condition E and diversification, a rise in k or ℓ has a positive effect on the home wage rate but a negative effect on the home rental rate. Similarly, a rise in k or ℓ has a negative effect on the foreign wage rate but a positive effect on the foreign rental rate.*[22]

The lemma is due to a rise (or drop) in the output of good 1 caused by the mentioned factor movement. The national income levels (GNP) of the home and foreign countries are given, respectively, by

(19a) $Y = \mathbf{Y}(p,p^*,k,\ell) = g(h(Q_1)p,K,L) + r^*(p^*,k,\ell)k - w(p,k,\ell)\ell$,

(19b) $Y^* = \mathbf{Y}^*(p,p^*,k,\ell) = g^*(h^*(Q_1^*)p^*,K^*,L^*) - r^*(p^*,k,\ell)k + w(p,k,\ell)\ell$.

---

[21]   Corresponding equations for the factor prices in foreign can be determined in the same way.

[22]   If a country specializes in producing one good only, the effects of factor movement on factor prices can be analyzed using the production function directly.

Note that in the definition of the functions in (19), free trade in goods has been assumed. The derivatives of home national income are[23]

(20a) $\mathbf{Y}_p = \dfrac{Q_1(1-\varepsilon)}{\Phi} - \dfrac{w\eta_{wp}(1-\varepsilon)}{p\Phi}\ell = \dfrac{h(1-\varepsilon)\left(\tilde{Q}_1 - W_{\tilde{p}}\ell\right)}{\Phi}$,

(20b) $\mathbf{Y}_{p*} = \dfrac{r*\eta_{r*p*}(1-\varepsilon*)}{p*\Phi*}k = \dfrac{h*R_{\tilde{p}*}^*k(1-\varepsilon*)}{\Phi*}$,

(20c)

$\mathbf{Y}_k = -\dfrac{\varepsilon\,pQ_1\eta_{1K}}{K\Phi*} + (r*-r) + \dfrac{r*}{K*}\left(\dfrac{\varepsilon*\eta_{r*p*}\,\eta_{1K*}}{\Phi*} + \eta_{r*K*}\right)k$

$\quad + \dfrac{w}{K}\left(\dfrac{\varepsilon\eta_{wp}\,\eta_{1K}}{\Phi} + \eta_{wK}\right)\ell$,

(20d) $\mathbf{Y}_\ell = \dfrac{\varepsilon\,pQ_1\eta_{1L}}{L\Phi} - \dfrac{r*}{L*}\left(\dfrac{\varepsilon*\eta_{r*p*}\,\eta_{1L*}}{\Phi*} + \eta_{r*L*}\right)k - \dfrac{w}{L}\left(\dfrac{\varepsilon\eta_{wp}\,\eta_{1L}}{\Phi*} + \eta_{wL}\right)\ell$.

LEMMA 4: *Given condition E and small values of k and ℓ, home national income depends positively on relative price of good 1 and the indicated factor movements. Furthermore, given a home capital outflow, a rise in the foreign commodity price of good 1 lowers home national income.*

The Marshallian demand for good i of home can be denoted by $\mathbf{C}_i(p,\mathbf{Y}(p,k,\ell))$, $i=1,2$. With homothetic preferences, both goods are normal. Define m as the marginal propensity to consume good 1:

$$m \equiv p\frac{\partial\mathbf{C}_1}{\partial\mathbf{Y}}.$$

The export of good i can be expressed as

(21) $\mathbf{E}_i(p,p*,k,\ell) = \mathbf{Q}_i(p,K,L) - \mathbf{C}_i(p,\mathbf{Y}(p,p*,k,\ell))$.

Note that by the Walras law, we can focus mainly on the equilibrium of the market for good 1. Subscripts are again used to denote partial derivatives of the export supply functions; for example, $\mathbf{E}_{1p} \equiv \partial\mathbf{E}_1/\partial p$. The price-export response is said to be normal if $\mathbf{E}_{1p} > 0$. The derivatives of the export supply function are equal to

---

[23]   The corresponding derivatives of foreign national income can be derived in the same way.

(22a) $\mathbf{E}_{1p} = \dfrac{h^2\tilde{Q}_{1\tilde{p}}}{\Phi} - \mathbf{C}_{1p} - \dfrac{mh\Theta(1-\varepsilon)}{p\Phi},$

(22b) $\mathbf{E}_{1p^*} = -\dfrac{mh^*r^*\mathbf{R}_{p^*}^*(1-\varepsilon^*)k}{p\Phi^*} > 0,$

(22c) $\mathbf{E}_{1k} = -\dfrac{h\tilde{Q}_{1K}(1-m\varepsilon)}{\Phi} - \dfrac{m}{p}[(r^*-r) + \mathbf{R}_k^*k - \mathbf{W}_k\ell],$

(22d) $\mathbf{E}_{1\ell} = \dfrac{h\tilde{Q}_{1L}(1-\varepsilon)}{\Phi} - \dfrac{m}{p}[\mathbf{R}_\ell^*k - \mathbf{W}_\ell\ell],$

where $\Theta \equiv \tilde{Q}_1 - \mathbf{W}_{\tilde{p}}\ell.$

LEMMA 5: *Given condition E and small values of* k *and* ℓ, $\mathbf{E}_{1k} > 0$ *and* $\mathbf{E}_{1\ell} > 0.$

Note that in (22b), $\mathbf{E}_{1p^*} > 0$. This is because an increase in p^* will lower foreign rental rate and thus home national income. Home will then consume less good 1, thus helping the export of the good. The foreign export supply function can be defined in a similar way: $\mathbf{E}_i^*(p, p^*, k, \ell)$.

3.2   Free Trade in Goods

Since we assume that in the present two-country model the commodity markets always clear, let us examine the free-trade equilibrium first. Suppose that international factor movements (k, ℓ) are given exogenously. Label the resulting free-trade equilibrium as **G**, with the following equilibrium conditions:

(23a) $\mathbf{E}_1(p, p^*, k, \ell) + \mathbf{E}_1^*(p, p^*, k, \ell) = 0,$

(23b) $p = p^*.$

Equations (23) are solved for the equilibrium free-trade price ratio, $p^g = \mathbf{P}(k, \ell)$, where superscript g represents the equilibrium value of a variable with exogenous international factor mobility. It is assumed that the two equations are always satisfied as capital/labor moves between the countries.

Consider first the special case in which $k = \ell = 0$. For simplicity, assume that both countries remain diversified under free trade. The equilibrium price ratio is denoted by $p_0^g = \mathbf{P}(0,0)$. Equation (13) shows that the larger home has a lower autarkic price ratio than the smaller foreign has. However, since the existence of multiple equilibria under free trade is possible in models with externality, it is sometimes difficult to predict the equilibrium. Wong (2001) shows that if the two-country system adjusts in a Marshallian way, a simple version of the law of comparative advantage holds: home will export good 1.[24] This will encourage the production of good 1 in home, implying that under free trade the production of good 1 will be higher in home than in foreign, $Q_{1,0}^g > Q_{1,0}^{*g}$. As a result, when both countries are facing the same real relative price of good 1, the virtual free-trade autarkic price ratio of good 1 is higher in home than in foreign, i.e.,

$$(24) \qquad \tilde{p}_0^g = h\!\left(Q_{1,0}^g\right) p_0^g > h\!\left(Q_{1,0}^{*g}\right) p_0^g = \tilde{p}_0^{*g},$$

where p_0^g is the free trade equilibrium price ratio with no international factor mobility. Equation (24) implies that factor price equalization does not hold for these two economies. Wong (2001) shows that with finite adjustments, the Stolper–Samuelson theorem holds for the present model. By (24), home will have a higher wage rate but a lower rental rate.

The above results are summarized as follows:

LEMMA 6: *In the absence of international factor movement, free trade in goods leads to a higher wage rate but a lower rental rate in home than in foreign.*

Substitute (23b) into (23a) and differentiate the latter totally to give

$$(25) \qquad \Omega dp + (\mathbf{E}_{1k} + \mathbf{E}_{1k}^*)dk + (\mathbf{E}_{1\ell} + \mathbf{E}_{1\ell}^*)d\ell = 0,$$

where subscripts denote partial derivatives, and $\Omega \equiv \mathbf{E}_{1p} + \mathbf{E}_{1p^*} + \mathbf{E}_{1p}^* + \mathbf{E}_{1p^*}^*$. For Marshallian stability of a free-trade equilibrium, Ω is assumed to be positive. Equation (25) is solved for the effect of factor movement on the free-trade price ratio:

---

[24]   Markusen and Melvin (1981) argue that under free trade between a large open economy and a small one, there exists at least one equilibrium at which the large economy exports the good that is subject to increasing returns.

(26a) $\mathbf{P}_k = -\dfrac{\mathbf{E}_{1k} + \mathbf{E}_{1k}^*}{\Omega},$

(26b) $\mathbf{P}_\ell = -\dfrac{\mathbf{E}_{1\ell} + \mathbf{E}_{1\ell}^*}{\Omega}.$

4   International Capital Mobility

Suppose now that in addition to free trade in goods, capital can also move between the countries freely. Labor movement, however, for the time being is treated exogenously. The equilibrium is now described by equations (23) plus the following:

(27) $\mathbf{R}(p, k, \ell) = \mathbf{R}^*(p^*, k, \ell).$

These three conditions can be solved for the equilibrium: substitute the free-trade price ratio into (27) to yield

(28) $\mathbf{R}(\mathbf{P}(k, \ell), k, \ell) = \mathbf{R}^*(\mathbf{P}(k, \ell), k, \ell).$

Equation (28) gives the equilibrium condition under free trade in goods and capital movement, when given international labor migration, ℓ. Let us call this equilibrium GK (for free trade in goods and international capital mobility), with ℓ given as a parameter. It can be solved for equilibrium capital movement, $k^{gk} = \mathbf{K}(\ell)$, where the superscript gk denotes the value of a variable at equilibrium GK.

To analyze the properties of the goods trade plus capital mobility equilibrium, let us begin with the special case of no labor movement, i.e., $\ell = 0$. Denote the equilibrium capital movement by $k_0^{gk} \equiv \mathbf{K}(0)$. We know from Lemma 6 that under free trade in goods but no international factor mobility, the rental rate is lower in home than in foreign. This means that at equilibrium G, when ICM is allowed, home capital tends to flow out to foreign, i.e., $k_0^{gk} > 0$.

At equilibrium GK, the two countries have the same commodity price ratio, but because home produces more good 1 than foreign does, the virtual commodity price ratio must be higher in home than in foreign. As a result, it is not possible to have diversification in production in both countries under free trade in goods and free capital movement.[25]

---

[25]   See Wong (2001) for more discussion of this result.

Since capital movement changes the factor endowments in the countries, we need to determine whether the initial patterns of trade remain unchanged. Note that as home capital flows out, production of good 1 in home at any given commodity prices will go up, as equation (5a) indicates.[26] Thus, the patterns of trade of the countries are not affected by the capital movement. The following three possible patterns in production in the countries at equilibrium GK can be identified:

K1:   home diversified, foreign specialized in good 2;
K2:   home specialized in good 1, foreign diversified;
K3:   home specialized in good 1, foreign specialized in good 2.

Let us examine these cases separately. In case K1, the zero-profit conditions of the sectors are

$$(29a) \quad c_1(w_0^{gk}, r_0^{gk}) = h(Q_{1,0}^{gk}) p_0^{gk},$$

$$(29b) \quad c_2(w_0^{gk}, r_0^{gk}) = c_2(w_0^{*gk}, r_0^{*gk}) = 1.$$

Equations (29a) and (29b) are represented by the curves labeled c_1 and $c_2 = c_2^*$ in panel (a) of Figure 2, respectively. Point K represents the factor prices in both countries at this equilibrium. It can be seen that both countries have the same rental rates and wage rates, $r_0^{gk} = r_0^{*gk}$ and $w_0^{gk} = w_0^{*gk}$.

In case K2, the zero-profit conditions of the sectors in the economies are

$$(30a) \quad c_1(w_0^{gk}, r_0^{gk}) = h(Q_{1,0}^{gk}) p^{gk},$$

$$(30b) \quad c_1(w_0^{*gk}, r_0^{*gk}) = h(Q_{1,0}^{*gk}) p^{gk},$$

$$(30c) \quad c_2(w_0^{*gk}, r_0^{*gk}) = 1.$$

Note that even though both countries are facing the same real commodity price ratio, the fact that home produces more good 1, $Q_1^{gk} > Q_1^{*gk}$, means that it is facing a higher virtual commodity price ratio. In panel (b) of Figure 2, the curves labeled c_1 and c_1^* represent the unit-cost curves of sector 1 in home and foreign, respectively, with the home curve uniformly beyond the foreign curve. By equation (30c), the foreign unit-cost curve for sector 2 is represented by the curve labeled c_2^* in the panel. The diagram shows that at equilibrium GK, the

---

[26]   We do assume mild externality, so that $\Phi > 0$.

two countries have the same rental rate but the home wage rate is higher than the foreign wage rate, $w_0^{gk} > w_0^{*gk}$.

In case K3, the two zero-profit conditions (sector 1 in home and sector 2 in foreign) are

(31a) $c_1(w_0^{gk}, r_0^{gk}) = h(Q_{1,0}^{gk}) p^{gk}$,

(31b) $c_2(w_0^{*gk}, r_0^{*gk}) = 1$.

The two conditions in (31) are shown by the curves labeled c_1 and c_2^*, respectively. The diagram shows that the two countries have the same rental rate but the home wage rate is higher than the foreign wage rate, $w_0^{gk} > w_0^{*gk}$. We summarize the above results in the following lemma:

LEMMA 7: *The two countries have the same rental rate at equilibrium GK with no labor movement. If both countries produce good 2 in equilibrium, they have the same wage rate as well. In other cases, the home wage rate is higher than the foreign wage rate.*

5   International Labor Migration

We now turn to the case of international labor migration. We still allow free trade in goods, but capital movement is taken as exogenous. In other words, variable k is now treated as a parameter. The equilibrium is described by equations (23) plus the following:

(32) $\mathbf{W}(p,k,l) = \mathbf{W}^*(p^*,k,l)$.

These three equilibrium conditions, when taking the level of capital movement k as given, can be solved for the equilibrium $(p^{gl}, p^{*gl}, \ell^{gl})$, where the superscript gl denotes the value of a variable at the equilibrium GL (for free trade in goods plus international labor mobility). Alternatively, the free-trade equilibrium price function can be substituted into (32) to give

(33) $\mathbf{W}(\mathbf{P}(k,\ell),k,l) = \mathbf{W}^*(\mathbf{P}(k,\ell),k,l)$.

Figure 2:
Factor Prices at Equilibrium GK

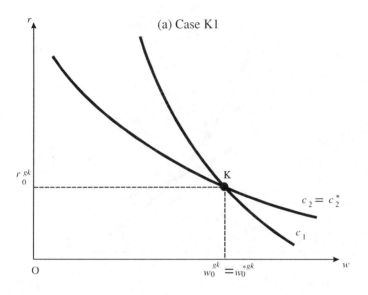

(a) Case K1

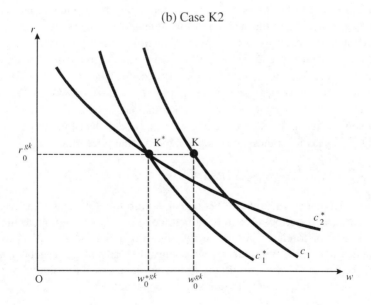

(b) Case K2

Figure 2:
continued

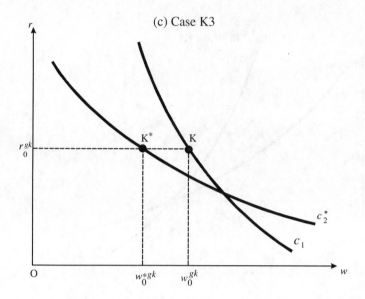

(c) Case K3

Equation (33) can be inverted to express the equilibrium international labor migration as a function of the capital movement level $\ell^{gl} = \mathbf{L}(k)$.

To facilitate our analysis of the effects of international capital movement, let us first focus on the special case with no international capital movement, i.e., $k = 0$, while free trade in goods and free movement of labor are allowed. The equilibrium labor movement can be denoted by $\ell^{gl}_0 = \mathbf{L}(0) > 0$. At this equilibrium, both countries are facing the same real commodity prices, but home, which exports good 1, has a higher production level of good 1 than foreign does, i.e., $Q^{gl}_{1,0} > Q^{*gl}_{1,0}$. Thus, home must be facing a higher virtual price ratio, i.e.,

$$(34) \qquad \tilde{p}^{gl}_0 = h\left(Q^{gl}_{1,0}\right) p^{gl}_0 > h\left(Q^{*gl}_{1,0}\right) p^{gl}_0 = \tilde{p}^{*gl}_0 .$$

One implication of equation (34) is that at equilibrium GL, with equalization of wage rates, it is not possible to have both countries diversified. Note further that the inflow of foreign labor encourages the production of good 1 in home. This implies that home will maintain its comparative advantage in good 1 as it receives foreign labor. As a result, the following three possible patterns of production of the countries at equilibrium GL can be identified:

L1:   home diversified, foreign specialized in good 2;
L2:   home specialized in good 1, foreign diversified;
L3:   home specialized in good 1, foreign specialized in good 2.

These three patterns of production are similar to those under free trade in goods and capital movement, but they have different implications on the factor prices in the countries. Let us analyze these patterns further. First, consider pattern L1. The zero-profit conditions of the sectors are

$$(35a) \quad c_1(w_0^{gl}, r_0^{gl}) = h(Q_{1,0}^{gl}) p_0^{gl},$$

$$(35b) \quad c_2(w_0^{gl}, r_0^{gl}) = c_2(w_0^{*gl}, r_0^{*gl}) = 1.$$

Equations (35) and the condition of identical technology imply that the two countries have the same wage rate and rental rate. This situation is illustrated in panel (a) of Figure 3. The unit-cost curve of sector 2, identical for both countries, intersects with the unit-cost curve of home sector 1 at point L, which indicates the same factor prices in both countries.

In case L2, good 1 is produced in both countries, but good 2 is produced in foreign only. The zero-profit conditions of the sectors can be written as

$$(36a) \quad c_1(w_0^{gl}, r_0^{gl}) = h(Q_{1,0}^{gl}) p^{gl},$$

$$(36b) \quad c_1(w_0^{*gl}, r_0^{*gl}) = h(Q_{1,0}^{*gl}) p^{gl},$$

$$(36c) \quad c_2(w_0^{*gl}, r_0^{*gl}) = 1.$$

These conditions are represented by curves c_1, c_1^*, and c_2^* in panel (b) of Figure 3. Because home exports good 1 and produces more of good 1 than foreign does, $Q_{1,0}^{gl} > Q_{1,0}^{*gl}$, implying that curve c_1 is uniformly beyond curve c_1^*. Foreign factor prices are given by point L*, the point of intersection between curve c_1^* and c_2^*. The equilibrium point of home is given by point L, which is vertically above point L*. From the panel, it is clear that the rental rate is higher in home than in foreign, $r_0^{gl} > r_0^{*gl}$.

In case L3, the countries are producing different goods, with home producing what it is exporting, good 1, and foreign producing good 2. The zero-profit conditions are

Figure 3:
Factor Prices at Equilibrium GL

(a) Case L1

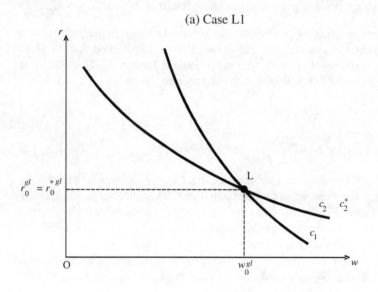

(b) Case L2

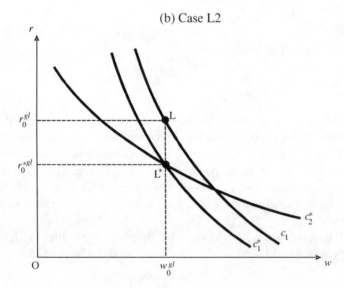

Figure 3:
continued

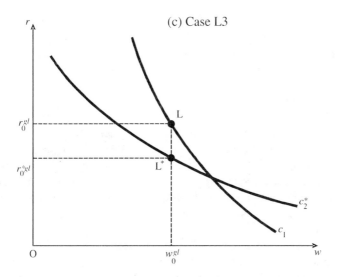

(c) Case L3

(37a) $c_1(w_0^{gl}, r_0^{gl}) = h(Q_{1,0}^{gl})p^{gl},$

(37b) $c_2(w_0^{*gl}, r_0^{*gl}) = 1.$

Equations (37a) and (37b) are represented by curves c_1 and c_2^* in panel (c) of Figure 3. The equilibrium factor prices in the two countries are shown by points L and L*. It is clear from the diagram that the rental rate is higher in home than in foreign, $r_0^{gl} > r_0^{*gl}$.

LEMMA 8: *The two countries have the same wage rate at equilibrium GL with no capital movement. If both countries produce good 2 in equilibrium, they have the same rental rate as well. In other cases, the home rental rate is higher than the foreign rental rate.*

6   Are International Capital Movement and Labor Movement Substitutes?

After analyzing some of the features of free trade in goods with either international capital movement or international labor movement, let us examine whether they are substitutes, in the senses defined above.

6.1   The Price Sense

We first examine whether they are substitutes in the price sense. Section 5 derives three possible equilibrium cases, depending on what each country is producing under free trade. It is shown that when good 2 is being produced in both countries (case K1), the two countries will have the same wage rate and same rental rate. This means that free trade in goods plus free international capital movement will equalize not only commodity prices and rental rates, but also wage rates as well.

In other cases when good 2 is produced in only one country (cases K2 and K3), then free trade in goods and free international capital movement will not equalize the wage rates. In these two cases, the wage rate is higher in home than in foreign.

When free trade in goods and free international labor movement are allowed, the equilibrium depends on the patterns of production in the countries. If good 2 is produced in both countries (case L1), then the commodity and factor prices are all equalized. In the other two cases, when good 2 is produced in foreign only, the commodity prices and the wage rates in both countries, but not the rental rates, are equalized.

PROPOSITION 1: *In cases K1 and L1, ICM and ILM are substitutes in the price sense. In other cases, they are complements.*

6.2   The Quantity Sense

We now examine whether international capital movement and international labor movement are substitutes in the quantity sense. We will analyze how the movement of one factor may be affected by an exogenous increase in the movement of the other factor.

6.2.1   International Capital Movement

Suppose now that there is an exogenous but small increase in ℓ. We want to find out whether, at the initial level of capital movement, while free trade in goods is allowed, the rental rate differential between the countries increases or decreases. Differentiate the equilibrium GK as described by equations (23) and (27), keeping k constant but allowing free trade in goods. We get

$$(38) \qquad \frac{d(r^* - r)}{d\ell} = (\mathbf{R}^*_{p^*} - \mathbf{R}_p) \frac{dp}{d\ell} + (\mathbf{R}^*_{\ell} - \mathbf{R}_{\ell}).$$

Let us consider the sign of the expression in (38). Locally, if the degree of increasing returns is mild, so that the Stolper–Samuelson theorem holds, and if the economies remain diversified, then both $\mathbf{R}^*_{p^*}$ and $\mathbf{R}_p$ are negative. We have also shown that, with diversification, $\mathbf{R}^*_{\ell} > 0$ and $\mathbf{R}_{\ell} < 0$. The sign of $dp/d\ell$ $= \mathbf{P}_{\ell}$, as given by (26b), is in general ambiguous. As a result, the sign of $d(r^* - r)/d\ell$ in (38) is ambiguous.

Since the local effects of more international labor movement on international capital movement are generally ambiguous, let us turn to finite changes. In Figure 4, point A depicts the value of k at equilibrium GK with no international labor movement, $k_0^{gk} > 0$. Schedule ABC in the diagram shows the locus of equilibrium capital movement under a different exogenously given level of international labor movement. It is represented by the function $k = \mathbf{K}(\ell)$. The slope of schedule ABC, which is given by the derivative of $\mathbf{K}(\ell)$, has the same sign as $d(r^* - r)/d\ell$. As equation (38) shows, the sign of the expression is ambiguous, meaning that the sign of the slope of schedule ABC is also ambiguous.

We can, however, show that the slope of ABC is on the whole negative. To show this, denote first point F in Figure 4, which indicates the value of ℓ at equilibrium GL with no international capital movement, $\ell_0^{gl} > 0$. Let us continue to consider international capital movement, but assume that an exogenous amount ℓ_0^{gl} of foreign labor flowing to home. Would capital move? The answer depends on the rental rates in the countries.

In case L1, an amount ℓ_0^{gl} of labor movement will equalize not just wage rates but also rental rates. This means that capital will not move between the countries even if allowed. As a result, point F represents an equilibrium point under international capital movement.

In cases L2 and L3, with an exogenous amount, ℓ_0^{gl}, of labor movement, the rental rate is higher in home than in foreign. This means that if capital is allowed

Figure 4:
Effects of International Factor Movements

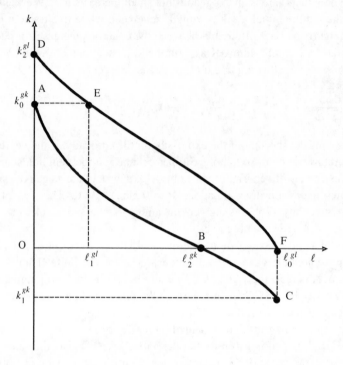

to move, it will move from foreign to home. Let us denote the final equilibrium capital movement by $k_1^{gk} < 0$. Let the equilibrium be at point C.

Continuity of the production and utility functions implies that function $k = \mathbf{K}(\ell)$ can be represented by the continuous curve ABC. In case L1, points B and C are on the horizontal axis and coincide with point F. In cases L2 and L3, point C is below the horizontal axis, and point B is where the curve cuts the horizontal axis. This situation is shown in Figure 4.

Even though the sign of the slope of schedule ABC is ambiguous, the fact that A is on the positive vertical intercept while C is either on the horizontal axis or in the negative k region means that at least part of the schedule is negatively sloped. In other words, over at least part of the region $(0, \ell_0^{gl})$ more international labor movement diminishes international capital movement.

6.2.2   International Labor Movement

Similar expressions can be obtained for an exogenous increase in capital movement when free trade in goods and free international labor movement are allowed. Differentiate the equilibrium conditions (23) and (32), allowing free trade in goods and keeping ℓ constant, to give

$$(39) \qquad \frac{\mathrm{d}(w - w^*)}{\mathrm{d}k} = (\mathbf{W}_p - \mathbf{W}^*_{p*})\frac{\mathrm{d}p}{\mathrm{d}k} + (\mathbf{W}_k - \mathbf{W}^*_k).$$

Assuming mild increasing returns and diversification in both economies, both $\mathbf{W}_p$ and $\mathbf{W}^*_{p*}$ are positive. We showed earlier that $\mathbf{W}_k > 0$ and $\mathbf{W}^*_k < 0$. The sign of $\mathrm{d}p/\mathrm{d}k$, as given by (26a), is in general ambiguous. In Figure 4, curve DEF shows the dependence of equilibrium labor movement on capital movement, or function $\ell^{gl} = \mathbf{L}(k)$. The slope of curve DEF is ambiguous.

We already know that curve DEF cuts the horizontal axis at point F, $\ell^{gl}_0 > 0$. Point E denotes the equilibrium labor movement, ℓ^{gl}_1, when capital movement is given exogenously as k^{gk}_0, which is the equilibrium capital movement at equilibrium GK with no labor movement. The position of point E depends on the feature of equilibrium GK.

In case K1, we showed that wage rates in the countries are also equalized. This means that at this point no labor movement will occur even if it is allowed. As a result, point E coincides with point A, and $\ell^{gl}_1 = 0$. In cases K2 and K3, at equilibrium GK the home wage rate is higher than the foreign wage rate. This implies that with an exogenous amount, k^{gk}_0, of capital movement, foreign labor will flow to home, indicating that $\ell^{gl}_1 > 0$. This means that in these two cases, point E is on the right-hand side of point A, and $\ell^{gl}_1 > 0$. However, in general, ℓ^{gl}_1 cannot be compared with ℓ^{gl}_0. To get more information about the slope of curve DEF, note that in cases K2 and K3, home specializes in good 1 and has a higher wage rate. Suppose we start with equilibrium GK with no international labor movement (point A in Figure 4). As Lemma 7 shows, the home wage rate is higher than the foreign wage rate. Suppose we move more home capital to foreign. The Inada condition implies that with at least very small amounts of capital stock, the home wage rate will be very low. This means that there exists at least one value of $k > k^{gk}_0$, so that $w = w^*$. Let this value be k^{gl}_2. If this amount of home capital moves to foreign, no labor movement will take place even if it is allowed. In other words, this value gives the vertical intercept, point D, of schedule DEF. This is shown in Figure 4. The continuity of curve DEF implies that at least part of it is negatively sloped. We now summarize the above results as follows:

PROPOSITION 2: *ICM and ILM are substitutes in the quantity sense at least over certain ranges of capital and labor movements.*

7   Concluding Remarks

This paper examines the relationship between international capital movement (ICM) and international labor movement (ILM) in the presence of national externality. Whether they are substitutes or complements has long been an important issue for those governments who are experiencing substantial amounts of international capital movement and international labor movement. Using a simple model, this paper analyzes the relations between ICM and ILM when free trade in goods is taking place.

Marshallian externality is assumed in this paper, and the model is used to analyze the roles of this type of externality in trade in goods and international factor movement. Such a type of framework is common in the literature, as Marshallian externality is compatible with perfect competition while the analysis can cover economies with external economies of scale.

This paper investigates how international capital movement and international labor movement are dependent on each other when free trade in goods is always allowed. In particular, this paper determines whether an increase in the movement of one of the factors will affect the volume of movement of the other factor.

The relationship between ICM and ILM is examined in two senses: the price sense and the quantity sense. This paper finds out that there are cases in which ICM and ILM are substitutes in the price sense and there are other cases in which they are complements. In the quantity sense, this paper argues that they are most likely substitutes, or at least there are ranges of capital and labor movements in which they are substitutes.

The findings in this paper seem to support the common perception that if the government allows more movement of a factor, then the movement of the other factor (usually in an opposite direction) will tend to decrease. Of course, if we are given two specific countries with which to analyze the relationship between ICM and ILM, then other factors of trade in goods and factor movements should be taken into consideration. In particular, some of the assumptions in the present paper, such as identical technologies and identical factor endowment ratio, should be relaxed in a more general model. It is also interesting to investigate ICM and ILM in other types of models: for example, the neoclassical framework and models with imperfect competition.

Bibliography

Ide, T., and A. Takayama (1991). Variable Returns to Scale, Paradoxes, and Global Correspondence in the Theory of International Trade. In A. Takayama, M. Ohyama, and H. Ohta (eds.), *Trade, Policy, and International Adjustments*. San Diego: Academic Press.

Ide, T., and A. Takayama (1993). Variable Returns to Scale, Comparative Statics Paradoxes, and the Theory of Comparative Advantage. In H. Herberg and N. Van Long (eds.), *Trade, Welfare, and Economic Policies: Essays in Honor of Murray C. Kemp*. Ann Arbor: University of Michigan Press.

Inoue, T. (1981). A Generalization of the Samuelson Reciprocity Relations, the Stolper–Samuelson Theorem and the Rybczynski Theorem under Variable Returns to Scale. *Journal of International Economics* 11 (1): 79–98.

Jones, R.W. (1968). Variable Returns to Scale in General Equilibrium Theory. *International Economic Review* 9 (3): 261–272.

Markusen, J.R. (1983). Factor Movements and Commodity Trade as Complements. *Journal of International Economics* 14 (3–4): 341–356.

Markusen, J.R., and J.R. Melvin (1981). Trade, Factor Prices, and the Gains from Trade with Increasing Returns to Scale. *Canadian Journal of Economics* 14 (3): 450–469.

Marshall, A. (1879). *Pure Theory of Foreign Trade*. London: London School of Economics and Political Science, 1930.

Marshall, A. (1890). *Principles of Economics*. 8th edition. London: Macmillan, 1920.

Mundell, R. (1957). International Trade and Factor Mobility. *American Economic Review* 67: 321–335.

Tawada, M. (1989). *Production Structure and International Trade*. Berlin: Springer.

Wong, K.-Y. (1986). Are International Trade and Factor Mobility Substitutes? *Journal of International Economics* 21: 25–43.

Wong, K.-Y. (1995). *International Trade in Goods and Factor Mobility*. Cambridge, Mass.: MIT Press.

Wong, K.-Y. (2001). *International Trade and International Capital Movement in the Presence of Production Externality*. Tamkang Chair Lecture Series 126. Taipei: Tamkang University.

Comment on Kar-yiu Wong

Jörn Kleinert

In a world of increasing globalization and increasing importance of all channels of international factor movements, the theoretical understanding of the relationship between migration, capital movements, and trade is necessary for both empirical analysis and policy advice. Economists have devoted some effort to the analysis of the relationship between trade and foreign direct investment (Brainard 1997, Blonigen 2001, Markusen 2002) and trade and migration (Gould and Findlay 1994) but less so to the relationship between different types of factor movements. However, the question how FDI affects international labor migration is an important one, since whether capital and labor movements are substitutes or complements yields different policy implications.

Kar-yiu Wong's paper uses a theoretical general equilibrium model with Marshallian externalities. In doing so, he considers resource allocation, income distribution, and intersectoral relationships.

Wong uses two substitution criteria to explore the relationship: substitution in the price sense and substitution in the quantity sense. He defines substitution in the price sense as when either international capital mobility (ICM) or international labor mobility (ILM) is sufficient to bring about the efficient allocation of resources in the world, i.e., when either of them leads to equalization of both factor prices. ICM and ILM are said to be substitutes in the quantity sense, according to Wong, when a small exogenous increase in the volume of flows of one factor leads to a decrease in the flow of the other factor, and vice versa. ICM and ILM are complements if a small exogenous increase in the volume of flows of one factor leads to an increase in the flow of the other factor, and vice versa.

Both factors, labor and capital, are homogenous, within and between the two countries. The production of a good uses both factors in a typical neoclassical production function, with substitutable input factors and falling marginal productivity of both factors. To generate Marshallian externalities, this production function is augmented in one sector by a term that increases the output of a single firm by an additional term that is a positive function of the size of the sector. Firms in the two countries use the same technology but differ in their factor intensities because both countries differ in relative factor endowment before integration. The home country is assumed to be relatively capital abundant. Sectors differ in factor intensities within a country. The more capital-intensive sector is subject to Marshallian externalities.

Since homogenous factors and identical technologies are assumed to obtain in both countries, perfect mobility of one factor is enough to achieve equalization of both rental rates and wages between the two countries. From the equalization of both factor prices through each channel follows that ICM and ILM are substitutes in the quantity sense of parameters. However, Marshallian externalities can cause ICM and ILM to be complements under certain conditions if the increase in the size of the sector through an exogenous increase in one factor overcompensates the decreasing marginal productivity. Although this case might arise, it is certainly rather the exception than the rule.

The results of the model are therefore strongly in favor of substitution between ICM and ILM. Yet, it is not obvious whether reality comes close to the conditions assumed in the models, and therefore, whether we should base policy advice on this analysis. A first warning not to use this assumption comes from the literature on the relationship between trade and FDI or trade and migration. Trade has been found to be a complement to both factor flows in various empirical analysis. Just as trade is predicted to be a substitute for both migration and capital movements in Wong's models, the result that migration and capital flows are substitutes might fail the empirical test as well. The main problems with the model are the assumption of identical technologies in both countries and the assumption of homogenous factors within and between countries. Wong admits this in his concluding remarks.

Davis and Weinstein (2002) come up with complementarity in their analysis. They use a Ricardian model instead of a neoclassical model. Thereby, they account for differences in technologies between the countries. Technological differences yield higher rental rates for capital and higher wages in the country with the higher level of technology than in the other country. Davis and Weinstein argue that possession of superior technology explains the inflows of labor and capital into the United States in the 1980s and 1990s. The empirical analysis that they present supports this view.

Gross and Schmitt (2003) explain immigration in an empirical analysis of OECD host countries using stocks of migrants from the same home country who are already living in the host country as a determinant. The theoretical reasoning behind this setup of the estimated equation is the observation that labor markets in many developed countries are fragmented. Migrants are mostly employed by people from the same country of origin. Gross and Schmitt explain this as being caused by information costs, which are smaller if employer and employees share the same cultural background. Heterogeneity in the labor force is therefore an important determinant of international migration according to Gross and Schmitt.

Buch et al. (2003) empirically analyze the relationship of FDI and migration using German data at the level of the German state (Bundesland). They show that FDI and migration are explained by the same determinants in gravity equations. In seemingly unrelated regressions (SUR), the FDI and the migration equations are positively correlated. Stocks of German FDI augment the explanation of German emigration. Granger causality tests show that German emigration Granger causes German firms' FDI flows. On the inward side, there is a two-directional relationship between immigration and FDI flows into Germany. FDI and migration are, according to these results, much more likely to be complements than substitutes in the German case. That is all the more likely, since Foders (2004) showed that a Ricardian approach to migration explains the German pattern quite well.

The analysis of Buch et al. (2003) reveals that it is necessary to differentiate migration flows with respect to Germans and foreigners and to explain immigration and emigration separately. Whereas Wong's models propose to estimate a specification that analyzes the determinants of net flows, Buch et al. estimate the effects for gross flows, separately for the inward and the outward side. That matches the policy debates in Germany and other developed countries which fear immigration from less developed countries and emigration to other developed countries at the same time. The former is feared and discussed as immigration into the welfare state, the latter as brain drain. Analyzing net flows is then misleading because the two effects do not cancel each other out.

A further reason why substitution might not be found in empirical analyses is the existence of impediment to factor or goods trade. Integration in Wong's models is perfect; political or physical barriers to trade in goods and factors do not exist. Although trade is fairly free, there are still surprisingly high border effects (McCallum 1995). International capital flows have been freed up in recent years from many impediments but they are far from being unrestricted. Migration is surely far less free than the other two. These political determinants also affect the relationship between ICM and ILM.

Wong's paper, building on his previous work (Wong 1995, Wong 2001), is an important contribution to the literature on the relationship between different channels of globalization. Wong emphasizes one driving force of integration: factor flows driven by factor price differentials. This is certainly an important channel but one among others. Wong shows that in a world in which only this channel exists, ICM and ILM would be substitutes. Since empirical analyses often find ICM and ILM to be complements, other channels might be more important. Technological differences, emigration networks, and political restrictions are other important determinants that shape the direction of migration and capital flows and thus the relationship between ICM and ILM. For purposes of providing policy advice, these factors must also be taken into account.

Bibliography

Blonigen, B. (2001). In Search of Substitution between Foreign Production and Exports. *Journal of International Economics* 53 (1): 81–104.

Brainard, S.L. (1997). An Empirical Assessment of the Proximity-Concentration Trade-Off between Multinational Sales and Trade. *American Economic Review* 87 (4): 520–544.

Buch, C.M., J. Kleinert, and F. Toubal (2003). Where Enterprises Lead, People Follow? Links Between German Migration and FDI. Kiel Working Paper 1190. Institute for World Economics, Kiel.

Davis, D.R., and D.E. Weinstein (2002). Technological Superiority and the Losses from Migration. NBER Working Paper 8971. National Bureau of Economic Research, Cambridge, Mass.

Foders, F. (2004). Long-Run Determinants of Immigration to Germany 1974–1999: A Ricardian Framework. *European Review of Economics and Finance* 3 (2): 3–29.

Gould, W.T.S., and A.M. Findlay (1994). *Population Migration and the Changing World Order.* Chichester: Wiley.

Gross, D., and N. Schmitt (2003). The Role of Cultural Clustering in Attracting New Immigrants. *Journal of Regional Science* 43 (2): 295-318.

Markusen, J.R. (2002). *Multinational Firms and the Theory of International Trade.* Cambridge, Mass.: MIT Press.

McCallum, J. (1995). National Border Matters: Canada–US Regional Trade Pattern. *American Economic Review* 85 (3): 615–623.

Mundell, R.A. (1957). International Trade and Factor Mobility. *American Economic Review* 47 (3): 321–335.

Wong, K-Y. (1995). *International Trade in Goods and Factor Mobility.* Cambridge, Mass.: MIT Press.

Wong, K-Y. (2001). International Trade and International Capital Movements in the Presence of Production Externality. Tankang Chair Lecture Series 126. Taipei.

Sheetal K. Chand and Martin Paldam

Some Economics of Immigration from an LDC to a DC: Stressing the Case of a Nordic Welfare State

Abstract:

The economic consequences of immigration from a less developed country (LDC) to a developed country (DC) are potentially very advantageous for both the immigrant and the recipient country. Cultural differences and the institutions of the DC can cause both a shortfall in and a redistribution of the potential advantage through two mechanisms: the selection of immigrants and the incentives for labor market participation. These effects are examined in three stylized cases: a Dubai-like guest worker society, a U.S.-like immigrant society, and a Nordic-like tax-based welfare state. The Dubai-like case is closest to the potential, while the Nordic-like evolved welfare case deviates the most. Major institutional changes will be required for the latter to better realize the immigration benefit potential.

1 Introduction

Millions of people move every year from the poor LDCs to the rich DCs. This flow is driven by two traditional gaps that have caused migration through the ages: the *income gap* and the *civil rights gap*. Failed states and civil conflicts have driven many to seek refuge in the DCs, but there is also a very strong economic motivation fueled by the income disparities between the LDCs and the DCs. As is well known from the theory of international trade, there are sizable potential gains to be had from immigration. While they are relatively easy to pin down for the immigrant, the benefits for the receiving country seem more diffuse and limited, and many DCs have responded to the immigrant flow by setting up barricades.

Remark: We want to thank Holger Bonin, Vani Borooah, Peter Nannestad, Michael Rosholm, and Harrie Verbon, among other discussants. As this paper is published in a volume that contains an excellent survey of the literature we keep references to a minimum.

This paper examines some aspects of the interaction between the LDC immigrant and the host DC. It attempts to quantify the potential economic gains from immigration for both parties and finds these to be sizable. However, the realization of the gains and their distribution between immigrant and host country appear to vary among the DCs. The contention of this paper is that institutional differences and their associated incentive structures largely account for the different realizations.

The institutional setup influences the immigrant type both directly in the host country's selection and in the self-selection of immigrants. Some DCs obtain immigrants that are more readily absorbed in their labor markets than do others, and gain accordingly. The rate of absorption is a function of several factors including how well the immigrants match the needs of the host country's firms, taking account of their skills, work attitudes and other culture-related factors, and also the nature of the selection process. The eagerness with which the immigrant seeks work is obviously central, but this can be adversely impacted by the availability of generous social subsidies and/or the perception of closed doors. The keenness with which firms acquire and train workers, a function of their competitiveness and the nature of labor market regulations that they operate under, is also critical.

The above-mentioned operative factors are complex in their operation. To obtain a handle on them, a framework is presented here that encapsulates their effects into two curves: the labor market *absorption* curve and an *income subsidy* curve, which covers the subsidy received by the immigrant until he is fully absorbed in the labor market. Using this framework, we consider three stylized policy packages taken to be the extreme cases that span the existing possibilities: (a) a Dubai-type case where the immigrant can be a guest worker only, and enters on a contract securing full labor market absorption, (b) a U.S.-type case of an immigrant society, and (c) a Nordic-type tax welfare state. By far the most problematic case is the Nordic welfare state, where the benefit to the DC could even be negative.[1]

Section 2 sets up the analytical framework, while Section 3 examines the potential gains from immigration, and Section 4 presents a standard or reference case. Sections 5 to 7 look at the three country cases. Section 8 considers the noneconomic variables, and Section 9 draws some conclusions. The Appendix contains a set of simulations.

---

[1]   We discuss the Nordic case in more detail in Chand and Paldam (2004), especially as regards the difficult policy choices.

2   Analytical Framework

The terminology distinguishes between natives and immigrants, or insiders and outsiders. The analysis begins at time $t = 0$, when the immigrant is accepted legally in the DC.[2] The analysis employs four assumptions to facilitate the presentation:

- It uses a simple overlapping generation framework, where the immigrant establishes a dynastic family and lives forever through succeeding generations. Consequently, we do not distinguish between first-, second-, and third-generation immigrants.
- It disregards economic fluctuations and assumes that each country grows at a steady state rate, generating an equilibrium rate of unemployment.
- It assumes that in the absence of immigration the intertemporal budget is intergenerationally neutral, i.e., the average native receives exactly the same in public consumption and transfers as he pays in taxes.
- All factors of production are paid their marginal product.

2.1   Absorption, $\lambda(t, \rho, \kappa)$, Excess Transfer, ρ, and the Wage, w

The analysis uses three key variables, which are functions of t and other variables. They are also the subject of much research, so we know something about the way these functions look. However, the paper will neither review the empirical literature nor estimate the functions. Instead it asks: Given that they look as assumed, what are the consequences for the welfare of the immigrant and the natives?

The absorption function, $\lambda = \lambda(t...)$, gives the relative employment of the stylized immigrant taken to reflect an average: some immigrants may be absorbed right away, while others take much longer than the norm. It is less than that of the native in two ways: (a) the labor market participation rate is lower, notably for women, and (b) the unemployment rate is higher. We assume that $\lambda = \lambda(t...)$ starts at 0 for $t = 0$ and then grows to 1 for $t = T$, whereupon the immigrant is fully absorbed in the labor market. Different cultural groups respond differently, and the complex matter of cultural integration, κ, is discussed in the next section. In addition, we take λ to be a function of the institutional package in the DC.

---

2   The first immigrant in a family is often male, so the male gender is used throughout. The decision of the immigrant to leave his (former) country and all intermediate stages between a full entry and no entry are disregarded.

We represent the relevant package of institutions of DC by ρ, the social policy. It gives the excess social transfer provided to the immigrant, while $\lambda < 1$, i.e., before he is fully absorbed.[3] ρ has two parts: ρ_1 is the minimum received by everybody in need, including a newly accepted immigrant. If the transfer has an insurance element, ρ grows to ρ_2, as t grows.

The labor income of the native is $w_t = \alpha e^{at}$. It is α at $t = 0$, and grows at a constant rate a. For short we call the income in the DC "wage." Both λ and ρ are taken to be fractions of w. The total "income" of the immigrant is thus $(\lambda + \rho)w$, while the native gets w. We take the wage structure to be constant. Also, in the discussion that follows, we consider primarily income from employment and not from self-owned enterprises.

2.2   Culture: The Concept of Integration

The immigrant arrives as an outsider with a different culture, language, often a different religion, and frequently looking different. We shall encapsulate these differences in the concept of *cultural distance*, $\kappa(t, i)$, starting at $t = 0$. The immigrant has to break into the society of the natives to be absorbed. This complex process demands integration and a mutual learning and adjustment process on the part of both immigrants and natives. We assume that $\kappa(t, i)$ falls monotonically for all i's as t increases, but the fall may stop at $\underline{\kappa}(i)$, when the immigrant is so integrated that he resists further integration.[4]

$\lambda = \lambda(t, \kappa...)$ is a complex function of κ. At present we take $\partial\lambda/\partial\kappa$ to be negative, so that the immigrant becomes more integrated as cultural distance diminishes. Some integration is surely needed before an immigrant can be fully absorbed. $\lambda = 1$ requires that $\kappa < \varepsilon$, where ε is the level of tolerance of the natives. It is interesting to contemplate if immigrant groups exist, where $\underline{\kappa} > \varepsilon$, making full absorption impossible, or if $\underline{\kappa}$ and ε must inevitably adjust in the long run to solve all problems of absorption.

Selection of the immigrant type determines initial cultural distance. The rapidity with which this is diminished will influence the speed of absorption. The DC may follow a policy that shortens the process, or pursue policies—for other reasons—prolonging the process, as we shall see.

---

3   It is thus assumed that the immigrant receives the standard social benefits and pays the corresponding taxes once $\lambda = 1$.

4   Epstein and Gang (2004) describe a process in which the cultural integration is cyclical.

2.3   Utility: Net Present Values of Income Flows and the Micro-Macro Puzzle

Two agents are considered: The immigrant (micro) and the DC country (macro). The old country of the immigrant is LDC. The decision of the immigrant to leave LDC and the economic consequences for LDC are not analyzed at present.

The utility gain of each of the two agents has economic and noneconomic parts. The economic part is taken to be a positive monotonic function of the net present values of the changes in the income flows calculated at the time of immigration $t = 0$.

For the immigrant the change in utility is $U = U(NVP_I, S, D)$, where NVP_I is the net present value of the changes in his income, as analyzed below. The other variables S and D are the possible increase in personal security in moving to DC, while D is the noneconomic loss he experiences before he is absorbed. We assume that $S > D$, so that S and D increase the utility of the immigrant. S and D are discussed in Section 8.

For DC, the utility is $U = U(NVP_{DC}, Q)$, where NPV_{DC} is the net present value of two flows: (a) the surplus produced by the immigrant in excess of his salary. It is taken to be proportional to his salary λw by a factor z, discussed in Section 3.2, and (b) the excess social expenditures paid to the immigrant untill he is absorbed. The noneconomic variable Q accounts for the increase in social tensions caused by the immigration. This is taken net of any positive utility assigned to multiculturalism, and it is assumed negative. Q reduces the utility of the DC, as discussed in Section 8.

Notice that while the benefits to the individual immigrant are personalized, they are not for the DC native. If $U = U(NVP_{DC}, \ldots)$ is divided between all natives in DC, it is negligible for any one native. This creates a typical puzzle, which may also be termed a micro-macro personalized versus generalized benefits puzzle. A native may want to forbid immigration, but still be in favor of allowing specific persons to enter, e.g., to work in his business or if a touching story is told in the media.

3   The Potential Gain of the Two Parties

The highest gain to both sides occurs when the immigrant fills a vacant job commensurate with his qualifications and aspirations at arrival at $t = 0$, and from that day has $\lambda = 1$. That is, in terms of employment he becomes just like a native.

3.1   The Potential Gain to the Immigrant, NPV_I^*

The immigrant shifts from the LDC wage to the DC wage. His gain from the decision is therefore the net present value of the DC wage minus the LDC wage. Using the two formulas for the wages from Table 1 and the standard expression for a perpetual annuity, given that $r > a, b$, we get:

(1) $$NPV_I^* = NPV(w - w_L) = \int_0^\infty (w - w_L)e^{-rt}dt = \alpha \int_0^\infty e^{-(r-a)t}dt$$

$$- \beta \int_0^\infty e^{-(r-b)t}dt = \frac{\alpha}{r-a} - \frac{\beta}{r-b} \approx \frac{\alpha - \beta}{r-a} = \alpha\frac{1 - \beta/\alpha}{r-a} .$$

The last two expressions hold if $a \approx b$.

Table 1:
Variables and Curves Analyzed

Curve	Definition (all variables consider one immigrant)	Depends upon
t, T	Time from entry $t = 0$. The immigrant is absorbed at $t = T$.	Decision is made at $t = 0$.
w	Wage in DC: $w = \alpha e^{at}$. For $t = 0$, $w = \alpha$.	Grow at constant real rate a.
w_l	Wage in LDC: $w_L = \beta e^{bt}$. For $t = 0$, $w = \beta$.	Grow at constant real rate b.
$\lambda(t, \rho, \kappa)$	Absorption curve, labor income of immigrant is λw.	t, ρ, culture, and labor market.
$\rho(t, \dots)$	Excess social subsidy to immigrant for $t < x$. Subsidy is ρw.	t and institutions of DC.
NPV	Net present values for immigrant NPV_I and natives NPV_{DC}.	Calculated at time $t = 0$.
NPV^*	Potential net present values, if no absorption problems.	$\lambda = 1$ and $\rho = 0$ for all t.
z	Surplus to natives of immigrant product. Fraction of product.	Typical value $z \approx 0.25$.
x	Time of social break-even, excess subsidy zero.	Intersection of λ and ρ curves.
L	Loss of DC production due to slow absorption.	λ-curve.
R	Excess transfer to immigrant, between $t = 0$ and T.	λ-curve and ρ-curve.
ϑ	Shortfall (ratio) of NPV due to slow absorption.	$\vartheta = (NPV^* - NPV)/NPV^*$

Note: Excess is above the normal amount received by the native. Surplus is gain of the natives. While the labor market absorption takes place at T, the social sector absorption already occurs at x.

From this expression, it is easy to reach some orders of magnitudes. The typical ratio between GDP per capita in PPP terms of the two countries suggests that β is in the range of 15 percent ±10 percent of α. The real rate of interest may be used as an approximation to the rate of discount. We use $r = 5$ percent, which is probably on the high end of the scale, and $a \approx b$ of around 2 percent. With these values, $NPV_I^* \approx \alpha(1 - 0.15)/0.03 = 28\alpha$. Even for a low α such as $25,000, NPV_I^* exceeds \$⅔ mill. NPV_I^* falls to half if r is high at, say 8 percent. NPV_I^* rises if r falls toward a. A rough estimate would therefore be

$$(2) \qquad NPV_I^* = \$\frac{2}{3} \pm \frac{1}{3}\text{mill.}$$

The large size of NPV_I^* is the economic incentive that drives the supply of immigrants.

However, to gain that benefit the immigrant faces three problems:

(p1) He may fail to get through the barriers to entry (see Section 8).
(p2) He may have to pay commissions to agents to get through the barriers (see Section 8).
(p3) During the absorption period, some of NPV_I^* is lost (see Section 4).

Nevertheless, given the large estimated size of the potential NPV_I^*, many are likely to think it is worth trying to emigrate.

3.2   The Potential Gain for the Host Country, NPV_{DC}^*, and the World

The potential gain for the DC is the net value of the surplus production of the immigrant—the overheads he produces. It is taken to be proportional to λw, by the factor z. The simplest interpretation of z is that it is the share of capital, so that $z \approx 0.25$. [5]

As $\lambda = 1$, there are no excess social expenditures incurred over and above those normal for natives. The potential value is thus

$$(3) \qquad NPV_{DC}^* = NPV(zw) = z\frac{\alpha}{r-a} = z(NPV_I^* + NPV(w_L)) \approx z\frac{\alpha}{\alpha-\beta}NPV_I^*,$$

derived as equation (1).

---

[5]   The paper assumes that the capital stock is owned by the natives. However, in many parts of the world immigrants have often proved to be more entrepreneurial in setting up businesses and acquiring capital.

For the values of the variables used, this is about $0.3\,NPV_I^*$, which is still considerable. This is the economic gap on the demand side that is also important for the flow.

(4) $NPV^* = NPV_I^* + NPV_{DC}^* \approx \$1$ mill.

The large potential gains for both parts have led many observers to think that the labor flows are beneficial for the world. Many stories can be told in which this has actually been the case.[6]

3.3   Realizing the Potential: Three Archetypal Societies

The potential gains are only reached in exceptional cases (see Section 5). It normally takes some time $(t = 0, ..., T)$ for the immigrant to be absorbed into the labor market. During the interval, he earns λw, where $\lambda < 1$. Hence, there is a loss in terms of the potential, L, to the immigrant or, zL, to the natives. In that period, he may also receive social transfers, R, according to the ρ-curve. R partly compensates the immigrant, but it is a cost to the natives. The NPV calculations thus change:

(5) $NPV_I = NPV_I^* - (L - R),$

where L and R are given in equations (8) and (9)

(6) $NPV_{DC} = NPV_{DC}^* - (zL + R),$

(7) $NPV^* - NPV = (L - R) + (zL + R) = (1 + z)L,$ so that

$\vartheta = (1 + z)L / NPV^*.$

From (7) follows that when the immigrant has a period of labor market participation below that of the natives, it generates a loss as compared to the full potential. Equations (5) and (6) show that R affects the distribution of the shortfall between the immigrant and the natives: it reduces the shortfall of the immigrant and increases that of the natives; it does not affect its size once L is given.

Many institutions of DC are relevant for the shape of the λ-curve. Some are labor market rules, regulations and customs, systems for receiving and training immigrants, and last—but not least—social policies, formulated as a ρ-curve.

---

6   Finland converged to the West after it left the Russian Empire in 1918, to about 1970. During that period about 1 million Finns went to work in Sweden, which benefited the development of both countries. Much the same story can be told of Portugal and France, etc.

Here each DC presents a "package" of institutions. We have chosen three such packages to span the possibility space. In addition the adaptability of the immigrant counts, as well as his response to the incentives provided. As suggested by the title, we are most concerned with the Nordic-like case, which is by far the most problematic.

4   The Standard Case

This subsection first introduces the basic logic of the 4 curves of Table 1. The next two subsections look at the *NPV* calculations of the immigrants and the natives. This is followed by an assessment of factors that influence the *NPVs* of the decision.

4.1   A Slow Absorption λ, and a Social Policy ρ

The basic curves are likely to have the forms drawn in Figure 1a. The DC wage, w, is 5–10 times higher than the LDC wage, w_L. It takes time, T, to absorb the immigrant into the labor market. We assume that he starts without a job at $t = 0$, so the absorption curve, λ, starts at 0 and reaches w at T. At present the λ-curve is assumed to be near-linear in accordance with the empirics in the Nordic case.

When the wage of the immigrant is below a certain threshold, x, he is entitled to a social subsidy. The subsidy, ρ, is likely to have two parts: a subsistence payment at the rate ρ_1, and an insurance part that has to be saved up, so ρ rises from ρ_1 to the maximum ρ_2, which is a certain fraction of w. Hence, ρ depends upon t as drawn. The social policies of the individual DC determine the exact form of the ρ-curve.[7] At the break-even point, x, the immigrant ceases to be a net recipient of subsidies. To simplify, assume that the subsidy received is a simple monotonic function of the difference between the wage, w, and the income earned, λw.

From casual observation and many studies from different countries we know that T is often large. It depends upon the institutions in the DC and the difference between the culture, education, etc. of the immigrants and the natives. It may even be that several generations are needed.[8]

---

[7]   The Appendix uses $\rho_1 = 0.25$, 0.4, 0.8 and $\rho_2 = 0.6$, 0.7, 0.8 and a period of 15, 10, 0 years to get from the low to the high value.

[8]   The Appendix uses $T = 20$, 40, and 60 years. For the Nordic case, several estimates (see, e.g., Blume and Verner (2003)) suggest that $T = 60$ may be low, although it

Figure 1a:
Standard Case: Basic Curves

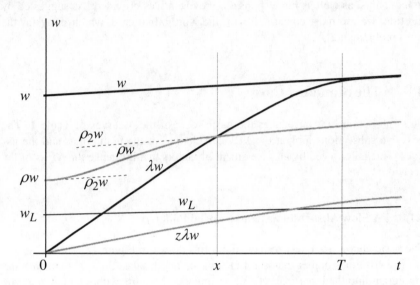

The slowness of absorption gives rise to two deviations from the ideal "potential" case: a production loss, L, and a social redistribution, R. The production loss, L, is the triangle between the w-line and the λ-curve—shown in Figure 1b below as the checkered area. The *NPV* is

$$(8) \qquad L = \int_0^T (1 - \lambda)we^{-rt}dt = \int_0^T we^{-rt}dt - \int_0^T \lambda we^{-rt}dt \approx \frac{q}{2}\frac{a}{r-a} = \frac{q}{2}NPV_I,$$

where q is the fraction of $NPV(w)$ between 0 and T. The derivation is shown in the Appendix. Table 2 shows some calculations of L in column (1).

The redistribution, R, from the natives to the immigrant is the area between the ρ-curve and the λ-curve from $t = 0$ to x. It is shown below in Figures 1b and 1c. The *NPV* is

$$(9) \qquad R = \int_0^x (\rho - \lambda)we^{-rt}dt = \alpha \int_0^x (\rho - \lambda)e^{-(r-a)t}dt \approx vL.$$

As R compensates for a part of L only, v must be a positive fraction, $0 < v < 1$. If the curves look as drawn in Figure 1c, $v \approx \frac{1}{3}$, but we shall meet

should be noted that this is an extrapolation, since none of the Nordic countries have had LDC immigration that long. Corresponding calculations for Sweden in Hansen and Lofstrom (2003) show a similar pattern.

Table 2:

The Decrease in the Two *NPVs* in Percent of NPV_I^*

	(1)	(2)	(3)	(4)	(5)
Absorption	Loss triangle L	Transfer $R = \frac{1}{3}L$		Transfer $R = \frac{2}{3}L$	
T (years)	For $r - a = 0.03$	ΔNPV_I	ΔNPV_{DC}	ΔNPV_I	ΔNPV_{DC}
20	26.4 percent	17.6 percent	15.4 percent	8.8 percent	24.2 percent
40	43.5 percent	29.0 percent	25.4 percent	14.5 percent	39.9 percent
60	55.5 percent	37.0 percent	32.4 percent	18.5 percent	50.9 percent

Note: $\Delta NPV_I = (L - R)\big/NPV_I^*$ and $\Delta NPV_{DC} = (0.25\,L + R)\big/NPV_I^*$; see equations (5) and (6). Section 3.2 showed that $NPV_{DC}^* \approx 30 \cdot NPV_I^*$. If $\Delta NPV_{DC} > 30$ percent, there is a net loss.

cases with larger v's below. Table 2 shows how the two *NPVs* change for three different duration λ-curves, and for $v = \frac{1}{3}$ and $\frac{2}{3}$. We shall refer to these calculations as we go along.

4.2   The NPV_I Calculation of the Immigrant

The immigrant's income gain from being accepted in DC is drawn as the dark-shaded NPV_I in Figure 1b—note that some NPV_I is checkered. The potential NPV_I^* is the area between the w-curve and the w_L-curve. The gray area of NPV_I is somewhat smaller, due to the loss triangle caused by the slowness of absorption. The exact formula is

(10) $NPV_I = \int_0^\infty (w - w_L)e^{-rt}dt - L + R = NPV_I^* - L + R$, as in (5).

The orders of magnitudes for the reduction in NPV_I relative to NPV_I^* are shown in columns (2) and (4) of Table 2. If R is only $\frac{1}{3}$ of the loss triangle, L, up to 40 percent of the potential may be lost for the immigrant, but with a more generous social compensation the loss falls.

4.3   The Calculation of the NPV_{DC} of the Natives

The corresponding calculation for the natives in the DC is shown in Figure 1c. The net surplus to the natives is assumed to be proportional to w, by the factor z, assumed to be 0.25.

Figure 1b:
Standard Case: NVP_I of Immigrants

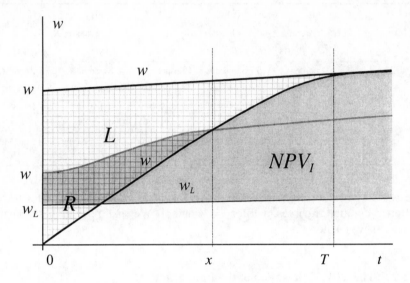

Figure 1c:
Standard Case: NPV_{DC} of Natives

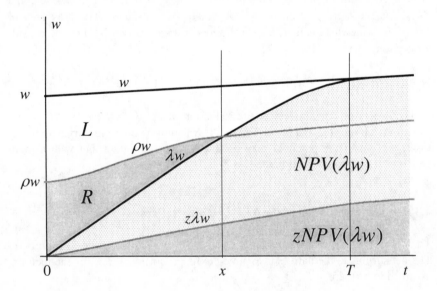

(11) $NPV_{DC} = z(NPV(w) - L) - R = NPV_{DC}^* - zL - R$, as in (6).

In Section 3.2 we found that NPV_{DC}^* was about 0.3 NPV_I^*, and from columns (3) and (5) in Table 2 we find that we have to deduct between 0.15 and 0.5 times NPV_I^*. Hence, with a fast absorption and stingy social benefits, NPV_{DC} is still positive, but with slow absorption and generous social support, NPV_{DC} becomes negative. In addition, most DCs pay reception and training costs to facilitate the absorption of the immigrant. They easily reach 0.05 NPV_I^*.

4.4   Three Effects on the λ-Curve: Selection, Incentive, and Other Regulation

Below, the λ-curve is taken to be roughly linear from 0 to T, but to have a slope that differs greatly between DCs. Three related factors affect their slopes:

(a) The *selection/self-selection* of the immigrants. Immigrants, depending on their type, will try harder to get into some countries than others, and countries also try to sort the immigrants they let in.
(b) The incentives generated by the package of institutions "offered" by the DC. Social policies are the key to the package, and they are therefore summarized in the ρ-curve.
(c) The labor market and business practices of the DC. Numerous studies have shown that firms in countries with deregulated labor markets and an aggressive profit-making culture tend to be more open in their hiring practices.

To analyze (a) consider two types of immigrants: type A has a high labor market value, and hence a fast absorption; type B has a low labor market value and a slow absorption. Type A immigrants will surely try to enter the countries where it is easiest to find work, and they will be less interested in the level of social support, while type B immigrants will have the reverse preferences. Hence, countries with long absorption times and generous support systems, but with a more distorted labor market and a negative attitude to hiring highly skilled foreign workers—as with the Nordic welfare states—generate adverse selection of immigrants. Also, some countries try hard to get the most economically valuable immigrants, while other countries—as the Nordic countries—try to choose the immigrants who have suffered most.

Figure 1d analyzes (b): the ρ-curve is determined by the organization of social security among the natives and the tradition for immigration into the country. The principle of nondiscrimination means that the rules for the natives apply to the immigrants as well. Figure 1d shows two ρ-curves and two λ-curves.

Figure 1d:

Incentives to Immigrants: Alternative Cases (Absorption: λ_f is *fast* and λ_s is *slow*. Social security: ρ_h is *high* and ρ_l is *low*.)

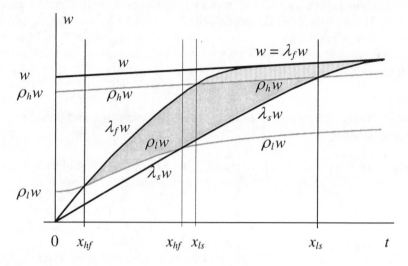

ρ_h is high, with no insurance part of the social payment, so the curve is parallel with and close to the w-line. ρ_l is low, with only a low basic social minimum payment, and the rest of social security is insurance based. The immigrant starts with no contribution to the insurance fund, and it only increases as time passes. The two λ-curves are also extreme: λ_f is fast, so that immigrants are quickly absorbed; λ_s is slow, so that immigrants are slowly absorbed. The four curves suggest three points:

(i) The differences between the curves have dramatic consequences for the intersection point x, and the three areas discussed in the two preceding sections. In particular the amount of social support received by the immigrant differs by about 20 times between the case in which the curves are (ρ_l, λ_f) and (ρ_h, λ_s). This will have large consequences for NPV_{DC}.

(ii) Incentives are different both for the immigrant worker and for the employer. The λ-curve is likely to be strongly influenced by the efforts and incentives of both parties. With high unemployment among natives, employers will be more reluctant to take on the possible added costs of hiring a nonnative, while the greater the social benefits the less hungry the worker is for employment. The λ_f-curve drawn here is a high-effort curve, and the λ_s-curve a low-effort curve. The two areas marked with gray show the differing incentives to making an effort. If the ρ-curve is the high alternative, then the immigrant's loss if he makes a small effort is the light gray area. However, if the ρ-curve is the low alternative, then the loss is the sum of the gray and the light gray areas—it is 5–6 times as much. Consequently, the logic of the curves is that if the ρ-curve moves upward, the economic pressures on the immigrant to find work decrease, and the λ-curve moves down, and vice versa. While there is no doubt that the two curves move in opposite directions, the magnitudes of the movements of the λ-curve are an empirical question.

(iii) Consider NPV_I in the (ρ_l, λ_f)-case and the (ρ_h, λ_s)-case. They are different as well, but less so. If incentive effects on λ are large, and they are combined with well-motivated employers, the seemingly brutal social policies may not cause large welfare losses. However, if incentive effects are small, as illustrated by comparing the (ρ_h, λ_s)-case and the (ρ_l, λ_s)-case, welfare losses are large for high discount rates.

The incentive effect and the adverse selection effect are difficult to distinguish in practice, and they reinforce each other.

5   A Society of Guest Workers: A Dubai-Like Country

It is difficult to find an ideal case of a rich country with a set of institutions allowing both sides to harvest all potential gains. The case closest to this "ideal" we have found is Dubai, although many of the Gulf states may also qualify.[9] Foreigners are invited in—by native sponsors for a fee—as guest workers on a contract that may be renewed if both parties agree. This appears to be widely done in Dubai, even though formal immigration is not allowed, and permanent residency is infrequently granted and then only for recognized services to the state. In Dubai the whole economy is based on the work of contract workers, as the society has 200,000 natives and roughly 800,000 guest workers.[10] In addition, immigrants pay taxes and sponsor fees that are a net gain to the natives.

---

[9]   Singapore, on a much smaller scale, could also be regarded as such a case.

[10]   The society appears to work rather well at present. However, it is dubious if the present setup is sustainable in the long run. Insofar as a proportionately huge foreign worker presence becomes a permanent feature of the economy, the workers could demand a more permanent relationship with associated civil rights.

5.1   The Basic Curves in the Dubai-Like Country

The guest worker has a contract from 0 to T_{C1}, subject to renewal. He works immediately after a brief introductory training period. Thus, λ rises steeply after that period, and then it becomes parallel to the w-line at the distance ts, which is the net tax expenditures and sponsor fees. The contract also contains all social security provided.

The $z\lambda$-curve used in calculating the gain to the natives is now easy to draw by shifting the λ-curve down as shown in Figure 2a. However, the two Figures 2b and 2c have to account for ts in a different way—it is a loss for the guest worker and a gain for the natives.

Dubai is a service economy in an oil-rich environment with a high capital-to-labor ratio,[11] and immigrants are thus necessary to operate that capital. We assume that z is much higher than in the case of Figure 1, and the natives also receive ts. However, the contract worker is likely to have greater remittances than an immigrant in the standard case. He not only remits to his family, but to himself, as it is likely that he has taken the contract precisely in order to make money for later use. Therefore, we still assume that $z + ts < 1$. Finally, the w_{IMM} is drawn higher than the w_L of the previous figures. Dubai makes contracts with people from many countries and tailors the contracts to the market.

Figure 2a:
Dubai-Like Case: Basic Curves

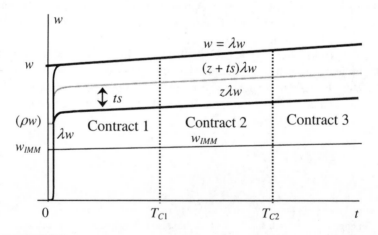

---

[11]   Dubai has much less oil per capita than its neighbors. Guest workers are allowed to bring family, but have to pay for their upkeep, including schools for the kids, health insurance, etc. Consequently, only the better paid workers are able to do so.

Figure 2b:
Dubai-Like Case: NPV_I of Guest Workers

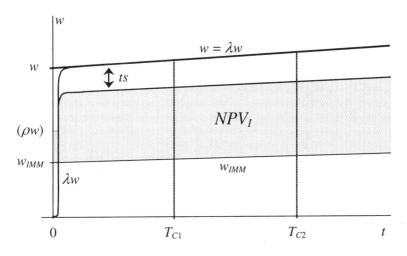

Figure 2c:
Dubai-Like Case: NPV_{Du} of Natives

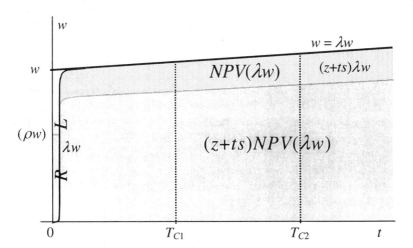

5.2   The Two *NPV* Calculations for the Dubai-Like Country

The gain for the guest worker is easy to calculate as done in Figure 2b. It is the area between the two wages for the duration of the contract, except for the small initial training period and *ts*—the net tax loss and the sponsor fee. Figure 2c calculates the gain of the natives. In this case, it is as large as (or even larger than) the one for the guest worker. It is the area below the $(z + ts)\lambda$ -curve minus a small correction for the training period.

In the Dubai-like case, contracts are market based and only made if mutually beneficial. It should be mentioned that the third part—the LDC from where the guest worker/immigrant comes—prefer that its surplus labor is temporary guest workers rather than permanent immigrants for two reasons: (a) it does not entail a permanent loss of human capital, and (b) it is the arrangement whereby remittances are maximized.

6   A Society of Immigrants: A U.S.-Like Country

The main characteristic of the U.S.-like country is that social security is based on an insurance principle and has a small basic payment only. Hence, immigrants have a strong incentive to find a job as quickly as possible, and it appears that the λ-curve rises relatively steeply. Immigrants with a foreign Ph.D. often start out driving a taxi or washing dishes in a restaurant to get a foothold in the labor market. Some do not succeed, but others do, and the second generation tends to be rather absorbed.[12]

Figure 3a shows the 4 curves in the U.S.-like case. The main difference is that the ρ starts low, but as time passes and the immigrant accumulates an insurance capital, ρ goes up. Also, the figure shows that thanks to the low ρ-curve from the outset, the incentive to find work is high, and the λ-curve rises relatively fast.

We shall not present what would have been Figures 3b and c, as they look like Figures 1b and c, though the loss, *L*, and the transfer, *R*, are both relatively small. Consequently, in the U.S.-like case immigration is an economic advantage for the natives. The United States is a country of immigration, which accounts for the way the curves look.

---

[12]   A large literature deals with immigration into the United States (see Borjas 1999, 2000).

Figure 3a:
U.S.-Like Case: Basic Curves

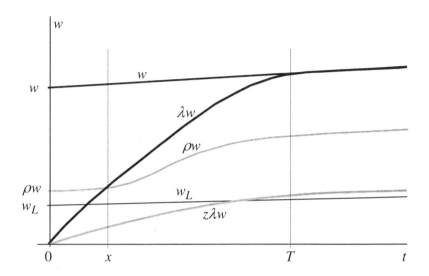

7   A Tax-Based Welfare State: A Nordic-Like Country

In a welfare state of the Nordic type, ρ is high and paid out of the general tax revenue, with hardly any insurance element included. Once the immigrant is accepted, he is, in principle, eligible for social benefits on a par with the natives. The benefits are made to equalize incomes, so they are highest at the low end of the income scale, where the immigrants are likely to be for some time.

The selection process for immigrants to the Nordic countries is adverse for two reasons: (1) immigrants are—in principle—only accepted for humanitarian reasons. It has even been said that the selection is now heavily biased towards those who have been heavily traumatized by torture and war. This is surely highly commendable from a humanitarian perspective, but it makes for slow labor market absorption in the absence of special actions, and for a high fiscal cost.

(2) The labor markets in the Nordic-like cases use the local language, which can only be acquired through a large investment on the part of the immigrant. Considerable time may thus have to elapse before the immigrant can get a job. During that time the immigrant is a client of the social system. The best educated immigrants will know English or French, but not Danish or Swedish. Hence,

they will try much harder to get into a country where they speak the language and are easy to absorb into the labor market and can get to work quickly.[13]

7.1   The Basic Curves in the Nordic-Like Country

Figure 4a shows the basic curves in the Nordic-like case. The curves have the worst possible shapes as regards the interests of the natives: the ρ-curve is unusually high, and the λ-curve is unusually low. As a result the loss triangle, L, is unusually large, and the share of the loss compensated for, v, is large too, so that the transfer, R, becomes very large as well.[14]

The ρ-curve is close to the w_N-curve for immigrants. Many calculations show that their income increases little—sometimes not at all—if they get a job of the type available to them.

The high ρ-curve is due to a high general level of support for the needy, both in general and with respect to special expenditures such as rent, kindergarten, etc. It is well known that immigrant groups quickly develop a solid knowledge of their entitlements, even when the social support legislation is complex. To partly offset the high path of the ρ-curve, some Nordic states have experimented with a special reduction in the subsidy for a new immigrant, ρ_{IN}. This is for a few years only and will be disregarded below.

7.2   The Two *NPV* Calculations for the Nordic-Like Country

Figure 4b shows an outcome that is better for the immigrant than in the standard case (Figure 1b) and the U.S. case as NPV_I is approximately 85 percent of NPV_I^*.

NPV_{DC} now looks as in Figure 4c. Both L and R are much larger than in the standard case, so it is obviously very difficult to reach positive values of NPV_{DC}. From all estimates, we know that $T = 60$ years is on the low side, and as shown in the Appendix, NPV_{DC} is always negative even for $T = 40$. With a high T, the Appendix shows that NPV_N becomes about -0.25 NPV_I^*. Finally, reception and training costs should be included. These costs are also unusually high, as they include language courses and the costs incurred by the state

---

[13]   Larger firms in the Nordic countries use English on a daily basis above a certain level, but it is a problem—especially for a family—to live in a Nordic country in the longer run without knowing the language, and for low-skill jobs a rather high proficiency in the language is essential.

[14]   In the Appendix the reader should look for the $T = 40$ and 60 case and the bottom line in the two sections where ρ is constant at 0.8.

Figure 4a:
Nordic-Like Case: Basic Curves

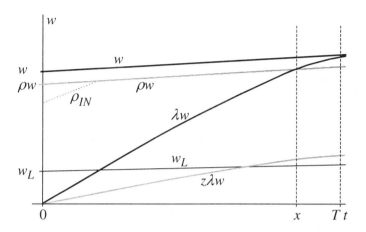

Figure 4b:
Nordic-Like Case: NPV_I of Immigrants

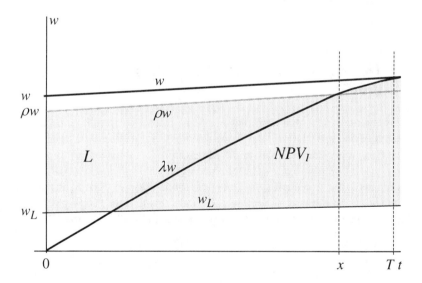

between the arrival of the prospective immigrant to the country and his actual admission. A ballpark estimate would be at least 0.05 NPV_I^*, increasing the total costs to –0.3 NPV_I^*.

Figure 4c:
Nordic-Like Case: NPV_N of Natives

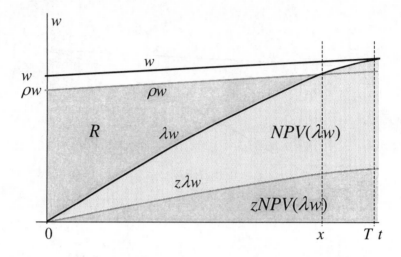

We thus conclude immigration is expensive for the natives in the Nordic-like case.[15]

8   The Noneconomic Variables: Additional Costs and Benefits

The introduction stated that the flows of people from poor to rich countries were directed by two gaps: the income gap and the civil rights gap. It further claimed that the two gaps generate flows in the same direction that are difficult to distinguish.

So far, we have considered the economic gap. We now turn to the noneconomic factors—introduced in Section 2.3—and show that the civil rights gap can be seen as a set of extra costs and benefits that should be added to the *NPV*s.

---

[15]   Several studies of the macro-orders of the magnitudes of these aspects have been made. See, e.g., Wadensjö and Orrje (1999) and Pedersen (2002) for Denmark, Storsletten (2003) for Sweden, and Roodenburg et al. (2003) for the Netherlands. They appear to be consistent with our assessments.

8.1   Noneconomic Costs and Benefits for the Immigrant: S, D

The assessment of the effect of the noneconomic variables affecting the immigrant is concentrated in two variables: S is the benefit for the immigrant of improved civil rights and political liberties, while D is the costs of being—for a (long) period—an outsider.

The standard measures for civil rights and political liberties are the two Gastil indices from Freedom House.[16] On the scale from 1 (all rights) to 7 (no rights), the average distance between the Western DCs and the LDCs is about 3 points. If the distance is weighted with the largest exporters and importers of immigrants, the gap grows to about 4. The typical immigrant hence has human rights in addition to economic reasons for trying to get into a DC.

In principle, the welfare gain of the permanent civil rights improvement can be calculated much as the gain in income, that is as the NPV of the improvement in civil rights, from $t = 0$ onwards. In money terms this is S.

However, the period from when the immigrant leaves his country until he is absorbed in the DC involves some mental hardship. We include only the loss from $t = 0$. The hardship is due to living in a country where he is an outsider. The shape of this loss is thus very much like the one of the loss, L. The NPV of the "mental" loss, in money terms, is termed D.

If the immigrant lived in fear for his life and freedom then surely $S > D$. Even if he was not actively repressed, we still think that $S - D > 0$. The administrative mechanisms sorting immigrants attempt to bias the selection toward immigrants who have been suppressed, and where consequently $S - D$ is large. The difference $S - D$ is, in principle, a noneconomic benefit that should be imputed and added to NPV_I. The noneconomic factors thus increase the gain of the immigrant:

$$(12) \quad NPVT_I = NPV_I + S - D > NPV_I,$$

where $NPVT_I$ is the total gain of the immigrant.

8.2   Noneconomic Costs for the Natives: Q

The assessment of the effect of the noneconomic variables affecting the natives appears to be dominated by one variable: S, the increase in social tensions. This effect will be subdivided in two items, (q1) and (q2), which are both "external-

---

[16] Paldam (2004) is a study of these indices. They are strongly correlated and show that the three big "enemies" of democratic rights and civil liberties are Communism, Islam, and poverty, where the latter explanation is the strongest.

ities" seen from the point of view of the immigrant and his employer, but as we consider all natives (and all other immigrants), all "externalities" are internalized. The point is that the DC has groups of nonabsorbed immigrants already and some social tensions between natives and immigrants.

(q1) An increase in the size of the immigrant group will marginally increase these tensions.

(q2) Also, the larger the immigrant groups, the easier it is to live separately from the natives,[17] making absorption more difficult. It lowers the λ-curve of everybody else.[18]

These effects are both costs. They may be imputed by the standard methods of cost benefit analysis, and be cumulated into a net present value Q that should be deducted form NPV_{DC}.

(13) $NPVT_{DC} = NPV_{DC} + Q < NPV_{DC}$,

where $NPVT_{DC}$ is the total gain of the natives.

In many cases, $NPVT_{DC}$ is small, and if Q is large $NPVT_{DC}$ may be negative. However, Q is high only if DC already has a (large) group of unabsorbed immigrants. If the immigrants already in DC are well absorbed, they may, in fact, help make absorption of new immigrants easier. These considerations may be used for developing a theory allowing us to calculate optimal rates of immigration.

8.3   Two Consequences: Administrative Controls and the Market for Agents

In money terms, immigration thus involves large amounts, and the amount is asymmetric. For the immigrant the amounts are substantial: $NPVT_I$ in the Nordic countries may be as much as 1 million dollars. For the natives in the Nordic-type countries, $NPVT_{DC}$ is either small or in some cases negative. This is both because adverse selection occurs and many incentives are wrong. While it could be argued that the resulting costs are the price that the Nordic-type countries

---

[17] This is a part of the dynamics of "ghettos" where nothing goes on in the language of the natives, making it impossible for the women to acquire that language, especially for the Muslim groups, who consider it important to shield women from the permissive secularized society of the natives.

[18] The two mechanisms also increase the problem of "second-generation" immigrants, who feel that they belong neither here nor there, and who are therefore more prone to crime or seek group identification in extreme politico/religious groups, thereby slowing down absorption even in the third generation.

must have decided to pay when they adopted their much publicized idealistic policy of helping refugees, there is an issue as to whether the costs were adequately anticipated.

This has created a situation in which the potential number of immigrants is huge, and led to a "panzer versus guns" process,[19] where most DCs keep raising administrative barriers to stop the flow, and the pressure generates a growing market for agents getting people through.

The administrative barriers are both international and national. They apply two criteria: humanitarian and economic. The decision is reached through a legal process based on the *legend* provided by the immigrant. The legends can only be checked by the DC bureaucrats to a limited degree. To check the legend they have to be able to investigate in the country the DC potentially accuses of persecuting innocent asylum seekers. It is obvious that in such cases decisions are based on a light burden of evidence, and consequently, it must have a large arbitrary element.

The agent market is partly legal and partly illegal. Legal agents are lawyers, NGOs, journalists, and politicians in the DCs helping immigrants for economic, humanitarian and political reasons. Some politicians and journalists specialize in running individual cases, etc.

Illegal agents perform two services: (i) they organize secret transport so that the immigrant turns up in the chosen DC without a legal exit from a country to which he can be sent back. (ii) They provide legends that tally to the rules of admission in the chosen DC. Most LDC immigrants come from countries with high levels of corruption (see Paldam 2002), with "bazaars" where many documents can be purchased.

In many DCs, laws increasingly criminalize and punish transport agents as "human traffickers"—the term sounds ominous, but it is difficult to convince most LDCs that this is a particularly immoral activity.[20] Nevertheless, these agents are becoming more ruthless and well organized.

It appears that the illegal agents often collect fees in the order of $5,000 to $10,000 from an immigrant—immigration is not for the poor in the LDCs. In addition, the legal process from when the immigrant enters the country until the decision is made, is likely to take half a year, over which period the immigrant loses, say, $\frac{1}{2}w_L$.

---

[19] The reader may remember that the technological history of war can be told as a competition between defensive "panzer" and aggressive "guns," where sometimes one was ahead and sometimes the other.

[20] The agents do not commit serious crimes in the LDC, and it appears that many countries do not consider "secret" transit to be a crime. The criminal part is thus only the end part in the DC.

The implication is that the immigrant may have invested a considerable sum in the attempt to obtain entry. Frequently, his family—that is, his extended family—has invested in him, so that the family can get a foothold in the DC. This investment is wasted if the application is rejected. Nonetheless, thanks to the large interests, the agents, the family networks, etc., some immigrants always manage to seep through the barriers.

The bureaucratization process, especially in the Nordic-type economies, is also inflicting an economic cost in hampering their ability to participate fully in the internationalization of business. The barriers discourage highly skilled personnel from the emerging countries from relocating to them, with the consequence that business is increasingly being moved away to several of these countries.

9   Conclusion: Unpalatable Choices

The introduction claimed that millions of people move from the LDCs to the DCs.

The analysis showed that while each immigrant getting through the barrier gets a very large premium—in *NPV* money terms maybe as much as a million dollars—most DCs get much less and in some cases may even incur a loss. In particular, this applies to the Nordic-type (tax-based) welfare system, and to those DCs characterized by high unemployment rates (over 10 percent) that already have large groups of unabsorbed immigrants.

The asymmetry of the advantage of the two parts has created the present panzer-gun-dynamics, where on the one side the DCs construct more and more impenetrable "panzer" in the form of barriers against the immigrants, while on the "gun side" the market for agents "shooting" people through the barriers is gradually increasing in size, sophistication, and ruthlessness. The simultaneous growth of the two sides appears to be a costly process that has led to all the welfare losses associated with dynamics of the growth of such illiberal practices.

The immediate reaction of the economist should obviously be that everything that can be done to decrease the economic advantage of the immigrant and increase the economic advantage of the natives will help reduce the pressures. However, it is morally and politically a difficult way to go.

Policies that decrease the economic advantage of immigrants have to be drastic to matter, and they would inevitably have the character of discrimination. Moreover, they would not sit well with an idealistic policy of refugee assistance. The problem for the Nordic-type economies is that a system meant for refugees is proving very attractive for nonrefugees. Perhaps a system could be made whereby immigrants had to pay a special tax—for a period—to earn the right to participate in the DC that has been built by the natives.

Policies increasing the economic advantage of the natives are potentially of two kinds: policies reducing payments from natives to immigrants, and policies increasing the speed of absorption. The latter can be done in three ways: by using the selection process, by pursuing positive discrimination for immigrants, and by freeing labor markets and promoting more flexible business practices.

Much more research and analysis is needed to develop policies that will effectively harness the potential benefit of the immigrant to the native population, especially in the context of rapid aging and its heavy social costs.

Appendix

Table: Simulations of *NPVs*

Social policy			T	NPV_I in percent of NPV_I^*					NPV_{DC} in percent of NPV_I^*				
Min ρ	Period	Max ρ		2 per-cent	3 per-cent	4 per-cent	5 per-cent	6 per-cent	2 per-cent	3 per-cent	4 per-cent	5 per-cent	6 per-cent
0.25	15	0.60		85.0	79.1	73.8	69.3	65.3	19.1	16.7	14.5	12.5	10.7
0.40	10	0.70	20	88.5	84.0	80.1	76.6	73.6	15.6	11.7	8.3	5.2	2.4
0.80	None	0.80		94.1	91.9	90.1	88.5	87.2	10.0	3.8	−1.7	−6.7	−11.2
0.25	15	0.60		76.6	69.1	63.2	58.6	54.9	10.4	5.2	1.1	−2.3	−5.1
0.40	10	0.70	40	82.3	76.8	72.5	69.1	66.4	4.6	−2.4	−8.1	−12.8	−16.6
0.80	None	0.80		89.8	87.0	85.0	83.6	82.5	−2.9	−12.6	−20.7	−27.3	−32.7
0.25	15	0.60	60	70.8	63.2	57.8	53.9	53.9	2.7	−3.9	−8.8	−12.5	−12.5
0.40	10	0.70		77.9	72.4	68.6	65.8	63.7	−4.4	−13.0	−19.5	−24.4	−28.0
0.80	None	0.80		86.9	84.1	82.5	81.5	80.9	−13.4	−24.8	−33.5	−40.1	−45.2

Assumptions (see also Table 1):

The "interest" rates 2 percent, ... , 6 percent are $(r - a)$, the rate of discount minus the growth rate of the real wage. With these "interest" rates, the NPV_I^* becomes 50, 33.3, 25, 20, and 16.7 times the DC wage rate, w, respectively. The λ-curve is linear, between $t = 0$ and $t = T$, where it becomes w and remains so. Social security (in percent of w) starts at Min ρ, and grows linearly during "period" to Max ρ. No reception and training costs are included.

The results to keep in mind are: (1) NPV_I is always positive and somewhere between 50 percent and 80 percent of the potential NPV_I^* (2) NPV_{DC} is small and easily becomes negative. The gray part of the table shows the negative section.

Derivation of L, equation (8):

$$\text{Let} \quad \lambda = \frac{t}{T} \times L = \int_0^T (1-\lambda) w e^{-rt} dt \, ,$$

$$L = \frac{1}{2} q NPVI^*, \quad \text{where} \quad q = \left(\frac{\alpha}{\alpha - \beta} \left(1 - \frac{1}{e^{(r-a)t}} \right) \right).$$

Derivation of R, equation (9):

$$R = \alpha \int_0^x (\rho - \lambda) \, e^{-(a-r)t} dtb = (\rho - \lambda) \left(\frac{\alpha}{\alpha - \beta} \left(1 - \frac{1}{e^{(r-a)x}} \right) \right) NPVI^* \approx vL \, .$$

Bibliography

Blume, K., and M. Verner (2003). Welfare Dependency among Danish Immigrants. Working Paper AKF. Seminar on Welfare Research, Nyborg Strand, December.

Borjas, G.J. (1999). *Heaven's Door. Immigration Policy and the American Economy.* Princeton: Princeton University Press.

Borjas, G.J. (ed.) (2000*). Issues in the Economics of Immigration.* National Bureau of Economic Research Conference Report. Chicago: University of Chicago Press.

Chand, S.K., and M. Paldam (2004). Immigration Policy and the Nordic Welfare States. Paper. Available at: http://www.econ.au.dk/vip_htm/mpaldam/Papers/Imm-Policy-4.pdf.

Epstein, G., and I.N. Gang (2006). Ethnic Networks and International Trade. This volume.

Hansen, J., and M. Lofstrom (2003). Immigrant Assimilation and Welfare Participation. *Journal of Human Resources* 38 (1): 74–98.

Hatton, T.J., and J.G. Williamson (2006). Refugees, Asylum Seekers, and Policy in Europe. This volume.

Paldam, M. (2002). The Cross-Country Pattern of Corruption: Economics, Culture and the Seesaw Dynamics. *European Journal of Political Economy* 18 (2): 215–220.

Paldam, M. (2004). The Big Pattern of Democracy. A Study of the Gastil Index. Working Paper available from the author. (Second version with V. Borooah under preparation).

Paldam, M., and G.T. Svendsen (2001). Missing Social Capital and the Transition in Eastern Europe. *Journal for Institutional Innovation, Development and Transition* 5: 21–33.

Pedersen, L.H. (2002). Befolkningsudvikling, integration og økonomisk politik. Dream Model Group, Copenhagen. Available at: http://www.dreammodel.dk.

Roodenburg, H., R. Euwals, and H.T. Rele (2003). Immigration and the Dutch Economy. CPB Netherlands Bureau for Economic Policy Analysis, Den Haag. Available at: http://www.cpb.nl.

Sinn, H.-W. (2003). EU Enlargement, Migration and the New Constitution. CES-ifo Conference Paper. Munich

Storsletten, K. (2003). Fiscal Implications of Immigration—A Net Present Value Calculation. *Scandinavian Journal of Economics* 105 (3): 487–506.

Wadensjö, E., and H. Orrie (2002). *Immigration and the Public Sector in Denmark.* Aarhus University Press: Aarhus.

Comment on Sheetal K. Chand and Martin Paldam

Holger Bonin

In the era of globalization, the model of the Nordic welfare states, which provide generous social amenities in exchange for high taxes, has come under pressure. It is disputed whether previous public transfer levels can be maintained when emerging low-tax and/or low-wage countries offer ample opportunities for investors of mobile capital. Against this background, mobility of labor has also become a matter of concern. The notion has developed that immigrants attracted by social redistribution are a burden for the host country and thus pose an additional threat to the welfare state. It appears that the new skepticism about the economic impact of immigration is a response to the relatively large immigration flows that have occurred over the last fifteen years. Figure 1 shows that net immigration into the Nordic countries has ranged above the long-term average since the fall of the iron curtain. Immigration rates now seem closer to those in traditional immigration countries like the United States. As a result, for example, the total population of foreign origin in Denmark more than tripled over the few years from 1987 to 2003. More importantly, the composition of immigrants has changed, as the share of refugees and asylum seekers from non-Western countries has risen substantially. Though Denmark tightened legal provisions in response to the historical peak of population growth from immigration in 1995, the country has still absorbed more asylum seekers per capita in recent years than, for example, Germany.

The paper presented by Martin Paldam provides a useful framework to rationalize potential gains and losses from immigration under different institutional settings. The key element is an account of the present value of production surpluses net of excess social subsidies accruing to the representative immigrant. Figure 2 illustrates the proposed model as it is used to perform numerical calculations of the immigration surplus in the host country. As a starting point, it is assumed that human capital is transferable between the sending and the receiving country and has a higher return in the latter. If the immigrant integrates, she eventually earns the host country wage, w^H, which is above the wage in the sending country, w^S. It is furthermore assumed that the wage absorption process is linear and starts at zero upon arrival.

Natives benefit from immigration if they can take the production surplus in excess of the immigrants' wage. This surplus is proportional to the current wage by assumption. An interpretation of this would be that natives own the capital employed by immigrants in production and receive a return according to the capital-labor ratio. The present value of the production surplus is the gross benefit of the host country from immigration.

Figure 1:

Net Immigration Rates to Denmark, Norway, and the United States, 1970–2003

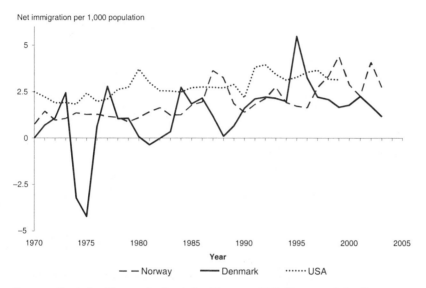

Source: Statistics Denmark, Statistics Norway, U.S. Bureau of the Census.

However, there may also be losses, if there is a social redistribution policy towards the poor. As drawn in Figure 2, the social policy consists of two components: a social transfer component and a wage-related insurance component. The latter implies that the transfer curve is a rising function of time spent in the host country. Excess transfers expire when wages exceed a certain income level guaranteed by social policy. The gap between the social subsidy and wage absorption curves before their intersection represents the gross loss for host country citizens due to immigration. Finally, the net benefit for the native population is the difference between the gross production surplus and excess social transfers during the start-up phase of immigrants.

Figure 2:

Net Surplus from Immigration for Native Population in the Chand–Paldam Model

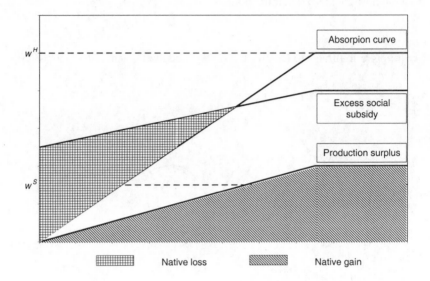

This framework is instructive, since it makes it easy to characterize different social and immigration policies, and their relation to the potential immigration surplus for the receiving country. In a guest-worker state admitting only immigrants with an approved labor contract, the absorption curve is naturally extremely steep. Consequently, the production surplus for natives is close to the maximum. The design of social policy is practically irrelevant, since immigrants would receive any excess social transfer only over a short period.

In a prototype immigration state, social transfers are predominantly organized through insurance. This means that the social redistribution curve has a positive slope but takes off from a low level. As a result, the loss for natives associated with social redistribution schemes is small even if the slope of the absorption curve is flatter than in a guest-worker state. However, as slower integration into the labor market reduces the present value of production surpluses extracted by the native population, the prediction of the model is that the net surplus from immigration in an immigration state is smaller than in a guest-worker state.

In a prototype Nordic welfare state, social policy prefers tax-financed transfers over insurance schemes, which leads to a rather flat social redistribution curve. This alleviating factor, however, is more than outweighed by the generous starting level of subsistence payments. Thus, natives' net surplus from immigration is smaller in a welfare state than in an immigration state, even if the speed of the absorption process is the same. Obviously, the difference becomes larger, if one assumes that the slope of the absorption curve is a negative function of the degree of social redistribution.

Does this mean that the surplus is negative under the conditions of a Nordic welfare state? The paper concludes that the answer to this question is "yes" on the basis of numerical simulations. However, it seems that the simulated framework is too stylized to derive valid approximations of the quantitative impact of immigration on host country welfare. Any action in the model is only described in reduced form, and takes place in a static environment. In particular, the model does not state exactly what factors determine the selection of immigrants into specific host countries, the speed of labor market absorption, the distribution of production surpluses among immigrants and natives, and the amount of social redistribution from natives to immigrants through the welfare state. The following remarks elaborate on these critical points.

In order to explain the supply of immigrants in the receiving country, the framework presented relies on the standard human capital model, where migration is an investment decision based on comparison of net present values of income in the sending and receiving countries. Immigrants move whenever the earnings differential net of mobility costs is positive. A deficiency of this approach is that it does not explain why a welfare state, in comparison to an immigration state, would systematically attract negatively selected immigrants who integrate into the labor market more slowly. An alternative model that explains this feature is the Roy model, applied to the case of international migration by Borjas (1987). In this model, the migration decision is based not only the means but also the variances of the income distributions in the sending and receiving countries. Immigrants are adversely selected if the income distribution is more compressed in the host country than in the country of origin. This means that an egalitarian welfare state may fail to attract immigrants from the top of the skill distribution who would have better (net) income opportunities in an immigration state with high income dispersion and low taxes. Similarly, a welfare state may only attract relatively risk-averse immigrants, since social policy provides better insurance against fluctuations in earnings than in an immigration state.

Allowing for immigrant self-selection of this type would be one important ingredient to explain absorption into the labor market within the proposed model. A second ingredient would be to make the link between the provisions for social redistribution and absorption explicit. The paper presupposes that immigrants deciding about labor supply and the acquisition of host-country-specific human capital respond to disincentives created by the welfare state. However, without a precise description of their optimization program, it is not obvious why immigrants, after controlling for self-selection effects, would act differently under the given institutional setting than natives. The resort to "cultural differences" in explaining that natives do not systematically exploit social redistribution through the welfare state, while immigrants do, does not seem entirely satisfactory in the context of an economic theory of immigration. More importantly, the reduced disincentive model cannot explain why immigrants are eventually absorbed. How do immigrants change their behavior over time spent in the host country if the disincentives that prevent them from acquiring human capital and supplying labor like natives are constant? Put differently, if a faster speed of labor market absorption, ceteris paribus, increases the present value gain of the individual immigrant from moving (as shown in the paper), why are the investments necessary for absorption made later rather than earlier?

One may counter these theoretical concerns with the empirical facts. There is indeed convincing evidence (see, for example, the analysis of Longva and Raaum (2003) for Norway) that earnings of immigrants from non-OECD countries assimilate slowly in the Nordic welfare states. Moreover, as shown by Rooth and Ekberg (2003) for Sweden, it appears that assimilation is not complete even among the second and third generation of immigrants. The authors' assumption that the absorption process of (a dynasty of) immigrants from less-developed countries may require as much as 60 years therefore does not seem out of range. However, empirically it does not seem likely that this absorption process would be linear, i.e., that even after 30 years, immigrants would reach only half of the average host country wage. Overall a concave absorption curve would look more plausible. At the micro level, even if immigrants do not acquire human capital specific to the host country, a concave wage function is the by-product of an age effect, provided that the labor market rewards experience normally. At the macro level, a concave absorption curve occurs if the probability of return migration is a convex function of the length of stay in the host country and economic failure is a reason for return. As the immigration surplus is expressed in terms of present value, the precise shape of the absorption process is crucial: a linear function, compared to a concave function, loads economic gains from immigration to the back where they are heavily discounted. Hence, at least a sensitivity test to check how the simulated immigration losses hinge on a particular, debatable functional form assumption seems in order.

Further clarification regarding the production surplus obtained by natives would also be valuable. In the paper, the surplus is a constant proportion of wages, approximated by the share of capital in production. This raises two questions. First, in keeping with this reasoning, the capital-labor ratio needs to be applied to gross wages as a measure of the marginal product of labor. The wage that appears in the model, however, is a net wage. It measures the salary net of standard net tax payments. The calculated surplus, therefore, may underestimate or overestimate the true gain of natives from immigration, depending on the direction in which the gross wage deviates from the model net wage. At the bottom end of the wage distribution, where immigrants are located during the absorption process, it appears more likely that gross wages are larger, which means that the calculated production surplus for natives is probably too small.

Second, to accurately gauge natives' production gains and losses, it seems essential to clarify the distribution of capital in the host country. As set up, the model framework implies that immigrant absorption does not relate to capital ownership. Immigrants enter the host country without capital and do not accumulate any during their stay. If they did, the production surplus for natives would decline while immigrants are absorbed. When the absorption process is completed, the period gain of natives from immigrants would be zero. In other words, the model does not capture the fundamental notion that immigration can only be beneficial for the receiving population if migrants are distinct from natives. The model, likewise, does not answer the related question as to what degree the relatively unskilled immigrant labor from a less-developed country could be a complement to or substitute for relatively high-skilled native labor. If it were a complement (substitute), the wage of the average native would go up (down) during the absorption phase of immigrants. Thus, the calculated surplus of the native population would be too small (large).

Overall, the paper may be too pessimistic about the burden on public budgets created by immigration. Conceptually, the framework seems to ignore that established immigrants partly refund social redistribution costs incurred after their arrival if the government has the ability to shift fiscal burdens over time.[1] The financing requirement associated with the integral of excess social benefits implies that the net tax rate of natives is higher than in the absence of immigration. As the government cannot systematically discriminate between immigrants and natives, the former bear the same elevated net tax rate after reaching the social breakeven. This effect, which reduces the immigration loss of natives, could be captured precisely only if a representation of the intertemporal budget constraint of the public sector were introduced into the model.

There are also empirical arguments supporting the view that the fiscal burden on natives due to excess transfer claims by immigrants is smaller than brought out in the simulations. First, social subsidy quotas of 60–80 percent as used in the numerical examples appear large even as a representation of the generous social policy in a Nordic welfare state. Considering that the denominator stands for the average income in the host country, transfer payments seem to reach far be-

---

[1]   This assumption is implicit in the model, considering that otherwise the slope of the net wage curve for immigrants would increase with the falling social transfers as immigrants assimilate.

yond the subsistence level. More critically, in order to be consistent with the model framework, the nominator must not represent actual transfers received by immigrants, but rather the resulting fiscal burden on natives, i.e., the part of the transfer bill that is not recovered by current tax or contribution payments by the immigrants. However, a nonnegligible share of paid transfers is usually recovered in the form of indirect tax payments, due to high consumption quotas among the recipients. Supposing that only 20 percent of transfer payments were recovered in this way, the subsidy quotas employed by the authors would imply that immigrants' gross earnings through transfers would basically equal natives' earnings, which seems unlikely.

Figure 3:
Differences in Welfare Participations, Native-Born Swedes and Migrants

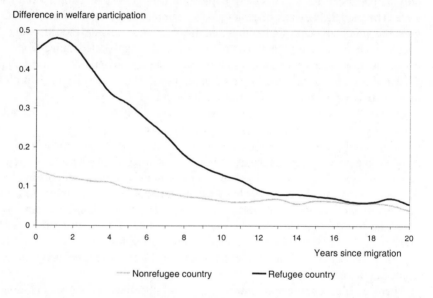

Furthermore, the combination of linear labor market absorption and linear excess subsidies implies that also the social benefits received by immigrants are a linear negative function of time spent in the host country. In contrast, empirical evidence suggests that the time path of welfare dependency is convex, which could reduce the fiscal burden in present value terms. Figure 3, using data reported by Hansen and Lofstrøm (2003), shows an example for Sweden. Although immigrants do not completely assimilate to the behavior of Swedish natives during the period under observation, most of the gap between the welfare participation rates of immigrants and natives is closed at an early stage. Convergence rates are high during the first ten years of the integration process before rapidly converging against zero. It is also interesting to note that over the long term, the difference between the welfare participation rates of immigrants and natives no longer depends on country of origin.

The observation made in this example that immigrants permanently exhibit slightly higher welfare dependency rates than natives does not allow the conclusion that they are by necessity net recipients of transfers over the time they spend in the host country. Detailed life-cycle calculations performed by generational accountants incorporating complete sets of taxes and transfers have revealed that immigrants may make large positive net tax payments even when they depend much more heavily on welfare and unemployment aid than natives (Collado et al. 2004; Bonin et al. 2000). The reason for this is that social transfers are small relative to overall public expenditure (or total public revenue) even in states with elaborate social policies. Of course, the outcome will be less positive in states that do not follow a tax-benefit principle with regard to old-age pensions, such as Denmark (Wadensjö and Gerdes 2004).

The measurement of fiscal gains from immigration through generational accounting points at another issue that is not fully clarified in the paper—the role of public nontransfer spending. Auerbach and Oreopoulos (2000) have demonstrated that simulated aggregate fiscal gains or losses from immigration hinge crucially on the assumptions made about the relation between immigration and per capita government consumption. The implicit assumption made in the current analysis is that all individuals consume the same amount of collective goods. Immigrants thus incur additional spending proportional to their population share. An alternative assumption would be that they trigger excess purchases, like spending on integration policies. Quantitatively, this effect is probably not important, however. Public investment in migrant-specific collective goods may be partly recovered through faster absorption, and will in general be small relative to the value of all collective goods purchased. On the other hand, one may assume the existence of economies of scale in government consumption: per capita public spending may decrease as population size increases. This aspect could be important given that the Nordic welfare states are aging societies facing substantial population decline. If downsizing the public infrastructure is costly, maintaining the size of the population through immigration could generate a positive fiscal externality on natives. To demonstrate the importance of this effect, it would be useful to simulate the model framework in a nonstationary demographic setting.

An even more important aspect of the demographic transition leading to higher old-age dependency is that current levels of social redistribution are not sustainable in the Nordic welfare states, as shown in studies collected by the

European Commission (1999). In order to pay off the existing intertemporal deficit in government budgets, it is necessary to lower transfer rates or increase tax rates in the future. In the given model framework, this type of nonstationary environment would immediately lead to a downward shift of the excess social subsidy curve, to the benefit of natives. Moreover, there is a tax base effect—if there is immigration, the amount required to close the intertemporal public budget deficit can be distributed among a larger population, which reduces the burden of adjustment per individual. The benefits for the native population from this effect can be large. In the German context, it has been found that it may account for as much as one half of natives' aggregate net present value fiscal gain from immigration (Bonin et al. 2000).

In sum, there are reasons to be optimistic that the recent wave of immigrants who cannot be integrated without difficulties into the Nordic welfare states is actually a smaller burden on the host countries than the authors seem to believe. In fact, one may interpret their simulation results in exactly this direction: though the given framework ignores several aspects that are to the advantage of natives, it requires quite extreme assumptions to generate substantial losses from immigration. Large negative results appear mostly under net of growth discount factors of four percent and more, which translate into uncommonly large real discount rates of six percent and more. Moreover, negative values mostly occur if excess transfer dependency of immigrants is not only large but also lasts long due to linear adjustment processes which seem unlikely from an empirical perspective. In any case, most of the simulated losses for the host country are not particularly large, especially when expressed as a per capita burden on natives. In this regard, the model results are similar to those Borjas (1995) has obtained by calibrating a supply and demand framework.

Even if one does not share the view that immigration into the welfare state is a serious threat, one would have to give an answer to the question how to handle immigration policy to the benefit of natives. After all, as the work by Chand and Paldam clearly demonstrates, the surplus of immigrants moving from a less developed to a more developed country is potentially very large, whereas the surplus for natives if not negative is potentially not so large. In other words, even in a situation where both parties gain, a potential conflict arises from the unequal distribution of profits between population groups that decision makers may have to address. My policy recommendations are threefold. First, for immigrants who have already entered into the country, it is crucial to ensure early integration into the labor market as soon as the expected probability of return migration is recognized as small. A requirement for this would be to remove the administrative hurdles to labor market participation. For example, immigrants with unsecured residence status like asylum seekers or refugees are often banned from the labor market, in order to deter disguised economic migration. But a forced delay of integration certainly does not increase the speed of integration later. Second, considering immigrants who do not seek permanent residency, it may be relatively easy to tax away part of their gain and redistribute it to natives. This could be done via an auction system that demands that employers pay a fee if they hire a temporary migrant.

This system does not work for permanent migrants, as their value in production is often spread over more than one employer. The third recommendation, therefore, is to make the potential production surplus generated by permanent migrants as large as possible. This target could be achieved by using rules for selecting those immigrants in a pool of applicants who are the best complements to natives. In other words, Nordic welfare states would preferably introduce discriminating point systems on the basis of observable characteristics, and thereby become more similar to immigration states. In order to avoid exploitation of generous social redistribution, immigrants admitted using the point system could be required to pass a waiting period before getting full access to the benefits provided by the welfare state. During this waiting period, it seems advisable to grant special reduced tax rates in order to compensate for incomplete social insurance against negative earnings shocks. This combination of low taxes and low social transfers would again mimic the institutional setting of a prototype immigration country. In this manner, the Nordic welfare states might also manage to attract positively self-selected immigrants who may currently be deterred by the prospect of a compressed earnings distribution.

Bibliography

Auerbach, A.J., and P. Oreopoulos (2000). The Fiscal Impact of US Immigration: A Generational Accounting Perspective. In H. Poterba (ed.), *Tax Policy and the Economy*. Cambridge: MIT Press.

Bonin, H., B. Raffelhüschen, and J. Walliser (2000). Can Immigration Alleviate the Demographic Burden? *Finanzarchiv* 57 (1): 1–21.

Borjas, G. (1987). Self-Selection and the Earnings of Immigrants. *American Economic Review* 77 (4): 531–553.

Borjas, G. (1995). The Economic Benefits from Immigration. *Journal of Economic Perspectives* 9 (2): 3–22.

Collado, M.D., I. Iturbe-Ormaetxe, and G. Valera (2004). Quantifying the Impact of Immigration on the Spanish Welfare State. *International Tax and Public Finance* 11 (3): 335–353.

European Commission (1999) (ed.). *Generational Accounting in Europe*. European Economy, No. 6. Brussels.

Hansen, J., and M. Lofstrøm (2003). Immigrant Assimilation and Welfare Participation. *Journal of Human Resources* 38 (1): 74–98.

Longva, P., and O. Raaum (2003). Earnings Assimilation of Immigrants in Norway—A Reappraisal. *Journal of Population of Economics* 16 (1): 177–193.

Rooth, D.-O., and J. Ekberg (2003). Unemployment and Earnings for Second Generation Immigrants in Sweden—Ethnic Background and Parent Composition. *Journal of Population Economics* 16 (4): 787–814.

Wadensjö, E., and C. Gerdes (2004). Immigrants and the Public Sector in Denmark and Germany. In M.L. Schultz-Nielsen, T. Tranæs, and K.F. Zimmermann (eds.), *Migrants, Work and the Welfare State*. Odense: University Press of Southern Denmark.

II.

Integrated Labor Markets and
Global Governance

Sanjay Jain, Devesh Kapur, and Sharun W. Mukand

Outsourcing and International Labor Mobility: A Political Economy Analysis

Abstract

We analyze the political economy of worker displacement, in an environment characterized by individual-specific uncertainty about the precise distributional consequences of a change in the economic environment. This change allows the displacement of high-paid Northern workers by low-paid, skilled Southern workers who were previously barred from competing with Northern workers, due to restrictions on the mobility of workers, and/or because of technological limits on the mobility of jobs. But while a policy of relative openness may be economically efficient, it may also have adverse distributional consequences. The dilemma faced by the Northern politician is that limiting the inflow of human capital might exacerbate the outflow of jobs, as firms "outsource" or "offshore" tasks that had previously been performed domestically. In particular, why does the outsourcing of service sector jobs have greater political resonance than the loss of manufacturing jobs? Why does the displacement of information technology workers seem to generate a disproportionate amount of political backlash? We trace the political implications of differences in the "vulnerability" of workers, and suggest that one answer may lie in the general-purpose nature of information technology, which allows greater mobility of workers and tasks across sectors than an improvement in sector-specific productivity.

Remark: For helpful comments and discussion, we are especially grateful to our discussant, Johannes Bröcker, and to Federico Foders, Tim Hatton, Henning Klodt, Wilhelm Kohler, Doug Nelson, Martin Paldam, and Horst Siebert. For assistance with the research, and in the preparation of this manuscript, we are grateful to Radu Tatucu and Anjali Salooja. Jain thanks the Bankard Fund for financial support. All views and remaining errors are those of the authors, and should not be attributed to their employers or anyone else.

1   Introduction

In February 2004 the U.S. Council of Economic Advisers (CEA) issued its annual Economic Report of the President. The CEA chair, Gregory Mankiw made what appeared to be a commonplace statement:

> Outsourcing is a growing phenomenon, but it's something that we should realize is probably a plus for the economy in the long run. We're very used to goods being produced abroad and being shipped here on ships or planes. What we are not used to is services being produced abroad and being sent here over the Internet or telephone wires. But does it matter from an economic standpoint whether values of items produced abroad come on planes and ships or over fiber-optic cables? Well, no, the economics is basically the same.[1]

The statement sparked an uproar. In an election year with anemic jobs growth, politicians and the media leapt at the statement.[2] Leaders of both parties, in the House and the Senate, called for apologies, resignations, and reversals of policy. Anti-outsourcing websites sprang up (some proclaiming that they had been constructed purely by American labor—presumably others had not been), denouncing the practice and the financial and emotional distress it was causing to American workers. The media fanned the flames. For instance, CNN anchor Lou Dobbs highlighted outsourcing in his shows and parlayed his concerns into a book, *Exporting America: Why corporate greed is shipping American jobs overseas*. Thus, outsourcing had become "America's national economic obsession."[3]

Many of these commentators, who responded to what they perceived as popular pressures against outsourcing, are also the same ones who oppose the expansion of quotas on the migration of skilled workers. We dub this the 'Northern politician's dilemma.' The dilemma is occasioned by technological change that makes possible the outsourcing of jobs to the South, and provides economic opportunities and a potential Pareto improvement for citizens of the North. However, our analysis below also suggests that it presents no easy choices for a politician in the North. He faces a choice between two policies, both of which boost national income and can be considered to be substitutes. The incumbent politi-

---

[1]   See the report in the *New York Times*, Feb 11, 2004, page A26.

[2]   Presidential candidate John Kerry accused CEOs of those firms that were outsourcing jobs overseas of being "Benedict Arnolds," referring to the notorious traitor in the American war of independence (Drezner 2004).

[3]   See Rattner (2004). It should be pointed out that the political backlash against outsourcing (or more accurately, "off-shoring") had been building for a while. See, for example, the *New York Times* op-ed piece co-authored by Sen. Charles Schumer of New York State (Schumer and Roberts 2004) and the discussion in Drezner (2004).

cian can allow a relaxation of immigration restrictions on the import of scarce (especially skilled) labor. Alternatively, he can watch jobs being outsourced to lower wage developing countries. These are politically difficult choices, since both are likely to engender a political backlash. From a politician's perspective, each poses a dilemma.

Consider a relaxation of immigration restrictions. Greater labor immigration into the country, especially of skilled workers, has the potential to boost national income.[4] In addition, another upside of inward migration is that it is more likely to result in the retention of jobs within the country. To see this especially sharply, consider an example where the production technology is such that each skilled labor job supports a relatively large nontraded sector. In such a case, even if immigration lowers wages, it boosts overall labor demand through an increase in demand for these ancillary support jobs. Of course, relaxation of immigration restrictions is likely to be politically costly. In the short run at least, an expansion in the labor supply can adversely impact the wages of incumbent workers with similar skills (Borjas 2003). Ethnic and cultural differences also typically make immigrants more "visible," which may amplify chauvinism among voters, and has been blamed for the rise of right-wing parties in several European countries.[5] Finally, unlike flows of capital, immigrants are also potential future voters.

The outsourcing of jobs, on the other hand, poses a slightly different problem. As with the immigration of human capital, outsourcing is likely to boost national income by increasing, for example, corporate profits and investment. Nevertheless, this beneficial impact is likely to be somewhat muffled by the degree to which outsourcing results in a loss of ancillary jobs. Hence, the impact of outsourcing on income distribution in the developed country is likely to be much more acute.

Nevertheless, it is surprising that there has been very little discussion of the key difference, from a political economy viewpoint, between job losses in the services versus manufacturing sector. In this paper, we focus precisely on this puzzle: why does the displacement of service sector workers, especially in information technology-intensive occupations, seem to generate a disproportionate amount of political backlash? Put another way, most economists would agree with Mankiw's assessment: "Outsourcing is just a new way of doing international trade."[6] Yet this statement was widely reviled by politicians from across

---

[4]   It is often argued that the gains, even to the developed countries, from liberalizing labor flows are far greater than those from further liberalizing the flow of goods, or even capital. See Rodrik (2002) for a discussion.

[5]   See, for example, O'Rourke and Sinnott (2003), Kapur (2003), Scheve and Slaughter (2001), and Mayda (2002).

[6]   See Drezner (2004).

the political spectrum. Why does the outsourcing of some jobs, most notably in information technology, have greater political resonance than that associated with the loss of manufacturing jobs?

In trying to understand this puzzle, we focus on a key feature of information technology: the fact that it is a general-purpose, rather than a sector-specific, technology. While we define this more specifically below, when we lay out our theoretical model, here we can simply define it loosely as something that is transferable across different sectors in ways that, for example, the manufacturing skills of assembly-line workers are not. One aspect of this general-purpose skill, which we focus on in this paper, is the size of the pool of "vulnerable" workers.[7] In our analysis below, we examine the political ramifications of the differing extent of "individual-specific uncertainty" engendered by different kinds of technological innovation.[8]

In the next section, we present a simple model to analyze the political economy of worker displacement, in an environment characterized by uncertainty about the precise distributional consequences of a change in the economic environment. This change allows the displacement of high-paid Northern workers by low-paid, skilled Southern workers who were previously barred from competing with Northern workers, due to restrictions on the mobility of workers, and/or because of technological limits on the mobility of jobs. We first describe the structure of the economy in the "preglobalization" world. Subsequently, we describe the impact of the technological revolution on workers, and the interaction of the (potential) displacement of workers with the politics of the responses to that potential displacement. In Section 3, we discuss the available evidence, and consider alternative explanations for the political backlash. Section 4 concludes with some observations about the importance of designing insurance and compensation mechanisms to ease the intersectoral transition of displaced workers.

2   The Benchmark Model

Consider a developed economy where technological changes now make it possible to outsource skilled labor jobs to developing countries with much lower wages. As will become clearer in our model below, this is analytically similar to a policy change that relaxes restrictions on the inward migration of skilled labor.

---

[7]   One widely cited study by Bardhan and Kroll (2003) suggested that the number of U.S. workers "vulnerable" to having their job outsourced was in the range of 14 million.

[8]   The seminal paper on the political importance of individual-specific uncertainty is Fernandez and Rodrik (1991), which we discuss in greater detail below.

Suppose that all citizen-workers own equal shares of each firm in the economy.[9] Then this technological change immediately creates potential "winners" out of the owners of firms, and of complementary inputs, on the one hand, and "losers" in the form of workers who may get displaced into a lower paying job. The distributional consequences of this outsourcing have the potential to create an unwanted political backlash for the incumbent government in the developed country. In what follows we construct a simple framework to capture the basic trade-offs faced by such a politician. While the politician does want to increase national income, this may entail the outsourcing of skilled labor jobs, and/or the immigration of skilled labor. Clearly, there is an adverse impact on the wages of those workers who lose their jobs. In other words, the increase in the size of the pie might simultaneously have adverse distributional consequences—much like all technological change.

2.1   Production and the Labor Force: The Predisplacement Economy

The developed economy is a small open economy that has $N + 1$ sectors, consisting of N "modern" sectors and one "traditional" sector. Since our focus is on the distributional consequences of technological change, we make the simplifying assumption that production is carried out solely by labor inputs. Extending our simple model to include the provision of capital, entrepreneurial skills, etc., would complicate the analysis without adding significantly to the insight. Accordingly, the traditional sector uses constant returns to scale technology and requires only low-skilled labor. The traditional sector's production function is given by $y_t = tL_t$, where L_t is the number of units of labor employed and t is the marginal product. Workers in this sector therefore earn the competitively determined wage $w_t = t$.

In contrast, each of the "modern" sectors uses two distinct kinds of labor input: labor that possesses sector-specific skills and labor that has general-purpose skills.[10] For simplicity, we assume that the skills of each worker are exogenously given and in fixed supply within the country (at the given wage). If sector-specific workers become unemployed for any reason, they can find employment only in the traditional sector, and not any of the other modern sectors. In contrast, workers with some general-purpose skills are mobile across the modern

---

[9]   In what follows, we use the terms "voters," "citizens," and "workers" interchangeably.

[10] It does no harm to think of the tasks being performed by these two types of workers as being, loosely, (sector-specific) manufacturing tasks, and (general-purpose) "information-processing" tasks.

sectors. The idea is that workers with an ability to work with (for example) computers, software, and information technology in general, have skills that can be carried relatively easily across the modern sectors. Thus, while a medical doctor may find it difficult to find a job that requires his medical skills outside the health care sector, an information technology expert may find it easier to migrate from the health care to the hotel services sector. Further, we make the analytical simplification that the production function displays perfect complementarity of workers. Accordingly, using L_i to denote the amount of the sector-specific factor, and L_{ig} for the number of "mobile" workers with general-purpose skills, the production function in sector i is given by

$$y_i = [\min\{a_i \cdot L_i, b_i \cdot L_{ig}\}]^\rho ,$$

where y_i denotes output, and setting $\rho < 1$ ensures that the production function has decreasing returns to scale. The constants a_i and b_i reflect the relative importance of the two types of labor in the production process. The total labor force in the modern sector is thus $\sum_i (L_i + L_{ig})$.

The technology of production is such that while workers in the modern sector are subject to moral hazard, workers in the traditional sector are not. This implies that in order to control the agency problem, the modern sector firm has to pay its workers a premium above the market-clearing wage.[11] Accordingly, there is a floor to the wages in the modern sector such that $w_g, w_i > w_t$, where w_g, w_i denote the equilibrium efficiency wage earned by general-purpose and sector-specific workers, respectively.[12]

Therefore, each firm hires workers with the aim of maximizing profits, where firm profits in sector i are given by

$$\pi_i = p_i[\min\{a_i \cdot L_i, b_i \cdot L_{ig}\}]^\rho - w_i L_i - w_g L_{ig} .$$

Observe that, since the firm will always combine the sector-specific and general-purpose workers in fixed proportions, the firm's maximization problem can be written as

$$\pi_i = \max p_i y_i - \frac{w_i}{a_i}(y_i)^{\frac{1}{\rho}} - \frac{w_g}{b_i}(y_i)^{\frac{1}{\rho}} .$$

---

[11]   This formulation is standard in the efficiency wage literature—see Shapiro and Stiglitz (1984) for a classic application. Accordingly, we assume that a worker who is found to shirk is thrown back into the labor force and suffers a lower wage. The wage premium is the minimum wage required to deter him from shirking.

[12]   Note that the intersectoral mobility of the general-purpose workers means that their wage will be the same across all sectors.

This gives the first-order condition with respect to output, y_i, that price will equal marginal cost:

$$p_i = \frac{w_i}{a_i}\frac{1}{\rho}y_i^{\frac{1}{\rho}-1} + \frac{w_g}{b_i}\frac{1}{\rho}y_i^{\frac{1}{\rho}-1} = (\frac{w_i}{a_i} + \frac{w_g}{b_i})\frac{1}{\rho}y_i^{\frac{1}{\rho}-1}.$$

Finally, we make the simplifying assumption that the number of firms, n_i, in each of the modern sectors is fixed, even though the incumbents may be making positive profits. Alternatively, one could assume the existence of fixed costs large enough that the incumbents just break even. Another alternative would be to posit the necessity of some "entrepreneurial capital" for starting up a firm, and the supply of this resource may be limited, at least over the period of analysis.

2.2   Production and the Labor Force: The Postdisplacement Economy

Suppose that a technological innovation makes it possible to have the work of a modern sector worker done by a (lower paid) worker in a foreign (developing) country. As mentioned above, an alternative would be to think of this possibility, of hiring a cheaper substitute, as arising from the new availability of (perhaps temporary) migrant workers.[13] The analytics of both these alternatives is qualitatively similar. Hence, although we model the comparative statics in terms of the outsourcing of jobs, it may be useful to keep in mind that the analysis of the new equilibrium arising from labor migration would be similar.

We contrast two kinds of "job losses": (a) what might be described as the "old outsourcing," in which there is a loss of manufacturing jobs, and (b) the outsourcing of information technology (service sector) jobs. In terms of our model, to facilitate the comparison of the political implications, we keep constant the number of jobs lost, of these two different kinds of job losses. In one case, the job losses are concentrated among sector-specific workers, while in the other, the job losses are concentrated among general-purpose workers.

Suppose there is a technological change that enables part of the production to be outsourced to a foreign (South) country. However, due to limited production capacity in the South, sector j firms still produce some units in the home country. Consider first a situation in which the job losses are solely confined to sector-

---

13   Further, these temporary migrants' wages are lower than those of the developed country workers. In terms of an efficiency wage model, the incentive constraints they face are determined by their (lower) reservation wage—if caught shirking, they will revert to their source (developing) country wage, and do not have recourse to the traditional sector wage, w_t, in the developed country.

specific workers. The cost function is otherwise unchanged, so that the new marginal cost function shifts down for part of its range, as shown in Figure 1.[14]

Figure 1:
Reduction in Marginal Cost

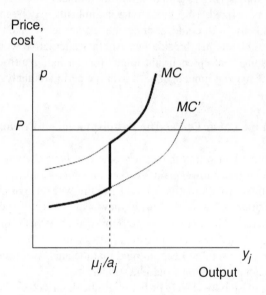

More formally, let μ_j denote the number of workers that each firm in the jth sector can hire more cheaply abroad, at a wage of $w'_j < w_j$. Further, suppose that $w'_j \leq w_t$. In other words, the output created by the displaced worker in the traditional sector is greater than the payment to the foreign factor of production. This can also be thought of as an "efficiency condition," which ensures that national income rises as a consequence of outsourcing. An alternative interpretation is to note that this is equivalent to assuming that $(w_t - w_j) + (w_j - w'_j) \geq 0$, i.e., that the wage loss of the displaced worker is exceeded by the increase in the profits of the outsourcing firm.

In that case, the total cost of producing y_j units in the jth sector, assuming that y_j exceeds the productive capacity of the foreign producers, is given by

---

[14]   The easiest way to see this is to consider a sector, j, in which $y_j = [a_j \cdot L_j]^\rho$. In other words, output is constrained solely by the employment of sector-specific workers, i.e., b_j can be thought of as effectively being equal to infinity.

$$C(\underline{y}_j) = (\frac{y_j^{\frac{1}{\rho}}}{a_j} - \mu_j) \cdot w_j + \mu_j \cdot w_j' + \frac{y_j^{\frac{1}{\rho}}}{b_j} \cdot w_g$$

$$= (\frac{y_j^{\frac{1}{\rho}}}{a_j}) w_j - \mu_j \cdot (w_j - w_j') + \frac{y_j^{\frac{1}{\rho}}}{b_j} \cdot w_g,$$

where the second term shows the cost savings accruing to the firm. The key point to note is that the marginal cost of producing the y_jth unit of output is unchanged, since the cost reductions come on the inframarginal units. Hence, each firm's optimal output is still determined by equalizing price to the (unchanged) marginal cost at its old output level. Of course, the fact that the cost of the inframarginal units has fallen, means that there is a windfall increase in each firm's profits. Hence, the "winners" from this outsourcing are sector j firms, and society at large, since the ownership of each firm is spread evenly across each citizen of the country. The potential losers are the displaced sector-specific workers. Since the total output of the jth sector is unchanged, and because the μ_j displaced workers are unable to bid down the wages of the other sector-specific workers,[15] they are forced to resort to employment in the traditional sector, at a lower wage of w_t.[16]

Next, consider a different form of outsourcing, in which job losses come from the outsourcing of the general-purpose workers' jobs. These workers, by the very nature of their skills, are mobile across sectors. Like the displaced sector-specific workers, one implication of the efficiency wage model is that the losses to these workers come from the reduction in employment (rather than in a decline in wages for all general-purpose workers). To sharpen the contrast with the loss of sector-specific jobs, suppose that the number of general-purpose jobs lost is the same as in the above case, viz., μ_j. Now, however, both the job losses, as well as the gains to employers, are spread across all sectors (albeit more thinly). As in the earlier case, the gains come from the fact that some of the (inframarginal) units become cheaper to produce using lower paid foreign general-purpose workers. The losers are, once again, those (general-purpose) workers whose reduction in earnings (to w_t from w_g) is greater than their gains from the increased firm profit.

---

[15] Due to the efficiency wage considerations alluded to above, they are unable to credibly promise to exert effort without a wage premium above the traditional sector wage.

[16] Suppose that, the loss in the wages of these particular workers exceeds their gains from the higher firm profits, so that overall, they emerge as losers from this policy. We derive an explicit condition for this below, in the next section.

2.3   The Political Economy of Worker Displacement

We can now compare the political economy of the two kinds of job losses. Recall that all citizen-workers own equal proportions of all the firms in the economy. Hence, for any given worker, there are two countervailing forces at work, in both the case when the job losses are sector-specific and when they are in the general-purpose skilled jobs. On the one hand, all workers gain from the higher firm profits that are realized as a consequence of the availability of lower cost modern-sector workers. On the other hand, those particular workers who are displaced by these newly available skilled workers, will turn to lower wage employment in the traditional sector.

Since workers within each type (sector-specific and general-purpose) are identical to other workers of their type, suppose that the displaced workers are picked randomly from the category of workers whose jobs are being outsourced. In that case, no worker in the affected sector can be certain *ex ante* that he will be a loser. However, the key point to note is that the number of *vulnerable* workers is greater when the layoffs occur in the general-purpose sector.

More formally, the number of workers who are potential losers, in the case when the labor displacement occurs among the sector-specific workers in the ith sector, is given by L_i. Although it is known *ex ante* that a majority of them may well turn out to be *ex post* "winners" from the process, it is straightforward to see that their *expected* payoff may be negative. The probability of being a loser is given by: μ_i/L_i. Using $\Delta\Pi$ to denote the increase in aggregate firm profits and L to denote the total number of the citizen-workers, the expected payoff of a representative sector-i-specific worker is given by

$$\frac{\mu_i}{L_i}(w_t - w_i) + \frac{\Delta\Pi}{L},$$

where the first term represents the expected wage loss in the event that the worker is displaced, and the second term represents the expected increase in firm profits that accrues to each worker in the economy. If the diffused general benefit, $\Delta\Pi/L$, is sufficiently small relative to the expected personal loss of wage from being displaced, $\mu_i(w_i - w_t)/L_i$, as seems likely, then the expression will be negative.[17]

---

[17]   A sufficient condition is that $(1/L) \cdot (w_i - w_i') \leq (1/L_i) \cdot (w_i - w_t)$. This can be seen by noting that $\Delta\Pi = \mu_i \cdot (w_i - w_i')$. Now, the efficiency condition guarantees that $(w_i - w_t) \leq (w_i - w_i')$. Hence the assumption is that $L_i \ll L$, i.e., that the employment share of the ith sector is relatively small.

By contrast, the number of workers who are potential losers, in the case when the labor displacement occurs among the general-purpose workers, is given by $\sum_j L_{jg}$. Again, although it is known that a large majority of them will turn out to be "winners" from the process, it is straightforward to see that their *expected* payoff may be negative. More formally, the probability of being a loser is given by $\mu_i / \sum_j L_{jg}$, and the expected payoff of a representative general-purpose worker is given by

$$\frac{\mu_i}{\Sigma_j L_{jg}} \cdot (w_t - w_g) + \frac{\Delta \Pi}{L}.$$

Once again, the terms represent, respectively, the loss of wage in the event that the worker is displaced and the gain from the general benefit of higher firm profits. If the diffused general benefit, $\Delta \Pi / L$, is sufficiently small relative to the expected personal loss of wage from being displaced, $\mu_i (w_g - w_t) / \sum_j L_{jg}$, as seems likely, then the expression will be negative. This is true even when the likelihood of being displaced, $\mu_i / \sum_j L_{jg}$, is relatively low.

The key point to note is that (so long as $\sum_j L_{jg}$ exceeds L_i) the political opposition to the adoption of the labor-displacing policy is likely to be much greater in the latter case than in the former. In terms of the model above, the opposition to this innovation will come from L_i workers in the case when the job losses are confined to the sector-specific workers in the ith sector, whereas all the $\sum_j L_{jg}$ general-purpose workers will be in opposition when the job displacements are diffused across a wider pool of workers.

Thus, even though the probability of being displaced, and the expected loss in wages, may be lower in the latter case, the number of *potential* losers is greater. This *individual-specific uncertainty* about the effect of potential outsourcing is the key to understanding why political resistance is likely to be greater in the latter case. The idea that individual-specific uncertainty can hinder the passage of even those reforms that voters know *ex ante* will lead to an increase in national income, and will benefit a majority of voters, is one that can be attributed to Fernandez and Rodrik (1991). Here, we apply that insight to suggest that even if one controls for the *number* of layoffs, the differences in the vulnerability of workers to these shocks might explain the very different political pressures generated in response.

For simplicity, here we have modeled workers as voting directly on policies. But the general idea can be easily embedded in a model in which voters choose representatives who decide policy, as in the widely used "representative democracy" framework (Besley and Coate 1997, 1998); Osborne and Slivinski (1996). Again, for simplicity we have also ignored the possibility of compensation of displaced workers. Of course, if winners could compensate losers without cost, then any "potentially Pareto-improving" policy (Besley and Coate 1997, 1998) would be adopted by voters. However, as Jain and Mukand (2003) have argued, redistributive compensation may be difficult to implement. Promises of compensation must be credible, but all voters know that once the winners have been realized, they face an *ex post* time-consistency problem, in that they will be reluctant to give up part of their gains. If there are a large number of realized winners, then the government's sensitivity to this reluctance is likely to be especially acute. Nevertheless, the compensation of displaced workers, for example, in the form of unemployment benefits, or retraining subsidies, is an important part of the policy debate, to which we turn next.

3   Discussion and Policy Implications

Traditionally, outsourcing has described the subcontracting of services from one company to another—an activity as old as the first firms. Today, the term has come to encompass the specific trend of importing services from low-cost providers located offshore—"offshoring." Why has this phenomenon caused so much anxiety in the world's richest, largest, and most powerful economy? In terms of its effects on employment, it appears at first glance to be no different from the automation that worried U.S. workers after the Second World War, after which America went on to enjoy a long period of prosperity. And outsourcing of manufacturing jobs has been going on for decades. Conceptually, there is little difference between relocating manufacturing production abroad and relocating services abroad. Both increase productivity and living standards, but of course both have distributional implications.

In contrast to trade in goods, which has exceeded GDP growth over the past half-century, the spurt in services trade has been more recent. In part, this is because most countries have only recently begun to liberalize their services sectors. However, the critical driver has been the revolution in information and communications technologies. The extent to which a wide range of business processes can be broken up into component parts, digitized, and dispatched to any corner of the globe, instantaneously and exceedingly cheaply, is having major repercussions for a range of jobs that were previously regarded as nontradable. The cost savings are often too large to ignore in an increasingly competitive economic environment. A recent widely cited report by the McKinsey Global Institute estimates a net cost reduction of 58 cents on every $1 "offshored" by firms, "even as they gain a better (or identical) level of service."[18] The competitive pressures to outsource operations overseas (e.g., software development and back office work, to take two prominent examples) can be easily imagined. But similar incentives exist in other, often more technologically sophisticated, service sectors too. For example, estimates of cost savings from outsourcing select engineering, information technology, and other support functions in the automobile component industry range up to nearly 50 percent, compared with performing the same functions in the United States. Similarly, the cost of developing a new drug, currently estimated at between $600 million and $900 million, can be cut by as much as $200 million if development work is outsourced to India.[19]

3.1   The Political Backlash

The political backlash, as discussed earlier, has been strong, with a number of legislative initiatives geared to protect jobs in the United States and Europe (particularly in the United Kingdom). In the United Kingdom, British Telecom's employee union initiated a series of one-day strikes in 2003 to resist the company decision to set up a call center in India and to force the High Court to intervene to stop it. In mid-October 2003, the House of Commons launched an inquiry into offshore outsourcing, to assess to "what extent, and why, jobs that were intended for the UK have been lost to the Indian sub-continent." In the United States, at the federal level, a flurry of bills like the "Job Protection Act" were introduced in 2003, designed to eliminate the tax incentives for offshore production and instead to provide tax incentives to produce in the United States. In January 2004, the U.S. Senate passed an amendment that would prevent private companies from using offshore workers in order to compete successfully against government workers on some contracts opened up to competition. (It applied only to the U.S. Treasury and the Department of Transportation.) Simultaneously many states got into the act as well and, over the period 2003–2004, approximately 37 states introduced (or were considering introducing) legislation

---

[18]   For details on the estimates cited in this paragraph, see McKinsey Global Institute (2003).

[19]   More recently, the sheer scope of the new outsourcing is captured by an interesting phenomenon. A number of news sources have reported that churches in the United States and Europe are "outsourcing" Holy Mass to parishes in Kerala in India where it is now known as the "Dollar Mass." (For a recent report, see Rai 2004.) Mass intentions—requests for services, such as thanksgiving and memorial masses for the dead—made in foreign dioceses are frequently outsourced to churches in Kerala. Prayers for the dead have been outsourced for decades but the number has increased recently.

aimed at eliminating public contracting to offshore destinations, and at restricting foreign-based call centers.[20]

3.2   How Large Is Worker Displacement?

The reasons for the political backlash against the outsourcing of services might seem obvious if job losses were quantitatively large, but it is not at all apparent that this is the case. A wealth of evidence suggests that job losses caused by outsourcing have been very small relative to job losses due to the normal business cycle and because of changes in technology. For example, a widely cited report by the U.S. Department of Labor found that layoffs caused by outsourcing comprised about 2 percent of the total layoffs in the first quarter of 2004.[21] Federal Reserve Chairman Alan Greenspan has described offshoring as part of the "creative destruction" that leads to higher living standards. Ben Bernanke, vice-chairman of the U.S. Federal Reserve, has argued that the quantitative impact of outsourcing on the U.S. labor market has been relatively small. Instead, he argues, the main reason for the weak U.S. labor market has been the "astonishing gains" in labor productivity in the past few years.[22] Further, when one considers that the United States is a net exporter of services, there is a strong argument that the net, rather than gross, effect on job creation may well be positive. The balance of trade in services reflects a trade surplus in high-value services, including financial, legal, engineering, and software development services, while many of the services imported by the United States are less sophisticated and, hence, less costly.

3.3   Alternative Explanations for the Political Backlash

The combination of election year politics with the weak macroeconomic situation perhaps made some political backlash against outsourcing inevitable. Nevertheless, the question is why, even in a presidential election year, the issue of a

---

[20]   John Kerry, then one of the Democratic presidential frontrunners, also called for a "right to know" law that would require all call centers to disclose their location.

[21]   Although the study examined only mass layoffs (of more than 50 workers) in large establishments (of 50 or more workers), the numbers were sufficiently small that there did not appear to be any indication of large-scale job relocations. For details, see Bureau of Labor Statistics (2004).

[22]   "Quantitatively, outsourcing abroad simply cannot account for much of the recent weakness in the U.S. labor market and does not appear likely to be an important restraint to further recovery in employment" (as quoted in Balls and Swann 2004).

relatively small number of job losses is so politically potent. While we have of-fered an explanation based on the uncertainty regarding winners and losers, we do not mean to suggest that this is the sole, or even the leading factor. Other al-ternative explanations include the idea that the political potency of the loss of white-collar, service-sector jobs is especially great. Implicit in that argument is that there is, in some sense, a "ladder" of jobs: as manufacturing jobs were off-shored, workers moved to service jobs. Hence, the insecurity created by the loss of service jobs becomes especially great.

Another reason for greater fears amongst IT workers is that, unlike their counterparts from the manufacturing industry, who under the Trade Adjustment Act get unemployment benefits as well as paid education for up to two years if they cannot get another job (as well as job-hunting services and expenses, assis-tance to pay health insurance, and retraining), IT workers who lose jobs due to offshoring are left without similar benefits. The law does not consider their out-put to be the equivalent of a manufactured product. Fiscally strapped govern-ments fearing the financial costs of such new entitlement benefits may prefer to instead turn to policies and legislation against offshoring.

These fears are magnified by other factors, such as the jobs' destination: per-haps if they were going to an OECD country, the fears would have been less. However, the destinations highlighted tend to be such developing countries as India, with a large pool of skilled English-speaking labor, and a growing invest-ment in higher education, particularly in engineering and in information tech-nologies. Second, unlike manufacturing, the wage disadvantages are not com-pensated by productivity disadvantages. India's service sector productivity is close to (and in some cases matches and exceeds) western levels. Finally, the shift is not just in commoditized work but also in highly skilled jobs. Indeed, the wage differential (after factoring in other costs) at a call center in India and an equivalent center in the United States is relatively modest. However, since the wage differential is much larger in high-skilled occupations, the economies of scale for higher value-added work like equity research, chartered accountancy, legal services, medical consultations, and publishing can be achieved at much lower levels.[23]

Finally, the rising fixed costs of granting retirement and medical benefits to new workers means that either the state provides greater social insurance or the privately rational course for firms will be to move offshore. This might explain why there is greater offshoring by Anglo-Saxon companies than by western European companies, where the state picks up a greater part of the overhead costs of firms.

---

[23] For a discussion of these issues, see Alden et al. (2004).

4   Conclusions

In this paper, we have attempted to set out some of the tradeoffs that politicians, and voters more generally face, in choosing between policies that may be economically beneficial in the aggregate, but that may have adverse distributional consequences. In order to focus on the tradeoff between labor mobility and outsourcing, we have constructed an extremely stylized model that abstracts from many important related issues.[24] Given the lack of hard data on the magnitude of the phenomenon, any rigorous assessment of its global impact will have to await the availability of better data. Yet, even in the absence of "hard numbers," the public debate that has been generated is in danger of obscuring the powerful technological and organizational changes driving this phenomenon. Few large companies are now prepared to discuss their outsourcing strategies in public. The lack of firm data has led some skeptics to question whether there is anything new about outsourcing beyond providing a fresh excuse for protectionism among populist politicians.

We have argued that one explanation for the greater political resonance of worker displacement in service sector jobs, whether as a consequence of offshoring or expanding labor migration for skilled workers, is precisely that the vulnerability of workers to those adverse distributional consequences may be greater. Thus, even though the economic benefits of expanded migration and outsourcing may be very large in the aggregate, so may the political costs. Hence, the development of compensatory, or insurance, mechanisms to soften the adverse shocks to workers may be especially necessary for the kinds of displacements that have been occasioned by advancements in general-purpose technologies such as information technology.

Bibliography

Alden, E., E. Luce, and K. Merchant (2004). The Logic Is Inescapable. *Financial Times*, Jan. 28, 2004: 19.

Balls, A., and C. Swann (2004). Fed's Bernanke Says Outsourcing Not Responsible for Weak U.S. Jobs Growth. *Financial Times*, March 31, 2004: 10.

---

[24] For example, in our model, the winners and losers from outsourcing are quite clear. More generally, however, a more nuanced analysis requires a full general equilibrium model, and the incorporation of the possibility of foreign direct investment as an alternative to outsourcing. See, for example, Kohler (2001, 2004).

Bardhan, A., and C. Kroll (2003). The New Wave of Outsourcing. Fisher Center Research Report 1103. Fisher Center for Real Estate and Urban Economics, University of California at Berkeley.

Besley, T., and S. Coate (1997). An Economic Model of Representative Democracy. *Quarterly Journal of Economics* 112 (1): 85–114.

Besley, T., and S. Coate (1998). Sources of Inefficiency in a Representative Democracy: A Dynamic Analysis. *American Economic Review* 88 (1): 139–156.

Borjas, G.J. (2003). The Labor Demand Curve *Is* Downward Sloping: Reexamining the Impact of Immigration on the Labor Market. *Quarterly Journal of Economics* 118 (4): 1335–1374.

Bureau of Labor Statistics (2004). Extended Mass Layoffs Associated with Domestic and Overseas Relocations, First Quarter 2004. Available at: http://stats.bls.gov/news.release/reloc.nr0.htm

Drezner, D.W. (2004). The Outsourcing Bogeyman. *Foreign Affairs* 83 (3): 22–34.

Fernandez, R., and D. Rodrik (1991). Resistance to Reform: Status Quo Bias in the Presence of Individual-Specific Uncertainty. *American Economic Review* 81 (5): 1146–1155.

Jain, S., and S.W. Mukand (2003). Redistributive Promises and the Adoption of Economic Reform. *American Economic Review* 93 (1): 256–264.

Kapur, D. (2003). Comments on Paper by K. O'Rourke and R. Sinnott, Migration Flows: Political Economy of Migration and the Empirical Challenges. Comments presented at ABCDE 2003, World Bank.

Kohler, W. (2001). A Specific-Factors View on Outsourcing. *North American Journal of Economics and Finance* 12 (2001): 31–53.

Kohler, W. (2004). International Outsourcing and Factor Prices with Multistage Production. *Economic Journal* 114 (March): C166–C185.

Mayda, A.M. (2002). Who Is against Immigration? A Cross-Country Investigation of Individual Attitudes toward Immigrants. Mimeo. Harvard University, Cambridge, Mass.

McKinsey Global Institute (2003). Offshoring: Is It a Win-Win Game? San Francisco. Available at: http://www.mckinsey.com/knowledge/mgi/rp/offshoring/perspective/.

O'Rourke, K., and R. Sinnott (2003). Migration Flows: Political Economy of Migration and the Empirical Challenges. Paper presented at ABCDE 2003, World Bank.

Osborne, M.J., and A. Slivinski (1996). A Model of Political Competition with Citizen-Candidates. *Quarterly Journal of Economics* 111 (1): 65–96.

Rai, S. (2004). Short on Priests, U.S. Catholics Outsource Prayers to Indian Clergy. *New York Times*, June 13, 2004: A15.

Rattner, S. (2004). Offshoring Should Be the Least of America's Worries. *Financial Times*, March 31, 2004: 15.

Rodrik, D. (2002). Final Remarks. In T. Boeri, G. Hanson, and B. McCormick (eds.), *Immigration Policy and the Welfare System*. New York: Oxford University Press.

Scheve, K., and M. Slaughter (2001). Labor Market and Individual Preferences over Immigration Policy. *Review of Economics and Statistics* 83 (1): 133–145.

Schumer, C., and P.C. Roberts, (2004). Second Thoughts on Free Trade. *New York Times*, January 6, 2004: A23.

Comment on Sanjay Jain, Devesh Kapur, and Sharun W. Mukand

Johannes Bröcker

This paper asks why the recent wave of job movements to low-wage foreign countries has provoked such a strong political backlash in the United States, stronger than the movement of manufacturing jobs that has been observed ever since the United States has been a part of the world market. The authors' answer is briefly this: even taking the case of an equal number of workers that lose their job in both industries, are more persons potentially threatened in the service industry. In other words, even with an equal number of those actually hurt ex post, there are more "vulnerables" ex ante in the service sector. Why? Because their qualifications are of a "general purpose" type, while those of manufacturing workers are "specific purpose" qualifications. If shoe production is supposed to relocate to Mexico, say, than only the small group of shoe producing workers is "vulnerable." If services are relocated to India, say, then the large group of IT workers is vulnerable and produces more unrest than the small group of shoe producers. This, as the authors claim, holds true even if the number of those eventually loosing their job is the same in both cases.

The argument is borrowed from Fernandez and Rodrik (1991), who pointed to the fact that a majority can prevent a reform from being enacted, even if it generates positive net benefits and a majority benefits ex post. This happens if (1) losers are randomly chosen from a subset of the society (the vulnerables) that is a majority, (2) actual losers are a minority, and (3) gains outweigh losses in expectation for the society as a whole, but not within the group of vulnerables.

Is the story plausible in the case at hand? I have four questions to raise: *First*, why is the number of vulnerables larger, if general purpose rather than specific purpose workers are affected? For each specific purpose, the number of workers who have the respective abilities may be small. But adding up workers for all different specific purposes, the number may become large. In manufacturing, dismissed workers are not just randomly drawn from the employees in one industry, but it may hit many different industries. Which number is larger is an empirical issue. I would have liked to see more on this empirical issue in the paper.

Second, if we accept there are more vulnerable general purpose than specific purpose workers, then the expected loss for members of the former group is smaller than that of the latter. The degree of political unrest should be somehow related to the size of the expected loss, and should not just depend on whether there is some loss to be expected or not. Hence, there may be more people potentially affected in the general purpose group, but each one is affected less, thus having less incentive to raise his voice.

Third, to some extent, any kind of resistance and political backlash is subject to a collective action dilemma. Raising the voice in the name of the vulnerables is a collective good for this group. The larger the group of people sharing a given expected loss, the more difficult it is to overcome the free-riding problem. Would not the Olson (1965) prediction just be the opposite of what the authors claim, that is, more resistance from a group sharing a given total expected loss among a few rather than among many?

A *fourth* question, closely related to the latter two, is whether the Fernandez and Rodrik (1991) argument really applies to the issue at hand. Their argument is made in the context of majority voting. For the argument to have a bearing on the case at hand, it is vital that the group of vulnerables is not just large, but a majority that can effectively prevent a political decision by their vote. This is in fact questionable with regard to general purpose workers. It is also vital for the argument that only the sign of the expected effect for an individual is important, not its size. Voting against reform incurs no cost; hence, a majority votes against reform, even if the expected loss per voter is tiny. What we are trying to explain in the case at hand, however, is not voting, but political backlash, that is, activity of any kind in the public. This sort of activity is facing a free-rider problem. It is less likely if the expected loss per individual is small.

I conclude by suggesting a competing explanation along classical lines. The backlash may be strongest among information technology workers because the U.S. economy faces the strongest decline in relative prices in those sectors using this type of labor most intensively. This is because other countries, in particular English-speaking ones, are gaining a comparative advantage in these sectors for three reasons: (1) The respective technologies and complementary factors (computers) become readily and cheaply available all over the world. (2) Other countries have accumulated human capital in this labor market segment. (3) Transportation cost—in this case, communication cost—is declining dramatically. Hence, the simple explanation is that this is what is always observed in the case of a changing pattern of comparative advantage. Factor owners facing a loss according to the Stolper–Samuelson proposition raise their voice.

This may also explain why a similar concern about job losses in IT services is not observed in Europe, possibly with the exception of the United Kingdom and Ireland. Instead, a similar debate is going on with respect to manufacturing. The German chancellor recently accused German entrepreneurs and managers of lacking patriotism, as they plan to move jobs to Central and Eastern Europe. Traditional manufacturing is currently losing its comparative advantage in Western Europe because trade barriers (tariff barriers a decade ago, nontariff barriers now) are falling, endowment with human capital in the respective segment is large in some Central and Eastern European countries, and capital needed as a complementary factor is flowing in rapidly.

Summarizing this argument, I come back to Mankiw's statement cited in the introduction (p. 188) of the present paper: whether it is manufacturing or services, "... the economics is basically the same."

Bibliography

Fernandez, R., and D. Rodrik (1991). Resistance to Reform: Status quo Bias in the Presence of Individual-Specific Uncertainty. *American Economic Review* 81 (5): 1146–1155.

Olson, M., Jr. (1965). *The Logic of Collective Action*. Cambridge, Mass.: Harvard University Press.

Stefania Pasquetti

Do We Need an International Regime for Migration?

Abstract:

The extent of labour migration is overwhelming and cross-border flows of people have been constantly growing during the past decades, so that in 2000 there were 175 million international migrants. Nowadays, more and more countries are involved with migration, either as origin, destination or transit countries, or all of these simultaneously. Migration is an international phenomenon that requires multilateral, rather than unilateral, action among all concerned states. The European Union is developing a unique regional model with respect to mobility of EU citizens working and residing in another EU member state, as well as with respect to immigration and asylum policies, including a new approach to integration of third-country citizens. This paper will focus mainly on the achievements of the EU migration policy on legal migration and on cooperation with the countries of origin. This paper will also try to explain why the Commission is convinced that a more efficient management of legal migration flows, in particular labour migration, is necessary and cannot be done exclusively at national level, but requires a coordinated strategy and common rules. It will also analyse the reasons why the development of an EU legal migration policy has so far been so limited, and try to discuss the future of such policies at the end of the five-year Tampere agenda.

1   Introduction

The extent of labour migration is overwhelming. Cross-border flows of people have been growing constantly during the past decades, so that in 2000 there were 175 million international migrants, of which 86 million (including refugees) were migrant workers.[1] The latter are often joined by their families and they may

---

Remark: The views expressed in this paper are my own views and do not necessarily represent those of the European Commission.

1   ILO report for the 92nd session of the International Labour Conference (2004) "Towards a Fair Deal for Migrant Workers in the Global Economy".

or may not be legally residing in the country of work. Economic differences between developed and developing countries/regions, globalization, trade, cheaper and easier travel, political problems and instability in the countries of origin, and ageing population in the developed countries are among the main reasons for this increase in labour mobility.

Labour migration is becoming increasingly complex, since its shape and dynamics have varied substantially over time. One of the main changes is the growing weight of immigration within the developing world, even though the traditional movement South–North is still very important. Furthermore, in the past it was mainly unskilled workers who migrated. Currently, migrant workers range from unskilled women working as domestics to highly skilled workers and specialists. Trafficking of human beings for labour and sexual exploitation is widespread. A growing number of migrants are in vulnerable situations, and not only because of irregular status, and many face different levels of discrimination. The social upheavals that migration produces in both sending and receiving countries can be far-reaching and destabilizing. Furthermore, many countries, including EU countries, have tightened their immigration legislation, thus reducing the possibility of legal admission for work reasons. As a consequence, since the 1970s we have mixed flows of immigrants who use asylum as a way of legally entering the European Union, thus abusing the system.

Migration is, by its very nature, an international phenomenon that needs a coordinated response. More and more countries are involved now with migration, either as origin, destination or transit countries, or all of these simultaneously. This requires multilateral, rather than unilateral, action among all concerned countries.

Since War World II, there have been various attempts to regulate migration flows and/or to establish common rules, mainly regarding migrants' rights, at the bilateral, regional and multilateral level.

International regulation has been taking the form of conventions drafted by international organizations, such as the two ILO conventions on migrant labour[2] and the UN Convention on the Rights of All Migrant Workers and Their Families of 1990. While the ILO conventions are based on a minimum standards approach to international regulation of migrant labour, the UN Convention adopts a human rights, nondiscriminatory approach: migrant workers must be treated in a nondiscriminatory way regardless of nationality. The ILO conventions are criticized because they are widely perceived as being limited in comparison with the current labour migration issues; the UN convention is, on the contrary, farreaching on the rights it recognizes for migrant workers and it is not too well accepted by the receiving countries also because it recognizes an extensive set of

---

[2]   Convention No. 97 of 1949 and Convention No. 143 of 1975.

rights for all migrants, including illegal migrants. Both the ILO and UN conventions have been ratified only by a limited number of countries, mainly sending countries. Another attempt to manage a specific kind of labour migration has been made with the GATS mode 4 (movement of natural persons supplying services), but this framework is still in development and, moreover, GATS commitments are only binding vis-à-vis GATS nationals.

At the regional level there have been two main experiences so far, the North American Free Trade Association (NAFTA) agreement and the European Union system.

While the primary objective of the NAFTA is the facilitation of trade between the three states concerned (Canada, Mexico and the United States), it also contains extensive articles about the entry of business persons into the respective states. It does not, however, cover any other kind of mobility for migrant work.

As to the European Union, it is developing a unique regional model with respect to the mobility of EU citizens working and residing in another EU member state and also with respect to immigration and asylum policies. It has also established principles and concluded agreements to promote better management of migration. All this may provide some inspiration for other countries and regions of the world, even if it has to be recalled that this is the result of an almost 50-year-old process of growing integration in all areas.

2   The European Model: Free Movement of Persons Who Are EU Citizens

As a preliminary observation, it is important to keep in mind that within the European Union there are two different regimes for migrant workers: a first more complete set of migration rights which applies almost exclusively to EU citizens (called "EU migrants" for the purposes of this paper) and a second one, still in development, which relates to non-EU citizens (which is properly defined as the "EU migration policy"). In this section, I will deal only with the free movement of EU citizens within the territory of the European Union, which is indeed the most liberal "migration" system developed by sovereign countries at regional level.

Freedom of movement of workers of EU nationality within the territory of the European Union is one of the four fundamental "freedoms" on which the EC Treaty is based. Mobility of labour within the European Union is one of the means by which a worker is guaranteed the possibility of improving his living and working conditions and promoting his social advancement. Initially, freedom of movement in the European Union was essentially directed towards economically active persons and their families. Today, the right of free movement within EU territory is also granted to other categories of EU citizens such as students, pensioners and also a residual category of "other" EU citizens. Whilst all EU citizens have a basic right to free movement, the scope of this right may differ, including the conditions under which they can exercise it.

Article 39 of the EC Treaty states that

1.   Freedom of movement for workers shall be secured within the Community.
2.   Such freedom of movement shall entail the abolition of any discrimination based on nationality between workers of the Member States as regards employment, remuneration and other conditions of work and employment.
3.   It shall entail the right, subject to limitations justified on grounds of public policy, public security or public health:
      (a) to accept offers of employment actually made;
      (b) to move freely within the territory of Member States for this purpose;
      (c) to stay in a Member State for the purpose of employment in accordance with the provisions governing the employment of nationals of that State laid down by law, regulation or administrative action;
      (d) to remain in the territory of a Member State after having been employed in that State, subject to conditions which shall be embodied in implementing regulations to be drawn up by the Commission.
4.   The provisions of this article shall not apply to employment in the public service.

In Article 39(4), the treaty provides for a specific exception, which must be interpreted restrictively: member states' authorities are allowed to restrict to their own nationals only those posts in which the exercise of public authority and the responsibility for safeguarding the general interest of the state is involved.

These basic rights have been fleshed out in secondary legislation: Regulation 1612/68 amplifies EU migrant workers' rights as regards eligibility for employment, equality of treatment and protection of workers' families, whereas Directive 68/360 fleshes out the abolition of restrictions on movement and residence of workers and their families.

The most elemental rights to which an EU migrant worker is entitled under EU law can be summarized as follows: (a) eligibility for employment: the right to obtain access to the labour market of another EU member state; (b) residence rights: the right to take up residence in the host member state; (c) family reunification: the right to be joined by family members, regardless of their nationality; (d) the right to equal treatment (i.e., the right to be treated as a national of the host state) in all employment related matters; (e) the right to equal treatment as regards other social and tax advantages to which workers or residents who have the nationality of the host state are entitled; (f) the right to equal treatment as regards social security benefits and entitlement to the rules on coordination of social security systems under EU law. Social security is obviously a key issue for persons exercising their right to free movement. Under Article 42 of the EC Treaty,[3] the Council is charged with enacting measures in the field of social security "necessary to provide freedom of movement for workers". This was accouplished by regulations 1408/71 and 574/72 on the coordination of social security schemes. The primary purpose of this legislation is to ensure that EU migrant workers are entitled to equal treatment in the host member state and do not lose their entitlement to social security benefits if they exercise their right to free movement. Accordingly, none of the social security contributions should be lost by virtue of the exercise of free movement, and the EU migrant worker is normally covered by the social security system of the member state in which he or she works.

The right of the EU migrant worker to live with his or her spouse, children and parents is extended to these family members "irrespective of their nationality". These third-country family members have the right to enter and reside in the country of residence of the worker. The spouse and children have free access to employment in that country. The children have access to general education and vocational training under the same conditions as the nationals of that country.

Migrant workers who possess the nationality of one of the EEA member states (25 EU states plus 3 EFTA states) are entitled to the full panoply of migration rights set out above when they settle in a EEA country, subject to the restrictions set out in the 2004 Treaty of Accession.

As concerns EU migrant workers from the new member states, a transitional regime is in place now. In fact, as a result of the accession negotiations between the EU-15 and the 10 new member states, temporary derogations to the principle of freedom of movement of workers may apply across the EU for a period of maximum 7 years.

As a result, the introduction of a part of the EU acquis on free movement of workers across the enlarged European Union will be delayed. The arrangements are complex, and include safeguard and reciprocity provisions. The restrictions can only be applied to migrant workers, and not to any other categories of EU citizens. Further, the restrictions can only apply to the obtaining of access to the

---

3   "The Council shall ... adopt such measures in the field of social security as are necessary to provide freedom of movement for workers; to this end, it shall make arrangements to secure for migrant workers and their dependants:

(a) aggregation, for the purpose of acquiring and retaining the right to benefit and of calculating the amount of benefit, of all periods taken into account under the laws of the several countries;
(b) payment of benefits to persons resident in the territories of Member States."

labour market, and can only limit the eligibility for employment in a particular member state. Once a worker has obtained access to the labour market of a particular member state, EU law on equality of treatment as regards remuneration, other employment related matters and access to social and tax advantages applies. Further, there are no transitional arrangements for the application of the EU acquis on the coordination of social security schemes.

3   Why Develop an EU Common Migration Policy?

In recent years migration has become a major theme on the international agenda and it can be expected that its size, impact and complexity will rise over the coming years. As already stressed, migration is, by its very nature, an international phenomenon that needs a coordinated response. Given the growth of the young adult population in many third countries, and economic and social differences, as well as political instability, migratory pressure is unlikely to fall in the foreseeable future. In the European Union, migration policies of one country inevitably affect the other member states. Another common characteristic is demographic ageing. For the above reasons, the Commission is convinced of the need for a coordinated approach, which should cover all the different aspects of migration.

In an overall economic and social context characterized by a number of skill and labour shortages, competition for the highly skilled in a globalized economy and accelerating demographic ageing, immigration is taking on a new profile in the European Union. Since immigration is caused by "pull" as well as "push" factors, it is therefore important to relate it to the employment situation and the profile of future labour market needs. More sustained immigration flows will be increasingly likely and necessary and it is important to anticipate these changes.

The EU member states have a long tradition of immigration, which, on the whole, has contributed positively to economic growth and labour market adaptability, although its shapes and dynamics have varied substantially across countries and over time. The total number[4] of third-country nationals living in the 15 member states in 2001 was estimated to be 14.3 million, the equivalent of 3.8 per cent of the total population. Looking at the 25 member states, the total number of nonnationals in 2001 was estimated to be around 15 million, which is the equivalent of 5.0 per cent of the total population. Belgium, Germany and Austria have sizeable nonnational populations (around 9 per cent). Next come Greece

---

[4]   For the data quoted in this section, see Communication from the Commission on Immigration, Integration and Employment (COM(2003)336 final) and First Annual Report on Migration and Integration (COM(2004)508 final).

and Sweden with, respectively, about 7.0 per cent and 5.5 per cent. Luxembourg and Latvia are unusual cases, with nonnationals accounting for just over one-third and one-fourth of the population, respectively. It should be noted that differences between countries in terms of nonnational populations partly reflect differences in national legislation on the acquisition of citizenship. Among the non-nationals, around one-third are citizens of another EU-25 member state and the remaining two-thirds (9 million people) are third-country nationals.[5] In 2001 the largest group of third-country nationals living in the European Union was Turkish citizens (around 2.4 million, of which two million in Germany).

During the 1990s, positive net migration became the largest component of population change in most member states, fluctuating around a total for the European Union of 850,000 net international migrants (including returning EU citizens) per annum by the end of the decade. To illustrate the contribution of migration to sustaining employment growth, the number of people employed in the EU-15 between 1997 and 2002 increased by about 12 million, 2.5 million of which were third-country nationals. While their share in total employment amounted to 3.6 per cent in 2002, third-country nationals contributed to employment growth by 22 per cent.

The period also witnessed a broadening and diversification in the typology of migrants, of the patterns of flows and of the mix of sending and receiving countries. Changes affecting asylum seekers resulted in peak numbers of applications in 1992 and 1997, largely as a result of the wars in former Yugoslavia and of armed conflicts around the world. In addition, former countries of emigration (southern member states and Ireland; more recently the new member states) became—or are becoming—countries of immigration.

The ageing and declining population in Europe and its impact on the European economy are of crucial importance when considering immigration policy for the longer term. Even if the Lisbon targets set for employment are met by 2010, and assuming no increase in net migration, an overall decline in employment could be expected after 2010 as a result of demographic change. According to the latest estimates, the fall in the number of employed people between 2010 and 2030 would be in the order of 20 million workers for the EU-25 (from 303 million now to 280 million by 2030). At the same time, the number of older people will rise from 71 million to 110 million. Germany is one of the member states which, along with several of the Mediterranean countries, will be most severely affected by these changes. Germany, with a very low birth rate, will have one of the highest numbers of older people and the lowest proportion of those of working age by 2030. Labour and skills shortages, already noticeable in a num-

---

5   Belgium and Luxembourg are the only countries where other EU-25 nationals outnumber third-country nationals.

ber of sectors, will tend to increase in the whole European Union. From an economic point of view, this decline in employment will impact negatively on economic growth. To compensate for this decline and achieve sustained economic growth, the EU economy would require a drastic increase in productivity. However, it is questionable whether such an increase will occur and could actually compensate for the foreseen decline in employment.

Against this background, the Commission believes that more sustained immigration flows are likely and necessary. It is of course not claiming that immigration can fully compensate for the impact of demographic ageing on the labour market; nevertheless, it does need to be part of the package of responses. First of all, the European Union must first tap into its existing human resources, including third-country nationals already residing here (also second and third generations). In Europe, the working age population would already have begun to shrink in some member states had it not been for the inflow of immigrants.[6]

Given the above, Europe must be capable of managing present migration flows, must take the necessary steps to promote a better integration of migrants present on its territory and must prepare for future immigration in an effective and responsible way. All this cannot be done exclusively at the national level, but requires a coordinated strategy and common rules.

4   The Legal Base for the Common Policy on Migration and the Tampere Council

The real competences of the European Union in the field of migration date back to only five years ago, with the entry into force of the Amsterdam Treaty on 1 May 1999 and the adoption of the Tampere European Council's conclusions in October of the same year.

With the Amsterdam Treaty, the European Union acquired competence as regards a series of actions in justice and home affairs, including legal and illegal immigration, with the aim "to establish progressively an area of freedom, security and justice".[7] Moreover, Amsterdam has opened up the possibility of not

---

6   The recent increase in immigration into Ireland seems to have contributed to the sustained growth performance in this country, where it followed a change in the regime of employment permits to ease labour shortages.

7   Title IV, Article 61 of the EC Treaty:

"In order to establish progressively an area of freedom, security and justice, the Council shall adopt:

(a) within a period of five years after the entry into force of the Treaty of Amsterdam, measures aimed at ensuring the free movement of persons in accordance with Article

only having a real immigration policy within the borders of the European Union, but also of developing an external action towards third-countries and international organizations in this area, since asylum and immigration are now under community competence, even though not exclusively.

Focused on the progressive establishment of an area of freedom, security and justice, the European Council of Tampere gave the same importance to this process that was previously given to establishing the Single Market. The heads of state and government therefore asked the Commission to elaborate a plan of action for the following 5 years.

The European Union is thus committed to developing a common policy on immigration and asylum with a view to ensuring more effective management of migration flows to the European Union. This common policy is based on a number of principles agreed to in Tampere:

- A *comprehensive approach to the management of migration flows*, which acknowledges the necessity of developing measures to deal simultaneously with all the different aspects of migration and which tries to find a balance between humanitarian and economic admission. This was emphasized by the European Council in Seville in June 2002, when it underlined the need for a balanced approach to migration management which combines measures on legal immigration and integration hand in hand with reinforcing action to combat illegal immigration and strengthening respect for the rights of asylum seekers and refugees;
- *Fair treatment for third-country nationals*, aiming to give them comparable rights and obligations to those of nationals of the member state in which they live. The need to strengthen integration policies has been stressed on a number of occasions by the Council, and the Thessaloniki European Council, in June 2003, adopted a number of important conclusions on the integration of migrants;

14, in conjunction with directly related flanking measures with respect to external border controls, asylum and immigration, in accordance with the provisions of Article 62(2) and (3) and Article 63(1)(a) and (2)(a), and measures to prevent and combat crime in accordance with the provisions of Article 31(e) of the Treaty on European Union;

(b) other measures in the fields of asylum, immigration and safeguarding the rights of nationals of third countries, in accordance with the provisions of Article 63;

(c) measures in the field of judicial cooperation in civil matters as provided for in Article 65;

(d) appropriate measures to encourage and strengthen administrative cooperation, as provided for in Article 66;

(e) measures in the field of police and judicial cooperation in criminal matters aimed at a high level of security by preventing and combating crime within the Union in accordance with the provisions of the Treaty on European Union."

- The development of *partnerships with countries of origin* and transit, including policies of co-development, as an important element in migration management strategies;
- *A separate common policy for asylum* which fully respects the terms of the Geneva Convention and member states' obligations under international treaties and which should lead to a common asylum procedure and a uniform status, valid throughout the European Union, for those granted asylum.

The EU policies include, therefore, action on the whole range of aspects of the migration phenomenon: legal migration, including the admission of labour migrants, illegal migration, integration of migrants, cooperation with third-countries, and asylum policy. In this paper, focus will be put mainly on international labour migration and international cooperation and dialogue.

5   The Need for Better Management of Migration at the Global Level

As underlined above, the Tampere conclusions called for a comprehensive approach to migration, addressing political, human rights and development issues in countries of origin and transit. This was based on the recognition that no migration or asylum policy can be fully effective without cooperation with the countries from which people come. This approach was reinforced in June 2002 by the Conclusions of the Seville European Council (§ 26–39): "It is crucial for the European Union and its member states that migration flows should be managed in accordance with the law, in cooperation with the countries of origin and transit of such flows", and further stated in Thessaloniki.

Improved dialogue with third countries is a major element of EU migration policy to facilitate orderly migration flows, to fight illegal immigration more effectively, to develop new policies to manage labour migration and to mitigate the negative effects of migration on the countries of origin.

The EU activities in this area were supported during three years (2001–2004) by a specific budget line for cooperation with third countries in the area of asylum and migration (for a total of €42 million). A new programme of cooperation with third countries, adopted in March 2004 and called AENEAS, will be launched this year with a total budget of €250 million over the next 5 years (2004–2008). The programme will cover all dimensions of migration, including legal and labour migration from, within or between third countries.

Migration issues have been progressively gaining higher priority in EU relationships with third countries. In December 2002, a Commission communication[8] examined the interaction between migration and relationships with third countries and set out a strategy for reinforcing the dialogue, which should focus not only on illegal immigration but also on channels for legal immigration in exchange for reinforced cooperation in preventing illegal migration. The dialogue resulted in a number of concrete activities related to various aspects of migration, including legal and labour migration, especially with the Mediterranean countries, the Balkan States, Russia and Ukraine.

Moreover, the European Union is now entitled to sign readmission agreements with third countries. Mandates have been given to the Commission to negotiate readmission agreements with 11 countries,[9] but only three agreements have been concluded so far (Macao, Hong Kong and Sri Lanka) and one has been initialled (Albania). Such negotiations are of course quite difficult and do require time.

Finally, the Commission now has the obligation to include a migration clause in any international general agreement to be signed with third countries and/or regional entities. This clause deals with all dimensions of migration, including legal and labour migration. In this context, this clause has been included in the Cotonou Agreement and in an agreement with the Andean Pact, while others are currently being negotiated (an agreement with Mercosur, for example).

6   The Development of a Common Policy on Legal Immigration

The Commission is progressively developing a set of rules covering immigration and asylum in which the rights of the legally resident third-country nationals are clearly stated and incremental in respect of the length of stay. According to Article 63 of the EC Treaty, the European Community has the competence to adopt measures on the entry and stay of third-country nationals, as well as on measures defining the rights and conditions under which nationals of third countries who are legally resident in a member state may reside in other member states. Two directives have been adopted so far in this area (on family reunification and on the status of long-term residents, both of which are not yet applicable), while another two should be adopted by the Council by the end of the year (on the admission of students and on the admission of researchers).

---

[8]   Communication from the Commission on Integrating Migration Issues in the EU's Relations with Third Countries (COM(2002)703 final).

[9]   Morocco, Turkey, China, Russia, Albania, Pakistan, Ukraine, Macao, Hong Kong, Sri Lanka and Algeria.

There are several reasons why only this legislation has been adopted so far. First of all, the decision-making procedure requires unanimity amongst the member states in the Council: such a condition has often limited the scope and the ambitions of the Commission's proposals. Secondly, the issues to be dealt with are extremely sensitive and governments must take into account public perceptions. Finally, this is a new policy area, so there is the added difficulty of harmonizing very different national legislations and administrative practices, especially because the Commission's interlocutors are the Ministries of the Interior, whose primary concern is to defend the integrity of the national territory. Working together and agreeing on common standards and procedures is not an easy task.

As a preliminary remark, it is important to recall that there continue to be two different regimes within the European Union for migrant workers, a first more complete set of migration rights which applies almost exclusively to EU citizens (see Section 2) and a second one, still in development, which relates to non-EU citizens. However, EU directives on issues such as occupational health and safety or working conditions are in principle applicable to all workers, irrespective of their nationality. The same goes for most of the articles of the European Charter on Fundamental Rights and for the EU antidiscrimination legislation.

As a second point, it is important to stress that the Commission does not intend to determine volumes of admission, which remain the strict competence of the member states,[10] nor to create a right to immigration (except in the case of family reunification): the intention is to establish at the European level the rights of the different categories of migrants and to define rules and procedures for the admission of third-country migrants.

The Directive on Long-Term Residents[11] aims to determine the terms for conferring and withdrawing long-term resident status, as well as the conditions of residence of third-country nationals in member states different from the one which conferred to them the long-term resident status. There are therefore two different rights, even though linked to one another: on one side, the right to be granted long-term resident status if the person has been legally and continuously residing in a member state for five years and, on the other, the possibility (provided that certain conditions are fulfilled) to move and settle with his/her family in a second member state for study, work or other purposes. This last possibility is in no way comparable to the right to free movement enjoyed by EU citizens.

---

[10]   The draft treaty establishing a Constitution for Europe does exclude it explicitly in Art. III-168, § 5: "This article shall not affect the right of Member States to determine volumes of admission of third-country nationals coming from third countries to their territory in order to seek work, whether employed or self-employed".

[11]   Council Directive 2003/109/EC, to be transposed into national law by 23 January 2006.

Nevertheless, taking into account the shortages in skills and labour existing in most member states, this conditioned right to move into the European Union for third-country long-term residents could be positive for the economies of both countries concerned and could compensate at least partially for the limited mobility of the EU citizens.

Apart from mobility, the directive ensures equal treatment of long-term residents with nationals as regards access to employment and self-employed activities, and conditions of employment and working conditions, including conditions for dismissal and remuneration; education and training, including studying grants; recognition of professional diplomas and other qualifications; social security, social assistance and social protection; tax benefits; access to goods and services available to the public, including housing; freedom of association and affiliation; free access to the territory of the member state of residence.

The Directive on Family Reunification[12] is also an essential instrument for the successful integration of third-country nationals, including refugees, since it determines the basic harmonized conditions for exercising the right to family reunification and for granting family members access to employment and self-employed activities, education and vocational training.

Furthermore, since 1 June 2003, any third-country national and his or her family members legally residing in a member state can rely upon the coordination provisions regarding social security when moving within the EU/EEA territory.

Political agreement was reached in March 2004 on a proposal for a directive on the admission of students and volunteers,[13] while a proposal for a directive on facilitating the admission of third-country researchers[14] is currently being negotiated in the Council. For both third-country students and researchers, the proposals foresee a certain right to mobility, in order to be able to pursue their studies/research in another EU member state. Furthermore, for students, the final text foresees the possibility of being employed or exercising a self-employed economic activity within a maximum number of hours per week or days per month to be established by the member state.

The only sector in which an agreement in the Council has not been reached so far concerns the proposal for a directive on the conditions of entry and residence by third-country nationals for the purpose of paid employment and self-employed economic activities.[15] The Commission considered that regulation of admission of economic migrants is a cornerstone of any immigration policy and

---

[12] Council Directive 2003/86/EC, to be transposed into national law by 3 October 2005.

[13] COM(2002)548.

[14] COM(2004)178 final.

[15] COM(2001)386 final.

that the development of a coherent common policy needs to address this issue at the EU level, since decisions to admit economic migrants into one member state do actually affect other member states (the right to travel within the Schengen area; the right to deliver services in other member states; the right to move to other member states once long-term residence status has been acquired under Directive 2003/109/EC; the impact of the admission of third-country workers on the EU labour market). Moreover, a comparative study of national practices[16] has shown that even though the rules on admission of third-country nationals to work in the European Union differ from member state to member state, there are several key similarities.

As to the specificities of this proposal for a directive, it was the first nonsectoral one put forward in this field, as it intended to establish a common framework for the admission of economic migrants to an EU member state, both for self-employment and for paid employment, including seasonal and transfrontier third-country workers, intracorporate transferees, trainees and youth exchange/au pair. The proposal for a directive was based on the idea that a third-country national could be admitted for paid employment in an EU member state if it could be demonstrated ("economic needs test", i.e., the situation of the domestic labour market) that a specific job vacancy could not be filled by an EU citizen or by third-country nationals who already enjoyed a consolidated access to the EU labour market. Three optional procedures were also proposed, in order to give more flexibility to the general system and provide for specific needs in specific regions, sectors, etc. A similar logic, but based on the evaluation of a detailed business plan, was proposed for self-employment.

It must be noted that the proposal took into account the commitments of the European Union and its member states under GATS mode-4 in two ways: on the one hand, a general clause clarified that commitments under international law (such as GATS) would prevail over the provisions of the directive. On the other, some substantive GATS commitments, in particular the commitment not to require the "economic needs test" for allowing the temporary presence (for a maximum of five years) of intracorporate transferees, were explicitly included.

Finally, the draft directive also laid down a set of basic rights, including equal treatment with EU citizens at least as concerns working conditions, including dismissal and remuneration; access to vocational training; recognition of diplomas, certificates and other qualifications issued by a competent authority; social security, including health care; access to goods and services and the supply of goods and services made available to the public, including public housing; trade

---

16   European Commission, *Admission of Third-Country Nationals for Paid Employment or Self Employed Activity*, Office for Official Publications of the European Communities, 2001 (ISBN 92-849-1689-0).

union rights. Enjoyment of some rights (in particular public housing) could be made conditional on a certain minimum stay, in line with the principle that the rights of third-country nationals should be incremental with their length of stay. No "right to mobility" between member states was foreseen.

With the aim of relaunching the issue of economic migration, the Commission is drafting a green book (which should be published in autumn 2004), in which different alternative options for a new proposal for a directive will be outlined for an open discussion.

7   The Future of European Policies on Legal Migration

Considerable work has been done in the development of a common migration policy since the Tampere European Council in October 1999, even through much still remains to be done. The Commission believes that a sound basis has been laid on which the European Union can build in the next five-year period. The European Union is in fact developing a unique regional model with respect to the mobility of EU citizens working and residing in another EU member state and also with respect to immigration and asylum policies, including a new approach to integration of third-country citizens. This model is founded on the establishment of rights and obligations for the legally residing third-country nationals and on a shared acceptance of the fundamental norms and values of a democratic society. It calls for adjustment by both immigrants and society. Moreover, the European Union has also established principles and concluded bilateral agreements to promote better management of migration. This model will have to be further developed and the debate is open on what the priorities and guidelines for future action will be.

In fact, since the new Commission will be appointed during the summer and will take office on 1 November 2004, the new Commissioner, who will soon succeed Mr Vitorino as Commissioner for Justice and Home Affairs, will have to define his political agenda for the mandate. Furthermore, we are getting close to the end of the Tampere mandate and new political guidelines will have to be agreed on by the European Council of 5 November 2004. The Commission will actively contribute to this debate, and present a number of policy papers containing concrete proposals in all sectors of justice and home affairs. Regarding immigration, the Commission is convinced that the economic and demographic evolution of our continent will require the adoption of a strategy based in a balanced way on legal admission for employment purposes, the promotion of the integration of legally residing third-country nationals and the fight against illegal immigration and trafficking in human beings.

Another question mark is represented by enlargement, as for the time being it is difficult to foresee in this specific field what the political orientations in the new member states will be and what their positions during the autumn debate will be. In this respect, it may be useful to keep in mind that the consequences of enlargement in terms of migration flows from the new member states are not an issue for the common migration policy, as defined in the European Union, i.e., dealing exclusively with third-country citizens. The transitional measures agreed to during the accession negotiations are actually derogations to the free movement of EU workers, not to the immigration acquis.

The shape of future developments in the area of immigration and asylum also depends on the institutional context. The entering into force of the Treaty Establishing a Constitution for Europe will be very important with respect to decision-making at the EU level in the immigration and asylum areas. The need for unanimity in the voting in the Council has been one of the main reasons for the low level of harmonization that some see in the current EU legislation. As already acknowledged, it is true that the standards do not meet the ambitions set out in the original Commission proposals; nevertheless they do create a European basis on which to build and a framework of rights for legally resident migrants. Already since the Nice Treaty, the Commission has been responsible for taking the initiative to put forward proposals, and most decisions on asylum will in future take place by majority voting and in co-decision with the European Parliament. The extension of qualified majority voting to immigration would facilitate the adoption of any new legislation that might be necessary in the future for the European Union to manage migration more effectively. Moreover, the Charter of Fundamental Rights, included in the draft constitution, sets out a number of basic human rights that will underpin the further development of the area of freedom, security and justice.

We must also keep the broader picture in mind. The issue of managing migration flows will continue to be a priority. Given the new focus of international attention on the impact of globalization on migration, the European Union, as a leading global player, must have an active role in the debate on, and in the development of, solutions to improve management of the movements of people around the world. There is now a growing interest in many third countries in taking a real part in migration management strategies. For many, this depends on the targeting of aid and financial support by the developed world, and the European Union is putting substantial programmes in place to encourage the activities of third countries in migration management. Serious attention to the possible negative effects of migration on the countries of origin is also increasingly being paid. In this context, the Commission is convinced of the importance of a coherent approach linking migration to external and development policies.

Comment on Stefania Pasquetti

Doris König

1 The Need for Migrant Labor

First of all, let me say that I fully agree with Ms. Pasquetti that many of the EU member states need migrant labor to prevent labor shortages in the future and even today. At first sight, this statement seems to be paradoxical, given the current high unemployment rate in many of these countries. I only want to mention the situation in Germany, which I am most familiar with: According to the Federal Labor Agency, the unemployment rate in May 2004 was 9.8 percent overall, 8.2 percent in western Germany, and a staggering 18.3 percent in eastern Germany. More than 300,000 young people leaving school within the next weeks will be looking for jobs which currently do not exist (Bundesagentur für Arbeit 2004). These statistics are meant to show you that the issue of labor migration is a highly explosive topic on the German political agenda. Public opinion is strictly against regulations allowing more labor migrants into the country and into the EU for fear of losing ever more jobs to aliens.

Nevertheless, recent OECD and other studies come to the conclusion that there is a need for immigrants. As far as potential labor shortages in the future are concerned, the two main reasons are an aging workforce and a declining overall population in many OECD countries. But even today, migrant workers are needed in some sectors. This is partly due to a mismatch between the low qualifications of numerous unemployed workers in a given country, and the high qualifications required in innovative technology industries. In these sectors, highly skilled foreign labor is needed. Elsewhere, there are numerous low-paid jobs, for example, in agriculture, where low-skilled labor is needed (OECD 2003: 104). As a consequence, some OECD countries and EU member states have already seen an increase in labor-related immigration, even though some of these countries are affected by an economic downturn.

It is also noteworthy that we can observe an increasing diversity both of migrants' nationalities and of the migration channels they use. This reflects a trend towards an increasing internationalization of migration flows worldwide (OECD 2003: 103). For these reasons, we need a coherent international regime to deal with this complex and multidimensional international phenomenon.

2   The Current Framework in International Law

Due to the limited time, I can only give you a short summary of the basic characteristics of international migration law. The most important factor is that currently there is no such thing as a coherent international migration law (Wolfrum 2001). What we find is rather a piecemeal approach to different facets of migration ranging from the rights of migrant workers to the war against trafficking in human beings, especially women and children, and the protection of refugees and asylum seekers. Since Ms. Pasquetti has already mentioned some of the relevant international conventions, I will refrain from repeating them. In addition, the universal and the regional human rights instruments, such as the International Covenants on Civil and Political Rights (ICCPR) and on Economic, Social, and Cultural Rights, and the European Convention on Human Rights (ECHR), are also applicable to migrants.

Even though there exists a human right to leave any country, including one's own,[1] there is no corresponding right to enter into the territory of any other state. International law leaves the access of aliens and the issues of immigration, nationalization, and the granting of asylum to the discretion of each and every state. Since these issues are politically and economically highly sensitive ones, states are extremely reluctant to give up their sovereign right of regulation for the benefit of common solutions. We, therefore, find a wide range of different national immigration regimes. On the one hand, there are traditional immigration countries like the United States, Canada, Australia, and New Zealand, which actively manage labor migration in their own interest.[2] On the other hand, there are quite a few EU member states that have become immigration countries, but have not yet adapted their legal system to the new situation. Again, Germany is a good example. The German Aliens Law Act is part of what we call "police law" (Polizeirecht) or administrative law on the prevention of dangers to the public (Recht der Gefahrenabwehr). Its main purpose is to control the entry, the stay, and the expulsion of aliens. The objective of managing labor migration is neither intended, nor can it be achieved. And although the government and the opposition parties succeeded in reaching a political compromise on the adoption of a modern migration law (Zuwanderungsgesetz) in mid-2004, substantial parts of the political establishment and of the population still refuse to accept that Germany is an immigration country. We, therefore, need to change our perception of international migration—not only in Germany!

---

[1]   Art. 12 sec. 2 ICCPR; Art. 2 sec. 2 Additional Protocol No. 4 of the ECHR.

[2]   See the state reports in Giegerich and Wolfrum (2001: 337–478).

3   The EU Approach

As Ms. Pasquetti has elaborated, we have a special situation in Europe. Because of the European integration process, national immigration and asylum policies in one state directly affect those policies in other member states. In my opinion, and here I fully agree with the European Commission, it is indispensable to develop a common immigration and asylum policy and to harmonize the different national legal regimes. In this process, the Commission is trying, as Ms. Pasquetti has mentioned, to find a balance between the humanitarian and economic admission of migrants. Measures on legal immigration and integration should go hand in hand with the respect for the rights of refugees and asylum seekers. These measures should be accompanied by reinforced action to combat illegal immigration and the trafficking of human beings.

So far, as we have heard, the European Community has adopted a number of regulations and directives in this field.[3] When evaluating these legislative activities, one has to keep in mind that the community competence is not exclusive and that up to now unanimity among the member states is necessary as far as legal immigration and the admission of legal third-country nationals to the labor market is concerned. Since these issues are highly sensitive, it is extremely difficult to reach agreement on common standards and procedures. In view of these difficulties, it is not surprising that an agreement between the member states could be reached best in the field of combating illegal immigration (Byrne et al. 2004: 359–362). Common standards could also be found with regard to the right to family reunification and the status of long-term residents.[4] In this respect, it is positive that the Community and its member states are willing to secure the legal status of third-country nationals who have been residing in Europe for 5 years and to promote family reunification for legal immigrants. There seems to be a common political understanding to improve the status and integration of those foreigners who are already living in the EU. However, matters seem to become more complicated when agreement has to be reached on the issue of access to the labor market by newcomers. The relevant Commission proposal dates back to 2001, and obviously agreement on this issue is still lacking.[5]

---

[3]   For an overview, see Knauff (2004).

[4]   Council Directive 2003/86/EC (on family reunification), to be transposed into national law by 3 October 2005; Council Directive 2003/109/EC (on long-term residents), to be transposed into national law by 23 January 2006.

[5]   Proposal for a directive on the conditions of entry and residence by third-country nationals for the purpose of paid employment and self-employed economic activities, COM(2001)386 final.

Another sensitive issue is the admission of asylum seekers and refugees to the European Union. In April 2004, the Council adopted the *Directive on minimum standards for the qualification and status of third-country nationals and stateless persons as refugees or as persons who otherwise need international protection.*[6] It is still negotiating a directive on minimum standards for procedures in member states for granting and withdrawing refugee status. The current proposal adopts the concepts of safe third countries and safe countries of origin,[7] which have been well known in German asylum law since 1993. Germany as one of the main target countries of refugees fought hard for the incorporation of these concepts into EU law. Both concepts have been criticized by the United Nations High Commissioner for Refugees (UNHCR), who came to the conclusion that the EU member states have agreed to continue with the worst national practices instead of harmonizing asylum law by using a best practices approach.[8]

To sum it up in a provocative way, EU common immigration and asylum policy seems to aim at improving the integration of migrants who already live and work in the EU, whereas the access of newcomers—with the exception of highly skilled labor—will be reduced as far as possible. Further, let me add two provocative questions: Does the European Union thereby refuse to accept its share in a global burdensharing? And does the facilitated admission of highly skilled labor migrants lead to a "brain drain" in third world countries?

4   Conclusion

Allow me three concluding remarks:

1. Since increasing migration and refugee flows affect the international community as a whole, an international migration regime is essential. On the regional level, the development and implementation of a common immigration and asylum policy in the European Union is indispensable. One of the main objectives of such a common policy should be a future-oriented management of labor migration into EU countries.

2. On the one hand, a common EU immigration policy has to take into account the fear of EU citizens and residents that already scarce job opportunities will be lost and that social security systems will be abused by foreigners. On the

---

[6]   See Council Directive 2004/83/EC.

[7]   On safe third countries and safe countries of origin, see Piotrowicz (2002) and Giegerich (2001: 509).

[8]   EU-Asylharmonisierung: UNHCR bedauert verpasste Chance, *UNHCR Aktuell,* 30 April 2004.

other hand, EU migration policy should take into account the effects it has on the situation in the countries where labor migrants come from.

3. A common EU asylum policy should take part in a global burden sharing and not leave third world countries alone with massive refugee problems. The recent *Communication from the Commission on the managed entry in the EU of persons in need of international protection and the enhancement of the protection capacity of the regions of origin*[9] is a step in the right direction.

Bibliography

Bundesagentur für Arbeit (2004). Monatsbericht der Bundesagentur für Arbeit (Monthly Report of the Federal Labor Agency). May 2004.

Byrne, R., G. Noll, and J. Vedsted-Hansen (2004). Understanding Refugee Law in an Enlarged European Union. *EJIL* 15 (2004): 359–362.

Giegerich, T. (2001). Rechtliche Steuerung der Einwanderung—Vergleichende Analyse nationaler Modelle im Spiegel zunehmender internationalrechtlicher Vorgaben. In T. Giegerich and R. Wolfrum (eds.), *Einwanderungsrecht—National und International*. Opladen: Leske & Buderich.

Giegerich, T., and R. Wolfrum (eds.) (2001). *Einwanderungsrecht—National und International*. Opladen: Leske & Buderich.

Knauff, M. (2004). Europäische Einwanderungspolitik: Grundlagen und aktuelle Entwicklungen. *ZeuS7* (2004): 11–42.

OECD (2003). *Trends in International Migration. Part II: Labor Shortages and the Need for Immigrants: A Review of Recent Studies*. Paris: OECD.

Piotrowicz, R. (2002). Safe Third States and Safe States of Origin in UK and Australian Practice: Exercises in Pragmatism. In K. Hailbronner and E. Klein (eds.), *Flüchtlinge—Menschenrechte—Staatsangehörigkeit*. Heidelberg: Müller.

Wolfrum, R. (2001). Völkerrechtliche Rahmenbedingungen für die Einwanderung. In T. Giegerich and R. Wolfrum (eds.), *Einwanderungsrecht—National und International*. Opladen: Leske & Buderich.

---

[9]   See COM(2004)410 final (4 June 2004).

Holger Wolf

Do Values Matter for Intra-EU Migration?

Abstract:

Europeans are relatively immobile across borders. This reluctance to move could reflect formal and/or informal barriers, low perceived benefits, or high perceived costs. This paper explores the importance of some of these determinants, giving particular attention to the role of location-specific utility.

1   Introduction

Europeans are famously immobile across national borders.[1] Their immobility can reflect either an unwillingness or an inability to move. While legal and institutional barriers to movement were once sizable, they have been substantially reduced over the last two decades. It thus seems reasonable to conjecture that the persistent low mobility within the European Union is to a significant extent voluntary and should thus be analyzed in a choice framework.

Migration theory in its most general form models individuals (or households) as optimizing expected utility across multiple decision variables, including location. The choice of location affects utility through two separate channels. First, for a given skill of the individual, income (and hence market consumption) differs across locations. Second, location itself may have a utility effect, reflecting proximity to friends and family, weather, or, the issue explored in this paper, feeling "at home" in a sense to be defined more closely below. If it is assumed that individuals experience the highest level of this income-independent location-specific utility at home, then migration involves a utility loss that must be compensated through higher expected income. The size of the threshold depends on

Remark: As a neophyte in the field of migration, I am particularly grateful for the many comments received during the conference, and in particular to Herbert Brücker and Jeffrey Williamson. Corey Campion provided excellent research assistance. I am also indebted to Samuel Barnes and Bimol Ghosh.

[1]   The size of the literature forestalls adequate citation. See Fertig and Schmidt (2002) for a critical review of the evidence.

the psychic cost of moving. If the cost varies across host countries, so does the wage threshold triggering migration.[2]

The focus on this location-specific utility has a long heritage. Adam Smith already remarked about individuals' hesitancy to move. Sjastaad's influential work (1962) refers to the "psychic cost" of being far from family and friends and a "preference for familiar versus strange surroundings." On an empirical level, these psychological costs are very difficult to quantify.

Among the proxies that have been used are distance, linguistic ties, and the stock of prior immigrants or lagged flows.[3] Distance captures a number of effects, including moving costs, information costs in the mental map tradition (Gould and White 1992) and, if cultural differences are assumed to increase with distance, also psychological costs. Under all three interpretations, distance is expected to be negatively associated with bilateral migration. Linguistic ties are assumed to ease assimilation and reduce search costs; they are expected to affect migration positively. The stock of prior migrants can be interpreted both in terms of network effects (through reduced search costs) and in terms of psychological cost (through improved access to home goods, culture, etc.).[4] Under both interpretations, it is expected to be positively associated with bilateral migration.

The empirical evidence suggests that distance effects are very important, a feature that has been documented both for Canadian and U.S. migration patterns (Helliwell 1998), for migration into Canada and the United States (Karemera et al. 2000; Clark et al. 2004), and for immigration into the OECD (Mayda 2004). The literature also documents the importance of the stock of prior immigrants or lagged flows (Mayda 2004; Clark et al. 2004). Linguistic ties appear to have somewhat weaker explanatory power (Mayda 2004). Among other variables, Kamerera et al. (2000), studying migration to North America, find that political variables in the country of origin matter; Mayda (2004), studying a broad panel of immigration into the OECD, finds past colonial ties are important, while Helliwell (1998) documents a possible climate effect through immigration to sunbelt states.

This paper aims to contribute to this literature by adding explicit measures of "values" to the other determinants. The focus of the paper is quite restricted: I look at bilateral migration between twelve EU members in cross section. The restriction causes some of the richness in broader datasets to be lost, but has the

---

2   As an implication, such thresholds provide one explanation for the persistence of real income gaps across European countries. Other explanations include agglomeration effects and adjustment costs.

3   Recent empirical studies include Helliwell (1998), Clark et al. (2004), and Mayda (2004).

4   See Ben-Porath (1980), Boyd (1989), Fawcett (1989), Kritz et al. (1992), Bauer et al. (2002), Clark et al. (2002), Pedersen et al. (2004), Mayda (2004), among others.

advantage that legal barriers to migration are arguably of lesser importance. I use the value measures to examine two questions:

- Is bilateral migration, ceteris paribus, influenced by the values of the host country?
- Is bilateral migration, ceteris paribus, influenced by the difference in values between the home and the host country of the migrants?

To be sure, the approach involves substantial interpretative risks. Value systems differ across individuals as well as potentially across regions. Constructing value variables for entire populations provides at best an approximation for the perception of individuals.

The next section describes the standard controls and the migration data. Section 3 turns to the measurement of values. Section 4 presents the results, and Section 5 concludes.

2   Migration Data and Traditional Controls

Before turning to the issues involved in measuring values, this section briefly describes the migration data and the traditional controls. The sample includes all (pre-2004) EU countries with the exception of Greece, Ireland and Luxembourg, for whom either the value data or the migration data were not available. The dataset thus consists of 132 bilateral observations.

2.1   Migration Data

The paper focuses on gross bilateral migration between the sample countries. It does not deal explicitly with issues associated with return and repeat migration. Migration data are known to be subject to a number of serious caveats, which can be no more than acknowledged here. The migration data were obtained from Haver Analytics (www.haver.com) and are based on Eurostat data. For the flow data (MIG_FLOW), I computed the mean of three consecutive years to avoid outlier bias. The years were 1996, 1997, and 1998 in most cases.[5] For the stock data (MIG_STO), I used 1995 data when available.[6] Both measures are in logs.

---

5 For Belgium, 1998 data were unavailable. I instead used 1995. For France 1996 data were unavailable. I instead used 1999.

6 For the United Kingdom, 1994 stock data were used. For Austria, the mean of the 1991 and 2001 stocks was used. For France, the mean of the 1990 and the 1999 stock

2.2   Traditional Controls

The controls are largely standard in gravity-type regressions. DISTance is defined as the log of the distance between the central cities in the home and host country in km.[7] As discussed above, distance proxies for information quality, the financial costs of relocation, and potentially for the loss of nonmarket location-specific utility. It is expected to enter negatively. As a second spatial measure, I add a common BORDER dummy, expected to enter positively.

POP_HOME and POP_HOST are defined as the logs of the population levels. Both scale variables are expected to influence migration positively. YG_HOST and YG_HOME measure income in the host and home country as the log of annual gross income in purchasing-power-parity dollars.[8] YG_HOST and YG_HOME are expected to enter positively and negatively, respectively. WEL_HOST is defined as the log of the maximum monthly amount of net income under social assistance in the host country for a single individual in purchasing-power-adjusted dollars.[9] The benefit data are not available for Portugal.

Unemployment in the home and in the host country can act as a push factor and as a deterrent. The UM_HOME and UM_HOST variables equal the 1996 unemployment rate for males aged between 15 and 24, the traditionally dominant migrant group.[10] Finally, the AGE variable, defined as the share of the population aged between 20 and 29 in the home country, captures the relative size of the traditionally dominant migrant group.[11]

3   Measures of Psychological Cost and Values

In order to introduce cultural and psychological terms into the empirical evidence, "psychological costs" and "values" must be quantified. These terms are of course multi-dimensional; the focus here is on a small, nonexhaustive subset of numerically measurable aspects that might reasonably be expected to be relevant for migration choice.

---

was used. In both cases a small problem of endogeneity may thus arise. The in principle preferable alternative of updating start-of-decade figures with cumulative migration flows was not feasible, as net migration figures were not available.

[7]   www.indo.com/distance.

[8]   OECD (1997), *The Tax/Benefit Position of Employees*, Table 18.

[9]   OECD (2002), *Benefits and Wages*, Table 2.10.

[10]   OECD (1997), *Employment Outlook*.

[11]   United Nations (1999), *Demographics Yearbook*.

3.1   Language

Perhaps least controversial is the view that a common language, by enhancing the ability to participate in society, reduces the psychological cost of migration.[12] Linguistic linkage has traditionally been measured by a dummy set equal to one if the home and host country share a common primary language, and zero otherwise, implicitly assigning no weight to the possibility of an immigrant communicating in a third language. As the latter pattern becomes more prevalent with the emergence of English as a professional language in much of Europe, the dichotomous approach risks understating the linguistic connection between home and host countries not sharing a primary language. To allow for this feature, the LANGUAGE measure is defined as 1 if home and host country share a common primary language, and as LANGUAGE$(i,j) = \alpha_{i,\text{ENGLISH}}\, \alpha_{i,\text{ENGLISH}}$ otherwise, where i and j denote the home and host country, and $\alpha_{i,\text{ENGLISH}}$ denotes the fraction of the population in country i speaking English. $L(i,j)$ thus proxies for the probability that a random resident of country i can communicate with a random resident of country j either in the host country language or in English.[13]

3.2   Religion

To the extent that religious views are closely intertwined with values, a common dominant religion can be used as a proxy for similarity of values. RELIGION is a dummy set equal to one if the same religion is dominant in both the home and host country. A religion is assumed to be dominant if it has at least a sixty percent share among individuals identifying themselves as religious.[14]

3.3   Direct Value Measures

The measures of values are based on the responses to a set of questions contained in the World Value Survey, as reported and discussed in Inglehart et al. (1998).[15]

---

[12]   Alternatively, one might view language as a predictor of income prospects.

[13]   CIA Factbook at www.cia.gov/cia/publications/factbook and Ginsburgh and Weber (2004).

[14]   CIA Factbook at www.cia.gov/cia/publications/factbook.

[15]   In the following, V-xxx refers to the question number in Inglehart et al. (1998). Western German data are used for Germany.

3.3.1   Emphasis on the Individual

The first set of measures aims to capture the relative weight given to individual effort and responsibility. IND_HOST and IND_DIFF are numerical scores proxying, respectively, for the emphasis on individualism in the host country and the difference in emphasis on individualism between the home and the host country. The measures are based on the responses to the following statements/questions:

V-250   "There should be greater incentives for individual effort."

V-247   "I find that both freedom and equality are important. But if I were to choose one or the other, I would consider personal freedom more important, that is, everyone can live in freedom and develop without hindrance."

V-228   Do you consider it especially important for children to learn hard work at home?

V-97   The reason that there are people in this country who live in need is because of laziness and lack of will power.

V-125   "Imagine two secretaries, of the same age, doing practically the same job. One finds out that the other earns $50 a week more than she does. The better-paid secretary, however, is quicker, more efficient, and more reliable at her job. In your opinion, is it fair or not that one secretary is paid more than the other?" (percent answering "fair")

V-254   "Competition is harmful. It brings out the worst in people." (Disagree)

V-337   Do you strongly agree that "We are more likely to have a healthy economy if the government allows more freedom for individuals to do as they wish?" (Agree)

In conjunction, it is hoped that the answers to these seven statements/ questions will allow the construction of a meaningful cross-country proxy for the relative weight placed on "individualism," broadly defined. To ensure comparability, the responses for each question are first transformed into deviations from the median for that question, and are then divided by the standard deviation of the deviation from the median. The variable IND_HOST is then constructed as the average across all questions. IND_DIFF is measured as the absolute difference between IND_HOST and IND_HOME, the latter constructed analogously to IND_HOST. By construction, a high value implies that the respondents in the country place a relatively higher emphasis on individual effort and responsibility.

Gender Roles

The gender variable aims to capture attitudes towards gender roles and equality in the workplace, based on four statements/questions in the World Value Survey:

V-128   When jobs are scarce, men have more right to a job than women.

V-218   Do you agree/strongly agree that "a working mother can establish just as warm and secure a relationship with her children as a mother who does not work?" (100 minus fraction responding "agree" or "strongly agree")

V-219   Do you agree/strongly agree that "a pre-school child is likely to suffer if his or her mother works?"

V-220   Do you agree/strongly agree that "a job is alright but what most women really want is a home and children?"

The GEN_HOST and GEN_DIFF are constructed analogously to the variables described in the previous section.

3.3.2   *Materialism versus Postmaterialism*

In addition to these two measures based on a subjective selection of questions, I also use an aggregate value measure constructed by Inglehart et al. (1998). The two measures aim to capture, respectively, the prevalence of "materialist" and "postmaterialist" values. The variable POS_HOST is defined, as in Inglehart et al. (1998), as the numerical value of the postmaterialism indicator in the host country. The variable VAL_DIF is defined as the sum of the absolute differences of the postmaterialist and the materialist score between the two countries.

3.3.3   *Openness towards Foreigners*

OPENNESS measures host country attitudes towards foreigners and towards immigration, which may reasonably be expected to affect the utility of a migrant. The Special Eurobarometer Opinion Poll No. 47.1, carried out in March and April of 1997,[16] explores these attitudes in greater detail. I use three of the responses to the Eurobarometer Poll and one question from the World Value Survey to construct an aggregate OPENNESS indicator. The first three questions address views on minority groups. Their usefulness in the current context thus depends on whether intra-EU migrants are perceived, and perceive themselves, as belonging to a minority group. The last question directly addresses migration.

---

[16]   http://europa.eu.int/comm/public_opinion/archives/ebs/ebs_113_en.pdf.

(i) *Discrimination*. Respondents were asked whether *"people from minority groups are discriminated against in the job market."* The submeasure used is the fraction of "yes" responses (nonresponses are excluded).

(ii) *Assimilation*. Respondents were asked whether *"in order to be fully accepted members of society, people belonging to these minority groups must give up their own culture."* The submeasure used is the fraction of respondents answering yes (nonresponses are excluded).[17]

(iii) *Capacity*. Respondents were asked to assess the statement that *"our country has reached its limits; if there were to be more people belonging to these minority groups we would have problems."* The submeasure used is the fraction of respondents answering yes (nonresponses are excluded).

(iv) *Preference*. The World Value Survey (Inglehart et al. 1998), Q. V-130 asked whether "when jobs are scarce employers should give priority to own nationality over immigrants." The submeasure used is the percentage agreeing with the statement.

The aggregate OPENNESS is defined as the average of the four responses, again rescaled as the deviation from the median divided by the standard deviation of the median.

Before turning to the results, two important potential problems in using these value measures deserve mention. First, the measures for the host country are used to proxy for the views of immigrants about the host country. For this to be a good assumption, self-assessment must be fairly close to external assessment. Second, by using the home country views to construct the difference measure, it is assumed that potential emigrants share the views of the population at large.

4   Empirical Results

This section turns to the empirical evidence. The gravity equation is estimated using least squares with White errors. The results are reported in Table 1. The first two columns report the baseline regression using only the spatial, income, and unemployment controls. The variables enter as expected, with the exception

---

[17]   The question contained two parts. The second question was, *"In order to be fully accepted members of society, people belonging to these minority groups must give up such parts of their religion or culture which may be in conflict with the law."* Respondents had the option to disagree with both statements, to agree with the first, and to agree with the second question (Eurobarometer Vol. 47, No. 1, 1997, Special Survey 113, p. 6).

Table 1

	(1)	(2)	(3)	(4)
Constant	−4.458	−9.663	−20.204	−18.881
	(0.62)	(0.93)	(2.58)**	(3.71)***
Distance	−0.684	−0.682	−0.499	−0.238
	(3.24)***	(3.07)***	(2.94)***	(1.90)*
Border	0.235	0.294	0.271	−0.170
	(0.84)	(1.01)	(1.24)	(1.08)
Home population	0.660	0.633	0.630	0.166
	(6.90)***	(6.01)***	(7.57)***	(2.27)***
Host population	0.886	0.907	0.531	−0.141
	(8.57)***	(9.23)***	(4.14)***	(1.27)
Gross income home	−0.916	−0.973	−0.679	−0.171
	(2.08)**	(2.10)**	(1.56)	(0.65)
Gross income host	1.364	1.840	3.203	2.879
	(4.99)***	(2.24)**	(6.57)***	(9.53)***
Male U-rate home	0.013	0.017	0.010	0.008
	(1.03)	(1.18)	(0.87)	(1.14)
Male U-rate host	−0.045	−0.036	−0.059	−0.046
	(4.19)***	(2.91)***	(4.73)***	(5.69)***
Age	−25.042	−26.348	−23.797	−16.978
	(2.23)**	(2.21)**	(2.63)***	(2.82)***
Welfare host		0.148		
		(0.48)		
Language			1.105	0.163
			(1.92)*	(0.45)
Religion			0.091	−0.109
			(0.38)	(0.69)
Individualism host			−0.601	−0.477
			(2.68)***	(3.50)***
Gender host			0.700	0.671
			(4.25)***	(6.78)***
Individualism difference			−0.331	0.061
			(1.55)	(0.49)
Gender difference			−0.382	−0.160
			(2.74)***	(1.82)*
Postmaterialism host			−0.114	−0.133
			(4.74)***	(9.17)***
Broad value difference			0.015	0.008
			(1.71)*	(1.23)
Openness			−1.524	−1.949
			(3.66)***	(7.33)***
Stock of immigrants				0.636
				(10.80)***
R^2	0.704	0.674	0.807	0.915
Observations	132	121	132	132

of the age variable.[18] Among the spatial variables, distance is negatively and a common border is positively associated with bilateral migration, though the latter effect is insignificant. The negative distance effect matches the findings of the prior literature, as discussed above. The two scale variables, home and host population enter positively and significant, as expected. The incentive variables also enter as expected: higher home income is negatively associated with migration, higher host income positively, and both are significant. A higher home unemployment rate is positively (though insignificantly) associated with migration, while a higher unemployment rate in the host country is significantly negatively associated with bilateral migration. The overall fit is good in the context of gravity regressions. Column two adds the welfare variable, which reduces the degrees of freedom, as data for Portugal are not available. As the variable does not enter significantly, it is not used in the subsequent regressions.

The third column adds the value/culture variables. Comparing columns one and three, the inclusion of the value/culture variables reduces the negative distance elasticity, consistent with the view that distance to some extent proxies for cultural effects. The inclusion of values also reduces the importance of the host but not the home population as a scale variable, and enhances the size and significance of the host income variable.

Turning to the value/culture variables themselves, greater linguistic links and a common major religion are positively associated with bilateral migration, though only the former effect is significant at even the ten percent level, again consistent with prior findings (Mayda 2004). Less openness to immigrants is negatively and significantly associated with bilateral migration. A greater emphasis on individualism and a postmaterialist orientation in the host country are negatively associated with bilateral migration, while more traditional views on gender are positively associated with bilateral migration. All three measures of differences in values between home and host countries are negatively associated with bilateral migration, two of them significantly. Taken together, the results, while obviously only scratching the surface and in some cases being counterintuitive, suggest that a deeper exploration of the effect of values on migration may be worthwhile.

Column four adds the stock of immigrants. As discussed above, the stock can be viewed as a proxy for (lower) search costs through ethnic network effects, or as a proxy for reduced psychological cost of moving. Under both interpretations, the stock enters positively, as it does in the regression. The finding is again consistent with the prior literature. Comparing columns three and four reveals that

---

[18]   An explanation may be that the age structure does not differ dramatically across the sample countries: the young share ranges from 12.3 percent in Finland to 16.6 percent in Spain.

the distance effect shrinks further. The stock of prior immigrants also appears to act as a scale variable, as the coefficient on the host population becomes insignificant. Among the value/culture variables, the inclusion of the stock of prior immigrants reduces the importance of a common language. It has relatively small effects on the coefficients on the host country values, though the importance of the value differences shrinks. In interpreting this last equation, it must of course be borne in mind that the stock of immigrants is trivially the accumulated flow, and as such is linked to the explanatory variables.

In conclusion, a caveat. The above discussion, to the detriment of readability, consistently used the term "associated with" to describe the linkages. While it is tempting to place causal interpretations on the linkages, the evidence presented here is not sufficiently rich to allow such an interpretation. While the variables are temporally structured to minimize endogeneity issues, there are clearly a number of fundamental linkages between migration flows and the explanatory variables, including income, population, and unemployment, which are themselves the subject of a lively literature. Indeed, at least some of the values may themselves be endogenous to migration over time.[19]

5   Conclusion

The theoretical literature on migration has long held "soft factors" to be important determinants alongside the traditional "hard" determinants such as wage differences, unemployment rates, etc. Recent empirical work has supported the importance of distance, linguistic ties, past migration, colonial links, and political instability in the home country.

This paper aims to add to this literature by exploring whether values in the host country and differences in values between the host and the home country affect migration, controlling for other factors. The analysis is focused on a very narrow and fairly homogeneous country group, twelve members of the European Union. Measuring "values" is of course tricky. To the extent that the measures proposed here indeed pick up such value/culture differences, they indicate that while the traditional determinants of migration account for the lion's share of explanatory power, values provide additional explanatory power at the margin. This paper no more than scratches the surface, much deeper analysis is required to fully understand the role of host-country values and value/culture differences.

---

[19]   See, for example, Mayda (2003) for an exploration of views on immigration in a political economy context.

Bibliography

Bauer, T. (2002). Migration, Sozialstaat und Zuwanderungspolitik. Working Paper No. 505. IZA, Bonn,

Bauer, T., and K. Zimmermann (eds.) (2002). *The Economics of Migration*. Northampton, Mass.:, Edward Elgar.

Bauer, T., G. Epstein, and I. Gang (2002). Herd Effects or Migration Networks? IZA Discussion Paper No. 551. Bonn.

Ben-Porath, Y., (1980). The F-Connection: Families, Friends, and Firms and the Organization of Exchange. *Population and Development Review* 6 (1): 1–30.

Blundell, R., V. Fry, and I. Walker (1988). Modeling the Take-Up of Means-Tested Benefits. *Economic Journal* 98 (390): 58–74.

Borjas, G. (1994). The Economics of Immigration. *Journal of Economic Literature* 32 (4): 1167–1717.

Borjas, G. (1999a). Immigration and Welfare Magnets. *Journal of Labor Economics* 17 (4):607–637.

Borjas, G. (1999b). The Economics Analysis of Immigration. In O. Ashenfelter and R. Layard (eds.), *Handbook of Labor Economics*. Vol. 3A. Amsterdam: North-Holland.

Boyd, M. (1989). Family and Personal Networks in International Migration. *International Migration Review* 23 (3): 638–670.

Brücker, H., G. Epstein, B. McCormick, G. Saint-Paul, A. Venturini, and K. Zimmermann (2001). Managing Migration in the European Welfare State. In T. Boeri, G.H. Hanson, and B. McCormick (eds.), *Imigration Policy and the Welfare System*. Oxford: Oxford University Press.

Burda, M. (2001). Factor Mobility, Income Differentials and Regional Economic Integration. Mimeo. Humboldt University, Berlin.

Carrington, W., E. Detragiache, and T. Vishwanath (1996). Migration with Endogenous Moving Costs. *American Economic Review* 86 (4): 909–930.

Clark, X., T. Hatton, and J. Williamson (2002). Where Do U.S. Immigrants Come from, and Why? NBER Working Paper No. 8998. Cambridge, Mass.

Eurostat (2000a). Push and Pull Factors of International Migration. Luxembourg: Eurostat.

Eurostat (2000b). Patterns and Trends in International Migration in Western Europe. Luxembourg: Eurostat.

Fawcett, J.T. (1989). Networks, Linkages and Migration Systems. *International Migration Review* 23 (3): 671–680.

Fertig, M., and C. Schmidt (2002). Mobility within Europe—What Do We (Still Not) Know? IZA Discussion Paper No. 447. Bonn.

Ginsburgh, V., and S. Weber (2004). Language Disenfranchisement in the European Union. Nota di Lavoro 4: 1–17.

Gould, P., and R. White (1992). *Mental Maps*. 2nd. ed. London: Routledge.

Helliwell, J. (1998). *How Much Do National Borders Matter?* Washington, D.C.: Brookings Institution Press.

Inglehart, R., M. Basañez, and A. Moreno (1998). *Human Values and Beliefs: A Cross-Cultural Sourcebook*. Ann Arbor: The University of Michigan Press.

Karemera, D., V. Oguledo, and B. Davis (2000). A Gravity Model Analysis of International Migration to North America. *Applied Economics* 32 (13): 1745–1755.

Kritz, M., L. Lim, and H. Zlotnik (eds.) (1992). *International Migration Systems: A Global Approach*. New York: Oxford University Press.

Mayda, A.-M. (2003). Who Is against Immigration? IZA Discussion Paper No. 1115. Bonn.

Mayda, A.-M. (2004). International Migration. Mimeo. Georgetown University, Washington, D.C.

Pedersen, P., M. Pytlikova, and N. Smith (2004). Selection or Network Effect? IZA Discussion Paper No. 1104. Bonn.

Ravenstein, E. (1885, 1889). The Laws of Migration. *Journal of the Statistical Society* 48 (June): 167–227, and 52 (June): 241–301.

Sjaastad, L. (1962). The Costs and Returns of Human Migration. *Journal of Political Economy* 70 (5): 2: 80–93.

Zipf, G. (1941). *National Unity and Disunity*. Bloomington, Indiana: Principia Press.

Comment on Holger Wolf

Herbert Brücker

The free movement of labor and other persons has been defined as one of the four fundamental freedoms of the Single Market in the European Union (EU) since the Treaty of Rome. It was introduced for the six founding members of the then European Economic Community (EEC) with a joint population of some 180 million in 1968, and has been applied to the members of the European Economic Area (EEA) since the beginning of the 1990s, which includes all EU members and three other countries with a joint population of some 380 million. Moreover, in the course of the present enlargement round, the free movement will be extended to the accession countries from Central and Eastern Europe when the transitional periods have expired. Nevertheless, although the barriers to the mobility of labor and other persons are largely removed, migration within the EU is rather low: no more than 1.5 percent of the population of the EU-15 reside in other EU member states. Although differences in income levels between the member states of the "old" EU and EEA are, at least from a global perspective, rather low, this figure is nevertheless small. Since institutional barriers to migration have largely been abolished, the low migration within the EEA seems to reflect a number of social, cultural, and historical factors which hinder the mobility of labor and other persons in Europe.

The paper by Holger Wolf addresses an important aspect of these nonpecuniary barriers to migration: differences in social and economic values. The general hypothesis of the paper that nonpecuniary arguments enter the utility function of individuals or households and, hence, affect migration decisions, has a long tradition in the migration literature. Starting with Ravenstein (1889), all major contributions to the migration literature stress the nonpecuniary migration costs ("psychological costs") that result from a loss of family and other social ties, cultural alienation, etc. (Sjaastad 1962; Mincer 1978; Ben-Porath 1980; Massey et al. 1993). What is missing, however, in the literature, and this holds true for this paper as well, is a coherent theoretical framework which considers pecuniary and nonpecuniary arguments in a systematic manner. Although the paper provides a number of interesting insights, the lack of a theoretical framework creates some difficulties for the empirical analysis of the role of values in migration decisions.

In the remainder of my comment I focus on three issues: firstly, the problems which are created by the missing theoretical framework of the paper, secondly, the empirical specification of the model, and, finally, the discussion and interpretation of the regression results.

Why Do Values Matter?

The paper goes beyond standard migration models which explain migration by income and (un-)employment variables, distance as a proxy for the monetary and psychological costs of migration, migration stocks as a proxy for migration networks, and language dummies. Based on the World Value Survey, the attitude of the populations in the host and home countries regarding the roles of individuals, the role of the state and society, gender equality, materialism and postmaterialism, and openness to immigration is considered here. With the exception of the last variable, the role of most of these variables with regard to the benefits and costs of migration remains unclear, however. In particular, it is hard to derive meaningful hypotheses at the macro level, since little is known about the composition of the migrant population. If migrants are selected from the upper range of the income distribution, they may prefer values which are based on liberal concepts of individuality, while migrants who are selected from the lower range might prefer values which are positively related to welfare state protection.

The implicit assumption that a greater difference in values between host and home countries hinders migration need not be true either. As many migration episodes in history have shown, ethnic, religious, and political minorities may migrate or may be forced to migrate because they to not comply with the values of the majority in the home population. Note that such migration often exceeds economically motivated migration, as the mass migration waves from the former Yugoslavia and within the Commonwealth of Independent States (CIS) have recently demonstrated.

Is the Lack of a Theoretical Framework a Problem?

Many empirical papers deliver valuable insights without providing a coherent theoretical framework. However, depending on the migration model, the consideration of nonpecuniary arguments in the utility function of individuals can yield counterintuitive results. Consider the following simple model of temporary migration: individuals have a preference to live in their home countries because they have family and other social ties there and share the same set of social values with their home community. The income differential between the host and the home country is substantial. Depending on the elasticity of substitution between income and the nonincome arguments in the utility function of individuals, the time an individual will spend abroad will either increase or decrease with an increasing income differential between the host and the home country, since a certain amount of lifetime income can be achieved within a shorter period of time if the income differential is increasing (Djajic and Milbourne 1988). This result is similar to the income and substitution effect in consumption theory.

Another important aspect is heterogeneity across individuals. Not all individuals have the same preferences or share the same values. If preferences or values affect the migration decision, the propensity to migrate is thus not equally distributed across the population. As a consequence, the propensity to migrate declines, ceteris paribus, the higher the share of the population is which already lives abroad. This has important consequences for modeling migration: instead of an equilibrium between migration rates, an equilibrium between migration stocks and explanatory variables such as the income differential emerges. Using migration rates as the dependent variables may thus yield spurious regression results, since migration rates reflect the adjustment to an equilibrium rather than the equilibrium itself.

Finally, values can affect the benefits and costs of migration through various channels. As an example, they can affect both the setup costs as well as the variable costs of migration. Moreover, variables such as language may have a direct impact on the income of migrants. As a consequence, they can affect the intercept and the slope parameters of empirical models.

Altogether, the consideration of nonpecuniary arguments in the utility functions of individuals can have important consequences for modeling macro-migration models. A coherent theoretical framework is needed for both a sound specification of macro migration models and a meaningful interpretation of the estimation results.

Specification of the Empirical Model

The paper applies a traditional gravity equation to a cross-section of countries. More specifically, the model has the form

(1)
$$\ln m_{ij} = \alpha + \beta_1 \ln D_{ij} + \beta_2 POP_i + \beta_3 POP_j + \beta_4 \ln y_i + \beta_5 \ln y_j + \beta_6 u_i + \beta_7 u_j$$
$$+ \beta_8 \ln mst_{ij} + \gamma Z_i + \eta Z_j + \lambda Z_{ij} + \varepsilon_{ij},$$

where m denotes the net migration rate, D geographical distance between the host and the home country, POP population, y GDP per capita, u the unemployment rate, mst the migration stock as a percentage of the home population, Z a vector of values, institutional and socioeconomic characteristics, ε the error term, and the subscripts i and j the host and the home country, respectively.

The model no doubt has a long tradition in the literature, but it nevertheless involves some difficulties: firstly, it is hard to interpret the parameters for the migration stock variable. The standard explanation is that this variable captures so-called network effects. However, since the migration stock approximates cumulative net migration, it may simply capture all omitted variables of the model. Secondly, using the migration rate as the dependent variable may yield spurious regression results if the implicit hypothesis of an equilibrium relationship between the migration rate and the explanatory variables (e.g., the income differential) is wrong. Thirdly, the model considers only one cross-section. This excludes any dynamic specification of the model, which may result in problems if the adjustment of migration to changes in the explanatory variables is sluggish. Of course there are not many alternatives, since data for the value variables are hardly available on an annual basis. Fourthly, the model assumes a log-linear relationship between distance and the migration rate. In fact, migrants optimize over locations, which results in a nonlinear relationship between migration and distance. As an example, the distance between Frankfurt and Athens and Frankfurt and Lisbon is exactly the same, but more than 4 percent of the Greek population resides in Germany and less than 0.5 percent in France, while the reverse picture holds true for Portugal. The reason for this phenomenon is that migrants tend to cluster in the first country with a large absorption capability and only few move any further. In dynamic models, interaction dummies can capture these effects. Fifthly, and perhaps most importantly, the variables of interest, the value variables, are considered only as intercept dummies. Including slope dummies might provide additional insights for the reasons discussed above.

Regression Results

The regression results for the standard set of variables (distance, population, GDP per capita, unemployment) have the expected signs and appear, with exception of the home unemployment rate, significant. Note that many macro studies in the literature find that home unemployment is insignificant, which might be traced back to the fact that migrants are positively self-selected, and, hence, tend to be less affected by unemployment in the home countries. For the value variables, the paper finds a significant negative impact for both individuality and the state variables in the host country. Moreover, the individuality difference variable turns out to have a significant negative impact on migration. However, the interpretation of these results is puzzling: if migrants are selected from the lower range of the income distribution and have higher social risks than the population average, it would make sense for them to migrate to countries where societies rank individual values relatively low and social values relatively high.

However, to have a negative impact for both is hard to interpret. More convincing is the negative correlation between postmaterialist values and migration. If migrants come basically from relatively poor countries with traditional values, societies which rank postmaterialist values relatively high may increase the cultural alienation, and, hence, the psychological costs of migration. Moreover, one of the interesting findings of the paper is that the explanatory power of the distance variable declines in the regressions which include value variables. This is indeed an indication that the distance variable captures a number of non-geographical factors.

Altogether, the paper presents a number of interesting insights on the correlation between migration and value variables. Nevertheless, a theoretical foundation is urgently needed to both avoid misspecification of the empirical model and to interpret the findings convincingly. In this sense, the paper is a good starting point for a promising field of further research.

Bibliography

Ben-Porath, Y. (1980). The F-Connection: Families, Friends and Firms and the Organization of Exchange. *Population and Development Review* 6 (1): 1–30.

Djajic, S., and R. Milbourne (1988). A General Equilibrium Model of Guest-Worker Migration: A Source-Country Perspective. *Journal of International Economics* 25 (3–4): 335–351.

Massey, D., J. Arango, G. Hugo, A. Kouaouci, A. Pellegrino, and J.E. Taylor (1993). Theories of International Migration. *Population and Development Review* 19 (3): 431–466.

Mincer, J. (1978). Family Migration Decisions. *Journal of Political Economy* 86 (5): 749–773.

Ravenstein, E. (1889). The Laws of Migration. *Journal of the Statistical Society* 52 (2): 241–301.

Sjaastad, L. (1962). The Costs and Returns of Human Migration. *Journal of Political Economy* 70 (5): 80–93.

Timothy J. Hatton and Jeffrey G. Williamson

Refugees, Asylum Seekers, and Policy in Europe

Abstract:

The number of refugees worldwide is now 12 million, up from 3 million in the early 1970s. And the number seeking asylum in the developed world has increased tenfold, from about 50,000 per annum to half a million over the same period. Governments and international agencies have grappled with the twin problems of providing adequate humanitarian assistance in the Third World and avoiding floods of unwanted asylum seekers arriving on the doorsteps of the First World. This is an issue that is long on rhetoric, as newspaper reports testify, but surprisingly short on economic analysis. This paper draws on the recent literature, and ongoing research, to address a series of questions that are relevant to the debate. First, we examine the causes of refugee displacements and asylum flows, focusing on the effects of conflict, political upheaval, and economic incentives to migrate. Second, we examine the evolution of policies towards asylum seekers and the effects of those policies, particularly in Europe. Finally, we ask whether greater international coordination could produce better outcomes for refugee-receiving countries and for the refugees themselves.

1 Introduction

The worldwide number of refugees has increased by a factor of four since the early 1970s—from about 3 to 12 million. And the number seeking asylum in developed countries has increased by a factor of about ten over the same period—

Remark: This paper draws heavily on our own recent work (Hatton and Williamson 2003; Hatton 2004) and on our ongoing book World Mass Migration: Two Centuries of Policy and Performance. We are grateful to the organizers of the Kiel Week Conference, where an earlier version of this paper was presented, and to the participants at the conference for their comments. Hatton acknowledges support through a British Academy Research Readership and Williamson acknowledges financial support from the National Science Foundation SES-0001363. We are both grateful to the Australian National University for providing us with the opportunity and the environment for collaboration on this research project. Williamson also thanks the University of Wisconsin Economics Department, where this paper was completed while on leave from Harvard.

from about 50,000 per annum in the early 1970s to half a million in 2001. This is seen by many as a crisis of growing proportions, and for two reasons. First, there is the humanitarian issue. Most refugees are displaced across borders in the Third World, suffering oppression, poverty and disease. With each new humanitarian crisis comes new criticism of the unwillingness or inability of governments and international agencies to act more decisively to solve the refugee problem, or at least to better ameliorate the condition of the refugees. Second, the arrival of increasing numbers of asylum seekers on the doorsteps of the First World has led to fierce political debate about asylum policies, often fueled by parties of the far right. Despite protest from humanitarian groups, governments have responded to the rising political temperature with a range of measures aimed at deterring asylum applications.

This paper draws on the recent literature and some of our own analysis to address a series of questions that are relevant to these debates. First, what are the causes of refugee displacement? Are they mainly political or economic? Second, how far can wars, political crises and economic conditions explain the apparently inexorable rise in the number of asylum seekers, particularly in Europe, but in the rest of the OECD as well? Third, how has asylum policy evolved in Europe and has it been effective in deterring asylum seekers, or has it instead simply deflected them elsewhere? Fourth, could greater international cooperation lead to outcomes that are better for refugee-receiving countries as well as for the refugees themselves? And finally, are there better policies?

2   Refugees and Asylum Seekers

Refugee and asylum seeker figures come from estimates compiled by the United Nations High Commission for Refugees (UNHCR). The definition of a refugee is derived from the 1951 Geneva Convention on Refugees, namely someone who, owing to a well-founded fear of persecution, is outside his or her country of normal residence and who is unable or unwilling to return to it. The UNHCR estimates plotted in Figure 1 show a dramatic increase from the early 1970s to a peak of nearly 18 million in 1992, before falling by a third to 12 million in 2001.[1] Two further points are worth noting about these refugee totals. First, they exclude an additional 5 million who in 2001 were *internally* displaced and living

---

[1]   Estimates of the total number of refugees differ. The United States Committee for Refugees (2003: 3) provides a figure of 14.9 million for 2001, nearly 3 million higher than the UNHCR estimate. Some of the definitional issues in constructing these totals are discussed in UNHCR (2002: 71–75) and Crisp (1999). Nevertheless, while estimates of the total differ, the profile of change over time is essentially the same.

in refugee-like situations but who were not classified as refugees because they were not outside their country of origin. Second, these refugee stock figures undergo considerable turbulence and turnover. When the refugee stock fell by 5.8 million between 1992 and 2001, there were 10.7 million new refugee arrivals and 16.5 million exits.

Figure 1:
Worldwide Stock of Refugees

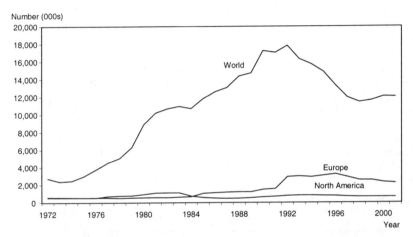

Source: UNHCR (2001: Annex 3).

The overwhelming majority of these refugees are located in the Third World, close to their country of origin. As Table 1 shows, there is a very strong correlation between the number of refugees that originated in a region and the number who are located within that region. In 2001, 49 percent of refugees originated somewhere in Asia or the Middle East and 46 percent were located there, while 30 percent originated in Africa and 27 percent were located there. Eastern Europe was the source of 11 percent of the refugees and host to 6 percent, some of whom were from outside the region. Western Europe hosted 1.7 million refugees from other regions in 2001 (14 percent of the worldwide total) while a further 646,000 (5 percent) were located in North America. As Figure 1 shows, the number of refugees in Europe rose sharply between the late 1980s and the early 1990s, while the number in North America declined. These trends are consistent with the rapid growth in the number of asylum seekers arriving in Europe.

Table 1:

Refugees by Region of Origin and Location, 1992 and 2001 (Thousands)

Region	Refugees by origin		Refugees by location	
	1992	2001	1992	2001
Great Lakes Region of Africa	700.2	1,055.3	983.6	1,190.7
West and Central Africa	960.1	540.4	950.5	570.1
East and Horn of Africa	1,928.8	1,364.7	1,784.7	966.8
Southern Africa	1,757.3	473.6	1,506.0	365.4
North Africa	245.5	206.7	257.2	183.6
The Middle East	1,454.4	901.4	266.3	463.4
South West Asia	4,682.0	3,914.4	5,840.0	4,066.8
Central Asia	60.0	63.4	3.0	97.8
South Asia	503.6	396.6	579.0	322.7
East Asia and the Pacific	731.6	667.4	473.0	616.1
Eastern Europe	708.8	372.9	546.0	294.3
South Eastern Europe	700.5	897.2	954.4	459.6
Central Europe and the Baltic States	60.1	62.8	147.8	18.7
Western Europe	0.0	1.8	1,841.0	1,731.5
North America and the Caribbean	23.8	26.7	769.7	646.1
Central America	129.1	30.9	853.4	25.8
South America	19.4	27.9	22.1	10.5
Stateless/Other/Unknown	3,132.0	1,025.7	20.7	–
Total	17,798.5	12,029.9	17,798.5	12,029.9

Source: UNHCR (2002: 84, 88).

Figure 2 plots the total number of new asylum applications lodged in 37 industrialized countries (a flow rather than a stock) by region of asylum.[2] It documents an enormous surge from about 150,000 per annum in the early 1980s to a peak of more than 850,000 in 1992, falling sharply to 380,000 in 1997 before rising again more recently. It also confirms once again that the bulk claimed asylum in Europe, principally in the 15 countries of the European Union (pre-enlargement). The EU accounted for 68 percent of all applications over the 20-year period, and North America accounted for most of the remainder. The sharp spike in the early 1990s (Figure 3) was accounted for by applications from Eastern Europe following the disintegration of the Soviet Union and the conflicts that followed the breakup of the former Yugoslavia. Still, there is evidence of an un-

---

2   These data are collected by the UNHCR, mainly from national governments. They are typically first instance claims and they represent the number of applications rather than the number of individuals. On average, each application represents around 1.2 to 1.3 individuals.

Figure 2:
Asylum Applications to Industrialized Countries, 1982–2001

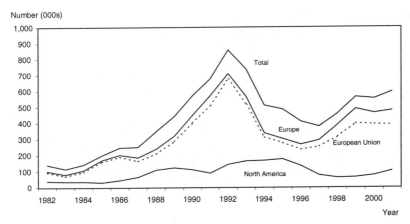

Source: UNHCR (2002: 112–113).

Figure 3:
Asylum Applications by Source Region, 1982–2001

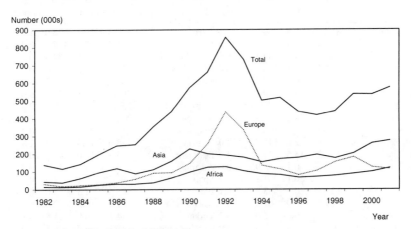

Source: UNHCR (2002: 115–116).

derlying upward trend, not only in applications from Europe, but also from Africa and Asia.

The left-hand panel of Table 2 reports the total number of applications from each of the top 20 source countries to the developed world by decade. Not surprisingly, Eastern Europe is well represented with large numbers arriving from Yugoslavia, Romania, Bosnia, and the Russian Federation, as is the Middle East with large numbers from Turkey, Iraq, Iran, and Afghanistan. Asia is also well represented by China, India, Pakistan, and Sri Lanka. While there is a clear correspondence between the number of refugees and the number of asylum seekers, some of the poorest countries (such as Angola, Rwanda, and Ethiopia/Eritrea) did not generate as many asylum seekers as might have been expected given the scale of the conflicts. Indeed, most African refugees do not get much further than a neighboring country, if they manage to leave at all. It is also notable that most of the countries that generated large numbers of asylum seekers in 1992–2001 also generated significant numbers in the previous decade. As we shall see, this historical persistence is an important feature of asylum flows, especially to Europe.

Table 2:
Top 20 Sources and Destinations of Asylum Seekers, 1982–2001

Source Country	1992–2001		1982–1991		Destination Country	1992–2001		1982–1991	
	No.	per 1,000	No.	per 1,000		No.	per 1,000	No.	per 1,000
Yugoslavia FR	817.2	77.5	269.8	17.0	Germany	1,597.3	19.6	996.9	1.7
Iraq	310.8	15.4	52.1	3.4	United States	869.0	3.2	437.7	0.2
Turkey	308.8	4.9	499.3	9.6	United Kingdom	576.6	10.0	164.5	0.3
Romania	304.7	13.1	195.4	8.6	Netherlands	358.6	23.2	95.0	0.7
Afghanistan	204.1	10.6	54.0	4.0	Canada	286.3	9.8	239.4	0.9
El Salvador	196.5	34.7	69.6	14.6	France	281.0	4.8	347.4	0.6
Bosnia and					Switzerland	243.5	34.2	170.2	2.6
Herzegovina	186.1	54.4	–	–	Sweden	228.6	25.9	183.2	2.2
Sri Lanka	168.9	9.5	176.8	11.3	Belgium	219.5	21.7	69.7	0.7
Islamic Rep. of Iran	161.1	2.6	195.5	4.0	Austria	128.0	15.9	134.0	1.8
Guatemala	154.8	15.5	38.1	4.9	Denmark	97.4	18.6	45.3	0.9
China	149.7	0.1	21.9	0.0	Australia	89.2	4.9	30.1	0.2
Somalia	147.6	20.1	51.1	7.7	Spain	84.2	2.1	37.5	0.1
India	124.4	0.1	63.2	0.1	Italy	83.4	1.5	55.0	0.1
Pakistan	113.2	0.9	67.9	0.7	Norway	71.1	16.3	32.3	0.8
Russian Federation	105.2	0.7	25.0	0.2	Turkey	54.5	0.9	27.8	0.1
Dem. Rep. of Congo	103.9	2.3	97.5	3.0	Czech Republic	48.1	4.7	3.8	0.0
Algeria	92.6	3.3	–	–	Ireland	39.7	11.0	0.03	0.0
Bulgaria	91.2	10.8	47.5	5.3	Hungary	37.5	3.7	4.4	0.0
Nigeria	77.1	0.8	33.0	0.4	Poland	25.0	0.6	2.4	0.0
Mexico	74.5	0.8	–	–					

Source: Asylum seeker numbers from UNHCR (2002: 112–113, 115–116); population totals for 1995 and 1985 from United Nations (2003: various tables).

The right-hand panel of Table 2 documents the top 20 countries in the developed world that receive asylum applications. Germany tops the list with a massive 1.6 million applications in 1992–2001, followed by the United States and the United Kingdom. Nine other EU countries also appear on the list, some of which have very large per capita rates (Belgium, Netherlands, Sweden, Switzerland). More notable still is the appearance on the list of Turkey, the Czech Republic, Hungary, and Poland, countries that were major sources of asylum seekers in the 1980s. Those countries might have become more attractive havens in the post-Soviet period, but it may also reflect the increasing difficulty of entering Western Europe. While most destination countries experienced an increase in the number of applications between the 1980s and the 1990s, the growth in those numbers varied widely. In Western Europe, large percentage increases occurred in the United Kingdom, the Netherlands, Belgium, and Ireland (from a base close to zero), while modest increases or small declines occurred in France, Switzerland, Sweden, and Austria. We shall examine the pattern of asylum claims in European destinations later, but first we turn to refugee origins.

3   The Causes of Refugee Flights

What causes refugees to flee their home country and seek sanctuary abroad? Perhaps the answer seems too obvious to warrant further discussion. For major refugee displacements such as those in Rwanda, Somalia, El Salvador, or Afghanistan the associated wars and conflicts are well known. Quantitative analyses typically focus on some measure of the incidence and intensity of conflict within the country as the main explanation. Table 3 offers an example using data from sub-Saharan Africa. Here the dependent variable is the total stock of refugees from a given country per thousand of the source country population, across 41 African countries annually from 1987 to 1992. There are 142 cases in this sample where no refugees are observed and another 104 with positive numbers of refugees. We therefore use tobit analysis. The explanatory variables exploit a variety of measures of violence and political instability from data assembled by Robert Bates (see Hatton and Williamson 2003).

Given that most of the variables in Table 3 are dummies, the coefficients can be read as the number of refugees per thousand created as a result of the violence event in question. Coups d'etat typically create an efflux of 35 per thousand, while government crises generate about 18 per thousand, but these effects are only on the borderline of significance. The incidence of guerilla warfare yields a more significant coefficient and the effect generates 25 refugees per thousand of the population. However, civil war is the most important variable generating refugees—about 35 refugees per thousand—while each military death in civil war (a proxy for the intensity of the war) generates another 35 refugees per thousand. Despite the strength of the civil war effects, the explanatory power of the regression as a whole is still rather low, as reflected in the pseudo R^2. This is because of the enormous heterogeneity in the size and intensity of the conflicts, and their refugee-generating effects, none of which is adequately reflected by these crude explanatory variables.

Table 3:
Explaining Refugee Displacements in Africa

Refs/Pop = −32.4	+35.7 Coups	+18.3 Crises	+25.2 GuerWar	+35.4 CivWar
(4.8)	(1.9)	(1.9)	(3.3)	(2.9)
+ 35.4 Deaths,		pseudo R^2 = 0.07, log likelihood = −595.6		
(4.4)				

Note: *t*-statistics in parentheses. – *Sample*: Balanced panel of 41 countries in sub-Saharan Africa by 6 years (1987–1992). – *Variable definitions*: Refs/Pop: number of refugees per thousand of source country population; Coups: dummy = 1 for years when there was a political coup d'etat; Crises: dummy=1 for years of government crisis; GuerWar; dummy =1 for years of guerilla warfare; CivWar: dummy =1 for years of civil war; Deaths: number of military deaths in civil war per thousand of the population. – *Method*: Tobit regression on 246 country/year observations.

Source: Hatton and Williamson (2003: Table 2), where the data are discussed in more detail. The original source for most of the variables is Robert Bates' Africa project, available at http://africa.gov.harvard.edu//.

Perhaps these results are unsurprising, but they raise a number of issues. First, if as some believe, refugee flights are determined by economic and demographic forces as well as by politics and violence, then these variables should also play a role. Indeed, some studies do find such effects, but they are generally weak in comparison to politics and violence. The African data also support that view. When variables such as real wage rates and the share of population aged 15–29 were added, they proved to be insignificant. Should we therefore conclude that economic and demographic factors play no role? Not necessarily, since war and violence are highly correlated with poor economic conditions and large young adult populations. And once the conflicts cease, the economy rapidly bounces back, so that their effects on refugees may not persist.[3]

---

[3]   Collier (1999) finds that the economies of war-ravaged states grow at 6 percent per year in the five years following the outbreak of peace. Pottenbaum and Kanbur (2001) find that the postwar bounce back in a range of socioeconomic indicators is

Second, the regression analysis is applied to the stock of refugees, rather than the flow into and out of refugee status. If refugees remain displaced for a number of years, even after the end of the conflict or crisis, then lagged values should also matter. However, when the regression in Table 3 is reestimated with the addition of explanatory variables lagged one and two years, the coefficients were not significant, suggesting that persistence is not important. This contrasts with the findings of some other studies where lags are found to matter (Schmeidl 1997; Azam and Hoeffler 2000). There are two possible explanations for our conflicting result. One is that the dynamics cannot be isolated in a short panel where most of the variance is in the cross-section. The other is that most refugee migrations in Africa occur just across borders; they are temporary and quickly reversed. Thus, of the14.2 million voluntary repatriations in 1992–2001, 8.3 million of them were in Africa.

It is worth dwelling on the second point for what follows later. Most of the refugee displacements occur when war breaks out or when there is a sudden rise in its intensity. Thereafter the flood subsides and the stock of refugees rises more gently. When the war or crisis abates, repatriation takes place, often quickly and on a scale that resembles that of the original displacement. This is particularly true in Africa, where refugees are often displaced to camps just across the border in which conditions are worse even than those in the refugee's war-ravaged homeland. In addition, refugees have in Africa sometimes been pushed back over the border by unwelcoming governments and hostile host populations (Rogge 1994). This response is less likely where the war is protracted and the refugees have assimilated into the host society. It is also less likely when refugees have gained asylum in a country where living standards are an order of magnitude higher than at home. This latter fact helps to explain the strong persistence of refugees in Europe that was observed in Figure 1. It can even be observed within Africa where those finding sanctuary in the Republic of South Africa have been less eager to return.[4]

---

significantly greater for low-income economies than for middle-income economies. They attribute this to the fact that the poorest countries have little infrastructure that can be destroyed during a conflict and they can therefore return to preexisting socioeconomic levels relatively quickly.

4   A 1994 survey of Mozambican refugees indicated that the majority did not want to repatriate. A UNHCR fact-finding mission showed that many of these Mozambicans whose families had joined them in the homelands were working on farms and in mines or were otherwise integrated and did not wish to return (Dolan 1999: 90).

4   Has the World Become a More Violent and Dangerous Place?

If war, violence, and political oppression are the fundamental causes that create refugees, then the refugee trends observed in Figure 1 and the pattern of asylum applications observed in Figures 2 and 3 should be explained largely by trends in war, violence, and persecution. The sources of "well founded fear of persecution" may, of course, take many forms that are not easy to quantify. Even if we consider wars alone, how do we combine the incidence, intensity, and the scale of wars in a way that captures the potential for generating refugees?

   One index of worldwide conflict is plotted in Figure 4. Each episode of conflict is given a score ranging from one to seven that reflects the scale of the conflict and the overall societal impact (Marshall 2002). A score of one denotes "sporadic or expressive political violence"—effectively, low-level violence by small militant groups. A score of seven denotes "pervasive warfare"—full-scale war that consumes the entire society. The total conflict index, which adds together all wars, followed an upward trend from 1965 until the late 1980s, a trend that dates back to the 1940s. Contrary to widespread belief, the cold war evinced a secular increase in violence, often associated with proxy wars, independence struggles, and post-colonial civil wars. These escalating levels of violence reached a peak between 1984 and 1992 and have since declined to levels similar

Figure 4:
Global Warfare Index

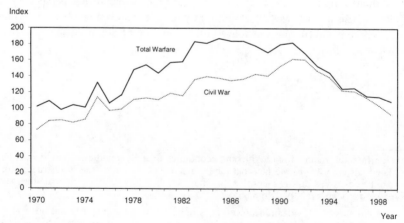

Source: Hatton (2004: 27).

to those of the early 1970s. The independence wars of the 1960s and 1970s gave way in the 1980s to intercountry wars, often involving newly independent states. While intercountry wars declined after the late 1980s, civil wars, which account for the bulk of worldwide violence, continued to rise until the early 1990s. These local conflicts often reflect long-standing ethno-political tensions, such as in the former Yugoslavia, that were unleashed by the ending of the cold war.

These patterns bear a fairly close resemblance to those observed in the total stock of refugees and in the flows of asylum seekers. The outbreak of new conflicts declined in the 1990s and the number of conflicts that were either contained or settled increased (Gurr et al. 2001). However, while the level of conflict fell in the 1990s back to that of the 1970s, the number of refugees and asylum seekers has not returned to its former level. This may reflect an increase in the ability of refugees to escape conflict. On the other hand, the number of refugees generated per conflict may have increased over time as a result of the growth of population at risk and, more importantly, due to greater access to weapons and to advances in weapons technology (Weiner 1997).

A further possibility is that refugee flights have increasingly been generated by causes other than full-scale war. Repressive political regimes, while not engaged in outright war, might nevertheless brutalize or persecute their populations. Measures of human rights abuse are correlated with lack of democracy and/or civil rights, and not only where there are wars and military regimes (Poe et al. 1999). One human rights measure is the Freedom House index, which scores the degree of political rights and of civil liberties on a scale of one to seven. The index is plotted in Figure 5, where lower numbers represent lower levels of human rights abuse and higher levels of freedom. They show a general increase in civil rights and political freedom with sharp improvements since the late 1980s.

These trends are also reflected in the evolution of political regimes. The percentage of all governments that were autocracies fell gradually from the 1970s and more sharply after the collapse of the Soviet Union and the ending of the cold war (Marshall 1999). Although the number and share of countries under democratic government increased, the greatest rise was—almost by definition—in the transitional regimes. The evidence suggests that transitional regimes are almost as prone to conflict as autocracies, but it may be easier to escape a chaotic transitional regime than an autocratic police state. That would be consistent with the experience of Eastern Europe after 1989, which accounts for most of the recent increase in the number of states that are labeled transitional. But while states that are not autocratic may be easier to flee, there may also be less reason to do so.

Figure 5:
World (Un)Freedom Index, 1975–1976 to 1999–2000

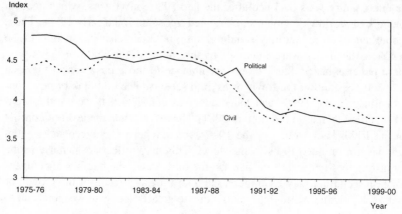

Source: Hatton (2004: 29).

5   From Refugees to Asylum Seekers in the West

As we have seen, the total number of refugees rose strongly until 1992 and then fell back, while the flow of asylum seekers followed the same pattern but with a steeper increase. This suggests that refugees (or those who claim to be refugees) have over time moved farther away from home conflicts and rights abuse and closer to the developed world, particularly Europe. Very few who claimed asylum did so in the developed world before the 1970s. In 1980–1982, the ratio of annual asylum claims to the worldwide stock of refugees was 1.7 percent; by 1999–2001 it had risen to 4.8 percent. So how and why do those displaced by conflicts in the Third World become asylum seekers in the First World?

While some manage to escape directly to Europe or America, costs and increasingly stringent visa requirements have made direct escape difficult. For most refugees, the first and only step is to escape over the border to a neighboring country. Poverty, disease, and risk of violence in refugee camps or shanty towns are among the reasons that so many return home as soon as war ends. Added to this, few of these neighboring countries offer the security of refugee status, since most are not signatories of the Geneva Convention. Often only temporary visas are given, with limited rights to move outside the camps, to gain employment, and to resettle into the host community. While these are good reasons to return home if circumstances permit, they are equally good reasons for onward migration in the hope of better conditions farther afield. Thus, although refugee displacements are almost always due to conflict and little else, economic factors play a much greater role in determining the numbers that emerge as asylum seekers in the West and the specific countries to which they apply—an issue that is explored further below.

For some refugees, the escape over the border to a neighboring country is the start of a much longer trip. But it is not simply a matter of applying for asylum at the embassy or consulate of the country of choice upon arrival in some transit country, since most Western nations do not admit asylum claims that are lodged outside their borders. Often the only prospect of gaining refugee status is through the refugee status determination procedure offered in the refugee camps or settlements by the UNHCR or even more indirectly through the fieldwork organizations of other NGOs. But the quota for direct resettlement in third countries is small—less than 100,000 per year worldwide—and it has become even more restricted after September 11, 2001. Hence, many potential asylum seekers bypass this process. As one recent report on conditions in East Africa and the Middle East puts it:

> Relatively large numbers of people, many in need of international protection and with valid asylum claims, choose not to avail themselves of the UNHCR's refugee determination procedures in the Middle East. Many fear making themselves known to the authorities out of concern of being detained pending refugee status determination and being treated like criminals by local police or security officials. Would be asylum seekers also know that generally only a fraction of asylum applications are granted. Concerned that the determination procedures are lengthy—lasting several months to several years in some countries—that they are unlikely to receive adequate social and economic assistance either from the host government or the UNHCR, and that they may have a better chance of getting to the West if they remain outside the official system, asylum seekers often turn to the services of smuggling organizations. (USCR and ECRE 2003: 13)

For many, this means clandestine travel, often across many borders and using many transport modes to reach the chosen destination. Routes into the EU include: from the north, through Russia and the Baltic; from the east, through Hungary, Poland, or the Czech and Slovak Republics, stretching back through to the Ukraine; or from the south, either directly from North Africa (the "blue route") or via Turkey and the Balkans. Although hard data are scarce, estimates suggest that more than half of those claiming asylum in countries like Germany, France, the United Kingdom, and the Netherlands are smuggled in (Morrison and Crosland 2001: 17). Estimates for the mid-1990s also suggest that the median payment to traffickers on European inward routes was around $4,000 to $5,000—the longer the route, the higher the cost (International Organisation for

Migration 2000: 94). Thus, it "is the poorest and most marginalized populations around the world that are least able to pay the price to enjoy asylum in Europe" (Morrison and Crosland 2001: 21).

Surveys of asylum seekers in Europe show that the degree of deliberation in the choice of route and destination depends on how sudden and unexpected the departure was and how limited the individual's resources were. Where there are choices, asylum seekers tend to gravitate to countries where friends and relatives have preceded them and along routes followed by other asylum seekers from the same source. Factors such as language or other cultural affinities matter too, as do perceptions of economic and social conditions at the destination.[5] For those who are smuggled in, the destination may be determined by the smugglers and sometimes the journey may end in a transit country rather than at the intended destination.

While a small number of refugees have arrived through organized programs, the vast majority are "spontaneous arrivals" who apply for asylum after having entered the country or at the border. Once having lodged a claim, the applicants must then wait for it to be adjudicated, a process that can take a long time. In the late 1990s, median processing times in the EU were about six months, although these durations have since fallen as processing has been speeded up. But, for a significant minority, the process can drag on for years, especially when there are appeals. At the end of this process, some are granted full refugee status under the Convention, while some who are not recognized are nevertheless given residency on humanitarian grounds (often with more restricted rights). The proportion who are successful has declined over the last 20 years. Among applications to 37 industrialized countries, the share of adjudications that resulted in Convention status fell from 50 to 20 percent between 1982 and 2001, while the share receiving any form of humanitarian status fell from 52 to 32 percent (UNHCR 2002: 121–122, 124–125). The EU-15 recognition rate for full Convention status was down to only 15 percent in 2001.

What happens to those who are rejected? In the late 1990s, removals and voluntary departures in major EU destinations were around half the number of claims that were rejected. Some may have simply left ahead of the threat of removal, but it is hard to escape the conclusion that most did not.[6] Most probably

---

5   See, for example, Böcker and Havinga (1997), Koser and Pinkerton (2001), and Robinson and Segrott (2002).

6   An average of 42,340 first instance claims were rejected in the United Kingdom over the years 1997–2001, while 23,200 were successful on appeal. Removals and voluntary departures were around 10,000 per annum in the late 1990s, rising to 13,460 in 2001, Thus, removals and departures account for only a little over half of the total number rejected. A parliamentary report noted with dismay that the government was unable to offer even a rough estimate of the number of asylum seekers whose claims

they either went underground or simply remained in a state of limbo because there was no possibility for legal migration elsewhere. It is also possible that the rising rejection rates have deterred some potential asylum seekers from making claims at all, preferring instead to remain underground rather than to risk rejection and removal. This is all the more likely for those with relatively weak claims and in countries where the flourishing underground economy makes it relatively easy to live and work undetected. For these migrants, low wages and uncertain employment in the EU are better than the conditions they would face in their country of origin. Hence, EU asylum policy has become increasingly bound up with the problem of illegal immigration.

6   Explaining Asylum Applications to the EU

Two-thirds of all asylum applications in the industrialized world are lodged in the 15 countries of the (pre-enlargement) European Union, and the absolute number of applications has risen dramatically over the last three decades. War and oppression may account for much of the rise but other things must matter too. It is often argued that flows of asylum seekers from poor origins to rich destinations are driven by the same economic and demographic fundamentals that determine other migration flows. Such evidence might be interpreted as support for the view that most asylum seekers are "economic migrants," but we think it has a bigger influence on the number of refugees (initially displaced for other reasons) that become asylum seekers in the West. Even so, it is far from clear that economic variables can account for much of the trend increase in asylum applications. And as we shall see below, there has been a massive tightening in policies aimed at deterring asylum applications. If these policies have been at all effective, then applications should have been falling rather than rising. There must be other, even stronger, forces offsetting the impact of economic variables and policy.

Quantitative studies of the determinants of asylum claims are scarce. Rotte et al. (1997) analyzed applications to Germany from 17 countries in Asia and Africa over the years 1987–1995. They found that the level of political terror in the source country was a key factor generating asylum seekers but that improvements in political rights and civil liberties tended to increase the numbers too. Economic incentives and constraints were also found to be important: the bigger the income gap between Germany and the source country, the greater the number of asylum applications; in addition, source country income by itself had a posi-

---

had been rejected but who nevertheless remained in the country (UK Home Affairs Committee 2003: 12).

tive effect, suggesting that poverty constraints were important. In the presence of these and other variables, they found that the key reforms in German asylum policy, in 1987 and 1993, had large negative effects on the number of asylum applications. Thieleman (2003) analyzed relative movements in asylum applications across 20 OECD countries from 1985 to 1999 to see whether the German policy results could be generalized. His pooled regression indicated that the key destination country variables were the unemployment rate, the existing stock of foreign nationals, and the country's reputation for generosity, as reflected by development aid. An index of the toughness of asylum policy had the expected negative effect on applications, but was not found to be very important.[7]

Existing studies focus either on one destination country (which may not be representative) or on the distribution of asylum claims between countries (thereby excluding source country effects and eliminating overall trends). The econometric result presented in Table 4 overcomes some of these limitations. The dependent variable is the annual number of asylum claims for 1981 to 1999 from three source regions (Africa, Asia, or Eastern Europe) and by 14 EU destinations. These flows are explained by variables representing economic forces, violence and oppression in source regions, and asylum policy in EU destinations. The coefficients imply that an increase of 1 percent in the ratio of source to destination GDP per capita reduces the number of asylum claims by 2.1 percent, while an increase in the unemployment rate of the destination country by 1 percentage point reduces asylum applications by 7.5 percent. A 10 percent increase in the index of source region conflict raises the number of asylum claims by 7.5 percent, while a 10 percent improvement in the index representing political rights (higher values represent less freedom) reduces asylum claims by 25 percent. Finally, the index of asylum policy (higher values represent tougher policies) confirms the view that more restrictive asylum policy reduces the number of applications.

These results indicate that economic forces, conflict, and policy all influence the number of asylum applications, but how do they account for the dramatic increase since the early 1980s? Table 5 provides a decomposition of the change in applications to the EU as a whole from the three source regions between 1981

---

[7]   There have also been a number of other studies that assess the effects of policy more qualitatively. A report from the Inter-Governmental Consultations on Asylum and Migration (1997: 22) concluded that the fall in asylum applications from its peak in 1992 was partly explained by the tightening of policy in a number of countries. More recently, a report commissioned by the UK Home Office found that, with the exception of policies relating to access to the country's territory, there is little evidence that policy has had the desired effects in stemming the flow applications (Zetter et al. 2003). But without using econometric methods, it is impossible to isolate the effects of policy from other variables that determine the number of asylum applications, nor is it possible to take account of the endogeneity of asylum policy.

Table 4:
Explaining Asylum Applications to the EU

Log Apps/Pop =	−2.12 log GDPRatio	−7.47 UDest	+17.17 Conflict	+0.51 PolRights
	(4.4)	(3.6)	(2.9)	(2.7)
	+0.26 logStock81	+0.77 EastEur90	−0.09 Policy	+0.20 Time
	(5.8)	(1.9)	(2.0)	(8.9)
	$R^2 = 0.78$;	No. obs. = 798		

Note: t-statistics in parentheses calculated from robust standard errors. – *Sample*: Annual data for three source regions, Africa Asia and Eastern Europe by 14 EU destination countries (EU-15 excluding Luxembourg), for 1981 to 1999. – *Variable Definitions*: Apps/Pop: asylum applications from source region to destination country/source region population (millions); LogGDPRatio: log ratio of GDP per capita, source region to destination country; UDest: unemployment rate in destination country; *Conflict*: Index of the scale and intensity of conflict in source region; PolRights: Freedom House index of political rights in source region; LogStock81: log population from source region living in destination country in 1981/source region population; EastEur90: dummy =1 for Eastern European source from 1990; Policy: index of toughness of asylum policy in destination country. – *Method*: Instrumental variables; Policy instrumented. Fixed effects for three source regions and 14 destination countries and dummy for Italy from 1990 (for Asia and Africa only) included but not reported.

Source: Hatton (2004: Table 8; see also the Appendix for details of the data sources).

and 1999. Population growth in source regions added about 50,000 to total applications. The impact of economic growth at home, however, was negative: African and Eastern European GDP per capita fell further behind that of the EU, but these effects were overwhelmed by improved economic performance in Asia, so that the net effect was a reduction in claims by 31,300. And because unemployment was higher in most EU countries in 1999 than it was in 1981, this reduced asylum claims by a further 60,000. Thus, the view that "economic migration" is the cause of rising asylum applications seems to be untenable. Economic incentives have substantial effects on asylum flows, but they cannot explain the long-term upward trend.

What about conflict and political oppression? The total effect of conflict across all three source regions was to increase applications by a modest 11,600. Although rising conflict contributed an increase of 83,000 to the annual flow between 1981 and 1992, this was largely reversed as the number and intensity of conflicts declined. Improvements in political rights in sending regions served to reduce the number of asylum claims dramatically, especially from Eastern Europe (−138,500). However, the improved political conditions that worked to keep Eastern Europeans at home were partially undone by the increased possibilities of exit. Thus, the dummy for Eastern Europe, which represents the period

Table 5:

Decomposition of Change in Asylum Applications by Source Region, 1981–1999 (Thousands)

	Africa	Asia	E. Europe	Total
Source region population	18.1	28.6	2.7	49.4
GDP per capita ratio	30.1	−79.1	17.7	−31.3
Unemployment in destination	−7.7	−28.6	−23.6	−59.9
Conflict index	−11.7	−28.3	51.3	11.3
Political rights index	−14.2	−11.6	−138.5	−164.2
Eastern Europe from 1989	–	–	70.9	70.9
Asylum policy	−25.5	−66.4	−63.4	−155.3
Total above effects	−10.9	−175.6	−82.8	−269.3
Actual change, 1981–1999	53.0	80.4	69.5	202.9

Source: Hatton (2004: Table 10).

Figure 6:

Asylum Policy Index, EU Average, 1980–1999

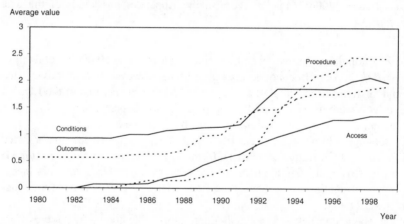

Source: Hatton (2004: 24).

from the fall of the Berlin Wall onwards, raised applications by 70,900 per annum after 1989.

Finally, the effect of the asylum policy index (Figure 6) was to reduce EU asylum applications by 155,300. This index consists of eleven components representing different elements of policy, each of which is a dummy variable taking the value 1 as policy becomes more restrictive. The result is a dramatic confirmation of the deterrent effects of policy but it leaves us with an even bigger puzzle. When the effects of policy are added to those of other variables, they predict a dramatic fall of 269,300 in the number of asylum applications between 1981 and 1999. Yet over the same period the annual flow actually *increased* by 202,900.

What lies behind this mysterious upward trend? One possibility is that policy has been far less effective in deterring asylum applications to the EU as a whole than the country-specific results in Tables 4 and 5 suggest. Rather than deterring asylum applications, the effect of tougher policies has been to deflect them from one EU country to another. If that were true, then the large negative policy effect for an individual country would be offset by the deflection effects of tougher policy elsewhere and so the EU-wide impact of policy might evaporate. To test this hypothesis, an additional variable for asylum policy in other EU countries (lagged one period) was added to the Table 4 regression. This took a positive sign as the deflection hypothesis would suggest but the coefficient was small and insignificant (0.04, $t = 0.5$). Deflection effects may be present but they are difficult to identify in the data. And even if net policy effects are zero for the EU as a whole, the overall increase in asylum applications would still remain unexplained.

The most plausible explanation for the underlying trend is that asylum flows have cumulative effects. These are analogous to chain migration effects that are widely observed in studies of migration, but here they operate a little differently. More than half of asylum applicants have arrived in the EU through illegal channels, often with the aid of increasingly dense and efficient networks of people smugglers. Migrant trafficking has grown since the late 1980s as smugglers have become more professional and expert, developments that have been coupled with the opening up of a variety of routes through Eastern Europe.[8] To test for these effects, a variable representing the cumulative flow of asylum applicants to the destination from the source region was added to the Table 4 regression. This took a large and significant coefficient (0.53, $t = 6.8$), and in its presence the coefficient on the time trend becomes small and insignificant. Not surprisingly, this effect is very powerful and it implies that every thousand of the cumulative stock of asylum applications generated a further eighty applications each year. This is

---

[8]   The process is well illustrated by a comment from an official of the Hungarian Border Guard: "In the beginning, only a few isolated individuals were involved in human trafficking, but as time passed they started cooperating, and step by step the business developed into an international one. Well-planned routes and well-organised groups have evolved, which are no longer coordinated from Hungary. Trafficking can be coordinated either from the destination country or from the migrants' country of origin. This is the result of a natural process of development; market demand and necessity have contributed to the development of certain branches of crime" (International Organization for Migration 2000: 196).

a larger effect than is typically found in studies of other migration streams and it can account for most of the otherwise unexplained upward trend.[9] While the interpretation of this "stock" effect may be open to question, the view that it represents the expansion of networks (legal and illegal) does seem consistent with much of the qualitative literature.

7   The Development of Asylum Policies in the EU during the 1990s

The fundamental basis for asylum policy in the EU and elsewhere in the developed world is the Convention Relating to the Status of Refugees, first signed in Geneva in 1951, and the Protocol that followed in 1967.[10] It has two key provisions. The first (Article 1) is to define a refugee as someone who is outside his or her country of normal residence and who is unable or unwilling to return to it "owing to a well founded fear of persecution." The second (Article 33) is that no person who has claimed asylum under the Convention should be forcibly returned to a territory where he or she may be at risk of persecution—the so-called principle of nonrefoulement. Any asylum claim submitted in a signatory state must be considered under due process irrespective of whether the applicant entered the country legally or not. Thus, the Convention provides access to asylum procedures for an unlimited number of applicants, once having gained access to the territory, irrespective of whether they enter legally or not.[11]

Nevertheless, there are a number of ways that individual countries can deter asylum claims: policies designed to restrict access to the country's borders by potential asylum seekers, reforms to the procedures under which applications are processed, measures relating to the outcome of claims, and changes in the treat-

---

[9]   Estimates for other migration streams generally suggest that every thousand of the stock generates a little over 20 additional migrants per year (Hatton and Williamson 2005). However, the *elasticity* of the flow with respect to the stock presented here is similar to that found in other studies (Pedersen et al. 2004).

[10]   The Convention, which became effective in 1954, was originally signed by 29 countries. Other countries have since signed bringing the total to 145 in 2004. Among EU-15 countries, the most recent signatories are Portugal (1976) and Spain (1978) and it is now a condition of EU membership. The right to asylum was earlier enshrined in Article 14 of the Universal Declaration of Human Rights (1948) and also in the European Convention for the Protection of Human Rights (1950), which contains a nonrefoulement clause. The main provision of the 1967 Protocol was to extend the coverage of the Convention to those displaced from sources outside Europe.

[11]   The Convention does not guarantee permanent right of residence in a host country except insofar as this is provided by the nonrefoulement clause.

ment of asylum seekers during processing. Measures of toughness in these different dimensions of policy are displayed in Figure 6. These are averages across 14 EU countries of variables that take a value of 0 before and 1 after the introduction of a restrictive measure. The index for "access" includes two components, whereas those reflecting "procedure," "outcomes," and "conditions" each include three components. These are averages of the constituent elements that were used to form the 11-point policy index for the individual EU countries that was used in the Table 4 regression. Across the EU as a whole, all these dimensions of policy show steep increases in restrictiveness, particularly in the first half of the 1990s.

The various elements of policy involved differing degrees of coordination between countries. Measures to tighten external border control followed from the relaxation of internal borders under the Schengen Convention (1990) and the Maastricht Treaty (effective 1993). Carrier sanctions were first introduced in the United Kingdom and Germany in 1987, and by the late 1990s they had become universal. Visa restrictions were gradually extended and by 1993 the Schengen signatories shared a joint list that included 73 countries, a figure that exceeded 150 by 1998.

The most important reforms to the processing of asylum applications followed from the 1990 Dublin Convention and the resolutions of a ministerial meeting in London. It was resolved in Dublin that an asylum claim would be dealt with by one state only, specifically the state of first entry. A consensus was developed in London on three further issues. The first was the "safe third country" concept that allowed member states to refuse to consider asylum claims if the applicant had transited through a country deemed "safe" where he or she could have sought asylum. The second was to determine that "manifestly unfounded" asylum claims could be summarily rejected without the right of appeal. The third was the designation of "safe countries of origin" where there is a presumption of no risk of persecution and where an expedited procedure could be used. In 1994 and 1995 the European Council of Ministers produced a series of further recommendations, the most important of which were on readmission agreements.[12]

These recommendations were not binding on member governments but they gradually diffused across the EU. The most notable case was Germany, where the measures introduced in 1993 required an amendment to the constitution (Basic Law), which contains a clause on the right to asylum. Particularly contentious was the adoption of the safe country of origin concept. Similar sets of policies were introduced in most other EU countries between 1991 and 1998 although the

---

12 These are bilateral agreements with nonmember states that allow asylum seekers to be sent back to countries they had transited. They have been heavily criticized for opening the door to serial refoulement.

toughness and the timing differed. In addition, there were reforms that affected the outcomes of the asylum procedures. These included the speed with which asylum claims are processed (which limits the opportunities for integration into the host community before a decision is reached), and increases in the toughness of deportation policies in the event of an unsuccessful claim. Some countries also moved to limit the granting of humanitarian status to those denied full Convention status.

Finally, various reforms were introduced relating to the treatment of asylum seekers during processing, in particular dispersal and detention, access to welfare benefits, and the right to seek employment. During the 1980s a number of countries permitted asylum seekers to work while their applications were being processed but these rights were largely withdrawn during the 1990s (e.g., France in 1991 and Belgium in 1993). A number of countries also restricted access to welfare benefits, substituting in-kind subsistence for cash benefits, often making them available only at designated reception centers. Such measures were often reinforced by the dispersal of asylum seekers to centers outside the major metropolitan centers and by increasingly strict rules on detention.

It is important to stress, however, that while a degree of harmonization developed during the 1990s, most of the recommendations made at intergovernmental conferences and by the EU Council of Ministers were not binding on member governments, at least until the end of the decade. In the absence of a binding EU-wide asylum policy, individual governments responded to mounting pressures, often with a succession of policy packages. Where some led, others followed. To a degree, EU-wide initiatives can be seen as attempts to harmonize policies that were developed by individual national governments from the late 1980s onwards. But true international coordination in the sense that policy is set at the international level, rather than percolating upwards from below, did not emerge until the end of the decade.

The capacity to set policy at the EU level stemmed from the 1997 Treaty of Amsterdam and the European Council meeting at Tampere, Finland in 1999. Under the latter, EU ministers reaffirmed that any common EU policy would be based on a "full and inclusive" application of the Geneva Convention and in particular that the principle of nonrefoulement would be honored. Under the former, the European Commission gained the exclusive right to propose legislation starting in 2002 in order to produce a set of harmonized asylum policies by May 1, 2004.[13] The first stage of the Common European Asylum System involved setting minimum standards in a number of areas. They include determining which state is responsible for considering an application (so-called Dublin II)

---

[13]   In the jargon of the EU, the Treaty of Amsterdam moved immigration and asylum from the Third Pillar (intergovernmental) to the First Pillar (Community).

and setting minimum standards for the reception and treatment of asylum seekers. Regulations establishing a common definition of refugee status and procedural standards have now also been agreed.

Much of the rhetoric surrounding the establishment of an EU-wide framework has been about jointly improving the plight of refugees. Although the first stage of the Common European Asylum system is often seen as a process of leveling down rather than up, there are some signs in the opposite direction. Limited steps on "burden sharing" include the setting up of the European Refugee Fund in 2000, chiefly to help defray the costs of projects for economic integration of refugees and to finance emergency temporary protection measures in the event of a mass influx of refugees. Also, the draft directive on the definition of a refugee explicitly includes those who are in fear of persecution by nonstate agents. If adopted, this would widen the definition used by France and Germany, which only includes as refugees those under threat of persecution by agents of the state rather than by, say, rebels or bandits.[14] But, while some progress has been made, EU-wide measures still fall far short of a thoroughgoing international asylum policy. A key issue now facing the EU is how the second stage of the common European and Asylum System should develop.

8   The Case for International Cooperation

Throughout the 1990s, international agencies, NGOs, and academic observers sympathetic to the plight of refugees and asylum seekers urged the case for international cooperation. They argued that, as a result of the limited degree of coordination, the evolution of policy has been a race to the bottom (see, for instance, Edminster 2000). In the absence of truly international policies there is essentially a noncooperative outcome that settles on the lowest common denominator. In his influential book, Gregor Noll (2000) described in detail the mechanics of what he saw as "the common market of deflection" within the EU. The implication is that individual governments acting alone have sought to protect themselves against floods of asylum seekers by tightening access, toughening their procedures, and affording less generous treatment to asylum seekers, thus deflecting them elsewhere. That raises two questions, one empirical and one theoretical. On the empirical side, we have seen that the deterrent effects of policy shifts in the 1990s are substantial, but the deflection effects are uncertain. On

---

14   A strict interpretation of that definition would, in principle, rule out many asylum seekers from countries like Somalia, where there is effectively no national government, or from countries like Angola and Sri Lanka, where many of the refugees are fleeing from rebel groups in areas outside the control of the government.

the theoretical side the case is yet to be made that a truly international policy would yield "better" outcomes and it is worth dwelling a little further on whether (and why) this might be the case.

The outcomes of policy must be judged from a welfare point of view, and the welfare in question is that of the citizens of states that control the admission of refugees through their asylum policies. In this respect, a sharp distinction must be drawn between asylum seekers and other (nonrefugee) immigrants. Immigration policy is determined by the interests of the host population, either by selecting those most likely to make an economic contribution and least likely to be a welfare burden, or by family reunification. By contrast, asylum policy is altruistic: asylum seekers are admitted because of the benefit it brings to *them,* not to the host society. Strong humanitarian motives for helping others escape persecution are widely reflected in public attitudes towards genuine refugees.[15] Thus, the "benefit" of refugees to the host country population comes through satisfying these altruistic motives, rather than through direct self-interest. Such benefit accruing to one individual does not preclude the same benefit accruing to others and hence providing a safe haven to refugees may be thought of as analogous to a public good. Furthermore, individuals with these humanitarian motives are likely to gain additional benefit from the knowledge that refugees also find safety in countries other than their own. However, there are also costs associated with asylum seekers that fall exclusively on the country to which they apply.

These elements can be captured in a simple model for two (identical) countries. The net benefit from refugees accruing to the citizens of refugee-receiving country 1 can be represented as

$$(1) \qquad V_1 = (r_1 + \lambda r_2)^b - c r_1,$$

where the valuation V_1 depends on the number that are received in the home country, r_1, and the number that are accepted abroad, r_2, minus the host country cost of refugees, $c r_1$. The parameter $\lambda < 1$ reflects a lower valuation for refugees accommodated abroad while $b < 1$ reflects diminishing marginal utility for (or diminishing tolerance of) refugees.

---

[15] An international opinion survey of 1995 shows that, in the developed world, public attitudes towards genuine refugees are much more positive than those towards immigrants and very much more positive than those towards illegal immigrants (Hatton 2004: Table 13; Hatton and Williamson 2004: Ch. 16). In most countries, a majority of respondents responded positively to the question whether "refugees who have suffered political oppression should be allowed to stay." Similar sentiments are revealed in a Dutch survey where 70 percent of respondents agreed that "a country like the Netherlands has a strong moral obligation to admit refugees" (Brons et al. 2001).

The number of refugees accepted in country 1 depends on overall "demand" for refugee places, on the generosity of asylum policy, and on deflection effects from policy in country 2:

(2) $r_1 = \gamma_1 A - \beta \gamma_2 A,$

where A is total refugee demand and γ represents the generosity of the country's asylum policy. The parameter $\beta < 1$ captures the deflection effect from policy in country 2 on refugees flowing to country 1. Thus, for a given level of demand, more refugees flow to country 1 the more generous country 1's policy is and the less generous that of country 2 is.

Substituting (2) and the identical equation for country 2 into (1) gives country 1's valuation of refugees as

(3) $V_1 = [\gamma_1 A(1 - \lambda\beta) + \gamma_2 A(\lambda - \beta)]^b - cA(\gamma_1 - \beta\gamma_2).$

The first-order condition for maximizing this valuation with respect to γ_1 gives the optimal policy for country 1, taking country 2 policy as given, as

(4) $\gamma_1 = \left[\dfrac{c}{b}\right]^{\frac{1}{b-1}} [1 - \lambda\beta]^{\frac{-b}{b-1}} A^{-1} - \gamma_2 \left[\dfrac{\lambda - \beta}{1 - \lambda\beta}\right].$

Thus, country 1's policy will be tougher (γ_1 is lower), the higher the cost per refugee, c, and the higher the overall demand for asylum, A. But the effect of toughening policy in the other country (a fall in γ_2) depends on the sign of $\lambda - \beta$. On the one hand, because people care about refugees in the other country, they might want to accept more if the other country takes fewer. On the other hand, the deflection effect from tougher policy in country 2 will cause country 1 to toughen its policy.

Solving the two identical reaction functions (4) together gives the noncooperative policy setting $\gamma_n = \gamma_1 = \gamma_2$ as

(5) $\gamma_n = \left[\dfrac{c}{b}\right]^{\frac{1}{b-1}} [1 - \lambda\beta]^{\frac{-1}{b-1}} A^{-1} [1 - \lambda\beta + \lambda - \beta]^{-1}.$

If instead asylum policy is set jointly to maximize the total valuation from refugees $V_1 + V_2$, the cooperative common policy parameter, $\gamma_c = \gamma_1 = \gamma_2$, will be

(6) $\gamma_c = \left[\dfrac{c}{b}\right]^{\frac{1}{b-1}} [1 - \beta]^{\frac{1}{b-1}} A^{-1} [1 - \lambda\beta + \lambda - \beta]^{\frac{-b}{1-b}}.$

In both the cooperative and the noncooperative regimes an increase in demand for refugee status causes toughening of policy. While this is consistent with the empirical evidence (Hatton 2004: Table 7), that evidence cannot discriminate between the alternative regimes.

What about absolute levels? As compared with the noncooperative outcome, the humanitarian benefit derived from refugees is higher, and policy is more generous, in the cooperative case. This can be seen by taking the ratio of (6) to (5):

$$(7) \qquad \frac{\gamma_c}{\gamma_n} = \left[\frac{1 - \lambda\beta + \lambda - \beta}{1 - \lambda\beta + \lambda\beta^2 - \beta} \right]^{\frac{1}{1-b}}.$$

Since this is greater than one, $\gamma_c > \gamma_n$, there are gains from cooperation. This is due to the public good spillover rather than to the internalization of deflection effects. Thus for $\beta = 0$ and $\lambda > 0$, the cooperative outcome produces higher welfare and more generous policy.[16] By contrast, if there are deflection effects but no public goods spillover, $\beta > 0$ and $\lambda = 0$, the cooperative and noncooperative outcomes are the same. Thus, the argument that cooperative policy will raise welfare chiefly because it internalizes deflection effects seems to be misplaced.

Of course, as the European experience shows, it may be hard (or it may take a long time) to reach agreement when there is an imbalance between countries in the level of refugee demand, in processing and support costs, or in tastes for humanitarian action. Such asymmetries are not considered in this simple model, and including them makes the analysis less tractable and the conclusions less clear-cut. In addition, there may be opportunities for strategic game playing by some countries in order to shift the burden to others. Nevertheless, the evidence reviewed above does suggest that centrally determined EU policies tend to be rather less restrictive than those of member governments. If so, then shifting the locus of power over asylum policy to supranational authorities should benefit both the humanitarian-inclined voters in receiving countries and the refugees themselves.

9   International Solutions

In recent years, there has been a vigorous debate about reforming asylum policies at the international level. The need for international cooperation is stressed

---

[16] Just to illustrate, in the case where public good spillover is large, say $\lambda = 1$, and with $\beta = 0$ and $b = 0.5$, the ratio γ_c/γ_n is 4.

on almost all sides of the debate. One view is that the main instrument of policy, the 1951 Geneva Convention, should either be replaced or reformed. Critics point out that the Convention was conceived in conditions very different from those that exist today. It was designed in the aftermath of wartime displacements in Europe and it operated in the shadow of the cold war when asylum seekers were few in number and when escapees from communism were welcomed. The arrival of large numbers of spontaneous migrants who can take advantage of the legal entitlement to enter the asylum process and are protected against refoulement is seen by some to compromise the entire edifice. Because the right to decide who can and who cannot enter is one of the defining features of a nation state, the clash between individuals' rights under the Convention and under national immigration and asylum laws has become all the more acute.

The trend in Western countries has been to deny access to the country's territory so that refugees' rights under the Convention do not become operative, to toughen up on Convention status determination, to substitute lesser forms of protection, using expedited processes, and to provide less favorable economic rights and conditions. While this may be consistent with the letter of Convention law, it nevertheless undermines its spirit. The weakness of the Convention's provision for international cooperation makes it seem all the more redundant in the eyes of some.[17] This is not principally a failure of the Convention itself but of cooperation within and around it. As one observer (referring to recent Australian experience) puts it, "if we fail to systematize a process of collectivized protection, we invite criticism of refugee law itself. Worse still we invite *de facto* withdrawal from refugee law" (Hathaway 2002: 44).

However compromised and conditional the current refugee regime may seem, it nevertheless puts a floor under what individual countries can do to avoid their obligations under it. In this minimal sense it forces countries to be more generous than they might otherwise be in the absence of the Convention or under alternatives that might be negotiated in its place. In the light of the previous section's argument that host countries acting alone fail to maximize the welfare even of their own citizens, the Convention, despite its loopholes, may still be seen as welfare enhancing. And even under the present pressures it seems unlikely to fall apart.[18] Ministers of signatory states gathered to mark the fiftieth

---

[17] Article 35 requires only that contracting states cooperate with the UNHCR in its duty of supervising the application of the provisions of the Convention.

[18] As the UK Government (2003: 9) candidly states: "The danger here is that a UK or European withdrawal would lead to the collapse of the Convention with developing countries reasoning that they need not tie themselves to obligations that the developed world is not prepared to keep. This would result in increased global flows of refugees with millions of people being left in limbo without protection. Therefore

anniversary of the Convention strongly reaffirmed their commitment to honoring it. The document that emerged from these "Global Consultations" called for a long series of enhancements, expressed as six goals, one of which was "sharing of burdens and responsibilities more equitably and building of capacities to receive and protect refugees."[19] Yet, for the most part, these represent good intentions rather than concrete plans for multilateral action.

It seems likely that the best prospects are for cooperation among regional groups of refugee-receiving states that face similar conditions. The European Union is the obvious example. Beyond the immediate harmonization that followed from Amsterdam and Tampere, the EU is still searching for a more workable policy for the second phase of its common European Asylum System. While the Commission has repeatedly stressed the need to develop a new system that is both comprehensive and humane, so far the focus has remained firmly on measures to control, efficiently process, and deter asylum seekers. Implicit in this is the recognition that expanding the opportunities for asylum seekers will simply lead to larger flows of illegal immigrants, most of whom fail to qualify as refugees but nevertheless remain in the country.

The European Council received two proposals in 2003, one from the United Kingdom Government and one from the UNHCR, each mapping out a future European Asylum System. The UK government's scheme concentrated on extraterritorial processing of asylum claims. Asylum seekers arriving in the EU would be transferred to a Regional Protection Area outside the EU (in a transit country or in the region of origin) where their refugee status would be determined (UK Government 2003). Those found to be in genuine need would then either be transferred back to developed countries according to pre-agreed-upon quotas, resettled elsewhere, or would remain until they could be safely repatriated. Aside from the practicalities of such a scheme, the proposal was widely criticized as burden-shifting rather than burden-sharing and it has since been dropped. [20]

---

any future withdrawal from the Geneva Convention needs to be coupled with an alternative regime for refugees."

[19] The other five goals were: strengthening implementation of the 1951 Convention and 1967 Protocol, protecting refugees within broader migration movements, addressing security-related concerns more effectively, redoubling the search for more durable solutions, and meeting the protection needs of refugee women and refugee children (United Nations 2002: 13). Details of the global consultations process and associated documents can be found at http://www.unhcr.ch/cgi-bin/texis/vtx/global-consultations.

[20] The United Kingdom's proposal was evaluated critically by the European Commission (2003) as well as in commentaries by NGO's such as the Refugee, Council, Amnesty International, the United States Committee on Refugees, and the European Council for Refugees and Exiles.

The UNHCR's proposal, which has received a more favorable reception, was presented as the "EU prong" of its wider so-called Convention Plus initiative (UNHCR 2003). Under this scheme, one or more closed Asylum Processing Centres would be set up within the borders of the EU, to act as community-wide clearing houses to which asylum applicants would be transferred from member states. At these centers, asylum seekers would be held and their claims determined on behalf of member governments by a new European Asylum Agency. Those whose claims are successful would be transferred for settlement in member states according to "agreed criteria" for burden sharing. Those whose claims are rejected would be returned to their countries of origin through collective action by member states, and the costs of administration would be defrayed by the pooling of resources in a relaunched version of the European Refugee Fund. While such a system would at first deal with only some claims (such as those deemed manifestly unfounded), it would progressively take on wider responsibilities for registering and screening applications and it would become increasingly independent of member governments.

There are a number of reservations even about this proposal. One is the legality of transferring asylum claims to be processed extraterritorially, especially if such functions are delegated to an agency that is not itself a responsible government. Another is the question of whether asylum applicants should be kept in mandatory detention at the Asylum Processing Centres, what freedoms they should have, and who would monitor them. There are also serious questions about whether such centers would become magnets for people-smugglers and traffickers, and about how to deal with unsuccessful applicants who, for one reason or another, cannot be returned to their country of origin. Related to these issues, there is the question of how individual countries might be persuaded to allow EU Asylum Processing Centres to be established on their territory.[21] Perhaps sufficient inducement might be provided to persuade one or more of the new members of the EU to act as hosts to such centers, which might be located conveniently close to entry points. And although a legal instrument on resettlement within the EU has been suggested, little attention has been given to exactly how successful claimants would be reallocated among member states.

The fact that member states would still be responsible for the resettlement of refugees suggests that the incentives for full cooperation (in the sense discussed above) would be limited. Our proposal would be a scheme that sets a fixed contribution to the European Refugee Fund (say, in proportion to the country's GDP) and a resettlement quota (say, in proportion to its population). For any EU member that took refugees in excess of its quota, there would be a per-refugee

---

[21] These and other criticisms of the (revised) UNHCR proposal have recently been discussed by the European Union Committee of the UK House of Lords (2004).

rebate that would effectively reduce the cost of resettlement at the margin. This would have two advantages. First, reducing the marginal cost of refugees would help to expand refugee numbers towards the fully cooperative level, even in the absence of full cooperation. Second, the number of refugees that a country accepted would be determined by its preferences for refugees and by the costs of resettling them, rather than simply on the number who happen to apply to that country.

While a system like this might provide the mechanism for efficient burden-sharing, there remains the question of whether the system as a whole would be perceived as more generous. On the one hand, centralized processing and greater enforcement of removals might make applying for asylum less attractive to those with weak claims, discouraging them from applying at all. On the other hand, if the processing of applications using an EU-wide standard led to a larger number being accepted for settlement, then according to the results in Table 4, that would add a boost to the total number of applications.

10   Tackling the Problem at the Source

It has been widely suggested that more resources should be devoted to providing aid to refugees closer to home, partly to prevent unwanted onward migration, but more importantly, to alleviate the plight of the vast majority of refugees who are in countries of first asylum in the origin regions. The UNHCR's Convention Plus agenda calls for situation-specific agreements to expand the opportunities for integration into countries of first asylum as well as for resettlement farther afield. It also seeks to create better conditions for voluntary repatriation.[22] While rejecting the idea of Regional Protection Areas that was proposed by the UK government, the UNHCR argues for rehabilitating refugees through cooperation within origin regions—the so-called regional prong. [23] But it also requires cooperation

---

[22]   Ruud Lubbers, until recently the UN High Commissioner for Refugees, introduced this approach as the "4R's"—repatriation, reintegration, rehabilitation, and reconstruction. Various documents describing Convention Plus are available at the UNHCR's website; see in particular "Convention Plus at a Glance," which is periodically updated.

[23]   Recent history provides some examples. One is the Comprehensive Plan of Action that was adopted in 1989 by countries in Southeast Asia, which provided for a combination of resettlement (predominantly in the United States), repatriation, and integration into the host countries in the region. Another is the International Conference on Central American Refugees, which involved a commitment by seven Central American countries, also in 1989, to recognizing and integrating refugees from conflicts in El Salvador, Guatemala, and Nicaragua as well as attempts to broker reconciliation and development (USCR and ECRE 2003: 33–38).

from the developed world in providing aid packages in order to improve the economic conditions for refugees as well as providing better access to refugee status determination procedures and more generous quotas for resettlement in the West.

If these enhanced procedures involved liberalizing refugee status determination to something approaching that of the developed world, then more would qualify. Given that 80 percent of refugees do not currently have access to these procedures as they operate in the industrialized world, this would lead to a vast increase in the number who would be eligible for resettlement. That number is likely to far exceed the willingness of Western countries to accept more refugees, however genuine they may be. It would also provide serious challenges to the neighbors of war-affected countries. One is that by providing superior access to asylum processes and perhaps higher living standards than are available in existing refugee camps, they would act as magnets to greater numbers of displaced persons, who may be less willing to return. Although the UNHCR proposes expanding the opportunities for permanent integration of refugees in countries within the region where they were displaced, many such countries are already hosting far larger numbers than they can (or wish to) absorb. While enhanced development aid tied to local resettlement and integration of refugees might help, those inducements would have to be provided (and policed) on a scale that would go far beyond existing aid budgets.

Policies that significantly improve access to asylum procedures and that enhance the opportunities for resettlement would undoubtedly benefit asylum seekers, especially those from the poorest countries of the Third World. But the incentives they provide are likely also to generate even greater cross-border migration from war-torn countries as well as increased pressure for onward migration. As part of its three-pronged approach to reforming the refugee regime, the UNHCR lays stress on promoting the voluntary return, reintegration, and rehabilitation of refugees in countries of origin. But widening the options for exit and improving the conditions for those who gain access to it (the second prong) would make it all the harder to foster voluntary return and reintegration. Not surprisingly, much lip service is paid to targeting development aid to countries in post-civil war situations, not only to ensure a more stable future, but also to make return migration more attractive.

While improving the conditions in source countries seems like the best of all solutions, it is the least well worked out. One issue is whether to devote resources directly to repatriation and reintegration programs, or simply to provide some form of economic incentive to return. Some observers argue that such packages should simply be part of broader strategies aimed at improving economic conditions generally. While these might help to foster cross-border remigration from the refugee camps in neighboring regions, they are less likely to stem the flow of long-distance illegal migrants, once such flows have become established. Although relative incomes matter in determining the flows of asylum seekers to the West, it would require dramatic increases in living standards at the source to seriously reduce the numbers. And even that may be too optimistic. Recent studies have suggested that, in the poorest countries, an increase in domestic living standards has conflicting effects on the pressure to emigrate (Hatton and Williamson 2005). While higher income at home may make emigration less attractive, it also makes emigration more feasible by easing poverty constraints.

The best option by far is to find ways of preventing civil wars or to stop them recurring. As we have seen, apart from the upheavals in Eastern Europe and the former Soviet Union, there are positive signs that the ending of the Cold War and the proxy wars associated with it has been associated with a decline in global conflict. Recent interventions in Sierra Leone and Liberia suggest that it is possible for Western governments to help promote the settlement of conflicts in the Third World. But the greater challenge is to prevent such conflicts in the first place.

Recent analysis of civil wars suggests that the causes are chiefly economic rather than political (Collier and Hoeffler 1998, 2004). If so, then political interventions that do not get to the root causes are less likely to be successful. In these studies the major causes of civil war are found to be low incomes, dependence on primary commodities, and the dominance of a single ethnic group. One further factor is that the diaspora from the source country, living in the developed world, raises the probability that war will recur. This is because diasporas are often former refugees from displaced minorities who have a vested interest in supplying economic aid to their particular faction. Thus, refugees, originally the consequence of war, may become a reason for its persistence.

This suggests a further reason why encouraging the return and reintegration of former refugees is an important priority. Those who return are more likely to have an interest in fostering peace than those who have gained a permanent foothold abroad. But the tools for promoting the successful reintegration of refugees in ways that also reduce the risk of war are the least well developed of all refugee policies.

11   Conclusions

European governments have reacted to the rising numbers of asylum seekers by introducing successive reforms in their policies in order to deter them. While these have had effects in the desired direction, they have been outpaced by the powerful cumulative forces that have kept up the flow of applications. Two things follow. First, had some of those policies been put in place a decade earlier, the numbers might not have increased so dramatically and the cumulative rise in asylum seeking would have been attenuated. As a result, there would have been less need for ever more draconian measures in the face of the growing pressure of numbers. Second, the numbers are still "too high" for countries that face strong political pressures to limit them. This may help explain why the transfer of asylum policy from the individual country level to the EU level has not so far resulted in the more generous policies that the theory suggests should result from genuine international cooperation.

In recent years, there has been a vigorous debate about the reform of asylum policies and refugee policies on an international scale. Given that existing asylum seeker flows probably exceed those that would be optimal even under more cooperative policies, a radical relaxation of asylum policies seems unlikely. Furthermore, proposals to shift asylum claim processing to reception centers in the regions of origin are also likely to meet with limited success. The resources put into such schemes might be better invested in efforts to help displaced populations when they return home and to create conditions that make civil wars less likely.

Bibliography

Azam, J.-P., and A. Hoeffler (2002). Violence Against Citizens in Civil Wars: Looting or Terror? *Journal of Peace Research* 7 (4): 461–485.

Böcker, A., and T. Havinga (1997). *Asylum Migration to the European Union: Patterns of Origin and Destination.* Luxembourg: Office for Official Publications of the European Communities.

Brons, M., K. Meijnen, and M.C. Schaap (2001). *Public Perceptions about Refugees, Asylum Seekers and Persons with Temporary Protection Status: Country Report: The Netherlands.* The Hague: International Organisation for Migration.

Collier, P. (1999). On the Economic Consequences of Civil War. *Oxford Economic Papers* 51 (1): 168–183.

Collier, P., and A. Hoeffler (1998). On the Economic Consequences of Civil War. *Oxford Economic Papers* 50 (4): 563–573.

Collier, P., and A. Hoeffler (2004). The Challenge of Reducing the Global Incidence of Civil War. Copenhagen Consensus Challenge Paper. Oxford University.

Crisp, J. (1999). Who Has Counted the Refugees? UNHCR and the Politics of Numbers. UNHCR Working Paper No. 12. Geneva.

Dolan, C. (1999). Repatriation from South Africa to Mozambique—Undermining Durable Solutions? In R. Black and K. Koser (eds.), *The End of the Refugee Cycle? Refugee Repatriation and Reconstruction*. New York: Berghan Books.

Edminster, S. (2000). The High Road or the Low Road: The Way Forward to Asylum Harmonisation in the European Union. In USCR *World Refugee Survey, 2000*. New York: U.S. Committee for Refugees.

European Commission (2003). *Towards More Accessible, Equitable and Managed Asylum Systems*. Brussels: Commission of the European Communities.

Gurr, T.R., M.G. Marshall, and D. Khosla (2001). Peace and Conflict, 2001. Center for International Development and Conflict Management, University of Maryland, College Park.

Hathaway, J. (2002). Refugee Law Is Not Immigration Law. In USCR *World Refugee Survey, 2002*. New York: U.S. Committee for Refugees.

Hatton, T.J. (2004). Seeking Asylum in Europe. *Economic Policy* 38 (April): 5–62.

Hatton, T.J., and J.G. Williamson (2003). Demographic and Economic Pressure on Migration Out of Africa. *Scandinavian Journal of Economics* 105 (3): 465–486.

Hatton T.J., and J.G. Williamson (2004). *World Mass Migration: Two Centuries of Policy and Performance* (forthcoming).

Hatton, T.J., and J.G. Williamson (2005). What Fundamentals Drive World Migration? In J.G. Borjas and J. Crisp (eds.), *Poverty, International Migration and Asylum*. London: Palgrave Macmillan.

Inter-Governmental Consultations on Asylum, Refugee and Migration Policies in Europe, North America, and Australia (1997). *Report on Asylum Procedures*. Geneva: Secretariat of the Inter-Governmental Consultations on Asylum, Refugee and Migration Policies in Europe, North America, and Australia.

International Organisation for Migration (2000). *Migrant Trafficking and Human Smuggling in Europe*. Geneva: United Nations.

Koser, K., and C. Pinkerton (2002). *The Social Networks of Asylum Seekers and the Dissemination of Information about Countries of Asylum*. London: UK Home Office.

Marshall, M.G. (1999). *Third World War: System, Process and Conflict Dynamics*. Boulder: Rowman and Littlefield.

Marshall, M.G. (2002). Measuring the Societal Impact of War. In F.O. Hampson and D.M. Malone (eds.), *From Reaction to Conflict Prevention: Opportunities for the UN System*. Boulder: Lynne Reinner.

Morrison, J., and B. Crosland (2001). The Trafficking and Smuggling of Refugees: The End Game in European Asylum Policy? UNHCR Working Paper No. 39. Geneva.

Noll, G. (2000). *Negotiating Asylum: The EU Acquis, Extraterritorial Protection and the Common Market of Deflection*. The Hague: Martinus Nijhoff.

Pederson, P.J., M. Pytlikova, and N. Smith (2004). Selection or Network Effects? Migration Flows into 27 OECD Countries, 1990–2000. IZA Discussion Paper No. 1104. Bonn.

Poe, S.C., C.N. Tate, and L.C. Keith (1999). Repression of the Human Right to Personal Integrity Revisited: A Global Cross-National Study Covering the Years 1976–1993. *International Studies Quarterly* 43 (2): 291–313.

Pottenbaum, D., and R. Kanbur (2001). Civil War, Public Goods and the Social Wealth of Nations. Unpublished paper. Cornell University.

Robinson, V., and J. Segrott (2002). Understanding the Decision-Making of Asylum Seekers. Home Office Research Study 243. UK Home Office, London.

Rogge, J.R. (1994). Repatriation of Refugees. In T. Allen and H. Morsink (eds.), *When Refugees Go Home*. London: Africa World Press.

Rotte, R., M. Vogler, and K. Zimmermann (1997). South-North Refugee Migration: Lessons for Development Co-operation. *Review of Development Economics* 1 (1): 99–115.

Schmeidl, S. (1997). Exploring the Causes of Forced Migration: A Pooled Time-Series Analysis, 1971–1990. *Social Science Quarterly* 78 (2): 284–308.

Thielemann, E.R. (2003). Why EU Policy Harmonisation Undermines Burden Sharing. National Europe Centre Paper 101. Australian National University, Canberra.

UK Government (2003). New International Approaches to Asylum Processing and Protection. Accessed as "New Vision for Refugees" from ProAsyl website: http://www.proasyl.de/texte/europe/union/2003/UK_NewVision.pdf.

UK Home Affairs Committee (2003). *Asylum Removals, Volume I: Report and Proceedings of the Committee*. House of Commons, London.

UK House of Lords, European Union Committee (2004). *Handling EU Asylum Claims: New Approaches Examined*. 11th Report of Session 2003–04. London: Stationery Office.

UNHCR (United Nations High Commissioner for Refugees) (2001). *The State of the World's Refugees: Fifty Years of Humanitarian Action*. Geneva: UNHCR.

UNHCR (United Nations High Commissioner for Refugees) (2002). *Statistical Yearbook, 2001*. Geneva: UNHCR.

United Nations (2002). *Agenda for Protection*. New York: UN General Assembly 53rd Session.

United Nations (2003). *World Population Prospects: The 2002 Revision*. New York: United Nations.

United Nations High Commissioner for Refugees (2003). Summary of UNHCR Proposals to Complement National Asylum Systems through New Multilateral Approaches, from Statewatch website at: http://www.statewatch.org/news/2003/jun/unhcr.pdf.

United States Committee for Refugees (2003). *World Refugee Survey 2003*. New York: USCR.

USCR and ECRE (United States Committee for Refugees and European Council on Refugees and Exiles) (2003). *Responding to the Asylum and Access Challenge*. New York: USCR and ECRE.

Weiner, M. (1997). Bad Neighbours, Bad Neighbourhoods: An Enquiry into the Causes of Refugee Flows, 1969–1992. In R. Münz and M. Weiner (eds.), *Migrants, Refugees and Foreign Policy: US and German Policies towards Countries of Origin.* Oxford: Berghahn Books.

Zetter, R., D. Griffiths, S. Ferretti, and M. Pearl (2003). An Assessment of the Impact of Asylum Policies in Europe, 1990–2000. Home Office Online Report 17/03, http://www.homeoffice.gov.uk/rds/horspubs1.html.

Comment on Timothy J. Hatton and Jeffrey G. Williamson

Martin Paldam

The H&W paper is a survey by two of the leading experts in the field and represents years of work. It is consequently a rewarding paper to read, especially as it belongs to the class of papers that raise more questions than they answer. This comment deals with the key question: What is driving the flow of immigrants from the poor LDCs to the rich DCs?

Framework: The Economic A-Gap and the Political B-Gap

It is obvious that the flows are driven by the two large gaps between the DCs and the LDCs: The A-gap in incomes and the B-gap in political rights and civil liberties. The puzzling claim of the H&W paper is that neither gap works in econometric modeling.

The rich countries keep raising barriers to reduce the flow, and it is difficult to imagine that the flow would not be much larger in the absence of these barriers, but it is still about 1 million people a year. The analysis of H&W can be summarized in a small figure (see below).

There are 3 distinct flows of immigrants from the LDCs to the DCs as shown:

(1)   Refugees who are accepted as such by the international authority UNHCR.
(2)   Asylum seekers who turn up in the DCs and are given asylum by national authorities.
(3)   Others who somehow enter the DCs—they "seep through" the barriers.

The figure includes two sets of authorities—UNHCR and the national ones—each using a "barrier" to regulate the flow. The barriers can be moved in and out of the flow, to allow it to run slower or faster. The barriers are drawn "checkered" to indicate that it is difficult to make it very "tight." Some are always seeping through.

Statistically, flow (1) is the best covered. Then follows (2), while (3) is largely in the gray. However, flow (3) appears to be the largest—the total flow is about 1 million people per year, of which flows (1) and (2) together are less than one-third. The H&W paper covers only flows (1) and (2)—and it is most detailed as regards flow (1) for data reasons.

Figure 1:
The Two-Gap Model of Hatton and Williamson

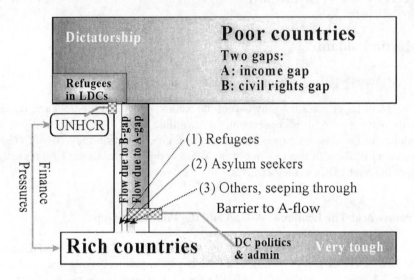

The decisions regarding (1) and (2) are made by administrative authorities using criteria meant to exclude the flow driven by the A-gap. Hence flows (1) and (2) are steered by authorities who take their decision—whether or not the applicant fulfills the criterions of being driven by the B-gap—based upon the legend of the applicant. The legends can only be controlled to a very limited extent by the authorities of the DCs, so we are dealing with decisions with a large stochastic element.

Hence, flows (1) and (2) should be the easiest to explain using variables that try to measure the B-gap, while (3) should be determined mainly by the A-gap. H&W have thus stacked the deck towards finding that the B-gap is important, but even then it does not work very well. However, they also claim that the A-gap does not contribute very much. Before we turn to that gap let us look briefly at the magnitudes.

Some Crude Orders of Magnitudes

The key measure used to represent the A-gap is GDP, defined as GDP per capita in PPP-terms. The B-gap is normally measured by the Gastil index (from the NGO Freedom House). The Gastil data have two annual observations per country: (i) democratic rights and (ii) civil liberties, both given as an integer from 1 to 7. The two observations are highly correlated, so the average is used (giving half points also). When the 6 billion in people in the world in 2000–2001 are divided using the two criteria, the two distributions given in Table 1 are obtained.

Table 1:
The World Population 2000–2001, Divided Two Ways

Income structure (based on GDP)		Political rights and civil liberties	
High income	957	All rights, Gastil 1–2	1,161
Higher middle income	504	Gastil 2½–4	2,311
Lower middle income	2,164	Gastil 4½–6	826
Low income	2,506	No rights, Gastil 6½–7	1,731
Total	6,130	Total for 171 countries	6,029

Note: The Gastil index is (almost) complete for 171 countries only, but the missing countries are small. The numbers given are the average for the index of political rights and civil liberties. Most of the missing countries are in the two low-income groups.

The two data—log GDP and the Gastil index—for the 171 countries have a correlation of about –0.6. All the rich Western countries receiving permanent immigration from the LDCs are in the high-income group, and they all have Gastil index scores below 1½. The correlation between the two indices is low especially in the lower-middle-income group. When the table in H&W showing the main exporters and importers of immigrants is considered, the GDP differences between exporters and importers are typically about 5–10 times,[1] while the Gastil index differs between the two groups by as much as about 4 points.

If the A-gap were permitted as a criterion for immigration, it would inevitably generate very large numbers of immigrants: When countries have 10 percent of the average income of the typical DC, it means that at least 80 percent of the population is poor by whatever definition used according to the DC standard. Hence, 2–3 billion people would qualify. This is why it is not an applicable criterion.

Consequently, only the B-gap is allowed, and it is not enough that the applicant lives under a political system with very few or no political rights and civil liberties. To qualify, people have to satisfy the criterion of having a "well founded fear of persecution." This is sufficiently vague to allow interpretations, but

---

[1]   With such large differences, small variations are unlikely to have much impact on the flows. Whether an LDC has 10 percent or 12 percent of a certain DC's standard of living makes only a marginal difference to the gain the immigrant obtains.

about 3½ billion people live under regimes giving them γ-scores of 4 and higher. Thus, even if the criterion is so restrictively applied that only 2 percent of those qualify, it is still 70 million. We shall return to that number.

Modeling the Effect of the Economic A-Gap: A Reverse Harris–Todaro Mechanism

The paper mentions that the relation between LDC income and immigration may be unclear, as an increase in the income may have two reverse effects on the flow: (1) It reduces the incentive to immigrate. (2) It means that more people are able to finance the journey. Whether 1 or 2 is strongest is not clear.

In the Harris–Todaro model people migrate more to the towns when town income goes up. This causes open unemployment to rise in the towns when employment rises. In the international case we are discussing, the mechanism operates almost in the reverse: immigration takes place when income goes up in the place from where the migration originates. People can immigrate only when they can afford it.

Imagine a situation in which the average extended family numbers 150 people, of whom an equivalent of 25 have a job outside the subsistence sectors, i.e., they have a "market" income. The family may want to establish a foothold in a DC; but to do so, they need to collect, say, $20,000 to pay agents for a legend and the journey, and to give their representative a minimum of starting capital. This is $800 per market job—an impossible investment if the average market income is, say, $2,000. However, imagine that economic growth causes the number of market jobs in the family to grow to 50, and the average income per such job increases to $4,000. Now the possibility of sending the smartest youngster away as an immigrant becomes a real possibility. And, of course, once the family has a foothold it becomes much easier to expand it to a real family base in the West. The Western family member can then marry a cousin and bring her in, and—if a good legend can be made for another brother—the one already in can finance the minimum starting capital and maybe the journey etc.

It is not straightforward to write down such a reverse Harris–Todaro model,[2] so all I shall do is point out that the relation between the A-gap and immigration is likely to be both *nonlinear and highly dynamic*, making it a very difficult relation to estimate.

---

[2]   Theoretically the Harris-Todaro model is just an arbitrage condition equilibrating a flow, but in our reverse case it is, rather, a minimum condition starting the flow.

Modeling the Effect of the Political B-Gap

If the Gastil index, γ, measures what it should, the fraction of people in each country that has a well-founded fear of persecution by the regime so as to be eligible for asylum by the rules of the DC countries should be a monotonous function of γ:

(1) $E(i) = f(\gamma)$,   where $\partial f / \partial \gamma < 0$.

However, we do not know what the function (1) actually looks like. Countries with γ-scores of 6 to 7 normally forbid outmigration and make it a serious crime. Hence, few people manage to escape, and they are normally accepted on face value as eligible. Nobody who came from Sadam Hussain's Iraq and requested asylum was sent back, so the assumption probably was that a rather sizable fraction of the Iraqi population was personally threatened by that regime.

Hence, it appears that at least 5 percent of the population in the countries with the worst Gastil score $\gamma = 7$ might be eligible to immigrate to the West. Figure 2 shows three curves which for a rectangular distribution (of people over the possible γ-values) have the same area. One is proportional at γ, one rises steeply with γ, and one is independent at γ.

Figure 2:
Theoretical Relations between the Share of Eligible People and the Gastil Index

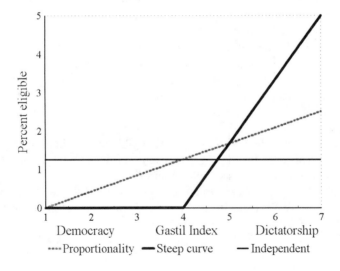

Figure 3:
The Number of People Eligible for Immigration Based on the 3 Curves of
Figure 2

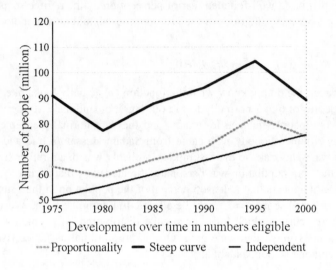

Development over time in numbers eligible

···· Proportionality   — Steep curve   — Independent

Figure 3 shows how many people the three E-curves in Figure 2 translate into
for the 171 countries every 5th year from 1975. The "independent" line is almost
straight, indicating that world population has increased almost linearly in the period.

The H&W paper shows that the Gastil index has improved, over the period it
has been collected, from 1972 onwards, and of course most strongly since 1989,
in connection with the collapse of Communism. However, Figure 3 shows that
the number of people living under low democratic rights and poor civil liberties
has nevertheless increased too. In spite of the relative improvement, there has
still been an absolute deterioration. Figure 3 points to two additional observations.

First, it shows that the number of people eligible for immigration from the B-
gap is large. This explains the big discussions surrounding the interpretation of
the "well founded fear of persecution" criterion.

Secondly, when the curves in Figure 3 are compared to the curves of actual
immigration in H&W's paper, there does not appear to be a clear connection.

Conclusion

This comment is not—as the reader will have noted—a critique of the paper by Hatton and Williamson. It is an attempt to discuss an unresolved and difficult issue raised by them: What is it that drives the flow of people from the poor to the rich countries that in spite of many attempts to reduce the flow still amounts to about one million people per year?

The comment argues that the key factor driving the flow is the huge difference in income. That would appear to be a trivial point, and it surely argues that people in the LDC world react in a perfectly rational way! However, it belittles much of the morally nicest policies in the field, which claim that the flows are due to much higher values than economic gain, i.e., that they are basically due to civil war and repression in the LCDs.

Behind this comment is the hope that perhaps it would lead to more successful policies if it were recognized that most of the flows are driven by perfectly ordinary economic motives. Consequently, we should be able to model the flows, and calculate how they react to policies, using standard methods.

III.

Labor Mobility and
Public Policy

David Greenaway and Douglas R. Nelson

The Distinct Political Economies of Trade and Migration Policy: Through the Window of Endogenous Policy Models, with a Focus on North America

Abstract:

The domestic politics of international trade seem to differ in fundamental ways from the domestic politics of immigration, but it is difficult to say exactly how and, more importantly, why. This paper uses a common frame of reference, simple endogenous policy models, as a way into this issue. These models capture the essential insight underlying much political economy analysis that material interests drive policy preferences. Part of the claim made in this paper is that trade politics appear to be essentially about material interest, while immigration politics are not. Related to this claim, however, is the complementary claim that the politics of these two seemingly similar issues are also organized in fundamentally different ways. The argument proceeds in five parts. The first part describes the general structure of endogenous policy models; the second provides a brief overview of theoretical and empirical work on trade; the third provides a similar overview of contemporary research on immigration politics; the fourth compares the political structures of the politics in these two domains; the fifth part concludes.

1 What Are Endogenous Policy Models, and What Are They For?

Endogenous policy models formalize the notion, widely applied for virtually as long as there has been systematic study of economic policy, that material self-interest has a sizable effect on the policy preferences of citizens, and that the

Remark: The authors acknowledge financial support from The Leverhulme Trust under Programme Grant F114/BF. The authors would like to thank Gerald Willmann, Jeffrey Williamson, Tim Hatton and the participants at the Kiel Week conference for useful comments.

policy preferences of citizens has a sizable effect on the policies chosen by rulers. Both of these statements should strike us as completely unexceptionable. In particular, they commit us neither to a thoroughgoing materialism, nor to any particular understanding of how citizen preferences are mapped into final policy determination. As such, they rule out virtually nothing and are, thus, virtually useless on their own as a theory of policy determination. The strategy of endogenous policy modeling proceeds from the radical simplification that these two attributes fully characterize the preferences of citizens and policy makers. All that remains is to develop the specific political and economic context, and results/predictions can be derived.

More formally, endogenous policy models build some form of explicit political structure into some form of neoclassical general equilibrium model. That is, the underlying economy is made up of households, characterized by preferences over final goods and portfolios of productive factors, and firms, which transform factors of production into final goods.[1] We can denote a neoclassical economy as $\mathcal{E} = \{\mathbf{Z}, \mathbf{F}, \mathbf{R}\}$, where $\mathbf{Z}$ is a matrix allocating factors of production among households, $\mathbf{F}$ a vector of technologies, and $\mathbf{R}$ a vector of household preferences over final commodities.[2] To this economy we attach a vector of possible interventions, $\mathbf{t}$, and a political mechanism, M, yielding a political economy: $\mathcal{P}= \{\mathbf{Z}, \mathbf{F}, \mathbf{R}; \mathbf{t}, M\}$. The easiest part of the analysis of a system like $\mathcal{P}$ involves the derivation of citizen preferences over policy. For a given household, h ($R_h \in \mathbf{R}$, $z_h \in \mathbf{Z}$), for a fixed $\mathcal{E}$, we simply ask how any relevant state of the policy variable, $\mathbf{t}$, affects household welfare. By answering this question for every feasible state of the policy variable, we trace out household political preferences over that policy.

Just as knowing preferences over final goods is not sufficient for a theory of market equilibrium, knowledge of political preferences is not sufficient to determine political-economic equilibrium. In principle, a model of political action must be combined with a model of policy determination to determine a full political economic equilibrium.[3] Here there are many possibilities. Two approaches

---

[1]   Under constant returns to scale and perfect competition the number of firms is indeterminate, but also irrelevant. That is, the industry acts as if it is being operated by a profit-maximizing/cost-minimizing firm under a zero-profit constraint. Thus the unit of analysis on the supply side of the economy is the industry. As a result, in the formal analysis, we need to keep track of: households ($h \in H$), factors of production ($i \in I$), and final goods ($j \in J$).

[2]   One of the extraordinary accomplishments of modern economic theory has been to prove that a decentralized equilibrium of this sort of system exists. However, to go beyond existence (and a couple of technical properties of the equilibrium) requires considerably more structure.

[3]   It should be noted that virtually no endogenous policy models involve politically active firms. This follows from zero profits, as discussed in footnote 1. In models with

short-circuit the need for models of this sort: the single-issue referendum approach and the political response function approach. Under the assumption that voting is costless (and the assumption that preferences are single-peaked over a one-dimensional t), the first approach simply determines the policy outcome at the most preferred point of the median voter. No resources are used up in the political process, and there are no gains from misrepresentation of preferences, so once citizen policy preferences have been determined, the step to final policy determination is trivial. This ease is achieved at the cost of radical simplification of both political action and policy determination.

Where referendum models adopt a radical simplification, the political response function approach simply does away with any attempt to theorize the supply side. Specifically, following Peltzman (1976), this approach represents unexplained (but completely plausible) differential group organization in terms of differential responsiveness of an untheorized function. Lobbying models, with a passive register state, introduce an explicit analysis of costs of political action. However, since policies are in the nature of public goods and expenditure on policy by any individual has an effect on all individuals, the theory of political action is far from compelling. Furthermore, it is not clear that simple venality (i.e., the selling of policy) is obviously superior to determination by referendum, and both lobbying and voting models can be seen as specific forms of Peltzman's black box. A recent innovation extends the Becker-type model to incorporate an active policy maker by applying the menu auction version of a common agency model (Bernheim and Whinston 1986), thus endogenizing the political response function (Grossman and Helpman 1994). That is, the policy maker offers a menu of policy outcomes associated with patterns of bids by various organized groups, and the equilibrium is determined by the menu offered and the pattern of bids, where these must form a Nash equilibrium. While formal theorists in political science have developed models of electoral competition and bureaucratic policy determination in considerably more detail, these have rarely been applied in the endogenous policy context. Where they have, in particular in models of endogenous macroeconomic policy determination, the underlying models of the economy tend to be radically simplified.

Endogenous policy theory, in virtually all applications, was first developed to account for "bad policy"—i.e., deviations from the optimal policies prescribed by economists. For example, the standard motivation for research on the political economy of trade policy proceeds by pointing out that virtually no contemporary or historical illiberal trade regime can be satisfactorily rationalized as welfare

---

specific factors, one might take the unit of organization to be the firm, just as in models with perfectly mobile factors we might take the unit of organization to be factor-based. However, fundamentally, these models run from citizen preferences, with no other input on the demand side.

maximizing.[4] Various political economy models illustrate the fact that plausible forms of political interaction *can* account for patterns of policy of the sort that we observe.[5] However, this is not much more than providing some substance to assertions of the form "that's a political economy problem." That is, it illustrates a possibility without providing a clear prediction about outcomes. As we have already noted, while bad policy choices are not at all uncommon, it is not clear that they are any more uncommon than good policy choices.

A closely related, also essentially negative, accomplishment is to help desimplify thinking about "good" and "bad" policy. Consider the following rather deep problem from Mayer's (1984) fundamental paper on the political economy of trade policy. For a small, open economy of the Heckscher–Ohlin–Samuelson sort, free trade welfare-dominates protection. However, in the case of single-peaked preferences over one-dimensional policy, majority rule satisfies all of Arrow's axioms for a democratic social choice function. And yet, except in the razor's edge case where the median voter has the same endowment as the aggregate endowment for the economy, the social choice will be for positive intervention. Thus, if we started from an imposed equilibrium at the welfare-maximizing policy of free trade, the democratically correct social choice would be some welfare-inferior level of protection. What are we to make of "good" policy in this context?

Qua social science, we presumably expect something more from a body of theory than the formalization of an argument or a cautionary tale. Research on endogenous policy modeling has moved beyond these essentially philosophical applications in most subfields, though the extent of motion varies quite widely across them. The most successful extensions from theory to systematic empirical research, and back again, are in local public finance and macroeconomics. In both cases, it can be reasonably argued that the policy environment is reasonably well understood and that policy is determined to some considerable extent by referendum. In the area of school finance, the policy really is often determined

---

4   This is just as true of illiberal elements of essentially liberal trade regimes. Thus, while there is a substantial literature on the political economy of administered protection in industrial countries, there is virtually no research by economists on the historically striking liberalness of all industrial countries. Apparently, there is no need to explain good policy. While the definition of "good" and "bad" policy may vary, essentially the same is true of political scientists. Thus, among those that see trade activism as "good" policy, the question is how government comes to adopt a relatively liberal policy.

5   There are now some very good general texts in what is essentially endogenous policy theory. The broadest in coverage is Persson and Tabellini (2000), while Drazen (2000) focuses on macroeconomic policy, Laffont (2000) develops informational and constitutional issues, and Dixit (1998) presents a transactions cost approach. Roemer (2001a) and Grossman and Helpman (2001) develop advanced methods of political modeling that are consistent with endogenous policy modeling.

by referendum and people really do see the issue quite straightforwardly in terms of material costs and benefits. As a result, there is now a substantial body of empirical research that quite successfully applies endogenous policy models in this area (Ross and Yinger 1999; Rothstein 1994; Epple et al. 2001). For macroeconomic policy the links are a bit looser, but the data are quite good and the stakes are high. Thus, macroeconomic models are relatively simple, if highly contested, and it is not too violent a simplification to see national elections as referenda on macroeconomic policy. As a result, there is an enormous literature on the political economy of macroeconomic policy which seems, under any reasonable definition of these concepts, theoretically and empirically progressive (Drazen 2000).

The story is less clear when we come to the cases that concern us most directly: trade and immigration policy. We will see that there are fundamental differences between the two in terms of both the extent to which citizen preferences can be represented by relatively straightforward materialist self-interest, and the policy-making environment can also be given a relatively simple representation. Finally, it will prove important for systematic empirical work that, as in the cases of local public finance and macroeconomic policy, policy choice is made repeatedly so as to permit the collection and analysis of data.

2   Trade Policy in Endogenous Policy Models

The theoretical and empirical literatures on the political economy of trade policy are both immense, though only very weakly integrated. In the last fifteen years, there have been no fewer than a dozen major surveys of one or another aspect of these literatures, and the papers on which they are based run into the hundreds.[6] The area of greatest success in the application of endogenous policy modeling to trade policy has been in the construction of plausible accounts of suboptimal policy of a general sort. That is, this work explains how policies different from welfare-optimal policy *could* be adopted, without making particularly strong predictions about what policies *would* be adopted. The proliferation of variants on referendum, response function, lobbying, electoral competition, and agency models has been rapid. However, given that the essential point is made quite

---

[6]   Among the major surveys: Anderson and Baldwin (1987), Ray (1987), and Gawande and Krishna (2003) emphasize the empirical work; Nelson (1988), Hillman (1988), Baldwin (1989 1996), Riezman and Wilson (1995), and Helpman (1995) emphasize theoretical work; and Rodrik (1995), Frieden and Rogowski (1996), Alt et al. (1996), Deardorff and Stern (1998), and Milner (1999) aim for critical synthesis.

clearly in the key contributions on voting (Mayer 1984) and lobbying (Findlay and Wellisz 1982), the value added of many of the later papers must be judged to be rather small. Similarly, much of the empirical research, while increasing our knowledge of the correlates of protection, is essentially ad hoc and, in particular, unrelated to theoretical models of political economy. This disjuncture should not surprise us given the very different demands on theory for these tasks: the abstract point-scoring task requires a minimal model that illustrates a plausible causal channel; while for a theory to be a compelling basis for empirical work, it must find some fundamental attachment to the empirical phenomenon.

Nonetheless, while recognizing that the literature on the political economy of trade cannot claim the sort of cumulative interaction between theory and research that characterizes work on the political economy of macroeconomic policy or of local public finance, there have been some genuine attempts to move in this direction: identification of policy preferences, identification of situations in which the model seems to bear some relatively close relationship to the actual environment, and efforts to bring more detailed institutional structure into the model in such a way as to produce plausible hypotheses that can be evaluated empirically.

One fundamental question that has recently seen a revival in interest is the empirical identification of preferences over trade policy. The theoretical problem is straightforward: under the maintained assumptions of the underlying model of the economy, the welfare of a given individual/household can be represented by it's *indirect utility function*:[7]

(1) $v^h(\mathbf{p}; \gamma_h) := \max_{x_h} \{u^h(\mathbf{x}_h) | \mathbf{px}_h \leq \gamma_h\}$,

where $\mathbf{p}$ is the vector of commodity prices, x_h is the household's consumption bundle, γ_h is the household's income, and $u^h(\cdot)$ is the household's utility function (derived from R_h–household preferences over possible consumption bundles). For our purposes, what is relevant is that utility is decreasing in the elements of $\mathbf{p}$ and increasing in γ_h. Furthermore, we suppose that household income is made up of factor income plus any governmental transfers:

(2) $\gamma_h = \mathbf{wz}_h + G_h$,

where $\mathbf{w}$ is the vector of returns to factors of production, $\mathbf{z}_h$ is the household's endowment bundle, and G_h is the government transfer to household h. Most trade interventions will affect $\mathbf{p}$ and any income transfers induced by the policy will enter through γ_h. These effects are easy to sign since the signs are not particularly

---

7   $v^h(\cdot)$ is the maximum value function associated with the consumer's optimization problem.

dependent on the structure of $\mathscr{E}$. The other major channel of effect, however, is generally dependent on the details of $\mathscr{E}$. The problem is that changes in **p** will cause changes in **w**, thus indirectly affecting γ_h. In the 2-factor × two-good Heckscher–Ohlin model, in which factors are costlessly mobile between productive sectors, the *Stolper–Samuelson theorem* makes a clear prediction that an increase in the relative price of one good will result in an increase in the real wage of the factor used intensively in the production of that good, and a reduction in the real wage of the other factor. That is, policy preferences will be driven by factor ownership. By contrast, if factors are completely immobile between sectors, the Cairnes–Haberler model, policy preferences will be determined by the sectoral allocation of factors. Between these extremes are a number of possibilities.[8] As is widely noted, it is a definitional attribute of the long run that all factors are fully mobile and of the short run that none are. Thus, as a practical matter, the issue of the relevant model for analyzing the politics of trade is not so much a matter of technology as of perception. That is, rational people will evaluate policies in terms of the time horizon over which they make political calculations (see, e.g., Hall and Nelson 1989).

Given the centrality of policy preferences to endogenous policy models, it is of considerable importance to know something about this time horizon, but this is an essentially empirical question. Here there are three kinds of evidence. There is economic evidence that capital responds to shocks as if it were relatively fixed. Specifically, an important paper by Grossman and Levinsohn (1989) used a capital-market event study methodology to examine the response of owners of firms to a variety of shocks, concluding that these responses were consistent with perceptions of relative capital fixity.[9] Magee (1978) developed a clever indirect methodology of using information on the trade lobbying behavior of labor and capital as evidence of revealed policy preference, and found that labor and capital tended to lobby together, concluding that the politically relevant time horizon was relatively short. There has recently been an upsurge of interest in this method with papers by Beaulieu (2002a, 2002b), Beaulieu and Magee (2004), and Hiscox (2001). Hiscox develops a sophisticated extension of Magee's method, and extends the analysis to the period 1824–1994, providing support for Magee's general conclusion, while showing considerable variance over time.

---

[8]   The most commonly studied, primarily because of its tractability, is the specific-factor (or Ricardo–Viner) model, in which some factor is costlessly mobile and all other factors are sector-specific. See Jones (1971) or Mussa (1974). Among others, Hill and Mendez (1983) consider the case of general imperfect mobility.

[9]   Thompson (1993, 1994) are similar studies. Recent papers by Ramey and Shapiro (1998, 2000) provide some direct evidence of capital fixity, while a substantial literature in labor economics finds labor to be quite fixed over economically relevant periods (e.g., Topel 1994a, 1994b).

Beaulieu and Magee use campaign contribution data, concluding that, while there is some evidence of both factor and industry effects, the effects of factor ownership (i.e., long-run calculation) seem to be dominant for capital, while labor may be more immobile over the politically relevant period. Finally, recognizing that these politically revealed preferences contain information about both preferences and political institutions, there have been some recent attempts to study preferences directly. Balistreri (1997), Scheve and Slaughter (2001a), Mayda and Rodrik (2005), and O'Rourke and Sinnott (2002) have all used public opinion data to examine the pattern of preferences on trade policy, with Balistreri and Scheve and Slaughter reporting findings supportive of the H–O/long-run/mobile factor model, O'Rourke and Sinnott also providing support of a more nuanced sort, and Mayda and Rodrik providing an argument in favor of a shorter-run perspective. The latter two studies also find considerable support for ideological factors in determining policy preferences. While there is still considerable disagreement in this literature, all of this work has attempted to more closely link the underlying theory to the empirical work in ways that hold great promise. However, the study of preferences is, in some sense, the easiest part of the program of systematically evaluating and applying endogenous policy modeling to trade policy.

The essential problem in developing empirical frameworks embodying endogenous policy models is that, over the period for which we have relatively reliable data on the relevant variables, trade policy has rarely been determined by referendum. However, there have been a small number of situations that were either, like school bonds, actual referenda on trade questions or electoral contests in which trade was a sufficiently prominent issue that, as with macroeconomic policy, they could be treated as referenda. In either case, there are two sorts of research question: the first asks whether the electorate behaves as predicted by the model; the second derives a comparative static implication of the model and asks whether the implication is observed. We have just seen that the first type of question faces certain difficulties in that there are no clear predictions about behavior without essentially empirical auxiliary assumptions about the underlying economic model in use by agents. The largest problem is the rarity of trade policy referenda. However, Switzerland has, on at least two occasions, held referenda on trade policy questions: a proposal to impose tariffs on processed food (1975) and a proposal to replace subsidies on sugar with tariffs (1986). Weck-Hannemann (1990) presents an analysis of these. The author focuses on industry as the basic unit of political organization/calculation, and finds statistically significant evidence of industry effects on proportion of vote in favor of both measures. That is, the presence of an industry protected by the tariff increased support for it. Other than this exceptional case, attempts to directly evaluate referendum models involve a claim that some general election, or set of general elections, turned to a considerable extent on a trade policy question. Most of these analyses involve periods prior to the development of Keynesian policy instruments. Thus, Johnston and Percy (1980) examine patterns of voting in Canada's landmark 1911 federal election in which liberalization of trade with the United States ("reciprocity") was a key issue, while Irwin (1994, 1996) considers British general elections in 1906 and 1923 in which Conservatives made "tariff reform" (i.e., increased protection) a key element of their platform. As with Weck-Hannemann, all three of these analyses find some support for an industrial basis of voting. Of particular interest is Irwin (1996), in which the author also attempts to carry out a class/factoral analysis of voting, ultimately concluding that "the occupational regressors explain the election outcome better than the class regressors" (p. 71).

An alternative approach to estimating/evaluating the referendum model involves deriving a comparative static proposition from the model. Dutt and Mitra (2002) focus on the relationship between inequality and tariff in a median voter model with an H–O structure. Dutt and Mitra consider a model, like that of Mayer (1984), in which every household is endowed with one unit of labor and some amount of capital k_h. Thus, they treat inequality as inequality in the distribution of capital. In this model, it is straightforward to show that increased inequality in a capital-rich country results in an increased tariff, and vice versa for a capital-poor country.[10] The authors, in fact, find support for the prediction in their empirical work. This work, however, makes the very strong assumption that trade policy (the average tariff) is determined in all countries in their sample by referendum. While the authors are explicit that this is not the case, the argument they give to support the assumption is weak. A somewhat less heroic approach is taken by Hall et al. (1998). As in the work of Johnston and Percy, and Irwin, the authors appeal to the historical record to argue that the tariff was a fundamental continuing issue between Republicans and Democrats in the period from the end of the Civil War (or at least from the 1880s) until the Reciprocal Trade Agreements Act of 1934. With this warrant to treat general elections as tariff referenda, the authors then argue that female franchise would tend to produce a downward shift in the equilibrium tariff. The empirical analysis presented in the paper is strongly consistent with this hypothesis.

The Hall et al. analysis constitutes a nice bridge to the final body of work seeking to forge a closer relationship between theoretical and empirical work: institutional comparative statics. The virtue of a comparative static analysis in the referendum case derives primarily from the lack of access to detailed data related

---

[10] That is, for the capital-rich country, a tariff raises the return to the scarce factor (labor) and, as a result of unequal distribution, the median voter has a large endowment of labor relative to the economy as a whole. Thus, as inequality rises, the median voter is increasingly capital poor and prefers an increasing tariff. Mutatis mutandis, the same logic applies to a labor-rich country.

to policy preferences. When we move into the modern period, the need for some form of comparative static analysis becomes more pressing. The problem is that, with the exception of the two Swiss referenda already mentioned, trade policy is virtually never the policy being considered by parties or voters. Trade policy is important continuing policy in many countries, but the form of politics is over-whelmingly lobbying. This implies two fundamental problems, one practical, and the other conceptual. Practically, the data on lobbying take two forms: public expressions of interest (mainly in the form of testimony) and general lobbying expenditures. The former give little information about intensity of interest, while the latter cannot generally be associated with a particular policy. At a conceptual level, while virtually all endogenous policy models applied to trade policy to date treat lobbying as simple venality, contemporary research on lobbying by political scientists seems to have increasingly moved away from this interpreta-tion in favor of interpretations stressing access and information transfer (Austen-Smith 1997).[11]

Thus, while there are a number of analyses of congressional voting on trade legislation that introduce contribution data into essentially ad hoc econometric models, along with a variety of other variables, it would be hard to treat these as derived in any way from an underlying model of the political economy.[12] By contrast, analyses that seek to introduce explicit institutional structure in such a way that lobbying incentives change, producing a change in the equilibrium permit explicit evaluation in much the same way as in the Hall et al. analysis. Here we briefly consider the two main cases that have been extensively ana-lyzed: the Reciprocal Trade Agreements Act of 1934 and changing terms of par-tisan competition. At least since Lowi's (1964) classic reconciliation of the ac-counts of trade policy making in Schattschneider (1935) and Bauer et al. (1963), it has been clear that trade policy making changed fundamentally around the time of the Reciprocal Trade Agreements Act of 1934. While much of the subsequent literature on the RTAA has sought to explain the legislation itself, several papers have looked directly at the effect of the legislation on the incentives to engage in lobbying. Broadly speaking, there are two approaches here: one emphasizes delegation to the executive branch, the other the adoption of a rules-based defi-nition of trade policy. Examples of the first are Lohmann and O'Halloran (1994), who argue that the executive is more prone to consider consumer costs than the legislature, and Bailey et al. (1997), who argue that general authority to negotiate

---

[11] A recent paper by Anderson and Zanardi (2004) develops a model of the political economy of antidumping as deflection based on a model with a sophisticated analysis of political money and information.

[12] Examples of such work include Goldberg and Maggi (1999), Bandyopadhyay and Gawande (2000), and Baldwin and Magee (2000).

trade agreements induced greater participation by liberalization-seeking firms. In either case, the analysis predicts a downward shift in the equilibrium tariff. Nelson (1989) and Hall and Nelson (1992) offer an account which, following Lowi (1964), emphasizes the changed incentives to lobby when trade policy is defined as a collection of private goods (distributive politics) and when it is a general rule to be applied across a number of industries (regulatory politics). Loosely speaking, this work accounts for a shift, though each implies somewhat different timing. Thus, there is the possibility of systematic time-series work on this topic.

An alternative institutional comparative static compares the incentives facing government under conditions in which the same party controls both the executive and the legislature, and conditions of divided government. In particular, O'Halloran (1994), Epstein and O'Halloran (1996), and Milner and Rosendorff (1997) argue that legislatures under divided government will want to delegate less authority to the executive than under unified government and, under the auxiliary hypothesis that the executive generally prefers greater liberalization than the legislature, conclude that divided government impedes liberalization. This conclusion has been criticized on empirical grounds by Coleman (1998) and Hiscox (1999), while Karol (2000) reinterprets the theory before undertaking a systematic analysis of the data, finding that simple divided government hypotheses are essentially groundless. More than any of the research considered to this point, the work discussed in this and the preceding paragraph seeks to construct a more fully satisfactory account of the political structure generating trade policy outcomes.

3   Immigration Policy in Endogenous Policy Models

When we turn to the analysis of immigration policy, we find considerably less application of endogenous policy modeling and most of that is of more recent vintage. The concomitant lack of empirical research on immigration policy with a direct link to endogenous policy modeling is partially a function of the relative immaturity of such modeling, but I will also argue that there are two kinds of problem beyond immaturity: weak empirical evidence of economic impact and strong evidence of noneconomic forces in determining preferences, and lack of regular, ongoing politics of immigration of the sort that permits systematic study.

As with trade policy, deriving individual/household preferences over immigration policy is, in principle, a simple task (see Bilal et al. 2003). Once again using the indirect utility function in equation (1), and the definition of income in (2), we can begin to see how immigration differs from trade. To focus directly on immigration, suppose that commodity prices, **p**, are fixed. Equation (1) makes clear that the only channel via which immigration can affect household welfare is its effect on income. Furthermore, since there is no initial revenue consequence of immigration, we start by assuming that $G = 0$. Now the underlying structure of the economy becomes even more important than in the case of trade policy. Without getting bogged down in the technical details, we note that if there are more factors of production than final commodities, changes in endowments of factors will generally have an effect on relative returns to factors, while in the case of more final commodities than factors of production, as long as certain commodities do not go out of production, a change in the factor endowment has no effect on relative wages.[13] This has implications for interpreting the results of econometric research on the link between immigration and wages as well as for political economy modeling.

Most of the sizable literature seeking to estimate the labor market effects of immigration proceeds from a many-factor × one-final-commodity model of the economy, where the commodity is interpreted as national output.[14] While a wide range of econometric techniques, data sets, definitions of the input vector, and time periods have been used, the results have pretty consistently found only very small effects on any native group, with the exception of least skilled workers (defined as high school dropouts) and previous immigrants with the same ethnographic and labor market traits as the current immigrants. Building on a substantial review of this literature, Gaston and Nelson (2002) argue for a presumption that, at least in the long run, there are more produced goods than factors of production, with the implication that, unless immigration transforms the production structure, adjustment to immigration occurs primarily on the output margin, not on the wage margin.[15] However, if we adopt this presumption, along with the standard assumptions that underlie endogenous policy models, there can be no

---

[13] This latter is often referred to as *factor-price insensitivity* (the single-country version of the more well known *factor-price equalization theorem*). An elementary presentation of this result can be found in Gaston and Nelson (2000), while the appendix to Jones and Scheinkman (1977) presents the relevant analytics in full detail. The expression "factor-price insensitivity," as well as an alternative presentation of the analytics, comes from Leamer (1995).

[14] See Hammermesh (1993) for a survey of the relevant methods, and Johnson (1998) or Borjas (1999b) for application to the labor market effects of immigration.

[15] At least some people at the Kiel conference thought notice should be taken of Borjas' (2003) most recent attempt to find large labor market effects of migration. From the perspective of this paper the essential fact is that this work presumes that the relevant labor market is national. That is, Borjas essentially argues that the measured local labor market effects are small due to their embeddedness in a national labor market. Thus, Borjas' results suggest that we should see national politics of immigration. However, as we shall argue below, the politics of migration seem to be much more local than the politics of trade.

material income distribution effects from immigration and, thus, no basis for an endogenous policy analysis. Of course, these results are far from dispositive with respect to the relevant assumption for political economic analysis. Perhaps most importantly, they say nothing about the politically relevant time horizon nor about the way in which adjustment costs are considered by agents in their political calculus.

With respect to the first, it is trivially true (as long as production generally involves the application of more than one factor of production and factors are not instantaneously mobile) that there is some period in which there are more factors and commodities. In such an environment, as well as in any environment in which there are some immobile factors in any industry, changes in endowments will generally have distributional effects. As with trade, it becomes important to the analysis to know the time horizon of political calculation. That is, regardless of the long-run consequences, if households generally focus on the short-term effects of immigration, there may well be a disjunct between the econometric results and effects revealed by political behavior. Similarly, the econometric analysis and endogenous policy theory are based on comparative static analysis. Neither allows us to raise the question of how adjustment costs enter the economic or political calculus. However, there is considerable evidence that losing a job entails considerable cost and, less compelling (because less general) evidence from ethnographic studies of the changing ethnic structure of very local job markets, that jobs are lost in ethnic transitions in these local markets (Waldinger 1996a, 1996b; Rosenfeld and Tienda 1999). Fears of such transitional costs could well be a substantial source of mobilization on the immigration issue.

Our empirical options for getting a grip on this question are fewer. We do not have studies, like Magee's (1978) and those that followed on trade, of the policy preferences revealed by political activity on immigration.[16] Similarly, while there are studies of labor mobility, on the whole they do not ask precisely the question we would like—i.e., how responsive internal/native migrants are to wage differentials—and we have nothing like the capital market studies that shed light on capital mobility in response to trade shocks.[17] Nonetheless, by appealing to the studies on trade, as well as the general studies of local markets (e.g., Topel 1994a, 1994b), we can conclude that there is some warrant to assume a nontrivial

---

[16] The occasional flaring up of active migration politics seems not particularly helpful in settling this question. The only strong explanatory factor seems to be economic hard times, not particularly moments of great immigration (in fact, Hatton and Williamson (1998), among many others, suggest that immigration seems to be cyclical—increasing in good times and falling in bad).

[17] Card's (2001) recent paper on the responsiveness of internal migration patterns to immigration shocks, however, strongly suggests that "intercity mobility rates of natives and earlier immigrants are insensitive to immigrant inflows" (abstract).

degree of stickiness in adjustment to economic shocks in general, and there is no reason to assume that migration shocks differ from other macroeconomic shocks in this regard. Thus, as with trade, we turn to public opinion data for some information that might help us understand the link between material conditions and policy preferences. Interestingly, unlike trade policy, where public opinion research has been rather scarce, the opinion literature on immigration is substantial.[18]

Most of the research attempts to distinguish between economic factors (labor market competition and fiscal redistribution effects) and social factors (proximity, political ideology, racism), not between factor-based and industry-based preferences. However, the results of this research are far from irrelevant. A fairly strong finding is that, while economic factors do have an effect on restrictionist attitudes, social factors have substantially larger effects (Espenshade and Calhoun 1993; Citrin et al. 1997; Burns and Gimpel 2000; Fetzer 2000; Dustmann and Preston 2001; Gang et al. 2002). Other studies have found larger effects of economic factors, while still finding significant effects from social considerations (Espenshade and Hempstead 1996; Kessler 2001; Mayda 2004). Finally, a recent paper by Scheve and Slaughter (2001b) finds strong evidence of a link between labor market skills and immigration preferences. However, since they do not particularly study the effects of social factors, the results are not strictly comparable with the other studies. Overall, just as it is hard to conclude that there is much systematic evidence of economic effect on labor market outcomes, it is hard to conclude from the public opinion literature that there is much evidence of economic motivation behind anti-immigrant politics. Before turning to endogenous policy models of immigration policy, it is worth noting an empirical finding reported in several of the above studies: Hispanic and black respondents tend to express more positive views of immigration than non-Hispanic whites (Espenshade and Hempstead 1996; Citrin et al. 1997; Scheve and Slaughter 2001b). Since these are precisely the groups that, at least according to the econometric studies of labor market impact, might experience measurable effects, results such as these strongly raise the question of the adequacy of labor market competition as an explanator of immigration policy attitudes.

Not surprisingly, virtually all theoretical treatments of migration policy in an endogenous policy framework adopt some assumption that generates material distribution effects from immigration. The most straightforward approach is to follow labor economists in treating the economy as producing a single final con-

---

18   Characteristic recent research includes Espenshade and Hempstead (1996), Citrin et al. (1997), Burns and Gimpel (2000), and Scheve and Slaughter (2001a) on the United States; Bean (1995) and Betts (1996) on Australia; and Lahav (1997), Dustmann and Preston (2001), and Gang et al. (2002) on the EU. Simon and Lynch (1999), Fetzer (2000), and Mayda (2004) provide a comparative perspective.

sumption good from the input of whatever factors the analysis chooses to consider. A number of analyses develop this in some detail. As we shall see, this is primarily an input to some form of analysis which seeks to identify political-economic equilibria or, more commonly, to perform comparative static analysis on such equilibria. If we accept, contrary to most of the empirical work that directly addresses this question, that immigration policy is driven by the indirect distributional effects of immigration, endogenous policy theory offers a number of relatively simple strategies for representing the political economic equilibrium.

As in the case of trade policy models, the approach with the least theoretical overhead assumes that policy is determined by direct referendum. If sufficient structure on preferences is assumed to yield single-peaked preferences, the equilibrium policy is determined by the most preferred point of the median voter. A number of analyses pursue precisely this approach (Benhabib 1996; Hillman and Weiss 1999; and Grether et al. 2001) Because of the simple political structure, referendum models are often a convenient reduced form representation of more complex political processes. As with trade, there are not many referenda on immigration, but there was one recent, highly visible and widely studied, example: Proposition 187 in California. Most of these studies emphasize the importance of social factors (Tolbert and Hero 1996; Alvarez and Butterfield 2000; Newton 2000; Hood and Morris 2000), broad macroeconomic conditions (Alvarez and Butterfield 2000), and linkage to welfare reform/race relations (Calavita 1996; Salvanto 1998), but provide only weak support for individual effects, party, or ideology (Alvarez and Butterfield 2000; though see MacDonald and Cain (1997) for the effects of partisan identification). Thus, at least with respect to the one clear example of a referendum on the question, standard endogenous policy models in which factor-market effects drive policy preferences must be seen as being more-or-less rejected by the data to date.[19]

While immigration politics, contemporary and historical, may be more naturally analyzed in the context of referendum models, it is also useful to consider lobbying-based models. Unlike voting models, in which preferences are costlessly transformed into policy outcomes via the referendum, lobbying is a resource-using activity. One specific policy that might be thought of as lobbying-related is the allocation of resources to enforcement of immigration law. Nelson and Xu (2001) build on the important work of Ethier (1986) and Bond and Chen (1987), to endogenize the determination of enforcement activities against illegal

---

[19] Timmer and Williamson's (1998) study of immigration policy in North and South America in the late 19th and early 20th centuries comes to exactly the reverse conclusions: income distribution effects dominate (at least in the United States and Canada), and neither broad macroeconomic trends nor racism play any role. While interesting, these results rely heavily on constructed data.

immigration. While they derive a number of formal results, they rely on a model with more factors and goods, which we have seen has dubious empirical foundations. Hanson and Spilimbergo (2001) develop a theoretical analysis of enforcement activities based on a similar model but focus on the implication that enforcement is negatively correlated with prices in sectors that are potentially high users of illegal immigrant labor (apparel, fruits and vegetables, livestock, and construction). Their empirical work is supportive of this hypothesis.[20]

Recent papers by Facchini and Willmann (2001) and Bellettini and Ceroni (2004) adopt a variant of the lobbying model based on treating political competition as a menu auction game (Bernheim and Whinston 1986; Grossman and Helpman 1994). Specifically, the authors consider factor protection in a multifactor × one-final-good economy in which government policy regulates both inflow and outflow of factors.[21] Facchini and Willmann use Grossman and Helpman's (1994) strong assumptions on both economic and political structure to derive a simple framework for estimation, which is then applied to data from OECD countries. While the model performs well empirically, it is difficult to know how to interpret the findings. Not only are the results apparently inconsistent with the existing small-to-zero estimates of labor market effects of immigration, but the reliance of the estimating framework on very strong economic and political assumptions is also problematic.

As with trade policy, lobbying models constitute a fairly natural motivation for empirical analyses of Congressional voting, on which there is a small literature. As part of a broad historical analysis of the political economy of immigration restriction from 1890–1920, Goldin (1994) presents an econometric analysis of voting on two bills (1913 and 1915) that would impose literacy tests on immigrants, and one vote to overturn a presidential veto (1915). In the first two analyses, vote is regressed on percent foreign born, percent urban, and immigration rate. The results show the first two negatively related to support for the literacy test and the last positively related. Once again, it is hard to rationalize such a re-

---

[20] Other empirical work has also examined the political economy of enforcement activities over time, focusing on broad macroeconomic variables as explanators: Shughart et al. (1986) also examine output measures (i.e., number deported) but motivate their analysis via a regulation-theoretic model, Moehring (1988) studies the evolution of the INS budget over time, and Dávila et al. (1999) use a Niskanen-type model of a budget-maximizing bureau to account for variation over time in the relative allocation of manpower to border versus interior enforcement activity.

[21] Where Facchini and Willmann consider a competitive labor market, Bellettini and Ceroni consider a unionized labor market. Given the active participation of unions in immigration politics, the latter is a particularly useful innovation. More recently, papers by Amegashie (forthcoming) and Espstein and Nitzan (2004) have also developed lobbying models in which the policy variable is the size of an immigration quota rather than the degree of enforcement.

sult in a standard endogenous policy model: while the increase in immigration rate might be associated with a negative impact on wages, the effect should be strongest on immigrants. Lowell et al. (1986) examine voting in the U.S. House of Representatives on the Simpson–Mazzoli bill (1984). In the context of concern with Mexican immigration, this analysis controls for Hispanic population, finding it negatively associated with support for restriction. The authors argue, correctly, that this is not consistent with explanations based on labor market effects. The most sustained analysis of Congressional voting on immigration issues is the important book by Gimpel and Edwards (1999), which reports econometric analysis of every major vote on immigration from 1965 through 1996. Consistent with the findings of Lowell et al., Gimpel and Edwards find little support for effects of indirect redistributive effects, but find that the issue becomes increasingly partisan over the period of study. Overall, then, nothing in the empirical work—whether focused on actual labor market outcomes, citizen preferences, or the political behavior of citizens or their representatives—provides support for a model of immigration policy making in which indirect redistributive/labor-market effects drive outcomes.

To this point, we have assumed that the government's only role is to set a level of immigration of some class of factor owner or to set some form of immigration enforcement. However, precisely because the measured labor market effects of immigration appear to be so small, a considerably greater effort has been made in the political economy of immigration to build in explicit redistributive mechanisms. That is, there is substantial evidence that the presence of welfare state policies, and the taxation necessary to support them, results in considerably larger redistributive effects from immigration than those deriving from labor market effects.[22] As a result, a substantial body of work analyzing the political economy of immigration in the context of a redistributive state has developed (see Cremer and Pestieau 1998). That is, in terms of equation (2), we need to consider the government transfer term, G, in considerably more detail. Building on important early work on local public finance, in which people can move among jurisdictions within a federation and then choose (by referendum) redistribution schemes knowing that this will affect interjurisdictional mobility, this work considers labor mobility between nations in which citizens vote on redistributive policies to which immigrants have access.[23] These papers tend to focus on level of immigrant admission (Lejour and Verbon 1994; Mazza and van

---

[22]   The literature here is large and contentious. Some representative studies are Simon (1996), Borjas (1995), VanHook et al. (1999), and Canova and Ravn (1998). Smith and Edmonston (1997: chapters 6 and 7) and Espenshade (1998) are useful overviews of the issues.

[23]   Representative examples of research in local public economics are Rose-Ackerman (1983), Yinger (1985), and Epple and Romer (1991).

Winden 1996; Flores 1997), generosity of transfers/magnitude of tax (Mazza and van Winden 1996; Scholten and Thum 1996; Haupt and Peters 1998; Cremer and Pestieau 1998; Razin et al. 1998), and the extension of the franchise to immigrants (Cukierman et al. 1994; Michel et al. 1998). Razin et al. (1998) contains an interesting empirical analysis, of European countries 1974–1992, in which they find support for the prediction that an increase in the number of unskilled immigrants tends to reduce the generosity of social insurance programs, even after controlling for overall generosity of the welfare state, demographic makeup of the country, and international openness.

By introducing a redistributive state, this research has introduced a plausible channel through which material self-interest can, at least in principle, drive the political economy of immigration policy. However, there are still at least two problems in making this link fully compelling: first, the politics of immigration policy were more public, more aggressive, and more sustained in the late 19th and early 20th centuries, when there was essentially no welfare state, than today; and second, not only are the politics of immigration broadly responsive to general business cycles, but they are only occasionally responsive. By contrast, the politics of trade policy appear to have been, at least since the end of the 19th century, substantially about their redistributive effects and, while the particular modes of domestic politics have changed, trade policy has never ceased to be a major issue.

4   Trade and Migration Policy

The argument, to this point, has been that a reasonably good first cut at understanding where trade policy comes from can be had by applying quite standard endogenous policy models. As with any first approximation, such models do not tell the whole story, but by capturing a fundamental element they help identify promising directions for extension and issues that need to be addressed outside the model. By contrast, endogenous policy models of migration policy seem to provide very little analytical leverage. While the patent failure of these models in their usual form did lead quickly to models emphasizing the role of a redistributive state, to date these models have not been the basis of much empirical work. Thus, this work is still at the stage of providing a plausible account of broad stylized facts, but as we argued, the stylized facts at which this analysis aims are themselves problematic. This state of affairs is troubling. Why should two obviously economic phenomena, both of which have been the focus of politics over long periods of time, have such different relationships to what is, after all, just a very stripped down version of what lies behind virtually any political economy analysis.[24]

In an effort to organize our thoughts about this problem, we begin with a distinction, due to Schattschneider (1960), between democratic politics and group politics. For Schattschneider, *democratic politics* refers to the public politics through which a democratic civil society constitutes itself and through which it is linked to the policy-making apparatus. While elections are the final defense of democratic politics, as well as the key stimulus to public discourse, as stressed by theorists of deliberative democracy, the core of democratic politics is the public discourse itself. Furthermore, the terms of this discourse emphasize public interest and downplay private/individual interest. There is considerable evidence that the public discourse, and its emphasis on some notion of public interest, affects both attitude formation and voting behavior (see Kinder and Mebane 1983). By contrast with democratic politics, *group politics* is explicitly about private interests. Furthermore, where democratic politics are public politics, group politics happen behind closed doors. Where democratic politics are inclusive, group politics is a game played by insiders. Because group politics are solidly rooted in relatively stable interests, they are predictable and they change in predictable ways in response to the, generally marginal, changes in the environment embedding those interests. Democratic politics are not tied down in the same way. While the location of individuals within the terms of the public discourse is certainly not independent of individual interest, not only do the terms of that discourse change, more quickly and on a much greater scale than the terms of group politics, but individual locations within that discourse (i.e., preferences) change as well.

Political economy analysis must proceed from the assumption that there is an ongoing material basis to the observed politics we seek to explain. At least since the emergence of the classic tariff system, trade policy has been, and has been understood to be, economic policy. In the public discourse the mix of fiscal, national development, industrial, and income distribution issues has varied, but the language of discussion has always been essentially economic. As a matter of group politics, trade policy has always been quite clearly understood as being about distribution broadly construed. During the period of classic tariff politics,

---

[24] As Timothy Hatton commented at the Kiel conference, the problems are even more complex. Given that the public opinion data seem to show a general public opposition to increased openness to any kind of globalization (trade or immigration), it is the politics of trade that are puzzling. That is, the average level of protection is surprisingly low and standard models have literally no compelling explanation for this (the currently popular Grossman–Helpman model simply treats this as a function of a government taste parameter). Immigration policy is rather more restrictive. On the other hand, the main focus of this paper has been on the ability of these models to explain "local" political economies.

it was widely understood that general elections were, to some extent, a referendum on "the tariff" (loosely the average tariff), an important issue of public policy that helped define the difference between Republicans and Democrats over the entire period. However, once a Congress was elected, dispersion around that average was going to be determined very much by group politics.[25] The self-interested nature of these politics is a constant linking classic tariff politics to the modern politics of the post–Reciprocal Trade Agreements Act system. There are important and difficult issues of accounting for shifts in these interests and shifts in the institutions that channel these interests, but at base the politics of trade policy making remain anchored in material interests.

We have already noted that, unlike trade, there is no systematic evidence of a material basis for ongoing politics of immigration. One of the most telling facts is that there is no equivalent, long-lived, group-based politics surrounding immigration. Following the establishment of the national origin quotas in the Johnson–Reed Act (1924), immigration more or less disappears as a political issue (democratic or group) for forty years. Interestingly, the Immigration and Nationality Act of 1965, which ended the quota system, reflected neither the emergence of new public pressure nor the operation of group politics, but rather derived from its attachment to civil rights issues and, to some extent, to a liberal framing of U.S. international obligations (Gimpel and Edwards 1999). By the time of the landmark Immigration Reform and Control Act of 1986, while there was a more established set of groups in play, these groups do not have the long history that groups on trade do (i.e., most of the established groups go back no further than the politics surrounding the 1965 act), and, more importantly, there is not the same straightforward material foundation, or the broad base, in immigration-related groups.[26]

---

[25] Even before the Civil War, at least from the early 19th century, narrative accounts emphasize the role of interest (e.g., Taussig 1931), while quantitative analyses of the income distribution effects (e.g., Pope 1972; Baack and Ray 1973/1974; James 1978) and a formal quantitative analysis based on a Chicago school political economy framework (Pincus 1977) all provide evidence of interest-based politics in the Ante-Bellum period.

[26] The best treatment of the politics of this period is Schuck (1992). A couple of exceptions require careful consideration. On the one hand, there are a small number of groups with clear material interests that have been involved in immigration politics on more-or-less the same terms as trade-related groups. Southwestern farmers, orchard owners, and ranchers have been actively involved in immigration politics. More recently are employers in the computer industry that have aggressively sought liberalization of entry for skilled labor. However, the narrowness of these interests relative to the wide base of economic interests makes the immigration groups exceptions that prove the rule. On the other hand, immigration lawyers have played an important role in the politics of immigration policy. In understanding their role, however, it is useful to compare the immigration bar with the trade bar. Both have an obvious interest in the details of the law regulating their areas of practice, but these two

It is interesting that, although there is interest-based organization on the immigration issue, this organization does not cover the wide range of economic interests that organization on trade does, and, as we have just noted, much of the organization focuses on issues that are essentially orthogonal to economic issues in general, and distributive issues in particular. Comparing the lack of both broad interest-based organization and sustained interest-based politics on immigration, to the presence of both on trade would seem to provide very strong evidence in favor of our central claim.[27]

In some ways, however, a comparison of the democratic politics of trade and immigration provide even more insight on their differences. In both the 19th and 20th centuries the public politics of trade and immigration are distinctive, in both centuries: trade is seen as national and essentially economic; while immigration is local and essentially social. First, consider the public politics of trade. Due to its position as one of the very few major sources of revenue for the federal government, the tariff had been an important issue to Congress from the founding of the nation. However, while there is evidence of partisan difference on the tariff even before the Civil War, it remained inchoate as an axis of systematic partisan conflict until the 1880s. During the 1880s, first the Republicans and then the Democrats seized on it as a central post-Reconstruction issue. From the 1888 election until the collapse of the classic tariff system with the Great Depression and the emergence of the modern trade policy system following the Reciprocal Agreements Act of 1934, the tariff was the most important continuing public issue between Republicans and Democrats. While the meaning of "the tariff" varied across regions—standing for, on the one hand, nation-building, economic development, national unity, and anti-imperialism, and, on the other, for sectional and industrial special interest, corruption, and centralism—the underlying claims were always economic, and understood as such. Then as now, there may well

---

groups of lawyers do very different things: the trade bar is essentially in the lobbying business, it represents broad parts of American industry and labor, the immigration bar represents a much less obviously material interest and what it does seems different. In addition, a range of humanitarian, religious, and other groups play large roles that they do not play in the trade context. Extremely useful discussion with Gary Freeman led to this footnote and to a substantial improvement in this whole section of the paper.

27 It may be that part of the reason the group politics of immigration appear so different from those of trade is that the opportunities to engage in group-based politics are so few. In addition to fairly regular legislation on trade issues, there are antidumping, countervailing duty, escape clause, unfair trade practices (301), (a few) national security cases, etc. In all of these the plaintiff is an industry. This is also, indirectly, true in the Court of International Trade cases. And we should not forget that there is virtually always Geneva-based action of one kind or another. All of these induce broad sector-based, and, since unions are actively involved, factor-based organization on the issue. There do not appear to be nearly the range of opportunities for group-based politics on immigration.

have been uncertainty about the economic effects of the tariff, and a certain amount of active disingenuity on the part of political leaders in their claims, but no one was confused that "the tariff" was a tax on imported goods, nor that the connection from the tariff to the broader goals it was being used to support had to rest on an essentially economic analysis.

The public politics of immigration in the 19th century were different from those of the tariff in almost every way. Most importantly, while the parties certainly differed, immigration was never a major axis of national partisan conflict. Where the tariff was always relatively central, immigration politics always seem to emerge from the margins of the political system. The first major move to restrict immigration (of Chinese, then Japanese), like the most recent one, emerged in California and elicited very little interest anywhere else. Not much later, fueled by pseudo-scientific notions of a "hierarchy of races," a small group of, mainly Boston-based, intellectuals began to lobby for general quotas. In both cases, the local concerns driving these movements were essentially political. That is, existing hierarchies seemed to be under pressure to change and a public rhetoric focused on an alien threat was an obvious way of reestablishing control. Thus, unlike trade, the public discourse was primarily about identity and community, with only the loosest claims about economic effects. As we have already noted, broad-based politics on the immigration issue have generally been related to broad macroeconomic or political conditions, not labor market conditions. Thus, the first major episode of national anti-immigrant politics, in the pre–Civil War period, was parasitic on fears associated with a collapse of the previous party system. Economic and political conditions were unsettled, and the enormous wave of, especially Irish and German, immigrants at mid-century created a more-or-less obvious focus for the politics of fear. The conclusion of Jones (1992) is worth quoting at length:

> In considering nativism it is important to distinguish between a general dislike of foreigners resulting from a recognition of cultural differences and a similar but more deep-seated antipathy based on emotions of fear and hatred. The former, present to some extent in all societies, has been a constant factor in America from colonial days to the present. Using stereotypes of the foreign-born which only rarely correspond to reality, this sentiment has been essentially passive, probably reflecting no more than a general ethnocentrism. Much more, however, has been involved in the usually short-lived but highly concentrated outbursts of xenophobia which have erupted in America from time to time. *These have been the product of loss of national confidence owing to internal stress of one kind or another.* Cyclical in character, strongly marked by hysteria and irrationality, and generally inspired by a specific political purpose, such nativistic movements have been essentially attempts to safeguard American nationality from the foreign influences which were believed to threaten it. . . . That the generation preceding the Civil war witnessed a recrudescence of nativism was not so much because the period was one of heavy immigration but that it too was one of internal cri-

sis, when national unity was increasingly threatened by sectionalism. (p. 126, our italics)

Olzak (1992) draws similar conclusions from her careful study of patterns of interethnic violence in the Unted States at the turn of the century. Thus, while occasionally intense, the public politics of immigration were essentially episodic and marginal, while the public politics of trade were constant and central. Combined with the constant presence of group politics of trade and the absence of broadly institutionalized group politics of immigration, and the fact that the group politics of trade have always revolved around economically defined interests and that the group politics of immigration (when they arise) are virtually never about economically defined interests, we begin to see why endogenous policy models seem to perform relatively well as a framework for organizing our thinking on trade, while they fail in this purpose for immigration.

5   Conclusion

This paper has sought to argue that endogenous policy models, and by extension any political economy analysis that rests essentially on material interest as derived from the effect of policy on the prices of goods consumed or the return on factor ownership, can be expected to aid our understanding of the politics of trade policy but not our understanding of immigration policy. This has been a schematic argument, and in particular the historical argument could do with close auditing and further development. It should also be very clear that we are not arguing against political economic analysis of immigration policy. Immigration may well have effects that work via more complex mechanisms. For example, Roemer (2001b) has developed an analysis of the welfare economics of migration in which immigration affects labor market outcomes via effects on working class solidarity (and thus union cohesion) and community identity (and thus willingness to support the welfare state). This certainly leads to an analysis of material interests, but it proceeds from an essentially social foundation—i.e., the links between immigration and both working class solidarity and community identity, for all their importance, are not ultimately material facts.

In thinking about the future of both of these issues, current work on the politics of immigration suggests additional directions for research in terms of the framing of issues that would be interesting to consider in a more formal analytical framework. For example, we might think of the effect of *positive framing*: trade in commodities induces a politics about commodities; immigration induces a politics about people. Unlike the claims in, for example, Hall and Nelson (1989) or Hiscox (1999), the temporal or material element may be trumped by framing effects. In addition, current research on the politics of immigration suggests the importance of *normative framing*: focus on foreign *countries* has no negative, and may have a positive, political affect; focus on foreign people, especially in a multiethnic society, may have a considerably negative affect in an era of strong rights-based normative notions. Thus, the normative framing effects may have been considerably weaker in the 19th century. Similarly, they may be weaker in countries in which the discourse of citizenship is defined less in terms of abstract rights and more in terms of descent (i.e., blood) or even cultural acceptance (the Roman tradition).

The prospects for an enriched political economy that applies the tools of formal theory to questions that are better grounded in social and political structures, and more sophisticated characterizations of social learning, suggest nearly boundless possibilities for growth.

Bibliography

Alt, J., J. Frieden, M. Gilligan, D. Rodrik, and R. Rogowski (1996). The Politics of International Trade: Enduring Puzzles and an Agenda for Inquiry. *Comparative Political Studies* 29 (6): 689–717.

Alvarez, R.M., and T. Butterfield (2000). The Resurgence of Nativism in California? The Case of Prop. 187 and Illegal Immigration. *Social Science Quarterly* 81 (1): 167–179.

Amegashi, J.A. (forthcoming). A Political Economy of Immigration Quotas. *Economics of Governance.*

Anderson, J., and M. Zanardi (2004). Political Pressure Deflection. CentER Discussion Paper 2004–21. University of Tilburg, The Netherlands.

Anderson, K., and R. Baldwin (1987). The Political Market for Protection in Industrial Countries. In A.M. El-Agraa (ed.), *Protection, Cooperation, Integration and Development.* New York: Macmillan.

Austen-Smith, D. (1997). Interest Groups: Money, Information, and Influence. In D. Mueller (ed.), *Perspectives on Public Choice: A Handbook.* Cambridge: Cambridge University Press.

Baack, B., and E.J. Ray (1973/1974). Tariff Policy and Income Distribution: The Case of the United States, 1830–1860. *Explorations in Economic History* 11(2): 103–121.

Bailey, M., J. Goldstein, and B. Weingast (1997). The Institutional Roots of American Trade Policy: Politics, Coalitions, and International Trade. *World Politics* 49 (3): 309–338.

Baldwin, R. (1989). The Political Economy of Trade Policy. *Journal of Economic Perspectives* 3 (4): 119–135.

Baldwin, R. (1996). The Political Economy of Trade Policy: Integrating the Perspectives of Economists and Political Scientists. In R. Feenstra, G. Grossman, and D. Irwin (eds.), *The Political Economy of Trade Policy*. Cambridge: MIT Press.

Baldwin, R., and C. Magee (2000). Is Trade Policy for Sale? Congressional Voting on Recent Trade Bills. *Public Choice* 105 (1/2): 79–101.

Balistreri, E. (1997). The Performance of the Heckscher–Ohlin–Vanek Model in Predicting Endogenous Trade Policy Forces at the Individual Level. *Canadian Journal of Economics* 30 (1): 1–17.

Bandyopadhyay, U., and K. Gawande (2000). Is Protection for Sale? Evidence on the Grossman–Helpman Theory of Endogenous Protection. *Review of Economics and Statistics* 82 (1): 139–152.

Bauer, R., I. de Sola Pool, and L.A. Dexter (1963). *American Business and Public Policy: The Politics of Foreign Trade*. Chicago: Aldine Publishing Company.

Bean, C. (1995). Determinants of Attitudes towards Questions of Border Maintenance in Australia. *People and Places* 3 (3): 32–39.

Beaulieu, E. (2002a). Factor or Industry Cleavages in Trade Policy: An Empirical Analysis of the Stolper–Samuelson Theorem. *Economics & Politics* 14 (2): 99–131.

Beaulieu, E. (2002b). The Stolper–Samuelson Theorem Faces Congress. *Review of International Economics* 10 (2): 343–360.

Beaulieu, E., and C. Magee (2004). Four Simple Tests of Campaign Contributions and Trade Policy Preferences. *Economics & Politics* 16 (2): 163–187.

Becker, G. (1983). A Theory of Competition Among Pressure Groups for Political Influence. *Quarterly Journal of Economics* 98 (3): 371–400.

Bellettini, G., and C. Berti Ceroni (2004). A Positive Analysis of Immigration Policy. Manuscript. Università di Bologna.

Benhabib, J. (1996). On the Political Economy of Immigration. *European Economic Review* 40 (9): 1737–1743.

Bernheim, B.D., and M. Whinston (1986). Menu Auctions, Resource Allocation, and Economic Influence. *Quarterly Journal of Economics* 101 (1): 1–31.

Betts, K. (1996). Immigration and Public Opinion in Australia. *People and Place* 4 (3): 9–20.

Bilal, S., J.-M. Grether, and J. de Melo (2003). Attitudes towards Immigration: A Trade-Theoretic Approach. *Review of International Economics* 11 (2): 253–267.

Bond, E. and T.-J. Chen (1987). The Welfare Effects of Illegal Immigration. *Journal of International Economics* 23(3/4): 315–328.

Borjas, G. (1995). Immigration and Welfare, 1970–1990. *Research in Labor Economics* 14 (1): 251–280.

Borjas, G. (1999a). *Heaven's Door: Immigration Policy and the American Economy*. Princeton: Princeton University Press.

Borjas, G. (1999b). The Economic Analysis of Immigration. In O. Ashenfelter and D. Card (eds.), *Handbook of Labor Economics*, Vol. 3A. Amsterdam: North Holland.

Borjas, G. (2003). The Labor Demand Curve *Is* Downward Sloping: Reexamining the Impact of Immigration on the Labor Market. *Quarterly Journal of Economics* 118 (4): 1335–1374.

Burns, P., and J. Gimpel (2000). Economic Insecurity, Prejudicial Stereotypes, and Public Opinion on Immigration Policy. *Political Science Quarterly* 115 (2): 201–225.

Calavita, K. (1989). The Contradictions of Immigration Lawmaking: The Immigration and Reform Act of 1986. *Law and Policy* 11 (1): 17–47.

Calavita, K. (1996). The New Politics of Immigration: "Balanced Budget Conservatism" and the Symbolism of Prop. 187. *Social Problems* 43 (3): 284–305.

Canova, F., and M. Ravn (1998). Crossing the Rio Grande: Migrations, Business Cycles and the Welfare State. CEPR Discussion Paper 2040. London.

Card, D. (2001). Immigrant Inflows, Native Outflows, and the Local Labor Market Impacts of Higher Immigration. *Journal of Labor Economics* 19 (1): 22–64.

Citrin, J., D.P. Green, C. Muste, and C. Wong (1997). Public Opinion toward Immigration Reform: The Role of Economic Motivations. *Journal of Politics* 59 (3): 858–881.

Coleman, J. (1998). Bipartisan Order and Partisan Disorder in Postwar Trade Policy. Manuscript. Political Science Department, University of Wisconsin.

Cremer, H., V. Fourgeaud, M. Leite-Monteiro, M. Marchand, and P. Pestieau (1996). Mobility and Redistribution: A Survey. *Public Finance* 51 (3): 325–352.

Cremer, H., and P. Pestieau (1998). Social Insurance, Majority Voting and Labor Mobility. *Journal of Public Economics* 68 (3): 397–420.

Cukierman, A., Z. Hercowitz, and D. Pines (1994). The Political Economy of Immigration. Foerder Institute for Economic Research Working Paper 17/93. Tel Aviv.

Dávila, A., J. Pagán, and M.V. Grau (1999). Immigration Reform, the INS, and the Distribution of Interior and Border Enforcement. *Public Choice* 99 (3/4): 327–345.

Deardorff, A., and R. Stern (1998). An Overview of the Modeling of the Choices and Consequences of U.S. Trade Policies. In A. Deardorff and R. Stern (eds.), *Constituent Interests and U.S. Trade Policies*. Ann Arbor: University of Michigan Press.

Dixit, A. (1998). *The Making of Economic Policy: A Transaction Cost Politics Perspective*. Cambridge: MIT Press.

Drazen, A. (2000). *Political Economy in Macroeconomics*. Cambridge: MIT Press.

Dustmann, C., and I. Preston (2001). Racial and Economic Factors in Attitudes to Immigration. CEPR Discussion Paper 2542. London.

Dutt, P., and D. Mitra (2002). Endogenous Trade Policy through Majority Voting: An Empirical Investigation. *Journal of International Economics* 58 (1): 107–133.

Epple, D., and T. Romer (1991). Mobility and Redistribution. *Journal of Political Economy* 99 (4): 828–858.

Epple, D., T. Romer, and H. Sieg (2001). Interjurisdictional Sorting and Majority Rule. *Econometrica* 69 (6): 1437–1465.

Epstein, D., and S. O'Halloran (1996). Divided Government and the Design of Administrative Procedures. *Journal of Politics* 58 (2): 373–398.

Epstein, G., and S. Nitzan (2004). The Struggle Over Migration Policy. Manuscript. Bar-Ilan University. Ramat Gan, Israel.

Espenshade, T. (1998). U.S. Immigration and the New Welfare State. In D. Jacobson (ed.), *The Immigration Reader: America in a Multidisciplinary Perspective*. Oxford: Blackwell.

Espenshade, T., and C. Calhoun (1993). An Analysis of Public Opinion toward Undocumented Immigration. *Population Research and Policy Review* 12: 189–124.

Espenshade, T., and K. Hempstead (1996). Contemporary American Attitudes toward U.S. Immigration. *International Migration Review* 30 (2): 535–570.

Ethier, W. (1986). Illegal Immigration. *American Economic Review* 76 (1): 56–71.

Facchini, G., and G. Willmann (2001). The Political Economy of International Factor Mobility. Stanford Institute for Economic Policy Research 00–20.

Fetzer, J. (2000). *Public Attitudes toward Immigration in the United States, France, and Germany*. Cambridge: Cambridge University Press.

Findlay, R., and S. Wellisz (1982). Endogenous Tariffs, the Political Economy of Trade Restrictions and Welfare. In J. Bhagwati (ed.), *Import Competition and Response*. Chicago: University of Chicago Press.

Flores, O. (1997). The Political Economy of Immigration Quotas. *Atlantic Economic Journal* 25 (1): 50–59.

Frieden, J., and R. Rogowski (1996). The Impact of the International Economy on National Policies: An Analytical Overview. In R. Keohane and H. Milner (eds.), *Internationalization and Domestic Politics*. Cambridge: Cambridge University Press.

Gang, I., F. Rivera-Batiz, and M.-S. Yun (2002). Economic Strain, Ethnic Concentration and Attitudes Towards Foreigners in the European Union. IZA Discussion Paper 578. Bonn.

Gaston, N., and D. Nelson (2000). Immigration and Labour-Market Outcomes in the United States: A Political-Economy Puzzle. *Oxford Review of Economic Policy* 16 (3): 104–114.

Gaston, N., and D. Nelson (2002). The Wage and Employment Effects of Immigration: Trade and Labour Economics Perspectives. In D. Greenaway, R. Upward, and K. Wakelin (eds.), *Trade, Investment, Migration and Labour Market Adjustment*. Basingstoke: Palgrave-Macmillan.

Gawande, K., and P. Krishna (2003). The Political Economy of Trade Policy: Empirical Approaches. In E.K. Choi and J. Harrigan (eds.), *Handbook of International Trade*. Oxford: Blackwell.

Gimpel, J., and J. Edwards (1999). *The Congressional Politics of Immigration Reform*. Boston: Allyn and Bacon.

Goldberg, P., and G. Maggi (1999). Protection for Sale: An Empirical Investigation. *American Economic Review* 89 (5): 1135–1155.

Goldin, C. (1994). The Political Economy of Immigration Restriction in the United States, 1890–1921. In C. Goldin and G. Libecap (eds.), *The Regulated Economy: A Historical Approach to Political Economy*. Chicago: University of Chicago Press.

Grether, J.M., J. de Melo, and T. Muller (2001). The Political Economy of Migration in a Ricardo–Viner Model. In S. Djajic (ed.), *International Migration: Trends, Policy, Impact*. London: Routledge.

Grossman, G., and E. Helpman (1994). Protection for Sale. *American Economic Review* 84 (4): 833–850.

Grossman, G., and E. Helpman (2001). *Special Interest Politics*. Cambridge: MIT Press.

Grossman, G., and J. Levinsohn (1989). Import Competition and Stock Market Return to Capital. *American Economic Review* 79 (5): 1065–1087.

Hall, H.K., and D. Nelson (1989). Institutional Structure and Time Horizon in a Simple Political-Economy Model: The Lowi Effect. *International Spectator* 24 (3/4): 153–173.

Hall, H.K., and D. Nelson (1992). Institutional Structure in the Political Economy of Protection: Legislated versus Administered Protection. *Economics & Politics* 4 (1): 61–77.

Hall, H.K., C. Kao, and D. Nelson (1998). Women and Tariffs: Testing Gender Gap in a Downs–Mayer Model. *Economic Inquiry* 36 (2): 320–332.

Hammermesh, D. (1993). *Labor Demand*. Princeton: Princeton University Press.

Hanson, G.H., and A. Spilimbergo (2001). Political Economy, Sectoral Schocks and Border Enforcement. Working Paper 44. CCIS, University of California, San Diego.

Hatton, T., and J. Williamson (1998). *The Age of Mass Migration: Causes and Economic Impact*. New York: Oxford University Press.

Haupt, A., and W. Peters (1998). Public Pensions and Voting on Immigration. *Public Choice* 95 (3/4): 403–413.

Helpman, E. (1995). Politics and Trade Policy. In D. Kreps and K. Wallis (eds.), *Advances in Economics and Econometrics: Theory and Applications*. Cambridge: Cambridge University Press.

Hill, J., and J. Mendez (1983). Factor Mobility in the General Equilibrium Model of Production. *Journal of International Economics* 15 (1/2): 19–25.

Hillman, A.L. (1988). *The Political Economy of Protection*. Chur: Harwood Academic Publishers.

Hillman, A.L., and A. Weiss (1999). A Theory of Permissible Illegal Immigration. *European Journal of Political Economy* 14 (4): 585–604.

Hiscox, M. (1999). The Magic Bullet? The RTAA, Institutional Reform, and Trade Liberalization. *International Organization* 53 (4): 669–698.

Hiscox, M. (2001). The Magee Test Revisited: Industry Lobbying Patterns and the Stolper–Samuelson Theorem. Manuscript. Harvard University, Cambridge, Mass.

Hood, M., and I. Morris (2000). Brother, Can You Spare a Dime? Racial/Ethnic Context and the Anglo Vote on Proposition 187. *Social Science Quarterly* 81 (1): 194–206.

Huber, G., and T. Espenshade (1997). Neo-Isolationism, Balanced Budget Conservatism, and the Fiscal Impacts of Immigrants. *International Migration Review* 31 (4): 1031–1053.

Irwin, D. (1994). The Political Economy of Free Trade: Voting in the British General Election of 1906. *Journal of Law and Economics* 37 (1): 75–108.

Irwin, D. (1996). Industry or Class Cleavages over Trade Policy? Evidence from the British General Election of 1923. In R. Feenstra, G. Grossman, and D. Irwin (eds.), *The Political Economy of Trade Policy*. Cambridge: MIT.

James, J. (1978). The Welfare Effects of the Antebellum Tariff: A General Equilibrium Analysis. *Explorations in Economic History* 15 (3): 231–256.

Johnson, G. (1998). The Impact of Immigration on Income Distribution Among Minorities. In D. Hammermesh and F. Bean (eds.), *Help or Hindrance? The Economic Implications of Immigration for African Americans*. New York: Russell Sage Foundation.

Johnston, R., and M. Percy (1980). Reciprocity, Imperial Sentiment, and Party Politics in the 1911 Election. *Canadian Journal of Political Science* 13 (4): 711–729.

Jones, M.A. (1992). *American Immigration*. 2nd Edition. Chicago: University of Chicago Press.

Jones, R. (1965). The Structure of Simple General Equilibrium Models. *Journal of Political Economy* 73 (6): 557–572.

Jones, R. (1971). A Three-Factor Model in Theory, Trade and History. In J. Bhagwati et al. (eds.), *Trade, Balance of Payments and Growth*. Amsterdam: North-Holland.

Jones, R., and J. Scheinkman (1977). The Relevance of the Two-Sector Production Model in Trade Theory. *Journal of Political Economy* 85 (5): 909–935.

Karol, D. (2000). Divided Government and U.S. Trade Policy: Much Ado about Nothing? *International Organization* 54 (4): 825–844.

Kessler, A. (2001). Immigration, Insecurity, and the "Ambivalent" American Public. Manuscript. Department of Government, University of Texas, Austin.

Kinder, D., and W. Mebane (1983). Politics and Economics in Everyday Life. In K. Monroe (ed.), *The Political Process and Economic Change*. New York: Agathon Press.

Laffont, J.-J. (2000). *Incentives and Political Economy*. Oxford: Clarendon Press.

Lahav, G. (1997). Ideological and Party Constraints on Immigration Attitudes in Europe. *Journal of Common Market Studies* 35 (3): 377–406.

Leamer, E. (1995). *The Heckscher–Ohlin Model in Theory and Practice*. Princeton Studies in International Finance 77. Princeton: Princeton University Press.

Lejour, A., and H. Verbon (1994). Labour Mobility and Decision Making on Social Insurance in an Integrated Market. *Public Choice* 79 (1/2): 161–185.

Lohmann, S., and S. O'Halloran (1994). Divided Government and U.S. Trade Policy: Theory and Evidence. *International Organization* 48 (4): 595–632.

Lowell, B.L., F. Bean, and R. de la Garza (1986). Undocumented Immigration: An Analysis of the 1984 Simpson–Mazzoli Vote. *Social Science Quarterly* 67 (1): 118–127.

Lowi, T. (1964). American Business, Public Policy, Case Studies, and Political Theory. *World Politics* 16(4): 676–715.

MacDonald, K., and B. Cain (1997). Nativism, Partisanship and Immigration: An Analysis of Prop. 187. In M. Preston, B. Cain, and S. Bass (eds.), *Racial and Ethnic Politics in California*. Berkeley: Institute for Governmental Studies.

Magee, S. (1978). Three Simple Tests of the Stolper–Samuelson Theorem. In P. Oppenheimer (ed.), *Issues in International Economics*. Stocksfield: Oriel Press.

Mayda, A.M. (2004). Who Is against Immigration? A Cross-Country Investigation of Individual Attitudes toward Immigrants. Manuscript. Georgetown University, Washington, D.C.

Mayda, A.M., and D. Rodrik (2005). Why Are Some People (and Countries) More Protectionist Than Others? *European Economic Review* 49 (6): 1393–1430.

Mayer, W. (1984). Endogenous Tariff Formation. *American Economic Review* 74 (5): 970–985.

Mazza, I., and F. van Winden (1996). A Political Economic Analysis of Labor Migration and Income Redistribution. *Public Choice* 88 (2): 333–363.

Michel, P., P. Pestieau, and J.-P. Vidal (1998). Labor Migration and Redistribution with Alternative Assimilation Policies: The Small Economy Case. *Regional Science and Urban Economics* 28 (3): 363–377.

Milner, H. (1999). The Political Economy of International Trade. *Annual Review of Political Science* 2: (2): 91–114.

Milner, H., and B.P. Rosendorff (1997). Democratic Politics and International Trade Negotiations: Elections and Divided Government as Constraints on Trade Liberalization. *Journal of Conflict Resolution* 41 (1): 117–146.

Moehring, H.B. (1988). Symbol versus Substance in Legislative Activity: The Case of Illegal Immigration. *Public Choice* 57 (3): 287–294.

Mussa, M. (1974). Tariffs and the Distribution of Income: The Importance of Specificity, Substitutability, and Intensity in the Short and Long Run. *Journal of Political Economy* 82 (5): 1191–1203.

Nelson, D. (1988). Endogenous Tariff Theory: A Critical Survey. *American Journal of Political Science* 32 (3): 796–837.

Nelson, D. (1989). Domestic Political Preconditions of US Trade Policy: Liberal Structure and Protectionist Dynamics. *Journal of Public Policy* 9 (1): 83–108.

Nelson, D. (1999). Problems in the Political Economy of Trade Policy Reform. *Journal of International Trade and Economic Development* 8 (1): 3–26.

Nelson, D., and Y. Xu (2001). The Political Economy of Illegal Migration. Manuscript. Tulane University and Georgia State University, New Orleans and Atlanta.

Newton, L. (2000). Why Some Latinos Supported Proposition 187: Testing Economic Threat and Cultural Identity Hypotheses. *Social Science Quarterly* 81 (1): 180–193.

O'Halloran, S. (1994). *Politics, Process, and American Trade Policy*. Ann Arbor: University of Michigan Press.

Olzak, S. (1992). *The Dynamics of Ethnic Competition and Conflict*. Stanford: Stanford University Press.

O'Rourke, K., and R. Sinnott (2002). The Determinants of Individual Trade Policy Preferences: International Survey Evidence. *Brookings Trade Policy Forum 2001*, 157–196.

Peltzman, S. (1976). Toward a More General Theory of Regulation. *Journal of Law and Economics* 19 (2): 211–240.

Persson, T., and G. Tabellini (2000). *Political Economics: Explaining Economic Policy*. Cambridge: MIT Press.

Pincus, J.J. (1977). *Pressure Groups and Politics in Ante-Bellum Tariffs*. New York: Columbia University Press.

Pope, C. (1972). The Impact of the Ante-Bellum Tariff on Income Distribution. *Explorations in Economic History* 9 (4): 375–421.

Ramey, V., and M. Shapiro (1998). Costly Capital Reallocation and the Effects of Government Spending. *Carnegie–Rochester Conference Series on Public Policy* 48: 145–194.

Ramey, V., and M. Shapiro (2000). Displaced Capital: A Study of Aerospace Plant Closings. *Journal of Political Economy* 109 (5): 958–992.

Ray, E. (1987). Changing Patterns of Protectionism: The Fall in Tariffs and the Rise in Non-Tariff Barriers. *Northwestern Journal of International Law and Business* 8 (2): 285–327.

Razin, A., E. Sadka, and P. Swagel (1998). Tax Burden and Migration: A Political-Economy Theory and Evidence. *Journal of Public Economics* 85 (2): 167–190.

Riezman, R., and J. Wilson (1995). Politics and Trade Policy. In J. Banks and E. Hanushek (eds.), *Modern Political Economy*. Cambridge: Cambridge University Press.

Rodrik, D. (1995). Political Economy of Trade Policy. In G. Grossman and K. Rogoff (eds.), *Handbook of International Economics*. Volume III. Amsterdam: North-Holland.

Roemer, J. (2001a). *Political Competition: Theory and Application*. Cambridge: Harvard University Press.

Roemer, J. (2001b). The Non-Parochial Welfare Economics of Immigration. Manuscript. Yale University, New Haven, Conn.

Rose-Ackerman, S. (1983). Beyond Tiebout: Modeling the Political Economy of Local Government. In G. Zodrow (ed.), *Local Provision of Public Services: The Tiebout Model After Twenty-five Years*. New York: Academic Press.

Rosenfeld, M., and M. Tienda (1999). Mexican Immigration, Occupational Niches, and Labor Market Competition: Evidence from Los Angeles, Chicago, and Atlanta, 1970 to 1990. In F. Bean and S. Bell-Rose (eds.), *Immigration and Opportunity*. New York: Russell Sage Foundation.

Ross, S., and J. Yinger (1999). Sorting and Voting: A Review of the Literature on Urban Public Finance. In P. Cheshire and E.S. Mills (eds.), *Handbook of Urban and Regional Economics*. Vol. 3 (*Applied Urban Economics*). Amsterdam: North-Holland.

Rothstein, P. (1994). Learning the Preferences of Governments and Voters from Proposed Spending and Voting in School Budget Referenda. *Journal of Public Economics* 54 (3): 361–389.

Salvanto, A. (1998). Initiatives as Running Mates: The Impact of a Candidate-Centered Initiative Campaign. Research monograph series paper, Center for the Study of Democracy, UC Irvine.

Schattschneider, E.E. (1935). *Politics, Pressure, and the Tariff*. Englewood Cliffs: Prentice-Hall.

Schattschneider, E.E. (1960). *Semi-Sovereign People: A Realist View of Democracy in America*. New York: Holt-Rinehart.

Scheve, K., and M. Slaughter (2001a). What Determines Individual Trade Policy Preferences. *Journal of International Economics* 54 (2): 267–292.

Scheve, K., and M. Slaughter (2001b). Labor Market Competition and Individual Preferences over Immigration Policy. *Review of Economics and Statistics* 83 (1): 133–145.

Scholten, U., and M. Thum (1996). Public Pensions and Immigration Policy in a Democracy. *Public Choice* 87 (3/4): 347–361.

Schuck, P. (1992). The Politics of Rapid Legal Change: Immigration Policy in the 1980s. *Studies in American Political Development* 6 (2): 37–92.

Shughart, W., R. Tollison, and M. Kimenyi (1986). The Political Economy of Immigration Restriction. *Yale Journal on Regulation* 4 (1): 79–97.

Simon, J. (1996). Public Expenditures on Immigrants to the United States, Past and Present. *Population and Development Review* 22 (1): 99–109.

Simon, R., and J. Lynch (1999). A Comparative Assessment of Public Opinion Toward Immigrants and Immigration Policies. *International Migration Review* 33 (2): 455–467.

Smith, J., and B. Edmonston (1997). *The New Americans: Economic, Demographic, and Fiscal Effects of Immigration*. Washington, D.C.: National Academy Press.

Sollner, F. (1999). A Note on the Political Economy of Immigration. *Public Choice* 100 (3/4): 245–251.

Stolper, W., and P. Samuelson (1941). Protection and Real Wages. *Review of Economic Studies* 9 (1): 58–73.

Taussig, F. (1931). *The Tariff History of the United States.* 8th Edition. New York: G.P. Putnam's Sons.

Thompson, A. (1993). The Anticipated Sectoral Adjustment to the Canada–United States Free Trade Agreement: An Event Study Analysis. *Canadian Journal of Economics* 26 (2): 253–271.

Thompson, A. (1994). Trade Liberalization, Comparative Advantage, and Scale Economies: Stock Market Evidence from Canada. *Journal of International Economics* 37 (1/2): 1–27.

Timmer, A., and J. Williamson (1998). Immigration Policy Prior to the 1930s: Labor Markets, Policy Interactions, and Globalization Backlash. *Population and Development Review* 24 (4): 739–771.

Tolbert, C., and R. Hero (1996). Race/Ethnicity and Direct Democracy: An Analysis of California's Illegal Immigration Initiative. *Journal of Politics* 58 (3): 806–818.

Topel, R. (1994a). Regional Labor Markets and the Determinants of Wage Inequality. *American Economic Review* 84 (2): 17–22.

Topel, R. (1994b). Wage Inequality and Regional Labour Market Performance in the US. In T. Tachibanaki (ed.), *Labour Market and Economic Performance: Europe, Japan and the USA.* New York: St. Martin's Press.

VanHook, J., J. Glick, and F. Bean (1999). Public Assistance Receipt among Immigrants and Natives: How the Unit of Analysis Affects Research Findings. *Demography* 36 (1): 111–120.

Waldinger, R. (1996a). Black/Immigrant Competition Reassessed: New Evidence from Los Angeles. *Sociological Perspectives* 40 (3): 365–386.

Waldinger, R. (1996b). Who Makes the Beds? Who Does the Dishes? Black/Immigrant Competition Reassessed. In H. Duleep and P. Wunnava (eds.), *Immigrants and Immigration Policy: Individual Skills, Family Ties, and Group Identities.* Greenwich, Conn.: JAI Press.

Weck-Hannemann, H. (1990). Protectionism in Direct Democracy. *Journal of Institutional and Theoretical Economics* 146 (3): 389–418.

Yinger, J. (1985). Inefficiency and the Median Voter: Property Taxes, Capitalization, Heterogeneity, and the Theory of the Second Best. *Perspectives on Local Public Finance and Public Policy* 2 (3): 3–30.

Comment on David Greenaway and Douglas R. Nelson

Gerald Willmann

In their contribution, the authors survey the literature on the political economy of trade protection and its counterpart, the literature dealing with the political economy of migration. This is a laudable endeavor. While the political economy of trade policy is relatively well developed, the literature on the political economy of migration is considerably less advanced, and a comparison of the two is a worthwhile undertaking. The only other comparison, known to this discussant, of the two areas is the recent contribution by Facchini (2004) who reaches different conclusions—a point I will return to below.

Since the paper surveys the two literatures in turn, I follow suit and consider the political economy of trade protection first. The extensive body of literature that exists on this topic has been summarized in previous surveys. Rodrik's (1995) article in the third Handbook of International Economics provides an instructive overview of different strands of the literature.

Helpman (1997) does an excellent job of relating them to the Grossman and Helpman (1994) protection for sale model. More recently, Gawande and Krishna (2004) focus on the empirical literature that has taken this particular model to the data.

While the present survey offers insights into the earlier literature and contains many interesting references to empirical work, it is surprising to see how little it says about the protection for sale framework. To be frank, this discussant disagrees—as most scholars working in the field would—with the authors' assessment that "the value-added of many of the later papers must be judged to be rather small" (p. 300).

Quite the contrary, the protection for sale model of Grossman and Helpman (1994) is the seminal contribution that has reinvigorated the field and led to many new insights. Grossman and Helpman (1994) use the menu auction or common agency approach of Bernheim and Whinston (1986) to model the interaction between industry lobbies and an incumbent government. In particular, the lobbies submit contribution schedules and the government then grants protection by setting the tariff vector and collects contributions. This approach does not only provide micro-foundations for earlier models of endogenous protection, it has also led to many interesting extensions and has given rise to numerous studies that perform structural estimations of the model. I refer to the surveys cited above for further details.

The other direction in which the present survey could be extended is the emerging new institutional political economy of trade policy. In line with developments in public finance, Willmann (2003) models the constitutional policy formation process and shows how the regional concentration of industries gives rise to tariff protection. Anderson and Zanardi (2004) also focus on the political process in greater detail, as do Grossman and Helpman (2005).

While the emphasis of the present survey may be selective, the conclusion it draws is valid: tariff protection is driven to a large extent by what the authors call material interest. There is ample evidence for this influence, no matter which subset of the literature one chooses to focus on. Having established this conclusion, the authors turn to consider the political economy of migration and argue that immigration policy differs in that it is not (or hardly) determined by material or economic interests.

For an economist this comes as a surprise. Yes, we tend to leave aside social or worse influences on migration policy, ritually acknowledging them briefly before concentrating on economic factors. But to dispute the economic impact? Borjas (2003) is an outstanding study that shows quite clearly that immigration does have economic effects on wages. Mayda (2003) analyzes how personal characteristics explain attitudes towards migration. Whereas one might conclude that it is the lack of education that causes xenophobia in rich countries, the results are the opposite for developing countries, where it is the poor who favor immigration and the rich who oppose it, very much in line with economic explanations. Why did Silicon Valley executives travel to Washington D.C. to demand more H1B immigration visas in the heyday of the Internet bubble if not for economic reasons. Were not the labor unions instrumental in enacting the first anti-immigrant pieces of legislation in the United States?

The other aspect of immigration policy that is underrepresented in this survey is the skill composition of immigration. Clearly, immigrants differ, from poor have-nots with hardly any education to rich entrepreneurs and highly educated engineers. This renders the problem of immigration policy considerably more complex: instead of a one-dimensional policy question it really is a multi-dimensional issue. As Benhabib (1996) shows, residents prefer immigration of a complementary type of labor. Empirically, shifts in the composition of immigration have been pronounced, from unskilled immigration in the form of family reunions to higher skilled immigrants in recent years. And these shifts often coincide with political changes. It is not by coincidence that it is the current leftist government in Germany that has reformed immigration laws to attract the bright and wealthy.

Surveys should be structured around guiding principles. The present one revolves around the point that trade policy is driven by material interest, whereas immigration policy is not. While the first part of this statement is hardly controversial, the second part is. It would have been preferable to establish differences in degree instead of making the case for such a stark contrast. One interesting additional dimension would be the question to what extent policy is determined by lobbying versus through institutional channels. The ultimate question remains why we come close to free trade, while closed doors prevail in the context of immigration.

Bibliography

Anderson, J., and M. Zanardi (2004). Political Power Deflection. NBER Working Paper 10439. Cambridge, Mass.

Benhabib, J. (1996). On the Political Economy of Immigration. *European Economic Review* 40 (9):1737–1743.

Bernheim, B.D., and M. Whinston (1986). Menu Auctions, Resource Allocation, and Economic Influence. *Quarterly Journal of Economics* 101 (1): 1–31.

Borjas, G. (2003). The Labor Demand Curve Is Downward-Sloping: Reexamining the Impact of Immigration on the Labor Market. *Quarterly Journal of Economics* 118 (4): 1335–1374.

Facchini, G. (2004). The Political Economy of International Trade and Factor Mobility: A Survey. *Journal of Economic Surveys* 18 (1): 1–32.

Gawande, K., and P. Krishna (2003). The Political Economy of Trade Policy: Empirical Approaches. In K. Choi, J. Harrigan, and W. Aldrich (eds.), *Handbook of International Trade*. Oxford: Basil Blackwell.

Grossman, G., and E. Helpman (1994). Protection for Sale. *American Economic Review* 84 (4): 833–850.

Grossman, G., and E. Helpman (2005). A Protectionist Bias in Majoritarian Politics. NBER Working Paper 11014. Cambridge, Mass.

Helpman, E. (1997). Politics and Trade Policy. In D. Kreps and K. Wallis (eds.), *Advances in Economics and Econometrics: Theory and Applications*. Vol. 2. Cambridge: Cambridge University Press.

Mayda, A.M. (2004). Who Is against Immigration? A Cross-Country Investigation of Individual Attitudes toward Immigrants. Jobmarket Paper. Harvard University, Cambridge, Mass.

Rodrik, D. (1995). Political Economy of Trade Policy. In G. Grossman and K. Rogoff (eds.), *Handbook of International Economics*. Vol. 3. Amsterdam: North-Holland.

Willmann, G. (2003). Why Legislators Are Protectionists: The Role of Majoritarian Voting in Setting Tariffs. Economics Working Paper 2003-10. University of Kiel.

Per Lundborg

Growth Effects of the Brain Drain

Abstract:

I analyze the theoretical effects on growth and welfare of emigration of educated and uneducated labor, of higher emigration probability, etc. Using a Grossman–Helpman growth model, I show that the prospects of emigration to high-wage countries raises the expected returns to education, stimulates human capital formation, and raises the growth rate in the emigration country. Given the expected returns, emigration of educated workers lowers growth and the welfare of those remaining. Thus, while the brain drain reduces welfare, the effects of globalization could nevertheless be positive. Emigration of low-skilled workers also reduces growth via adverse effects on education. Higher tuition fees counteract positive growth effects.

1   Introduction

Increasing international labor mobility is a salient feature of the internationalization of the world economy. Not only do migration rates increase among the low-skilled, low-paid workers, but available data, albeit of doubtful reliability, strongly suggest that emigration rates increase at even stronger rates among high-skilled workers. Docquier and Marfouk (2004) offer a recent measure of international skill migration. They show, among other things, that during the 1990s the brain drain increased at remarkable rates in many countries in Africa and Central America.[1] Emigration rates among the skilled are now extremely high in the Caribbean, reaching over 80 percent in countries like Haiti and Jamaica. Many people in the new EU countries of Eastern Europe fear that the "brain drain" will reduce growth and welfare in their home countries, as membership in the EU means that workers, including their best R&D workers, will

---

Remark: I wish to thank participants, and in particular Gabriel Felbermayr, at the conference for very insightful and useful comments.

[1]   Docquier and Marfouk (2004) represents an improvement as compared to the study by Carrington and Detragiache (1998), which builds on data in Barro and Lee (1993, 1994), the 1990 U.S. census data, and OECD migration data.

eventually be offered free access to all the EU's labor markets.[2] The propensity to emigrate is considerably higher among the high-skilled than among the low-skilled workers in the new EU countries (Docquier and Marfouk 2004). A factor that may contribute to stimulating emigration is that universities in the developed countries to a large extent educate students from less developed countries, which might raise the probability that many of the best students end up in the richer parts of the world.[3]

The brain drain issue has been a recurrent research theme ever since the 1960s,[4] but several recent developments in economic research have further raised the interest of the issue. First, empirical studies on economic growth, notably Barro (1991) and Hall and Jones (1999), have shown that the level of schooling across countries is a significant variable for explaining growth rates. This suggests that the brain drain could potentially have large adverse effects on growth.[5]

Secondly, the rise of endogenous growth theory has made it possible to analyze the consequences of outflows of skilled labor in a richer setting than was previously the case. A case in point is Mountford (1997), who studies the theoretical conditions for the brain drain to have positive growth effects in the source economy. His paper shows that when educational decisions are endogenous and if successful migration is not a certainty, a brain drain may increase productivity. Migration to a high-wage country raises the return to education, which favors human capital formation and can outweigh the negative effects of the brain drain. Beine et al. (2001) specify an OLG model with the same counteracting forces and find that the brain drain may favor the sending country if the domestic human capital is stimulated enough.[6] Using a cross-section of 37 developing coun-

---

2   See Lundborg and Rechea (2003) for a brain drain study with special reference to the transition countries.

3   For instance, Freeman et al. (2004) show that in 1966, 77 percent of science and engineering PhD graduates were U.S.-born males and 23 percent were foreign-born. In 2000, 61 percent of the graduates were U.S.-born and 39 percent were foreign-born.

4   See, for instance, Grubel and Scott (1966), Bhagwati and Hamada (1974), and Johnson (1967).

5   Bils and Klenow (2000) elaborate further on Barro (1991) by studying the dual relationship between schooling and growth. In their model, the expected growth rate reduces the effective discount rate that leads to an increase in demand for schooling. Their overall conclusion contradicts that of Barro by showing a very weak direct relationship between schooling and growth but a strong effect of growth on schooling.

6   Wong and Yip (1999) also examine an OLG model and find that the brain drain has an adverse effect on static income and reduces growth. In this case, the government must use a more aggressive education policy to compensate for emigration of highly

tries, they also find that the possibility of such a positive effect of the outflow of skilled labor cannot be rejected.

In this paper, we utilize an established endogenous growth model to analyze the brain drain issue. The model is a variety of the Grossman and Helpman quality ladders model (Grossman and Helpman 1991a, 1991b), which we extend to analyze the effects of migration of workers at different and endogenously determined skill levels. Like Mountford (1997) and Beine et al. (2001), we allow for the effect that emigration of skilled workers stimulates education but we show that this positive growth effect cannot fully counteract the negative growth effect as skilled workers leave the country. However, this does not mean that labor market integration necessarily lowers economic growth and welfare in the emigration countries, since the possibilities of emigration to a high-wage country per se has a favorable effect. Opening up the labor markets raises the probability of emigration to the high-wage countries, which in turn raises the returns to higher education. Hence, education is stimulated and the growth rate goes up. Welfare falls only if a large enough number of skilled workers emigrate.

We find that emigration also of unskilled workers lowers the growth rate in the emigration country and welfare among the remaining workers. While these workers do not enter the growth generating R&D departments, an outflow lowers the relative wage of R&D workers who react by cutting down on education. This reduces human capital formation and growth.

2   Migration and Growth

2.1   A Basic Model

Start by describing the behavior of consumers who maximize a common intertemporal utility function

$$(1) \qquad U \equiv \int_0^\infty e^{-\rho t} \log u(t) dt,$$

where ρ is the subjective discount rate and $\log u(t)$ is each consumer's static utility at time t. The instantaneous utility is given by

$$(2) \qquad \log u(t) \equiv \int_0^1 \log \sum_j (\lambda)^j d(j,t,\omega) d\omega,$$

---

skilled workers. See also Haque and Kim (1995). An earlier study that found possible positive effects of the brain drain is Miyagiwa (1991).

where $d(j,t,\omega)$ denotes the quantity consumed of a product of quality j produced in industry ω at time t. $\lambda > 1$ represents the extent to which innovations improve product quality.

Each consumer allocates expenditure E to maximize $\log u(t)$ given the prevailing market prices. Solving this budget allocation problem yields the unit elastic demand function

(3) $d = E/p,$

where d is quantity demanded and p is the market price for the product in each industry with the lowest quality-adjusted price. The quantity demanded for all other products is zero. Given this static demand behavior, each consumer chooses the path of expenditure over time to maximize (1) subject to the usual intertemporal budget constraint. Solving this optimal control problem (see Grossman and Helpman 1991b) yields

(4) $\dfrac{dE(t)}{dt} \Big/ E(t) = r(t) - \rho,$

that is, a constant expenditure path is optimal if and only if the market interest rate equals ρ. We will restrict attention to steady-state properties of the model. Then ρ is the equilibrium interest rate throughout time and consumer expenditure is constant over time. We let E denote aggregate steady-state consumer expenditures.

We have two types of workers: R&D workers, L_r, and production workers, L_p. Both are in fixed supplies but we shall allow for endogenous determination of the length of R&D workers' education. Thus, human capital supply is endogenous. One unit of production workers is required to produce one unit of output, regardless of quality. Hence, every firm has a constant marginal cost equal to one. We treat the wage rate of production workers as the numeraire and let w denote the relative wage of R&D workers.

Consider the profits earned. With the previous state-of-the-art producer charging a price of 1, the lowest price such that losses are avoided, the new quality good producer earns instantaneous profits

(5) $\pi(p) = \begin{cases} (p-1)E/p, & p \le \lambda, \\ 0, & p > \lambda, \end{cases}$

where p is the quality leader's price. These profits are maximized by choosing $p = \lambda$. Therefore, this quality leader earns as a reward for its innovative activity the profit flow $(1 - 1/\lambda)E$, and the other firms in the industry can do no better than break even by selling nothing at all.

Turning to firms' R&D activities, we follow Grossman and Helpman and assume a continuum of industries with individual industries indexed by $\omega R[0,1]$. In each industry, firms are distinguished by the quality j of the products they produce. Higher values of j denote higher quality and j is restricted to take on integer values. At time $t = 0$, the state-of-the-art quality product in each industry is $j = 0$, that is, some firm in each industry knows how to produce a $j = 0$ quality product and no firm knows how to produce any higher quality product. To learn how to produce higher quality products, firms in each industry engage in R&D races. In general, when the state-of-the-art quality in an industry is j, the next winner of an R&D race becomes the sole producer of a $j + 1$ quality product. Since firms are Bertrand price-setters, each R&D race winner is able to price lower quality competitors out of business and take over the world market in its industry. Thus, over time, product quality improves as innovations push each industry up its quality ladder.

The returns to engaging in R&D are independently distributed across industries and over time. In industry ω at time t, let ℓ_i denote firm i's employment of R&D labor and let $\ell \equiv \sum_i \ell_i$ denote the industry-wide R&D employment. Firm i's instantaneous probability of winning the R&D race and becoming the next quality leader is assumed to equal ℓ_i. Individual R&D firms behave competitively and treat ℓ as given.

Let υ denote the expected discounted rewards for winning R&D races. Then, each firm i chooses its R&D employment to maximize instantaneous profits $\upsilon \ell_i - w \ell_i$. In a steady-state equilibrium, firms will determine their R&D levels, so that $\upsilon = w$.

We will now determine the equilibrium rewards for winning R&D races. From equation (4), in any steady-state equilibrium, the market interest rate must equal ρ. Not only must we discount profits using ρ, but we must also take into account that every producer is eventually driven out of business by another firm that innovates. This occurs with instantaneous probability ℓ. Thus, we obtain as equilibrium R&D conditions:

(6) $$\upsilon = \frac{(1 - 1/\lambda)E}{\rho + \ell} = w.$$

This equation captures the idea that, in equilibrium, a producer is eventually driven out of business by innovation.

R&D workers can work in the lab and on the factory floor, while production workers only can work on the factory floor, but not in the lab. With $w_p = 1$, each producer employs E/λ workers for production. Full employment in the labor market for production workers then implies that

(7) $L_p = E/\lambda.$

So far, we have said nothing about demand for education and hence there is no adjustment on behalf of individual workers' human capital formation. Evidently, education for R&D is highly demanding and it seems inappropriate to assume that all individuals in an economy have the choice of becoming a scientist or R&D worker. As in the previous analysis, and in line with many other human capital studies, we therefore continue to assume that a number of workers, L_p, lacks the capability to acquire higher education, while L_r has this capability. The difference is that L_r now faces the decision to determine the number of years in higher education, S. An increase in L_r relative to L_p could represent either an increase in the number of workers capable of acquiring an R&D education, or some university reforms that would imply that less ability is needed for a given university education.

Each worker works a finite length of T years. With S years of schooling, the individual accumulates $h(S)$ of human capital, which is an increasing and concave function. S years of education yields a flow salary of $h(S)w$, where w is now the reward to one unit of human capital. However, with some probability m, which equals the emigration rate, the worker finds a job abroad that pays a fixed and higher wage $\overline{w}$. Thus, the expected flow salary becomes $h(S)(m\overline{w} +(1-m)w)$.

To determine the optimal number of years of schooling, the individual must consider the benefits and costs of marginal additional schooling, dS. The gains to be made from extra schooling equal the extra return in this state $(m\overline{w} + (1-m)w)h'(S)$. Thus, the marginal benefits $[(m\overline{w} + (1-m)w)h'(S)]dS$ can be reaped during the period $t+S$ to $t+T$ and the present value of these earnings equals $(e^{-\rho S} - e^{-\rho T})[(m\overline{w} + (1-m)w)h'(S)]dS/\rho.$

During dS, the student has no income and had he worked, expected income would have been $(m\overline{w} + (1-m)w)h(S)dS$. Moreover, for each year of study, the individual pays a tuition fee of θ. Hence, the marginal cost of an extra unit of schooling is the forgone earnings during the period $t+S$ to $t+S+dS$ and the annual fee, or $e^{-\rho S}[(m\overline{w} + (1-m)w)h(S)+\theta]dS$. The first-order condition, i.e., marginal benefits equal to marginal cost, yields

(8) $(m\overline{w} + (1-m)w)h'(S)(1 - e^{\rho(S-T)}) = \rho[(m\overline{w} + (1-m)w)h(S)+\theta].$

At each instant, we have $(S/T)L_r$ students in school and $(1 - S/T)L_r$ working in R&D departments.

The supply of human capital is the product of the number of educated R&D workers, their working life, and each individual's human capital, or

$$H \equiv L_r\left(1 - \frac{S}{T}\right)h(S).$$

As firms do R&D, they demand ℓ of human capital per industry. Thus, full employment of human capital in laboratories equals

(9) $\ell = L_r\left(1 - \frac{S}{T}\right)h(S) = H.$

We close the model by determining consumer expenditures, E, which must equal wage income plus interest income on assets owned. The value of all assets, A, equals the stock market value of all firms. From (6) we have

(10) $A = w.$

Then ρA is interest income. To determine consumer expenditures on goods we need to deduct the students' tuition fees but these fees pertain to the government that passes them back to the consumers in a lump-sum manner. Hence, these fees cancel out from the expenditures expression. The value of purchased goods then becomes

(11) $E = L_p + w\ell + \rho w = L_p + w(\ell + \rho).$

2.2   Growth and Welfare

We calculate consumer welfare (discounted consumer utility) starting from time $t = 0$ and noting that all consumers are assumed to have identical preferences. Consider first the utility of a consumer with steady-state expenditure e. At any point in time, this consumer only buys the highest quality product in each industry, and from (3), this consumer's static demand function is given by $d(j,t,\omega) = e/p(j,t,\omega)$. The consumer buys from a producer charging the price λ. Before we substitute this information into (2), we note that, in this equation,

$$\int_0^1 \log \lambda \, d\omega = t\ell \log \lambda.$$

ℓ is the instantaneous probability of R&D success. Substituting the above information into (2) yields the consumer's instantaneous utility

(12) $\log u(t) = t\ell \log \lambda.$

Differentiating (12) with respect to time yields growth as[7]

$$(13) \quad g = L_r\left(1 - \frac{S}{T}\right)h(S)\log\lambda = \ell\log\lambda.$$

To obtain overall consumer welfare we set $e = E$, and substituting (13) into (1) we get welfare as $W\rho U = \ell\log\lambda/\rho + \log(E/\lambda)$. Merging g with this expression, and utilizing (4) and that $p = \lambda$ we find that welfare is

$$(14) \quad W = g/\rho + \log d.$$

Welfare is thus the sum of discounted growth and static demand. Welfare per capita is $W/(L_p + L_r)$, which is relevant when we discuss the welfare effects as workers emigrate.

3   Results

The system of five equations, (6), (7), (8), (9), and (11), solves for four variables w, ℓ, E, and S. Obviously, with five equations and four variables the system is overdetermined. However, using (6) through (9) in (11) shows that this last equation also is satisfied. Hence, we can drop equation (11). By eliminating E, we reduce the remaining equation system to three equations. We first solve for w, ℓ, and S and can then straightforwardly obtain the effects on expenditures, growth and welfare. The remaining three-equation system yields a determinant

$$(15) \quad D = \left\{ \frac{\theta(m-1)(\lambda-1)\rho L_r L_p (h(S) + (S-T)h'(S))}{T(m\overline{w} + (1-m)w)^2(1+\rho)H'(S)} \right. $$
$$\left. -\rho\left(\frac{\theta + (m\overline{w} + (1-m)w)h(S)h''(S)}{(m\overline{w} + (1-m)w)h'(S)^2} - e^{(S-T)\rho} - 1\right)\right\}.$$

A sufficient, though not necessary, condition for this determinant to be positive is that $(h(S) + (S-T)h'(S))$ is negative. This condition can be rewritten as $\varepsilon > S/(S-T)$, where ε is the elasticity of human capital with respect to an increase in schooling years. This elasticity is reasonably positive, while $S/(S-T)$ is negative.

---

[7]   The growth rate of utility can be shown to be identical to the growth rate of real GDP. See Lundborg and Segerstrom (2002).

3.1   Opening up for Emigration

To workers in low-wage countries, opening up for emigration implies that with some probability, m, a worker may obtain a higher wage by emigrating and accepting a work abroad. This option will, by itself, have effects on the economy as it raises the expected gains from higher education, i.e., the expected university premium. The effects of increasing the probability of emigration on optimal schooling years obtain as

$$(16) \qquad \frac{\partial S}{\partial m} = \frac{1}{D} = \left\{ \frac{-\theta(w - \overline{w})\rho}{(m\overline{w} + (1-m)w)^2 h'(S)} \right\} > 0,$$

i.e., an increase in the probability raises the length of optimal education. We note from (16) that the effect is larger the larger the wage difference to the potential emigration country is. Notable is also that the effect hinges crucially on the tuition fee: if this is zero, the first-order condition is unaffected by the probability. (See equation (8).)

The increase in the probability of emigration to a high-wage country reduces the domestic R&D wage:

$$(17) \qquad \frac{\partial w}{\partial m} = -\frac{(\lambda - 1)L_p L_r (h(S) + (S - T)h'(S))}{-T(1+\rho)^2} \frac{\partial S}{\partial m} < 0.$$

The prospects of emigration to a high-wage country should lower the wage, which is the reward to one unit of human capital. This fall is consistent with the increase in schooling years that has increased the supply of human capital. The quantitative wage effect hinges crucially on the effects on optimal schooling.

How is growth affected? On the one hand, the higher probability of emigration means that R&D workers now spend more time in school, which reduces the number of R&D workers available in the laboratories. On the other hand, each R&D worker has a longer education that should raise human capital. The net effect is unambiguously positive:

$$(18) \qquad \frac{\partial \ell}{\partial m} = -\frac{T}{(h(S) + (S-T)h'(S))} \frac{\partial S}{\partial m} > 0.$$

The quantitative effect hinges crucially on the length of the working life, T. The longer the working life the larger the positive effect on growth is. A basic condition for the positive growth effect is, of course, that the higher probability of emigration has a positive effect on optimal schooling.

Assuming that there is a positive probability of emigrating, we can show that the effects of an increase in the R&D wage, $\overline{w}$, in the potential emigration country are quantitatively identical to those of an increase in the probability of emigration (at any positive m).

So far, we have kept factor supplies constant, which, of course, is an unrealistic assumption: for a given probability to be realistic for the long run, emigration should occur at the same rate as the probability. Below we focus on the effects of exogenous changes in the supplies of R&D and unskilled labor.

3.2   Emigration

Before we analyze the effects of the brain drain, i.e., decreases in the supplies of R&D workers, we shall first discuss the effects of emigration of production workers. The comparative static effects of a decrease in production workers on the R&D wage:

$$(19) \quad -\frac{\partial w}{\partial L_p} = \frac{(\lambda - 1)\rho}{D(\rho + \ell)} \left\{ \frac{(\theta + (m\overline{w} + (1-m)w)h(S))(h''(S) + \rho h'(S))}{(m\overline{w} + (1-m)w)h'(S)^2} \right.$$
$$\left. - e^{(S-T)\rho} - 1 \right\} < 0.$$

In a country from which production workers emigrate, the relative wage of the R&D workers goes down. As expected, the increase in relative supplies of R&D workers lowers the relative wage of R&D workers.

We next consider the effects on optimal schooling years:

$$(20) \quad -\frac{\partial S}{\partial L_p} = \frac{1}{D} \left\{ \frac{\theta(1-m)(\lambda-1)\rho}{(m\overline{w} + (1-m)w)^2 h'(S)(1+\rho)} \right\} < 0.$$

In a small emigration country, students will demand less education as production workers leave the country. This is in line with the decrease in the wage of R&D workers, which has lowered the university premium and thus reduced the incentives for schooling. However, we also see that the result hinges on the existence of the tuition fee (see equation (8)).

Emigration of production workers then implies that domestic R&D workers would find that their salaries are falling and that they will reduce the time spent in school. As domestic educated workers lose, this emigration policy tends to decrease the income differences between the skilled and unskilled workers. The income difference is $wh-1$ and the effects on the wage differences are

$$(21) \quad -\frac{dw}{dL_p} h \frac{dh}{dS} \frac{dw}{dL_p} w < 0,$$

i.e., domestic R&D workers lose as compared to production workers.

To explore the effects on the growth rate, we differentiate (13) with respect to a decrease in L_p to get

$$(22) \quad -\frac{\partial g}{\partial L_p} = -\frac{\partial \ell}{\partial L_p} \log \lambda = -\frac{L_r(h(S) + (S-T)h'(S))}{T} \log \lambda \frac{\partial S}{\partial L_p} < 0.$$

In many other growth models a decrease in production workers raises growth, since less workers can be put into R&D. Here, the effect is another, as it runs solely via decreased optimal education that lowers the growth rate.

Before we can evaluate the welfare effects, we need to determine the effects on expenditures. They obtain as

$$(23) \quad -\frac{\partial E}{\partial L_p} = -1 - \left[\frac{\partial w}{\partial L_p}(\ell + \rho) \frac{\partial \ell}{\partial L_p} w \right] < 0.$$

Expenditures decrease in an emigration country. From (14) we get

$$-\frac{\partial W}{\partial L_p} = -\frac{\partial g}{\partial L_p} \Big/ \rho - \frac{\partial \log E}{\partial L_p} < 0.$$

We are, however, more interested in how welfare per remaining worker, $W/(L_p + L_r)$, is affected. We find that

$$(24) \quad -\frac{\partial \left(W/(L_p + L_r) \right)}{\partial L_p} = -\frac{1}{(L_p + L_r)} \left[\frac{\partial g}{\partial L_p} \Big/ \rho + \frac{\partial \log E}{\partial L_p} + \frac{W}{(L_p + L_r)} \right] < 0.$$

Thus, welfare among workers left behind falls, since both the growth effect and the static consumption (expenditure) effect are negative.

3.3   Brain Drain

The central interest of this paper is the effects of an outflow of R&D workers. To explore these, we shall do the corresponding comparative static experiments as above but for R&D labor. We find the wage effects of a decrease in R&D workers to be

$$(25) \quad -\frac{\partial w}{\partial L_r} = \frac{\left(1-\frac{S}{T}\right)(\lambda-1)\rho h(S)L_p}{D(\rho+\ell)^2} \left\{ \frac{(\theta+(m\overline{w}+(1-m)w)h(S))h''(S)}{(m\overline{w}+(1-m)w)h'(S)^2} \right.$$
$$\left. - e^{(S-T)\rho} - 1 \right\} > 0.$$

As expected, the relative wage rises as the supply of R&D workers decreases. We expect this increase to be accompanied by an increase in the optimal schooling years. Indeed

$$(26) \quad -\frac{\partial S}{\partial L_r} = -\frac{1}{D} \left\{ \frac{\theta(m-1)(\lambda-1)\left(1-\frac{S}{T}\right)\rho h(S)L_p}{(m\overline{w}+(1-m)w)^2 h'(S)(\ell+\rho)^2} \right\} > 0.$$

As the number of R&D workers decreases, the students prefer a larger number of schooling years. We see that a positive tuition fee, θ, is a necessary condition for a change in the number of R&D workers to affect schooling years. The fee causes the wage to affect benefits of schooling more favorably than the costs of schooling.

This increase in years of schooling, in turn, suggests that growth could rise, counteracting the initial negative effect of the outflow of educated people. To obtain the net effect, we differentiate growth with respect to a decrease in L_r:

$$(27) \quad -\frac{\partial g}{\partial L_r} = \frac{\partial w}{\partial L_r} \frac{(\rho+\ell)^2}{\lambda-1} \log \lambda < 0.$$

Thus, there is an unambiguously negative net effect on growth. While the economy benefits from the increase in schooling years increase, it also loses from the outflow of R&D workers. The net effect is negative.

We turn now to the welfare effects. Since the demand curve is unit elastic, so is the demand curve for R&D workers. From this follows that expenditures are unaffected. From (11) this implies that welfare is solely determined by the growth effect, i.e., welfare decreases.

To sum up the results so far, we thus see that the emigration country loses from an outflow of unskilled production workers as well as from an outflow of R&D workers.

3.4   Effects of Education Policy

We noted that the effects of labor migration hinge crucially on the existence of the tuition fee. The existence of the fee in the model allows us to evaluate the effects of education policy. An increase in the tuition fee raises the costs of higher education, yielding an expected negative impact on the optimal years of schooling:

$$(28) \qquad \frac{\partial S}{\partial \theta} = -\frac{1}{D} \frac{-\rho}{(m\overline{w} + (1-m)w)h'(S)} < 0.$$

This drop in education years lowers the supply of human capital, which, in turn, raises the wage, i.e., return to human capital:

$$(29) \qquad \frac{\partial w}{\partial \theta} = -\frac{1}{D} \frac{(\lambda - 1)\rho L_p L_r (h(S) + (S-T)h'(S))}{T(m\overline{w} + (1-m)w)(1+\rho)^2 h'(S)} > 0.$$

As a direct consequence of the drop in years of schooling, the inputs of human capital should fall:

$$(30) \qquad \frac{\partial \ell}{\partial \theta} = -\frac{L_r (h(S) + (S-T)h'(S))}{T} \frac{\partial S}{\partial \theta} < 0.$$

As each R&D worker gets shorter education, the stock of human capital goes down and with it, the inputs of R&D in firms. This reduces the growth rate, since $g = \ell \log \lambda$. Since expenditures are unaffected (θ is returned to the consumers), there is also a negative welfare effect.

4   Concluding Remarks

In this paper, we first showed that opening up for the possibility of emigration to a high-wage country has important effects, as it raises the expected returns from schooling, and the worker would select a longer education which raises human capital and thus the growth rate.

To the extent that the possibility of emigration is manifested in the emigration of skilled workers, this brain drain would raise the wage of the skilled and thus stimulate more schooling among those who stay. While the economy is left with fewer skilled workers, which lowers growth, the workers left behind would be better educated, which raises growth. However, the net effect on growth is unambiguously negative and welfare is reduced.

This does not mean, however, that labor market integration between, for instance, the old EU members (EU15) and the new member countries (EU10) necessarily will lead to lowered growth and welfare in the EU10. The possibility of emigration to high-wage countries in the EU will per se stimulate education and thus growth. Clearly, the EU10 would benefit the most if the probability of emigration increased as much as possible and as few as possible of the skilled workers actually emigrated. It should be recognized, though, that a high probability cannot be maintained in the long run unless workers do emigrate.

We also find that an outflow of unskilled workers would lower growth and welfare. In this case, the lowered supply of unskilled workers lowers the relative wage of the skilled and thus reduces the incentives for higher education among skilled workers.

Bibliography

Barro, R. (1991). Economic Growth in a Cross-Section of Countries. *Quarterly Journal of Economics* 106 (2):407–443.

Barro, R., and J.-W. Lee (1993). International Comparisons of Educational Attainment. *Journal of Monetary Economics* 32 (3): 363–94.

Barro, R., and J.-W. Lee (1994). Sources of Economic Growth. *Carnegie–Rochester Series on Public Policy* 40 (June): 1–46.

Beine, M., F. Docquier, and H. Rapoport (2001). Brain Drain and Economic Growth: Theory and Evidence. *Journal of Development Economics* 64 (1): 275–289.

Bhagwati, J.N., and K. Hamada (1974). The Brain Drain, International Integration of Markets for Professionals and Unemployment: A Theoretical Analysis. *Journal of Development Economics* 1 (1): 19–42.

Bils, M., and P.J. Klenow (2000). Does Schooling Cause Growth? *American Economic Review* 90 (5): 1160–1184.

Carrington, W.J., and E. Detragiache (1998). How Big Is the Brain Drain? IMF Working Paper 98/102. IMF, Washington, D.C.

Docquier, F., and A. Marfouk (2004). *Measuring the International Mobility of Skilled Workers, 1990–2000*. Release 1.0. Washington, D.C.: World Bank.

Freeman, R.B., E. Jin, and C.Y. Shen (2004). Where Do New US-Trained Science-Engineering PhDs Come From? NBER Working Paper 10554. Cambridge, Mass.

Grossman, G., and E. Helpman (1991a). Quality Ladders in the Theory of Growth. *Review of Economic Studies* 58 (1): 43–61.

Grossman, G.M., and E. Helpman (1991b). *Innovation and Growth in the Global Economy*. The MIT Press: Cambridge, Mass.

Grubel, H.G., and A. Scott (1966). The International Flow of Human Capital. *American Economic Review* 56 (2): 268–274.

Hall, R.E., and C.I. Jones (1999). Why Do Some Countries Produce So Much More Output per Worker Than Others? *Quarterly Journal of Economics* 114 (1): 83–116.

Haque, N.U., and S.J. Kim (1995). Human Capital Flight: Impact of Migration on Income and Growth. *IMF Staff Papers* 42 (3): 577–607.

Johnson, H. (1967). Some Economic Aspects of the Brain Drain. *Pakistan Development Review* 7 (3): 379–411.

Lam, K.-C. (2002). Interaction between Economic and Political Factors in the Migration Decision. *Journal of Comparative Economics* 30 (2): 488–504.

Lundborg, P., and C. Rechea (2003). Will Transition Countries Benefit or Lose from the Brain Drain? *International Journal of Economic Development* 5 (3): 1–15.

Lundborg, P., and P. Segerstrom (2002). The Growth and Welfare Effects of International Mass Migration. *Journal of International Economics* 56 (1): 177–204.

Miyagiwa, K. (1991). Scale Economies in Education and the Brain Drain Problem. *International Economic Review* 32 (3): 743–759.

Mountford, A. (1997). Can a Brain Drain Be Good for Growth in the Source Economy? *Journal of Development Economics* 53 (2): 287–303.

Wong, K., and C.K. Yip (1999). Education, Economic Growth and Brain Drain. *Journal of Economic Dynamics and Control* 23 (5–6): 699–726.

Comment on Per Lundborg

Gabriel Felbermayr

Introduction

In the last two decades or so the academic literature on the economics of international labor flows has largely focused on the welfare and distributional effects of inflows of relatively poorly educated people into rich countries. The sending country's perspective has been adopted much less frequently and if so in a less rigorous way. This is a pity because the potential adverse effects of the brain drain could be dramatic for poor source countries, while the effect may be small in already rich receiving countries. Moreover, the numbers suggest that at least in some parts of the developing world the brain drain is certainly not negligible; see the data recently compiled and described in Docquier and Marfouk (2004). Hence, it is certainly most welcome if theorists and empirical researchers become interested in modeling the source country effects of emigration. Fortunately, this conference volume contains a contribution that does exactly this.

Per Lundborg's paper looks at the issue of emigration within the context of a model of endogenous growth. The Schumpeterian framework that he chooses has largely proven its quality and is accepted as a work-horse model in many applications. In a paper with Paul Segerstrom (Lundborg and Segerstrom 2002), Per has already demonstrated that this model can be fruitfully used to address questions of international labor mobility. His present paper comes to the conclusion that the mere possibility of outward migration has a positive effect on the growth rate of output per capita in the sending country but that a marginal change in the stock of either production or R&D workers has a negative effect on growth.

The older literature has been more pessimistic. It has often looked at outward migration in static one-sector models and has concluded that emigration usually comes to the disadvantage of those that are left behind. This result is an analogy to the positive welfare effects that immigration yields for the average individual in the receiving country. The older literature has dealt at length with the thorny question: to which country's welfare do migrant workers contribute? Typically, in theoretical studies, immigrants are excluded from the receiving country's welfare criterion. If we do not include them in the sending country's welfare, as Per seems to suggest, where do we count them? This question does not have an easy answer, and I do not intend to offer any answer here.

If researchers in the field of endogenous economic growth agree on one thing, they agree on the fact that the level and/or the growth rate of human capital is important for economic growth. The more recent empirical literature finds significant effects of the level of human capital on the growth rate of economies along their adjustment paths (Benhabib and Spiegel 2005) and on their balanced growth paths. Models of the AK variant which link the growth rate of per capita output to the growth rate of human capital have been less successful empirically.

In models in which the level of human capital is the driving engine of growth (or at least convergence), a rather natural conjecture would be that emigration of high-skilled workers is almost by definition bad for growth. Per's argument contrasts this easy intuition with the fact that the mere possibility of out-migration to a high-wage country raises the incentives for native workers in the source country to acquire human capital. This indirect effect of brain-drain is to be contrasted with the direct loss of human capital associated with out-migration. Thus, it may be possible that emigration raises an economy's growth rate.

This is an interesting and quite novel element in the discussion on growth effects of emigration, but certainly not the only one. Emigrants remit substantial fractions of their earnings and frequently return back to their source countries with rich experience and capital. All these effects may also turn out to be beneficial for growth, and, in contrast to the indirect education channel, they are first-order benefits.

The remainder of this comment contains two further parts. The first offers a critical recapitulation of Per's main results and uses a very simple puppet-house model for this purpose. The second section ventures into an empirical exercise where the effect of emigration is looked at in a Barro-type cross-sectional growth regression.

How to Model the Dynamic Effects of the Brain Drain?

For the sake of simplicity, let us neglect the rich details of Per's model and start immediately with an equation that relates the growth rate of per capita income to the relative stock of human capital in the economy along the balanced growth path. We also assume that the stock of production workers does not matter for the growth rate.[1] The stock of R&D workers is given by S and their average level of education is $\bar{h}$. The growth equation is then

---

[1]   In Per's model there is a scale effect: the larger the population of R&D and production workers, the larger aggregate demand; hence, the larger potential profits in the case of successful innovation, the larger the incentives for innovation.

(1) $g = g(\bar{h}S)$.

Clearly, $g'(\bar{h}S) > 0$ in any sensible endogenous growth model.

In the context of his model, Per conducts two separate comparative statics exercises. First, he looks at the effects of a higher probability to find a job in a foreign country, given the stock of R&D workers, S. The amount of education that a student wishes to purchase is a positive function of the expected wage rate. Let $w'(S)$ denote the domestic wage (with $w'(S) < 0$) and $w^* > w$ the foreign wage. Then, the wage that a student can expect to earn is just

(2) $\bar{w} = mw(S) + (1-m)w^*$.

The higher the probability of finding a job abroad, $m \in (0,1)$, the larger the expected wage and the stronger the incentives to get educated are: $d\bar{h}/dm > 0$ and, accordingly, $dg/dm > 0$ for a given S.

The second comparative statics exercise that he proposes is with respect to the stock of skilled labor in the economy. Clearly, in the present simplistic framework this amounts to an immediate reduction in S. However, since skilled labor is now scarcer, the wage rate is driven up and the average human capital level goes up. However, Per shows that this indirect effect is dwarfed by the direct effect, so that the level of effective R&D labor $\bar{h}S$ goes down and $dg/dS < 0$.

Per treats the above questions separately, but really they must be closely related: if people are to expect with some probability that they can find a well-paid foreign job, and therefore adjust their educational choices, there must be an actual outflow that exactly validates these expectations. Otherwise, the balanced growth path of the model would not satisfy rational expectations. Moreover, if over small intervals of time the probability of finding a foreign job is m, then the actual outflow per dt must be related to m. So the comparative statics exercise that should be carried out is one that studies the derivative $d(\bar{h}S)/dm$, allowing for variation in both $\bar{h}$ and S.

The key problem here is that a constant outflow cannot be compatible with a balanced growth path (BGP) since this would gradually deplete the economy and asymptotically lead to a zero-growth path. One way out of this difficulty is to think of $g(\bar{h}S)$ not as the growth rate along the BGP but during some adjustment process. Models of imitation such as the one in Benhabib and Spiegel (2005) would do the trick: there, education plays a key role in the speed with which a poor country catches up with the rich countries, while the asymptotic growth rate is exogenously given. In the context of emigration from poor countries, this setup may actually be preferable to the one chosen by Per, because poor countries typically do not grow because they invent new products or processes, but because they imitate and implement best practices from the rich countries.

The simplest version of the Nelson–Phelps hypothesis is modeled in Benhabib and Spiegel (2004), who postulate that

$$(3) \qquad g(\overline{h}S,t) = c(\overline{h}S)(A_t^* - A_t) + x,$$

where A_t^* is the state of the frontier technology (total factor productivity, TFP) which grows at some constant exogenous rate x and A_t is the state of the domestic technology which grows at the rate $g(\overline{h}S,t)$. We assume that the domestic economy initially has a lower TFP, $A_0 < A_0^*$. The term $c(\overline{h}S)$ captures the speed at which the laggard economy catches up to the frontier.

The stock of R&D labor depreciates at rate m_t, so that

$$(4) \qquad S_t = S_0 e^{-\int_0^t m_\tau d\tau}.$$

Let the wage difference between home and foreign countries depend on the technology gap $A_t^* - A_t$. If catch-up takes place, m_t asymptotes to zero over time. If the catch-up process fails, $c(\overline{h}S)$ falls over time and the wage gap remains positive (or even rises). In that case, m_t would remain positive and the economy would eventually lose all R&D workers.

Hence, the crucial question is how $\overline{h}S$ changes with m_t. In other words, does a higher probability of finding a well-paid job abroad trigger a sufficiently strong increase in the average level of human capital, so that the actual outflow of R&D workers is overcompensated?[2]

Per's analysis does not give an answer to this question. In most situations, one would expect some nonmonotonicity. The reason is that the brain-drain effect is a first-order effect while the brain-gain effect is a general equilibrium feed-back effect and likely to be a second-order effect. Before filling the model with more structure relating to the interplay between these two effects, it may be recommendable to see what the data say.

---

[2]   Clearly, in the proposed setup, m_t would be endogenous. The equilibrium outmigration rate would then be a function of the technology gap. In order to avoid corner solutions, one could also assume that the foreign country has limited absorptive capacity, so that the foreign wage rate falls in m_t. Comparative statics could then be carried out with respect to some parameter of the foreign wage offer function.

Emigration and Growth in the Data

Docquier and Marfouk (2004) have assembled a new data set for the period 1990–2000. These data are of substantially higher quality than earlier data. The authors provide information about the fraction of agents in some skill class born in some source country and living in some OECD country. There are some stylized facts that stand out from their analysis. First, the share of home-trained workers in the total home workforce who are employed abroad is larger in the segment of high-skilled workers than in the low-skilled and medium-skilled segment. Second, the brain drain is not a phenomenon observed only in poor countries. Quite the contrary is true; the highest emigration rates are observed in Europe.

There are several tough problems with the data. One is related to measurement issues and is intensively discussed by Docquier and Marfouk (2004). Another problem is interpretational in nature: emigration rates are not informative about the scale of the brain drain if they are not contrasted to immigration rates. In other words, what would be needed is information on the net outflow of skilled labor. Large emigration rates of high-skilled people may be evidence for a loss of human capital or they may just be an indicator for the degree of labor market integration that some economy enjoys.

Table 1 presents the data that will be used below. Except for the emigration rates, which are from Docquier and Marfouk (2004), all data are taken from the Penn World Tables 6. Summary statistics are provided for the full sample (118 countries) and for a subset of countries which are poorer than the median (60 countries).

Table 1:
Raw Data

Variable	Source	Full sample		Poor country sample	
		Mean	Std. dev.	Mean	Std. dev.
Ln GDP 1998	PWT 6	8.47	1.16	7.52	0.69
Ln GDP 1990	PWT 6	8.36	1.10	7.45	0.61
Inv. rate 1990	PWT 6	15.00	8.22	10.11	5.13
Emig. rate 1990	D&M	5.12	7.55	3.62	7.17
Pop. growth (1990–1998)	PWT 6	1.53	0.92	2.06	0.75

We use these data in a canonical cross-country growth regression of the type studied in Barro and Sala-i-Martin (1995). For simplicity, we use GDP per capita as a proxy for TFP and formulate equation (1) as a difference equation in the log level of per capita GDP. The term $\overline{h}S$ is not observed directly. However, the theory postulates that $\overline{h}S$ is affected by m. To this purpose, log per capita GDP in PPP terms as of 1998 is regressed on a constant, its 1990 value, the emigration rate in 1990 (m), the investment rate in 1990, and the growth rate of population (n) between 1990 and 1998. With the exception of n, all regressors are predetermined. This ensures that endogeneity problems are not too severe:

$$(5) \qquad \ln y_{1998} = \alpha_0 + \alpha_1 \ln y_{1990} + \alpha_2 m_{1990} + \alpha_3 \left(\frac{i_{1990}}{y_{1990}} \right) + \alpha_4 n + u.$$

We make the typical regularity assumptions on u and estimate the relationship by OLS. The Breusch–Pagan/Cook–Weisberg test rejects the null of homoskedasticity in u, so that we report robust (White–Newey) standard errors in the regression output. Note that subtracting the term $\ln y_{1990}$ from both sides of the equation yields an expression for the growth rate of per capita GDP between 1998 and 1990.

Table 2 reports the results of this regression. The number of countries in the cross-section is 118. As usual, there is evidence for conditional convergence, since $\alpha_1 < 1$. All variables enter with the expected signs and are statistically significant at least at the 10 percent level. The emigration rate enters with a positive sign; however, the coefficient seems rather small economically. We also estimate the regression including the term m_{1990}^2 in order to see whether the emigration rate has a nonmonotonic effect on growth. This hypothesis is not supported by the data.

Table 2:
Regression Results

Ln GDP 1998	Coef.	Std. err.	t	p > |t|
Ln GDP 1990	0.978	0.025	39.57	0.000
Inv. rate 1990	0.006	0.002	2.60	0.011
Emig. rate 1990	0.004	0.002	1.81	0.073
Pop. growth	−0.045	0.027	−1.66	0.100
Constant	0.256	0.236	1.08	0.280

Number of obs. = 118; F (4, 113) = 1143.54; Prob. > F = 0.0000; R-squared = 0.9755; Root MSE = 0.1851

The regression results discussed in Table 2 are run over the whole sample of 115 countries. This large cross-section includes rich countries, for which a high emigration rate does not indicate brain drain but rather brain exchange. Hence, it could be that the positive effect of the emigration rate on growth in Table 2 just reflects the economic benefits of international labor market integration rather than the effect of the brain drain. To address this issue, we limit the sample to that subsample of countries with a GDP per capita level in 1990 below the median and rerun the regression (Table 3).

Table 3:
Regression Results for Poor Countries

Ln GDP 1998	Coef.	Std. err.	t	p > |t|
Ln GDP 1990	0.995	0.059	16.84	0.000
Inv. rate 1990	0.008	0.006	1.31	0.194
Emig. rate 1990	0.000	0.005	0.03	0.978
Pop. growth	−0.111	0.042	−2.65	0.011
Constant	0.253	0.465	0.54	0.588

Number of obs. = 60; $F (4, 55) = 135.94$; Prob. > F = 0.0000; R-squared = 0.9061; Root MSE = 0.2192

In the sample of poor countries, it turns out that the emigration rate does not have any statistically significant effect on growth anymore. Including the squared emigration rate as an additional regressor reveals some evidence for a hump-shaped (inverse U) effect of the emigration rate on growth, albeit not at standard levels of statistical significance. Figure 1 plots this result. It suggests that the optimal rate of outward migration is around 12–15 percent. Countries with this rate of emigration should be able to capture a growth bonus of almost 3 percent.

One problem with the empirical approach is that only a rather short time interval is looked at, namely, 1990–1998. Another problem lies in the fact that theory associates brain drain to the net loss of human capital. However, the data contain only information about emigration rates.

However, a couple of conclusions may be drawn nevertheless: in the simple cross-section of countries, we do not find any particularly strong relation between the emigration rate as measured by Docquier and Marfouk (2004) and the growth rate of GDP per capita. If rich countries are included in the analysis, a (modestly) significant effect of emigration is detected. If only poor countries are looked at, the emigration rate is no longer statistically significant. However, there seems to be some (weak) evidence in favor of a hump-shaped relation between emigration and growth in the poor subsample. In order to draw stronger conclusions, one would need to look at a longer time period and use net emigration rates rather than the gross rates.

Figure 1:
Growth and Emigration Rates in the Subsample of Poor Countries

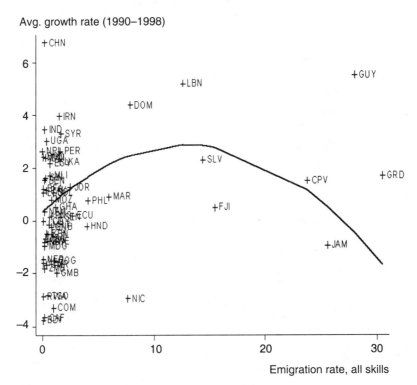

Avg. growth rate (1990–1998)

Emigration rate, all skills

Bibliography

Benhabib, J., and M. Spiegel (2005). Human Capital and Technology Diffusion. Forthcoming in P. Aghion and S. Durlauf (eds.), *Handbook of Economic Growth*. Amsterdam: North-Holland.

Docquier, F., and A. Marfouk (2004). Measuring the International Mobility of Skilled Workers (1990–2000) – Release 1.0. World Bank Policy Research Working Paper 3389. Washington, D.C.

Lundborg, P., and P.S. Segerstrom (2002). The Growth and Welfare Effects of International Mass Migration. *Journal of International Economics* 56 (1): 177–204.

List of Contributors

JUTTA ALLMENDINGER
Institute for Employment Research of the German Federal Employment Agency (IAB),
Nuremberg, Germany

FRANK BARRY
Department of Economics, University College Dublin, Dublin, Ireland

HOLGER BONIN
Institute for the Study of Labor (IZA), Bonn, Germany

JOHANNES BRÖCKER
Institut für Regionalforschung, Christian-Albrechts-Universität zu Kiel, Kiel, Germany

HERBERT BRÜCKER
German Institute for Economic Research (DIW) Berlin, Germany; Aarhus Business
School, Aarhus, Denmark; Institute for the Study of Labor (IZA), Bonn, Germany

SHEETAL K. CHAND
Department of Economics, University of Oslo, Oslo, Norway

GIL S. EPSTEIN
Department of Economics, Bar-Ilan University, Ramat Gan, Israel; CEPR, London,
United Kingdom; Institute for the Study of Labor (IZA), Bonn, Germany

GABRIEL FELBERMAYR
Internationale Wirtschaftsbeziehungen, Eberhard Karls Universität Tübingen, Tübingen,
Germany

CHRISTIAN GAGGERMEIER
Institute for Employment Research of the German Federal Employment Agency (IAB),
Nuremberg, Germany

IRA N. GANG
Department of Economics, Rutgers University, New Brunswick, New Jersey, United
States

DAVID GREENAWAY

School of Economics, University of Nottingham, Nottingham, United Kingdom

TIMOTHY J. HATTON

Faculty of Economics and Commerce, School of Economics, Australian National University, Canberra, Australia

SANJAY JAIN

Department of Economics, University of Virginia, Charlottesville, Virginia, United States

DEVESH KAPUR

Department of Government, Harvard University, Cambridge, Massachusetts, United States

JÖRN KLEINERT

Department of Economics, Eberhard Karls Universität Tübingen, Tübingen, Germany

DORIS KÖNIG

Bucerius Law School, Hamburg, Germany

WILHELM KOHLER

Department of Economics, Eberhard Karls University Tübingen, Tübingen, Germany

PER LUNDBORG

Trade Union Institute for Economic Research, Stockholm, Sweden; Department of Economics, School of Economics and Commercial Law, Göteborg University, Göteborg, Sweden

SHARUN W. MUKAND

Department of Economics, Tufts University, Medford, Massachusetts, United States

DOUGLAS R. NELSON

Murphy Institute of Political Economy, Tulane University, New Orleans, Lousiana, United States

MARTIN PALDAM

Department of Economics, University of Aarhus, Aarhus, Denmark

STEFANIA PASQUETTI

Immigration and Asylum Unit, Directorate General Justice and Home Affairs, European Commission, Brussels, Belgium

JOAQUIM RAMOS SILVA

Department of Economics, Instituto Superior de Economia e Gestão, Technical University of Lisbon, Lisbon, Portugal

JEFFREY G. WILLIAMSON

Department of Economics, Harvard University, Cambridge, Massachusetts, United States

GERALD WILLMAN

Department of Economics, Christian-Albrechts-Universität zu Kiel, Kiel, Germany

HOLGER WOLF

BMW Center for German and European Studies, Georgetown University, Washington, D.C., United States

KAR-YIU WONG

Department of Economics, University of Washington, Seattle, Washington, United States

KIELER STUDIEN · KIEL STUDIES

Kiel Institute for World Economics

Editor: *Dennis Snower* · Managing Editor: *Harmen Lehment*

326. **The Role of Multinational Enterprises in Globalization,** *Jörn Kleinert*
Berlin · Heidelberg 2004. 211 pp. Hardcover.

327. **Dynamic Efficiency and Path Dependencies in Venture Capital Markets,** *Andrea Schertler*
Berlin · Heidelberg 2003. 190 pp. Hardcover.

328. **Globalization of Financial Markets. Causes of Incomplete Integration and Consequences for Economic Policy,** *Claudia M. Buch*
Berlin · Heidelberg 2004. 249 pp. Hardcover.

329. **Demand and Supply of Aggregate Exports of Goods and Services. Multivariate Cointegration Analyses for the United States, Canada, and Germany,** Hubert Strauß
Berlin · Heidelberg 2004. 241 pp. Hardcover.

330. **Mehr Wachstum in Europa durch eine Koordination makroökonomischer Politik? Zur Kombination von Geld- und Lohnpolitik sowie zur Steuerharmonisierung in der EU,** *Alfred Boss, Klaus-Jürgen Gern, Carsten-Patrick Meier, Joachim Scheide*
Berlin · Heidelberg 2004. 141 pp. Hardcover.

331. **The Dynamic Macroeconomic Effects of Public Capital. Theory and Evidence for OECD Countries,** *Christophe Kamps*
Berlin · Heidelberg 2004. 238 pp. Hardcover.

332. **Privatisierung der Arbeitslosenversicherung: Ein Konzept für Deutschland,** *Hans H. Glismann, Klaus Schrader*
Berlin · Heidelberg 2005. 232 pp. Hardcover.

333. **Die Lohnansprüche deutscher Arbeitsloser. Determinanten und Auswirkungen von Reservationslöhnen,** *Björn Christensen*
Berlin · Heidelberg 2005. 208 pp. Hardcover.

334. **Monetary Policy and the German Unemployment Problem in Macroeconomic Models. Theory and Evidence,** *Jan Gottschalk*
Berlin · Heidelberg 2005. 287 pp. Hardcover.

335. **Ausbau der Flughafeninfrastruktur: Konflikte und institutionelle Lösungsansätze,** *Frank Bickenbach, Lars Kumkar, Henning Sichelschmidt, Rüdiger Soltwedel, Hartmut Wolf*
Berlin · Heidelberg 2005. 251 pp. Hardcover.

More information on publications by the Kiel Institute at http://www.ifw-kiel.de/pub/pub.htm, more information on the Kiel Institute at http://www.ifw-kiel.de

---

Berlin · Heidelberg: Springer-Verlag (springeronline.com)

Kiel Institute for World Economics

Symposia and Conference Proceedings

Globalization and Labor
Tübingen 1999. 320 pages. Hardcover.

The Economics of International Environmental Problems
Tübingen 2000. 274 pages. Hardcover.

The World's New Financial Landscape: Challenges for Economic Policy
Berlin · Heidelberg 2001. 324 pages. Hardcover.

Economic Policy for Aging Societies
Berlin · Heidelberg 2002. 305 pages. Hardcover.

Economic Policy Issues of the New Economy
Berlin · Heidelberg 2002. 251 pages. Hardcover.

Global Governance: An Architecture for the World Economy
Berlin · Heidelberg 2003. 276 pages. Hardcover.

Macroeconomic Policies in the World Economy
Berlin · Heidelberg 2004. 346 pages. Hardcover.

Monetary Policy and Macroeconomic Stabilization in Latin America
Berlin · Heidelberg 2005. 254 pages. Hardcover.

Labor Mobility and the World Economy
Berlin · Heidelberg 2006. 359 pages. Hardcover.

Berlin · Heidelberg: Springer-Verlag (springeronline.com)
Tübingen: Mohr Siebeck (http://www.mohr.de)